This catalogue went to print a few days after the untimely death of Fulvia Ferragamo Visconti, the daughter of Salvatore Ferragamo. It is to her, a lover of art and of culture in all its expressions, that we dedicate this exhibition, inspired by the years her father spent in California, where he outlined the values of commitment and creativity on which the brand's success is founded. The family has rigorously upheld these principles through the years and Fulvia applied them to her work in the world of silk, with passion and extraordinary flair.

ITALY IN HOLLYWOOD

EDITED BY STEFANIA RICCI

MUSEO Salvatore Ferragamo   SKIRA

ITALY IN HOLLYWOOD

Museo Salvatore Ferragamo
Palazzo Spini Feroni, Florence
May 24, 2018
March 10, 2019

Under the Patronage of
Ministero dei Beni
e delle Attività Culturali
e del Turismo
Regione Toscana
Comune di Firenze

Exhibition promoted
and organized by
Museo Salvatore Ferragamo
in collaboration with
Fondazione Ferragamo

Curated by
Giuliana Muscio
Stefania Ricci

Scientific Committee
Luca Scarlini
Rosa Sessa
Carlo Sisi
Maddalena Tirabassi
Daniele Tommaso
Elvira Valleri
and
Cinemazero, Pordenone
La Cineteca del Friuli, Gemona

Research
Simona Carlesi
Catherine Angela Dewar

Scenography
Maurizio Balò
in collaboration with
Andrea De Micheli

Project
TWO YOUNG ITALIANS
IN HOLLYWOOD
Yuri Ancarani
Manfredi Gioacchini
curated by Silvia Lucchesi for
Lo Schermo dell'Arte Film Festival

The texts of the explanatory
educational panels in the
exhibition are the work of
Alessandro Alberti, Costanza
Giovacchini, Marco Magini,
and Clara Pescatori, students
of the Liceo Classico
Michelangiolo (IV A) in Florence,
supervised by professor Maria
Teresa Leoncino within the
framework of the Alternanza
Scuola-Lavoro-MIUR program
in agreement with Fondazione
Ferragamo

Video installations
The Italian Citadel at the
Panama-Pacific International
Exposition in San Francisco, 1915
Italian Sound in America

after World War I
The Hollywood Boot Shop
Concept by Luca Attilii, Fabio
Iaquone, and Stefania Ricci;
art direction and production by
Iaquone e Attilii Studio, Rome;
multimedia service AVUELLE s.r.l.

Videos
All videos have been edited
by Daniele Tommaso

Coordination of
organizational staff
Paola Gusella

Organizational staff
Ludovica Barabino
Chiara Fucci
Gregorio Gabellieri
Eugenia Panettieri
Maria Rosa Ventimiglia

Mannequin dressing
CIVITA Group. Opera Laboratori
Fiorentini S.p.a., Florence
(Simona Fulceri)

Restoration
CIENNE S.N.C. di Gangemi
A.& C., Turin
DAMBRA laboratorio di restauro
di Forcucci Gabriella, Florence
Lucchini e Sanna Restauri
S.N.C., Turin

Multimedia technology
AVUELLE s.r.l.

Lighting
Watt Studio s.r.l.

Insurance
AON S.p.a. Insurance &
Reinsurance Broker, Florence

Shipping
Apice Firenze S.r.l.

Technical sponsors
AON S.p.a. Insurance &
Reinsurance Broker, Florence
Bonaveri Unipersonale S.r.l

Catalogue edited by
Stefania Ricci

Catalogue coordination
Eugenia Panettieri
Maria Rosa Ventimiglia

Graphic design
RovaiWeber design

Photography
Arrigo Coppitz, Enrico Fiorese,
Daniel Watson

Editorial coordination
Emma Cavazzini

Copy editor
Emanuela Di Lallo

Translations
Patricia Garvin
Sylvia Adrian Notini
Mark Eaton, Sergio Knipe,
Karen Tomatis, Susan Ann
White for *Scriptum*, Rome

First published in Italy in 2018
by Skira editore S.p.A.
Palazzo Casati Stampa
via Torino 61
20123 Milano
Italy
www.skira.net

FONDAZIONE FERRAGAMO · MUSEO Salvatore Ferragamo · Ministero dei beni e delle attività culturali e del turismo · REGIONE TOSCANA · COMUNE DI FIRENZE

Printed and bound in Italy.
First edition

ISBN: 978-88-572-3887-6

Distributed in USA, Canada, Central & South America by ARTBOOK | D.A.P. 75, Broad Street Suite 630, New York, NY 10004, USA.
Distributed elsewhere in the world by Thames and Hudson Ltd., 181A High Holborn, London WC1V 7QX, United Kingdom.

Acknowledgments

This exhibition could never have taken place without the wholehearted support of the Ferragamo family.

The curators of the exhibition and catalogue editors wish to thank: Ministero dei Beni e delle Attività Culturali e del Turismo Soprintendenza Archeologia Belle Arti e Paesaggio per le Province di Firenze, Pistoia e Prato Regione Toscana Comune di Firenze

Exhibition promoted and organized by Museo Salvatore Ferragamo with the collaboration of Fondazione Ferragamo and the following museums, institutions, and private collectors:

Cineteca di Bologna, Bologna Galleria d'Arte Moderna di Roma Capitale, Rome Galleria d'Arte Moderna Paolo e Adele Giannoni, Novara Galleria d'Arte Moderna Ricci Oddi, Piacenza Galleria Internazionale d'Arte Moderna di Ca' Pesaro, Venice Gallerie degli Uffizi, Galleria d'Arte Moderna, Florence Museo Civico Giovanni Fattori, Livorno

Museo del Paesaggio, Verbania Museo Internazionale Enrico Caruso, Comune di Lastra a Signa (Florence) Museo Nazionale del Cinema, Turin Natural History Museum of Los Angeles, Los Angeles The Metropolitan Opera, New York

Archivio Fornasetti, Milan Archivio Galleria Campari, Sesto San Giovanni (Milan) Roberto Devalle Collection, Turin Dolfi Collection, Florence Fondazione Cardinale Giacomo Lercaro, Bologna Fondazione Tirelli Trappetti, Rome Bryan Johns Collection, Pasadena Private collection, Heirs Bianca Capoquadri Tommasi The Collection of Motion Picture Costume Design: Larry McQueen, Los Angeles The Jimmy Raye Collection, Salem (MA)

The private collectors who preferred to remain anonymous.

We especially wish to thank: Academy of Motion Picture Arts and Sciences – Margaret Herrick Library, American Academy in Rome, Archivio Famiglia Matassi, Archivio Piacentini, Archivio Storico Fratelli Alinari, Biblioteca Nazionale Braidense, Biblioteca Nazionale Centrale di Firenze, Biblioteca Nazionale di Napoli, California Polytechnic State University, California State Library, California State University, Centro Altreitalie, Cineteca di Bologna, Fashion Institute of Design & Merchandising of Los Angeles, History San José Archives, Istituto Centrale Catalogo e Documentazione di Roma, Istituto Italiano di Cultura di Los Angeles, Italian American Museum of Los Angeles, Johns Hopkins University,

Los Angeles Public Library, The Metropolitan Opera, Museo Italo Americano of San Francisco, Museo Teatrale alla Scala, Occidental College of Los Angeles, San Francisco Public Library, Santa Barbara Historical Society Museum, Santa Barbara Public Library, The John D. Calandra Italian American Institute, Università degli Studi di Firenze. Silvia Alessandri, Giuseppe Anichini, Francesco Arianese, Martino Arianese, Michaela Asanger, Ross Auerbach, Angela Bagni, Chiara Baroni, Roberta Basano, Francesco Belaise, Elena Beltrami, Duccio Benedetti, Alessandro Bernardi, Silvio Bernardi, Sara Berto, Filippo Bigi, Enea Brigatti, Kevin Brownlow, Andrea Brugnoni, Marco Brusamolin, Laura Buonocore, Antonio Burello, Claudia Calò, Leonilde Callocchia, Letizia Campana, Simona Carlesi, Angela Carraro, Emma Cavazzini, Michele Cecchini, Giovanni Cerini, Elena Chiti, Giulia Ciappi, Alessandro Cinelli, Massimo and Sonia Cirulli, Anne Coco, Diane Connors, Riccardo Costantini, Ilaria Cozzuti, Vittoria Crespi Morbio, Luciano Curreri, Stella Dagna, Ilaria Della Monica, Emanuela Di Lallo, Marzio Di Pace, Elisabeth Dowling, Viola Fantoni, Sonia Farsetti, Virginia Ferragamo Schilling, Stefano Fiordi, Luigi Fiore, Barnaba Fornasetti, Marco Fortini, Sonia Francini, Gianna Frosali, Simone Frosecchi, Marianna Gatto, Elisa Ghelardi, Claudia Giannetto, Sofia Gnoli, Massimo Gravagno, Marco Graziano, Mina Gregori, Francesca Guerrini, Jan-Christopher Horak, Mario Ianeri, Aldo Innocenti, Stefania Ippoliti, Livio Jacob, Massimo Lari, Alessandro Lemmo, Simone Londero, Roberto Longi, Mauro Macario, Antonella Maggiorelli, Andrea Maglio, Fabio Mangone, Andrea Marchi, Ivan

Marin, Maria Giovanna Marletti, Eliana Marsico, Roberto Mascagni, Giuliana Matassi, Piero Matteini, Giuliano Matteucci, Germana Mentil, Valerio Massimo Miletti, Simone Monticelli, Tiziano Mugnai, Luca Mugnaini, Chiara Onniboni, Nicoletta Pacini, David Packard, Liliana Palmieri, Piero Pananti, Silvia Parretti, Marco Pesciullesi, Sandra Pietrini, Gianni Piolanti, Giuseppe Poeta, Elena Pontiggia, Giuliana Puppin, Federica Rabai, Michael Redmon, Alice Rispoli, David Robinson, Luciano Rosi Belliere, Simona Rossi, Maria Antonia Salom De Tord, Stefano Salvatici, Massimo Sanzani, Lapo Sergi, Molly Sjoberg, Antonella Soldaini, Andrea Terradura, Andrea Tessitore, Matthew Testa, Lucia Tito Zavagli Ricciardelli, Tommaso Tombelli, Veronica Tonini, Neri Torrigiani, Laura Trambusti, Roberto Troubetzkoy Hahn, Lia Trovelli, Marco Vianello, Giuseppe Viesti, Mara Vitali, Jay Weissberg, Beth Werling, Todd Wiener, Claude Zachary, Alessandro Zuri.

Special thanks to Piera Detassis and Daniela Fonti for their availability to help.

CONTENTS

8

STEFANIA RICCI

The *Italy in Hollywood* exhibition project was conceived a year ago, in April 2017, during preparations for the *1927 The Return to Italy* exhibition, which was dedicated to the period in which Salvatore Ferragamo, after twelve years spent in the United States, decided to return to his native country and settle in Florence, closing the American chapter and opening the way to other challenges, other opportunities, and other enterprises.

The examination of a number of photographs and documents that Ferragamo brought with him to Italy as a reminder of his impressive American interlude led to a reflection on the years he lived in California (1916–27), an intense period of experimentation and relationships, but still enveloped in the mists of time. This prompted an investigation in America—conducted by scholar Catherine Angela Dewar under the guidance of historian Elvira Valleri—that focused attention on important aspects of Ferragamo's Californian experience and confirmed not only his undoubted entrepreneurial ability, but also the determination and commitment of a man who tried to interpret change by shaping it to his own vision of the world.

Moreover, this historical reconstruction has greatly benefited from a further valuable resource: the recovered and restored audio tape that Salvatore Ferragamo recorded as an outline for the subsequent editing and printing of his autobiography, published in English in 1957. It is a flow of words from which the sense of a life emerges, the dedication and love for a craft that he carefully modeled like a work of art during the course of his intense life.

A number of fundamental stages define Ferragamo's Californian story: his departure from Italy in 1915, just as the country was entering World War I; the voyage in third class aboard the *Stampalia* to join his older brothers, who had left a few years earlier for North America, the preferred destination of immigrants from southern Italy; his transfer to Santa Barbara, California where he decided to join three of his brothers, Girolamo, Alfonso, and Secondino and with them open a shoe repair and custom-made shoe shop. Ferragamo's cooperation with the world of cinema began in this very shop, and in particular with some of the most famous directors of the time: David W. Griffith, James Cruze, Raoul Walsh, and Cecil B. DeMille. He made the shoes for the main characters and extras in their films, which earned him the respect of Californian society. Within a few years the young Italian had become both a shoemaker and a "shoe designer," as the American press referred to him, soon achieving fame and acclaim. When the film industry moved to Hollywood, Ferragamo followed, opening a new store on Hollywood Boulevard, called the Hollywood Boot Shop, patronized by the best-known stars of the day: Mary Pickford, Pola Negri, Charlie Chaplin, Joan Crawford, Lillian Gish, as well as Rudolph Valentino, with whom Ferragamo not only established a professional relationship but also a regular day-to-day friendship.

Many insights have therefore contributed to give shape to the exhibition, providing an opportunity to examine the phenomenon of Italian emigration to California during the first decades of the twentieth century, which in the process has become the main focus of the project. This important yet little-known historical period has given us an awareness and appreciation of the various and interesting activities of Italians in California, as well as a chance to

ITALY IN HOLLYWOOD

consider how their presence was perceived on the West Coast, and how Italian culture influenced that part of North America as regards architecture, art, craftsmanship, and the world of entertainment and cinema (the young Ferragamo's areas of interest), without ignoring the WASP society's opinion of Italians, which is also expressed in the pages of American literature from that period.

A large, late nineteenth-century painting by Raffaello Gambogi, on loan from the Museo Civico Giovanni Fattori in Livorno, makes a good introduction to the topic. It portrays an Italian family on the quay of a port, waiting to board one of the ships bound for the Americas, where they hope to find a better future. A video-installation comprised of excerpts from *L'emigrante* (1915) directed by Febo Mari, *Good Morning Babilonia* (1987) by the Taviani brothers, and *Nuovomondo* (2006) by Emanuele Crialese portrays the often painful experience of Italian emigration. Between 1880 and the first two decades of the twentieth century, millions of people from every region of Italy left their country, but not always with the desire to escape difficult socio-economic conditions. For many of them, emigration to another continent meant new opportunities to develop their professions. Such was the case with Salvatore Ferragamo, who decided to leave his homeland in order to broaden his knowledge of the art of shoemaking and, in particular, try out new methods of measuring feet, since he was intrigued by the achievements of the American footwear industry.

California, where Ferragamo arrived in 1916, was home to the best Italian colony in the United States—or so many have described this settlement of Italians in those lands. Photographs and films document this phenomenon, showing Italians working in many agriculture-related activities: vine growing, winemaking and horticulture, taking advantage of the presence of the railway. Recalling his four years in Hollywood, actor Alberto Rabagliati wrote: "About fifty miles north of Hollywood in San Bernardino, California, lies a huge estate belonging to Guasti, an Italian who owns the largest vineyard in the world. Every God-given abundance grows in the enormous garden, ninety miles long and even crossed by

Raffaello Gambogi,
Emigranti [Emigrants], 1894
Oil on canvas, 146 x 196 cm
Livorno, Museo Civico
Giovanni Fattori, inv. 1109

the Union Pacific, which transports all kinds of agricultural products."[1]

Ischian fishermen introduced sardine fishing to San Pedro using traditional *scorticaria* nets, while other Italians headed to the Sierra Nevada to work in the mines, or were employed in constructing the railways or in the flourishing timber industry. Some moved to the big cities where they found employment as road sweepers and barbers, or they took up small commercial or artisanal work.

The Italians in California also distinguished themselves in the publishing field, founding two newspapers in San Francisco: *La Voce del Popolo* and *L'Italia*, later followed by *Il Corriere del Popolo* and the anarchist *La protesta umana*. They also established themselves in the financial world, setting up four of San Francisco's major banks: the Columbus Savings Bank, Amadeo Peter Giannini's Bank of Italy (later the Bank of America), the Italian American Bank, and the Fugazi Bank.

The awareness and influence of Italian culture also involved architecture, inspiring design on various scales: from urban buildings and homes to furnishing to garden design for the villas of important cultural figures of the period, businessmen, politicians, and movie stars. It was not only Renaissance principles that guided the hands of the California architects but also more modest examples, such as the vernacular architecture of smaller Italian towns, farmhouses, and the fishermen's cottages along the Italian coasts.

A fundamental occasion that reaffirmed in America the artistic values of ancient and modern Italy, bringing legitimate pride to Italian immigrants throughout North America, was the Panama–Pacific International Exposition in San Francisco, organized in 1915 to celebrate the imminent opening of the Panama Canal. Italy took part in the event, entrusting the design and construction of its pavilion to architect Marcello Piacentini, who won first prize among the 110 competing buildings. The Italian Citadel, as the complex was called, was a compendium of Italian architecture appreciated by Americans, convincing and captivating in its intention to

recreate overseas not merely a building but the very atmosphere of an Italian town.

Many Italian artists, painters, and sculptors also took part in an exhibition organized in the Expo's Palace of Fine Arts, which hosted paintings, drawings, and other artworks from all over the world. The public greatly appreciated the Italian section, which won prizes and honors, thus reinforcing the American fascination with Italian art. A special section, set up in a building annexed to the main venue, was reserved for avant-garde art and hosted a selection of works by the Futurist movement, shown in the United States for the first time, thus opening new avenues for American art and art collecting.

The San Francisco exposition is at the heart of the Taviani brothers' *Good Morning Babilonia* and has provided a precious reference for the exhibition's itinerary sequence, which is like the storyline of a film. It has also inspired the staging by set designer Maurizio Balò, who carefully examined pictorial and photographic material documenting the Hollywood film studios in those years. In the film, the two Bonanno brothers, who work as restorers on Pisa Cathedral, are obliged to emigrate to the United States because of a crisis that has forced their father to close his workshop. They and other skilled Italian workers find jobs in the construction phase of the Panama-Pacific International Exposition. The Taviani brothers emphasize the culture of "well-made work" which characterized a particular, positive image of Italian immigrants like Ferragamo. Among visitors to the Expo is film director Griffith, who invites the two Italian craftsmen to work on the set of his new film *Intolerance* (1916), which clearly reveals a total

fascination with the film *Cabiria*, one of the most celebrated epic movies in the entire history of cinema, directed by Giovanni Pastrone in 1914 and produced in Turin by Itala Film, with intertitles by Gabriele d'Annunzio. Griffith's screenwriter Anita Loos later used them as an example.

Until that moment, Italian and French silent films had dominated the international scene. The typical Italian movie was a feature-length film with a large number of extras, suggestive landscapes, references to real monuments, and a production style that showed the influence of theater and opera. In this context *Cabiria* was the Italian historical film that received the broadest consensus in the United States. It was promoted as the most mature artistic product of a genre that would disappear only ten years later, leaving Hollywood cinema with a considerable number of its biblical and classical film legacies. This is why an entire exhibition room has been reserved for *Cabiria*, containing scene shots, promotional material, and Leopoldo Metlicovitz's extraordinary posters, all on loan from the Museo Nazionale del Cinema in Turin, together with costumes made for the actors by the Devalle theatrical tailoring company in Turin.

"Hollywood is the only city in the world to have subverted, modified, and infected the minds of most of the people who have experienced or still experience it. Hollywood spreads its songs and music everywhere, the images of its beautiful women and its talented actors, fables, stories, comedies, and the most sensational and romantic dramas of life. Hollywood both moves and makes almost all mortals laugh; it amuses them, entertains them and, for an hour, makes them forget the sorrows of life. Hollywood is the heavenly and hellish city, the crucible of joys and sorrows, pleasures and tortures, desires and mortifications, orgiastic extremes

Frames from the movie
L'emigrante, directed
by Febo Mari in 1915

Frames from the movie
Good Morning Babilonia,
directed by Paolo and
Vittorio Taviani in 1987

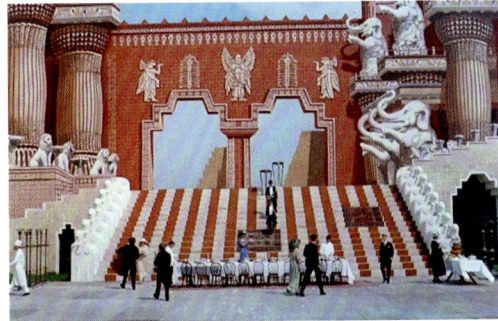

The final frame from *Nuovomondo*,
directed by Emanuele Crialese in
2006. The film deals with the massive
Italian emigration to the United
States in the nineteenth century,
focusing on the immigrants' long
and distressing detention on Ellis
Island. One particularly powerful
scene shows the immigrants in their
rags immersed in a milky white
sea, symbolic of their dream
of a happy country where they
could live peacefully

and extremes of wretchedness, and of gold in superabundance and the most squalid poverty." This was the description of the mecca of cinema in the 1920s by Alberto Rabagliati, an actor who, like other Italians, was invited to California.[2] After earning a certain fame in Italy and beyond, Italians in Hollywood—the children of immigrants and, in some cases, immigrants themselves—seemed able to make the most appreciated Italian qualities flourish in the world of American cinema: imagination, gaiety, ease of movement and stage presence, enthusiasm, warmth and a sense of harmony, as Gianni Puccini wrote in 1937.[3]

Even if generally known only to specialists, the panorama of Italians working in the American silent movies was extensive and vibrant: they were the creators of a culture of entertainment rooted in the ancient and versatile traditions of Italian theater. Among them were potential stars such as Lido Manetti, whose death in a car accident was one of the unsolved mysteries of the Roaring Twenties. There were actors from the immigrant theater, such as Frank Puglia; comedians like Monty Banks, the stage name of Mario Bianchi; character actors the likes of Henry Armetta, and dramatic performers such as Cesare Gravina, whom director Erich von Stroheim used in all his films. The American cinema also included Italian-born directors who had emigrated at a tender age, among them Frank Capra and Robert Vignola, or second-generation Italian Americans like Gregory La Cava and Frank Borzage. But also extraordinary cinematographers, such as Tony Gaudio and Sol Polito, figures who excelled in their job as cultural mediators and interpreters by combining their know-how with a positive image of Italy: the cradle of art with a cult of the past. In their work, "well-made" meant continuity with an age-old craft, as is claimed by the two Bonanno artisans, the main characters in *Good Morning Babilonia*, who explicitly link their training in art to the great masters of the Renaissance, Leonardo and Michelangelo.

Besides casting light on more or less well known names and personalities, the exhibition also aims to reveal WASP culture's ambivalent and often contradictory assessment of Italian Americans, divided between its appreciation of Italian history and culture and its contempt for certain stereotypical characteristics attributed to the immigrants, especially those from southern Italy: impulsiveness, passion, and excessive sentimentality. In their different ways, Lina Cavalieri and Enrico Caruso, Tina Modotti and Rudolph Valentino are perfect examples of how the duality of nature and culture was forged into a harmonious balance in their art. These artists knew

Lina Cavalieri in a
1890 photograph

Portrait of Enrico Caruso, n.d.

Tina Modotti in a scene
from the movie *The Tiger's
Coat*, directed by Roy
Clements in 1920

how to use to the full their natural talents of voice and body, finally refining them through study, technique, and art, to become the embodiment of Italian appeal and style.

Between 1919 and 1925, a period that saw the expansion and success of American cinematography and culture in Europe and the world and a corresponding decline in Italian cinema, American filmmakers and actors embarked on the Grand Tour of Italy, the celebrated journey traveled by European aristocracy beginning in the seventeenth century which included Rome, Florence, Venice, Naples, and sometimes Sicily, as was the case with Mary Pickford and Douglas Fairbanks on their visit in 1926, or with screenwriter Anita Loos, who, with her husband John Emerson, met Mussolini in Rome in the mid-1920s.

American film directors shot a dozen films in Italy, drawn by the artistic beauty of the country, its ever-changing landscape, and a population that was consistently able to stage its own life. The quality of Italian craftsmanship, which Americans have always lauded and prized, is evident in the work of Italian artisans employed in making the sets for *Ben-Hur*, the 1925 film directed by Fred Niblo, in which Tito Neri and his shipyard in Livorno played a fundamental role, constructing in record time the historical boats used in the production.

Romola, Henry King's 1924 film based on the famous novel by George Eliot (the nom de plume of Mary Ann Evans), is an extraordinary example of how Americans' interest in the Renaissance and its fascinating atmosphere and events brought together in Florence the resources of a large film production and the rich and varied range of Tuscan craftsmanship. Not only did places such as the Bargello and the Duomo become the genuine backdrop for the narrative, but also Florentine artists and craftspeople (costume designers, sculptors, joiners, and carpenters) contributed to reconstructing the fifteenth-century city as authentically as possible, including its vistas, the interiors of noble residences, and, above all, the much admired Palazzo Davanzati. Alongside a selection of film frames, chosen as the most representative sample of "neo-Renaissance Hollywood," this section of the exhibition presents paintings and sculptures that, in the climate of Renaissance revival stimulated by Bernard Berenson's studies, illustrate facts and characters based on the same compositional ideas found in King's film sequences. This produces a game of comparisons, in which a striking affinity in taste and iconographic sources emerges between Italian artists of the time favoring historical escapism and

Romola's screenwriters, who diligently consulted piles of books in American libraries before traveling to Italy: their imagery is almost identical. The film was shot in the V.I.S. film studios at Rifredi, in the suburbs of Florence, where the city's monuments were reconstructed on a set worthy of the great epic films of the day. Costumes and settings were entrusted to the historical and artistic consultancy of Guido Biagi (then the director of the Laurentian Library in Florence), to Gabriellino d'Annunzio, and to the Florentine aristocracy—qualified individuals who were called upon to contribute in their various capacities to the creation of sets that were clearly inspired by Italian Renaissance art or its romantic interpretation in nineteenth-century painting.

Italy was the source of many of the elements found in Hollywood's silent movies: the genre of historical films (like *Cabiria*) was first of all an ideal tool for linking cinema to art history and culture and Hollywood's stars looked overseas to examine styles of portraiture, to copy and reinvent poses. Using wood and paint, craftsmen brought the Renaissance

to California, while the temporary failure of the Italian film production system brought American stars to Europe as testimonials for the new Hollywood-made empire of images.

Italian music plays an important part in this analysis of the reciprocal influence of the two cultures, despite being little known, perhaps even less than the Italian contribution to American cinema. Whereas opera and classical music conquered American high society, recordings of traditional and popular songs, mostly Neapolitan and Sicilian, circulated among Italian immigrants: they document the life of Italian immigrants in America, the way they faced difficulties in the New World, the conflicts that arose between the new and older generations of Italian American families, the political problems that affected them, and the nostalgic memories of their cherished homeland. The musical tastes and style of these craftsmen-cum-musicians, such as the quartet led by Rosario Catalano from Sicily, one of the most important figures in the Italian American recording scene of the 1920s, heavily influenced North American dance music of the period.

No less important was the contribution of Italian immigrants to jazz, the soundtrack of the Roaring Twenties. Very many Italian musicians (or ones of Italian origin) played in the most important bands, either adopting new English names or Americanizing their own. Among them was cornetist Nick La Rocca, one of the founders of the Original Dixieland Jazz Band; Russ Columbo (Ruggiero Eugenio di Rodolfo Colombo), a baritone, violinist and actor; and Giuseppe Venuti, aka Joe Venuti, who introduced the violin to jazz and appeared in the film *King of Jazz* together with Eddie Lang (born Salvatore Massaro).

Italian musicians brought the Italian tradition of wind instruments in bands into jazz orchestras, paving the way for other Italian Americans destined to become famous, such as Louis Prima, Frank Sinatra, and

Rudolph Valentino and Vilma Bánky on the set of *The Son of the Sheik*, directed by George Fitzmaurice in 1926. The photo was chosen as the representative image for the exhibition

NATALIE TALMADGE
WM. S. HART
TALMADGE
ALLAN FORREST
McFARLAN
MARY PICKFORD
CHAPLIN
MRS. PICKFORD
JOE SCHENK
MRS. VALENTINO
RUDOLPH VALENTINO
TALMADGE
DOUGLAS FAIRBANKS
JOHN KONSODINE
CONNIE TALMADGE
LOTTIE PICKFORD
PROPERTY B.B.RAY
3827-L
WEAVE
40

Rudolph Valentino with his wife Natacha
Rambova at the gala dinner organized
by United Artists Associates, 1924. Guests
included Charlie Chaplin, Mary Pickford
and her husband Douglas Fairbanks,
producer Joe Schenck, Buster Keaton,
producer John W. Considine Jr., actress
Natalie Talmadge (Buster Keaton's wife),
actors William S. Hart and Allan Forrest,
George MacFarlane, Elise Charlotte Pickford
(Mary's mother), actress Constance "Connie"
Talmadge and Lottie Pickford (Mary's sister
and Allan Forrest's wife)

18

American actor William Haines
with Marion Davies and Charlie
Chaplin in a scene from the movie
Show People, directed by King
Vidor in 1928

Dean Martin. They were also among the first to adopt new technologies: Enrico Caruso was the precursor, recording opera arias on disc in Milan in 1902, whereas La Rocca made the first recording of jazz music on disc in New York in 1917.

Naturally, this exhibition could not fail to reserve a place for Salvatore Ferragamo, the source for this project. When the Italian craftsman left Santa Barbara for Los Angeles, Hollywood was little more than a village. The film studios were few, small, and had meager finances. Sumptuous residences could be counted on the fingers of one hand, among them those of Harold Lloyd, Mary Pickford, Pola Negri, Charlie Chaplin, and Rudolph Valentino. By the time

he left the United States in 1927, everything had changed: the studios had become more numerous and splendid, and the number of film productions, famous actors, and film sector employees had multiplied.

Ferragamo noticed a parallel between the development of his own business and that of the film industry, observing the changes that were turning Hollywood into a place that belonged to the collective imagination. Upon arriving in the city, he chose premises on Hollywood Boulevard where shoes were already sold under the Hollywood Boot Shop label. He kept the name but completely transformed the design, installing classical columns, neo-Renaissance furniture and a large sofa to help create a less commercial, more intimate atmosphere and give the space the appearance of an Italian palazzo. The store quickly became a point of reference for the entire market that revolved around the film industry: the most famous stars, but also dancers, showgirls, directors, actors, and producers.

Salvatore's arrival in Hollywood was marked not only by his close connection to cinema's brilliant trajectory, but also by a direct involvement in cultural activities and the promotion of the arts. Research conducted in California has highlighted various initiatives that document Ferragamo's original advertising campaigns and his growing familiarity with the huge Hollywood Bowl amphitheater, where his friend, orchestra director Pietro Cimini, often conducted.

We can therefore presume that alongside Ferragamo's professional involvement with the film studios was his pleasure and interest in the world of music, especially opera, a style of theatrical performance much appreciated in the Italian communities, which among other things greatly helped in going beyond the notion of regionalism. Unlike his competitors, Ferragamo understood the importance to his business of music and opera as an instrument of cultural emancipation. A convinced believer in the possibility of a union between art and craftsmanship, and economics and culture, he took part repeatedly and in various ways in the groups that were set up to found an Opera Company.

As with every exhibition at the Museo Salvatore Ferragamo, a present-day reflection on the chosen theme was included in our study of the subject. The *Two Young Italians in Hollywood* project, curated by Silvia Lucchesi (director of Lo Schermo dell'Arte Film Festival), involves two young Italian artists working in both Italy and the United States. Manfredi Gioacchini and Yuri Ancarani were invited to create two original works—a photographic series and a video installation—in close continuity with the past. One hundred years on, who are the Italians working in Hollywood today? What sights catch the eye of an artist arriving from Italy?

Manfredi Gioacchini has produced black and white portraits of a number of Italians working in the Hollywood cinema today; they are known to a greater or lesser extent by the general public and portrayed in their homes or work environments. Costume designers, editors, producers, cinematographers, screenwriters, actors, shoemakers to the stars and special effects technicians, either young or experienced, they are individuals whose

Joan Crawford in the Hollywood
Boot Shop with Salvatore
Ferragamo, 1920s

old or new professions still contribute, as they did a century ago, to the life of the most important film factory in the world.

For Yuri Ancarani, whose work moves freely between contemporary art and cinema and is included in the major international festivals, Hollywood is a recent discovery and an opportunity to develop new projects using specific skills in the field of new media. For *Italy in Hollywood* he proposes a video installation filmed at Zuma Beach, the famous location depicted in the final scene of the film *Planet of the Apes* (1968). The beach's spectacular natural setting and extraordinary colors at sunset make it a popular place for people to take selfies or be photographed. Ancarani captured these scenes with an iPhone in an apparently amateur way and later elaborated them to construct a visual narrative made up of brief stories interwoven with surprise references to Franklin J. Schaffner's famous cult film.

The exhibition has drawn on the expertise of co-curator Giuliana Muscio, a leading international scholar focusing on the Italian contribution to American cinema, and on a committee of experts in the various fields investigated. A number of artworks, photographs, films, costumes, and objects have been loaned by national and international museums and private collections, which have welcomed our project with enthusiasm. Indispensible cooperation on the subjects of Italian immigration and the history of Italian and American cinema has been received from specialized institutions, which, in addition to sharing original materials, have also generously offered their knowledge and advice. Particular thanks go to the Academy of Motion Pictures in Los Angeles, the Museo Nazionale del Cinema of Turin, the Cineteca di Bologna for their assistance with research, and to Cinemazero and the Cineteca del Friuli for their constant support and for

organizing the special event that completes this exhibition: the screening of King Vidor's film *Show People*, set in Hollywood and starring Marion Davies and Charlie Chaplin. Made in 1928, the film is a carefree look at Hollywood in the period when silent movies came to an end and includes entertaining cameos by famous actors and celebrities, such as the lead actors, who play themselves. One scene contains an image of Salvatore Ferragamo's store, the Hollywood Boot Shop, thus adding a valuable piece of evidence to the historical reconstruction of the period Ferragamo spent in the United States. This charming film helps us imagine the atmosphere that reigned in those years when Los Angeles and its Hollywood studios became the myth we have all come to know.

[1] In 1932 Rabagliati wrote an account of his Hollywood years; see Alberto Rabagliati, *Quattro anni fra le "Stelle". Aneddoti e impressioni*, ed. by Denis Lotti (Cuneo: Nerosubianco edizioni, 2017), 27.
[2] Ibid., 50.
[3] Gianni Puccini, "Italiani nel mondo del cinema," in *Cinema* 20 (April 25, 1937): 329.

Black, white, and gray two-piece snakeskin shoe created by Salvatore Ferragamo for Joan Crawford in 1932
Florence, Museo Salvatore Ferragamo

FULVIO CONTI

ERNESTO NATHAN AND THE 1915 SAN FRANCISCO INTERNATIONAL EXPOSITION

The last decades of the nineteenth century and the early part of the twentieth were characterized by seemingly contradictory social and political phenomena. On the one hand this period saw the triumph of nationalism, which precisely then revealed its worst face through the aggressive imperialism of the great powers, actively committed to apportioning the African and Asian continents, and through the tensions between the Balkan ethnic groups that triggered World War I. On the other hand, these were the years that saw the spread of an unstoppable tendency toward internationalization, with the establishment of supranational institutions and networks in the most disparate fields, seeking to respond to people's desire to travel and to get to know and fraternize with one another.[1] This desire was fostered and made possible by the profound transformations that took place in means of transport and communications technology, reducing or even cancelling distances and thus making the world smaller. Consider the construction of the large railway networks in North America or across Siberia, or the enormous spread of trans-continental voyages by steam ship (before the *Titanic* disaster in 1912 dampened enthusiasm), or the new connections guaranteed by the wireless telegraph and the radio.[2]

Nowadays we tend to define this period as the first "globalization," when the frequency and ease with which people, goods, and information began to move from one part of the world to another gave rise to a radically different perception, compared to the past, of the categories of space and time.[3] When Roald Amundsen reached the South Pole in 1911, it became clear that every part of the globe was now known and mapped. At the same time, and the first in the history of humanity, the new means of communication allowed people to conceive of the present as a set of events that took place concurrently all over the world: a new and inebriating notion of *global simultaneity*.[4]

A decisive impetus to this phase of major changes occurred in November 1869 with the inauguration of the Suez Canal, which allowed direct navigation from the Mediterranean Sea to the Indian Ocean, avoiding the perilous circumnavigation of Africa and producing an immediate increase in world trade. It is significant that the peak of this long season of economic growth and international traffic, or at least an equally important phase, coincided with the opening of another canal, the Panama, in August 1914. Its giant infrastructure, over 81 kilometers in length, was built and then managed by the United States, the country to which the Republic of Panama had entrusted the protection of its economic and military

Le grandi catastrofi: il terremoto e l'incendio distruggono la città di S. Francisco di California.
(Disegno di A. Beltrame).

L'incendio nel quartiere italiano di S. Francisco di California spento coraggiosamente col vino.
(Disegno di A. Beltrame).

interests after obtaining independence from Colombia in 1903. I speak of the "peak" because the inauguration of the canal followed only days after Austria's declaration of war on Serbia, which began World War I and brought down the curtain on the belle époque, on what Stefan Zweig later defined with ill-concealed regret as "the golden age of security."[5]

It was to this very event, the opening of the new communication route between the Atlantic and the Pacific, that the International Exposition held in San Francisco in 1915 was dedicated, which had amongst its main attractions a model of the Panama Canal reproduced in scale and fully functional. Officially called the Panama-Pacific International Exposition (PPIE), the event was also intended to celebrate the rebuilding of the city of San Francisco after the devastating earthquake that had struck it in 1906.

Ever since the 1851 London Exposition, held in the futuristic Crystal Palace, the universal world fairs had represented an extraordinary showcase for new achievements in science and technology and, more generally, of the economic and social progress of the Western world.[6] They had proved to be an effective tool for the dissemination of new knowledge and had offered an opportunity for mobility to millions of members of the middle classes—the most dynamic and most involved in the processes of change in the economy and society. The world fair in San Francisco, set up in the Marina District area along the north coast, took place from February 20 to December 4, 1915. Although the chosen period was certainly not the best, given that due to the war many European countries, including Great Britain, Russia, Austria-Hungary and Belgium, were forced to renounce their participation in the event, it was nonetheless a remarkable success, visited by about nineteen million people.[7]

Since Italy had declared itself neutral in the summer of 1914, it had no reason to cancel its participation. Therefore the Italian government, presided by prime minister Antonio Salandra, confirmed the appointment of Ernesto Nathan to the office of general commissioner and honorary plenipotentiary minister for the Exposition: Nathan had been nominated at the beginning of 1914 by Francesco Saverio Nitti, minister at the time for the Department of Agriculture, Industry and Commerce under the Giolitti government. Indeed, the choice could not have been better. Nathan had given excellent proof of his administrative skills while running the city of Rome as its mayor from 1907 to 1913. In this capacity, in 1911 he had found himself having to manage the so-called "Jubilee of the Fatherland," that is, the celebrations to mark the fiftieth anniversary of the Unification of Italy that had their most important events and greatest popular participation in the capital. As one of his biographers wrote, "Nathan was a strict and scrupulous administrator; he was a perfect gentleman and, due to his fluency in the English language, he was able to converse with American authorities and businessmen with no need of intermediaries. And because of the renown he had acquired . . . during the period in which he had governed the City of Rome, and also due to the high Masonic rank he held, he was not an unknown figure, even to the Americans."[8]

Nonetheless, his nomination aroused considerable protest and discontent in the United States, and it was not difficult to see behind this a reflection of the anti-Italian sentiment that had taken root in some immigrant communities, most notably among the Irish. Certain Catholic groups in particular argued that it was intolerable that a Jew and a

Covers of the April 29 and May 13, 1906 issues of *Domenica del Corriere* dedicated to the San Francisco earthquake and fire respectively

General Electric designed the lighting
for the San Francisco Expo. In the
foreground, the Tower of Jewels;
in the background, the rays spread
by the "Scintillator," a barge anchored
in San Francisco Bay

Cittadella italiana

(fig. 11) Veduta panoramica dell'Esposizione e della Baia di San Francisco.

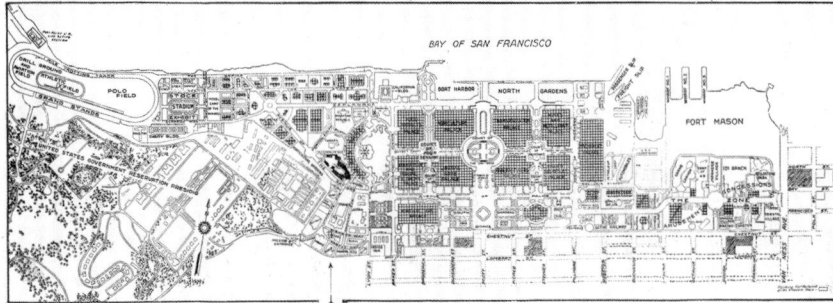

Cittadella italiana

(fig. 12) Planimetria generale dell'Esposizione.

Panoramic view of the Expo on the background of San Francisco Bay and the general layout, published in *Della Cittadella Italiana alla Esposizione di San Francisco* (Rome: Stabilimento Tipografico " Aternum" di Enrico Sabucchi, 1915), 11

Freemason (from 1896 to 1903 Nathan had been Grand Master of the Grand Orient of Italy), known for his anticlericalism, should lead the Italian delegation. This criticism was softer in San Francisco, where local Catholic organizations were more tolerant and less imbued with anti-Semitism than those of other American states, such as New Jersey or Illinois. Conversely, in addition to Jews, several Protestant and Masonic groups in Wisconsin and Chicago raised their voices in Nathan's favor, not hesitating to label Catholic protests as "Un-American."[9] In any event, the Expo governing bodies ignored the chatter and when Nathan took part in the official inauguration of the Italian Pavilion, which was attended by the archbishop of San Francisco among others, he was given a warm welcome. Indeed, in this and other respects, the former mayor of Rome's long visit to the United States turned out to be a success. In addition to being received by President Thomas Woodrow Wilson, he received invitations from many institutions and associations, and, as he said himself, everywhere he gave speeches and lectures he spoke

The crowd at the inauguration ceremony of the Panama-Pacific International Exposition

26

Ernesto Nathan at the consecration
ceremony of the Italian Citadel,
designed by Marcello Piacentini for
the San Francisco Expo
San Francisco, San Francisco Public
Library Historical Photograph
Collection

Ernesto Nathan receives
the first prize medal from
C. C. Moore, President
of the Expo
San Francisco, San Francisco
Public Library Historical
Photograph Collection

"of Rome, of our government, our political and administrative systems, enveloped in a fog of very imperfect notions; of our economic conditions, of emigration, and so forth." He wrote in a report sent to the minister: "I hope I have not performed a futile task by presenting them with a picture of the Third Italy that is a little more truthful than can be portrayed by images of the Colosseum and picturesque Neapolitans intent on spending their lives between a dish of macaroni and a tarantella."[10]

Nathan took his assignment very seriously, and in May 1914 he settled in San Francisco to take command of the area assigned to the Italian Pavilion, whose design was entrusted to architect Marcello Piacentini. The resulting group of buildings was much appreciated by the public and became one of the Expo's most visited locations, receiving the sole Grand Prix for Architecture instituted by the organizers.[11] Its symbolic heart was represented by a construction that Nathan described as the "Royal Tribune of the Risorgimento," which contained "a gallery of bronze busts and oil portraits featuring several of our greatest citizens" and "two charts in English with some statistical data" summarizing Italian progresses over the past thirty years. Among the busts and portraits were those of Dante, Leonardo da Vinci, Michelangelo, Galileo, Giambattista Vico, Alessandro Volta, Giuseppe Verdi and Guglielmo Marconi, which were joined by a series of explorers: from Cristoforo Colombo to John Cabot and Amerigo Vespucci, Alessandro Malaspina and Luigi di Savoia, Duke of the Abruzzi. These formed an introduction to the portraits of Giuseppe Mazzini, Giuseppe Garibaldi, Camillo Benso Count of Cavour and Victor Emmanuel II, whom Nathan called respectively "the apostle, the warrior, the statesman, and the king," grouped together as the great architects of the unity and independence of the Italian homeland according to an ecumenical vision of the Risorgimento fostered by the First Vatican Council. This iconography of national glories was completed by images of members of the royal family, from Charles Albert King of Sardinia to Victor Emmanuel III and Queen Elena.[12]

Nathan dedicated part of his report to a description of the Expo and the pavilions of other nations. Like many of the visitors, he was extremely impressed by the Tower of Jewels, the Expo's main building, which he described as "a very high, circular tower, about 150 meters in diameter at the base and ending almost in a spire." It earned its name because it was "covered in glass prisms of various colors, hung by iron wires that when waving in the wind reflected the light and shimmered almost as if they were precious stones. A simple and ingenious fairground toy conceived and executed on a gigantic scale."[13] He was equally impressed by the "lavish electric lighting": "Powerful electric projectors that sent out beams of dazzling light in various colors, arc lamps in the avenues, and a profusion of light bulbs everywhere transformed night into day, and day so bright as to be perhaps prejudicial to the visual faculties." He concluded: "Precise data have not been collected, but there were hundreds of thousands, millions, of electric candles consumed every evening, certainly not one of the least conspicuous operating costs."[14]

Among the other foreign pavilions, Nathan paid particular attention to that of Japan, because it seemed to him to reveal the enormous progress made in all areas by the Empire of the Rising Sun, and the potential threat it posed to the Western world. "Everything is attractive," he wrote, "all well finished and displayed so as to attract the visitor's attention; and, moreover, everything is cheap in order to challenge the competition: even the excellent-looking 'rackets' for 'tennis' are on sale at 30 percent below American or European prices. And I mention this persuasive competition in equipment for what is a very recent, essentially Western sport, because it is valid as an example for all the other various industries."[15] This Japanese display of the country's productive and technological capacity, however, evoked in Nathan some

worrying and farsighted considerations about its expansionist ambitions, and the conflict that would inevitably arise with the United States in competing for hegemony over the Pacific, and even over some Central American states. Nathan remarked: "If later on, in the desire or need for territorial expansion, conflicts should arise between yellow and white—Japanese and Americans—for the Philippines, for Cuba, or for the settlement of Mexico, then whether in such an eventuality a solitary, minimally combative America will find itself facing moments of grave anxiety, if not absolute danger, is one of the questions of international politics raised by the opening of the Panama Canal that sooner or later will require a solution, but which a commissioner of a peaceful international competition is not called upon to judge."[16]

On the whole, he gave an unenthusiastic evaluation of the San Francisco Exposition, or at least he felt he had to point up the lack of genuinely innovative products from a technological point of view: "In every branch of industry, from mechanics to food, there was an infinity of products worthy of admiration for the way they were prepared, packaged or presented, but almost none were new . . . More of a series of shops and stalls to attract customers, to sell things, than a display of the highest human ingenuity aimed at finding new and more perfect production processes."[17] In short, a Great International Fair, as people called the event, rather than an Expo capable of astounding visitors by the presence of new discoveries in science and technology.

What Nathan astutely noted in his report were the profound transformations that the American economy was undergoing in those years as it transitioned from a nineteenth-century manufacturing system to a great Fordist industry, and the subsequent consumer revolution that anticipated the new mass society.[18] His inquiring gaze rested on the disappearance of a number of traditional craftsmen's trades and others in the agricultural sector, and their replacement by machines or the advent of new forms of mass production. The passage he dedicated to shoemakers seems particularly significant, especially if we consider that only a few months earlier, a very young Salvatore Ferragamo had arrived in America from Italy and was to build his entrepreneurial success precisely due to the skill and genius with which he was able to interpret the craft.[19] "Just like the fossilized illiterate, the artisan is also in decline, yet large numbers of shoemakers still exist among

In the courtyard of the Italian Citadel. Left to right: Giacomo Giobbe, Marcello Piacentini, Matilde Piacentini-Festa, Bruno Ferrari, Arduino Colasanti (seated), Ettore Ferrari and Cesare Formilli, published in *Della Cittadella Italiana alla Esposizione di San Francisco* (Rome: Stabilimento Tipografico "Aternum" di Enrico Sabucchi, 1915), 26

The Plant Shoe Factory, the Boston-based company that produced machine-made shoes under the Queen Quality brand. Ferragamo worked there when he first arrived in the United States

us. The cobbler who patches the sole and the worn uppers, the shopkeeper who sells the artifact, is able to dress, live and thrive; but the shoemaker—properly speaking, the friend of the family who comes to the house, measures the children's growing feet, takes into account the father's calluses, proposes refinements for the heels of the mother's shoes—is disappearing or has disappeared. They are replaced by factories, among the major ones those in Massachusetts, which do not admit that individuality can exist in the human foot because it comes under the collectivity, graded by a series of numbers, from the Chinese pygmy to the giant. It is like a succession of Procrustean beds, where in one or the other the foot has to rest. There are colossal factories where people are replaced by machines that cut and sew, turning out hundreds of thousands of shoes a day onto the world market, satisfying the needs of two hundred million American feet. The large surpluses are shipped and offloaded onto the European markets, throwing our poor shopkeepers into turmoil because of the quality and competitive price of their product, imposing on them the death penalty that has already been enacted on those others back home."[20]

Emblematic of these changes that were overturning North America, and of which this California Expo offered a complete inventory, was the automobile industry. And, as Nathan did not fail to emphasize, "The triumph of American industrialism was attained at the show of the Ford car. In the automobile hall there was a department where they manufactured, or rather assembled, vehicles in front of the public, who could at their pleasure order and take away a car of almost any price, from 500 to 5,000 dollars. But let us be clear, the precision, finish, and durability of those cars cannot rival the best of our factories, such as Fiat, which has a workshop near New York, or Isotta Fraschini, etc.; nevertheless, the Ford workshop is among the most remarkable triumphs of American industrialism. They claim—perhaps exaggerating somewhat—that they produce a thousand cars a day, properly made, and at prices that not only challenge the competition but allow anyone who needs a vehicle to replace a draught animal with mechanical traction."[21]

When he visited Los Angeles, Nathan was impressed by the fact that the city even held veritable "car markets." In his report he noted: "We have cattle markets and horse fairs, they have a car market; and not only one but two markets, where every day in a dedicated public place, manufacturers, traders, owners and car 'users' meet for every type of sale, exchange, or trading that has to do with vehicles.

Italian miners at Angels Camp,
California, 1910
Courtesy of the Museo Italo
Americano of San Francisco

Italian street sweepers in
San Francisco, c. 1915
Courtesy of the Museo Italo
Americano of San Francisco
and Paola Sensi Isolani

Italian fishermen
in San Pedro
Los Angeles, Italian
American Museum of
Los Angeles, Los Angeles
Public Library, San Pedro
Bay Historical Society

Italian workers employed in canning fruit at the
California Fruit Canners Association (later Del Monte
Foods) founded by Marco Giovanni Fontana for
conserving and selling canned foods
San José (CA), History San José Research Library and
Archives

The Costantini store
in Los Angeles
Los Angeles, Italian
American Museum
of Los Angeles

The Di Carlo bakery
bread cart
Los Angeles, Italian
American Museum
of Los Angeles

Little Joe's restaurant
and grocery store
on North Broadway,
Los Angeles
Los Angeles, Italian
American Museum
of Los Angeles

The cart used for distributing
the Italian newspaper
L'Italia, 1910
Courtesy of the Museo Italo
Americano of San Francisco
and Paola Sensi Isolani

Amadeo Peter Giannini,
founder of the Bank
of Italy, later the Bank
of America, in his office
in 1923

A car can be bought there for 50 or even 5,000 dollars; you can hire them, swap them or have them repaired, engage a driver or a mechanic, fill them with petrol or fit tires, changing old ones for new."[22]

The former mayor of Rome then took the opportunity of his stay in America to brief the minister on the conditions of the Italian community in California.[23] According to the 1910 census, it was a community whose 102,618 individuals made it fourth in size after the German, Irish, and English, but different from them due to its more recent establishment: three-fifths of its members were first-generation immigrants. In the city of San Francisco alone, there were about 35,000 Italians, most of whom worked as manual laborers or artisans. Nathan observed: "Laborers make up the greater part of our colony, mostly self-employed. Unlike in New York, they are not an ignorant mob reduced to the worst servitude by the American and Italian mafia who, under the now notorious title of 'bosses,' recruit them as soon as they arrive, exploit them, keep them in a state of anxiety and terror, almost like sheep under the paws of a ferocious dog. In San Francisco they have freedom of action, they are independent men." Even in the Californian city, however, Nathan denounced the lack of an authentic "freedom to work," since the workers' organizations were of a corporate and trade union nature, mostly led by the Irish, and controlled and managed the labor market. He therefore commented: "Our masons, terrazzo workers, stonecutters, painters, carpenters, and all the building-related workforce have to follow that path, be accepted, pay their dues and obey the stringent regulations of the various corporations."[24]

Many Italians worked as porters ("some of the most influential members of the colony owe their brilliant careers to these humble origins") or as shoeshine boys, even though this last field "has been taken over, as in the case of domestic work, by the black and the yellow, the Japanese and

Chinese." Nathan further reported: "Where the Japanese are not so common is in the hotels: there, like in the major restaurants, the waiters, especially the head waiters, are by preference Italian." Noteworthy and well organized was the Italian presence among fishermen, where a sort of cooperative had been set up that specialized in crab fishing, mainly made up of southern Italians: "Neapolitans, Sicilians or Ligurians from the coast—from La Spezia to Chiavari."[25] Finally, there was a remarkable number of Italians among shopkeepers and traders, among hotel, restaurant, and café owners, and among florists, a sector that Nathan judged to be "very profitable," explaining that "the climate and soil lend themselves to floriculture, and Americans don't skimp on the price for having rare flowers in profusion. They want them to adorn the house; they want to give them away; they want to wear them in their buttonhole. Anyone invited to a meal at a private home may have a good, mediocre or bad one, depending on the skill of the cook, but they do not have it for free. As soon as the meal is digested, a guest is obliged to send a bouquet of flowers to the lady of the house. It is a tax that ranges from a minimum of three to a maximum of ten dollars. More often than not it is willingly paid; who most willingly receives it is our compatriot the florist."[26]

In San Francisco, two Italian daily newspapers were published. The first, *La Voce del Popolo*, was over fifty years old, launched in 1859; the other, *L'Italia*, founded and directed by engineer Ettore Patrizi, had appeared

The railroad at the Italian Vineyard Company, a winery founded by Secondo Guasti in 1883 in San Bernardino County (CA) Los Angeles, Italian American Museum of Los Angeles

in more recent times. Nathan remarked that "both papers share advanced views, without being an intense flaming red; they represent commendably and keep the flag of the Italian identity flying high in the colony." A colony that evidently by then contained a cultured, socially and economically evolved component, eager to preserve its identity and therefore able to guarantee the existence of two newspapers in Italian.[27] Nathan gave an account in his report of some compatriots noted for having undertaken entrepreneurial, commercial, and financial activities through which they had reached positions of absolute prestige. This was the case with Amadeo Peter Giannini, founder of the Bank of Italy, which would later become the Bank of America and one of the largest banking groups in the world,[28] or with Marco Giovanni Fontana and Andrea Sbarboro, both of Ligurian origin and respectively president and director of the Italian-American Bank. Fontana had set up the California Fruit Canners Association, a company producing and marketing canned foods that would go on to become the giant Del Monte; Sbarboro, together with Fontana, had started a thriving grape-growing and wine production business in the inland valleys of California.[29] Another illustrious Italian was Giovanni Fugazi from Lombardy, who built his fortune by managing the White Star Shipping Line; then created an agency to send immigrants'

funds home to Italy via telegraphic transfer, soon with branches all over the U.S.; and eventually founded the Italian People's Bank after the 1906 earthquake.

Amadeo Peter Giannini offered to accompany Nathan from San Francisco to Los Angeles by car, taking a different route there and back, so that the Expo commissioner could form a better idea of the region and meet other notable compatriots. One of these, Secondo Guasti, an émigré from Piedmont in 1881 and now one of the major figures in the wine industry in the whole of California, hosted him in his home in Los Angeles. "A shining example of homeland initiative,"[30] Guasti had established the Italian Vineyard Company, which at the time managed "about 2,000 hectares of vineyard" in the county of San Bernardino, employing hundreds of workers. A small village of sorts that had developed around the company's base had since grown to the size of a town and been named Guasti.

The journey through California's vast semi-desert expanses allowed Nathan to appreciate other aspects of modern American life, which, in his view, could help explain the success of the country. One of these regarded economic and technological progress, or, more specifically, the discovery and exploitation of a new source of energy: oil. The wells, scattered over a huge area and governed by a sort of "invisible hand," incessantly poured rivers of wealth in the national economy.[31] Another very important aspect concerned the efforts made by public and private institutions to promote education and combat illiteracy. Even in sparsely populated areas with only a few rare farms here and there, it was not difficult to come across a school. It was no coincidence that the 1910 census reported that in California only 3.7 percent of the population was illiterate, and most of these were immigrants.

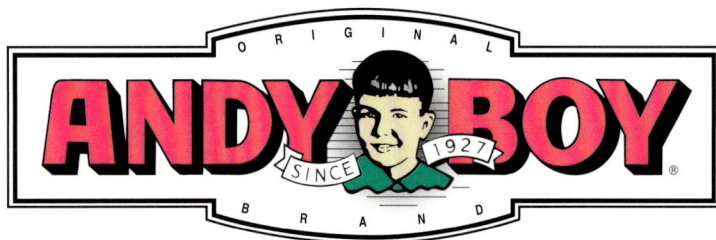

D'ARRIGO

CALIFORNIA

Nathan was able to make other discomforting comparisons between the American and Italian situations during his return train journey from San Francisco to New York, which he decided to hasten as soon as news reached him of Italy's entry into the war. It is worth mentioning that together with Nathan, another important member of the delegation also speedily returned home: Ettore Ferrari, who had held the office of president of the Italian Fine Arts Section at the Expo.[32] Since 1904, the well-known sculptor had taken over from Nathan as Grand Master of the Grand Orient of Italy, which had very much pressed for the nation's interventionist decision alongside the Entente.[33] It was unthinkable that at a moment like this, in the aftermath of the fatal May 24, 1915, the organization's two major executives would remain thousands of kilometers from the capital.

The rapid train race through the various American states and his encounter with a range of laws on the most disparate subjects (for example, the waiters in the restaurant car served or did not serve alcoholic drinks, depending on the legislation in force in the state the train was passing through in that moment) led Nathan to a number of considerations on the federal system, "where legislation is the responsibility of individual states and not of the nation's representatives." Above all, he wanted to emphasize the positive consequences of such a system with reference to certain civil rights, such as divorce, which he had fought in vain to introduce into the national legislative system when he was leader of the Grand Orient of Italy. "Granting freedom to citizens to drink or not drink vermouth, or to divorce and take another wife or not, is the responsibility of the numerous state legislative assemblies . . . Therefore, when a husband and wife who mutually come to find each other odious reside in a state that does not allow the dissolution of the marriage bond, they can go to live temporarily in another with broader views or more biblical customs."[34] With the result—Nathan cited tables and statistics that had been provided for Expo visitors—that over the course of forty years, the incidence of divorce in the United States had notably increased, passing from 3 percent in 1870 to 10 percent in 1910 ("for every ten marriages there is a divorce!"). Numbers significantly higher than those found in Europe, but also higher than those in Australia, New Zealand, and neighboring Canada.

However, not all of the glittering American civilization could be labeled under the banner of progress, and in some cases Europe and Italy emerged comforted from the comparison. Referring to an article in a New York newspaper that reported the sentence imposed on certain individuals for having sold cocaine to young people, Nathan commented: "Sometimes back home we also turn from wine to liquor as a stimulant, and when the effect is not so quick and easy with alcohol, we take lessons from the Chinese and turn to narcotics, but instead of smoking opium, we swallow or inject morphine or cocaine. But if that's what the devil wants, back home it is men and women, it is grown-ups with shattered nerves that give in to such excesses, whereas across the ocean it is minors, even kids! We haven't reached that point. In America everyone is in a hurry, they run and run and run; sometimes, as in this case, it is a race to the abyss."[35]

[1] See Glenda Sluga, *Internationalism in the Age of Nationalism* (Philadelphia: University of Pennsylvania Press, 2013). See also *The Mechanics of Internationalism: Culture, Society and Politics from the 1840s to the First World War*, ed. by Martin H. Geyer and Johannes Paulmann (Oxford, London, and New York: Oxford University Press, 2001); Madeleine Herren, *Internationale Organisationen seit 1865* (Darmstadt: Wissenschaftliche Buchgesellschaft, 2009).

[2] See Daniel R. Headrick, *The Tools of Empire. Technology and European Imperialism in the Nineteenth Century* (New York and Oxford: Oxford University Press, 1981); Id., *The Tentacles of Progress. Technology Transfer in the Age of Imperialism, 1850–1940* (New York and Oxford: Oxford University Press, 1988).

[3] See Stephen Kern, *The Culture of Time and Space, 1880–1918* (Cambridge, MA: Harvard University Press, 1983).

[4] Jürgen Osterhammel and Niels P. Petersson, *Globalization. A Short History* (Princeton: Princeton University Press, 2005).

[5] Stefan Zweig, *The World of Yesterday. An Autobiography* (1943) (Lincoln and London: University of Nebraska Press, 1964).

[6] For an account of the International Expositions, see Linda Aimone and Carlo Maria Olmo, *Le esposizioni universali, 1851–1900. Il progresso in scena* (Turin: Allemandi, 1990); Paul Greenhalgh, *Ephemeral Vistas: The Expositions Universelles, Great Exhibitions from London to Shanghai, 1851–1939* (Manchester: Manchester University Press, 1990); Id., *Fair World: A History of World's Fairs and*

Advertising for Italian brands: Italian Vineyard Company; Andy Boy, a canning company founded in 1927 by brothers Stefano and Andrea D'Arrigo from Messina; Del Monte Los Angeles, Italian American Museum of Los Angeles

Expositions from London to Shanghai, 1851–2010 (Winterbourne, UK: Papadakis, 2011); "Esposizioni in Europa tra Otto e Novecento. Spazi, organizzazione, rappresentazioni," ed. by Alexander C. T. Geppert and Massimo Baioni, monographic insert in *Memoria e Ricerca*, no. 17, 2004; Anna Jackson, *Expo: International Expositions, 1851–2010* (London: V&A Publishing, 2008); *Encyclopedia of World's Fairs and Expositions*, ed. by John E. Findling and Kimberly D. Pelle (Jefferson, NC: McFarland, 2008); Riccardo Dell'Osso, *Expo. Da Londra 1851 a Shangai 2010 verso Milano 2015* (Rimini: Maggioli, 2008); Alexander C. T. Geppert, *Fleeting Cities: Imperial Expositions in Fin-de-siècle Europe* (New York: Palgrave Macmillan, 2010); Luca Massidda, *Atlante delle grandi esposizioni universali. Storia e geografia del medium espositivo* (Milan: Franco Angeli, 2011); *Cultures of International Exhibitions, 1840–1940: Great Exhibitions in the Margins*, ed. by Marta Filipová (London and New York: Routledge, 2015).

7 On the San Francisco Exposition, see Sarah J. Moore, *Empire on Display: San Francisco's Panama-Pacific International Exposition of 1915* (Norman: University of Oklahoma Press, 2013); Laura A. Ackley, *San Francisco's Jewel City: The Panama-Pacific International Exposition of 1915* (Berkeley: Heyday, 2014); Abigail M. Markwyn, *Empress San Francisco: The Pacific Rim, the Great West, and California at the Panama-Pacific International Exposition* (Lincoln: University of Nebraska Press, 2014). For a general survey of the first International Expositions held in the U.S., see Robert W. Rydell, *All the World's a Fair: Visions of Empire at American International Expositions, 1876–1916* (Chicago and London: University of Chicago Press, 1984).

8 Alessandro Levi, *Ricordi della vita e dei tempi di Ernesto Nathan* (Florence: Ariani, 1927), 251–52. On Nathan, see my entry in *Dizionario biografico degli italiani*, vol. 77 (Rome: Istituto della Enciclopedia Italiana, 2012).

9 On these aspects, see Markwyn, *Empress San Francisco* 2014, 118–23.

10 *Relazione del R. Commissario Generale Italiano per l'Esposizione internazionale Panama-Pacifico di San Francisco a S.E. il Ministro di Agricoltura, Industria e Commercio Senatore Giannetto Cavasola* (Rome: Nazionale Tipografia G. Bertero e C., 1916), 11–12.

11 See *Della Cittadella Italiana alla Esposizione di San Francisco*, ed. by the Royal Italian Commission for the San Francisco International Exposition (Rome: Stabilimento Tipografico "Aternum" di Enrico Sabucchi, 1915). See also *Marcello Piacentini architetto, 1881–1960*, Conference Papers (Rome, December 16–17, 2010), ed. by Giorgio Ciucci, Simonetta Lux, and Franco Purini (Rome: Gangemi, 2015); and Maria C. Buscioni, *Esposizioni e "stile nazionale", 1861–1925. Il linguaggio dell'architettura nei padiglioni delle grandi kermesses nazionali ed internazionali* (Florence: Alinea, 1990).

12 *Relazione del R. Commissario Generale Italiano* 1916, 22–23.

13 Ibid., 27.

14 Ibid., 29.

15 Ibid., 38.

16 Ibid., 39.

17 Ibid.

18 From among a limitless bibliography, see Victoria de Grazia, *Irresistible Empire. America's Advance through Twentieth-Century Europe* (Cambridge, MA: Harvard University Press, 2005).

19 Salvatore Ferragamo, *Shoemaker of Dreams: The Autobiography of Salvatore Ferragamo* (Florence: Giunti Gruppo Editoriale S.p.a., 1985).

20 *Relazione del R. Commissario Generale Italiano* 1916, 43–44.

21 Ibid., 46.

22 Ibid., 84.

23 It is not possible to discuss here in detail the countless studies on the history of Italian immigration to America. I would just like to mention Sebastian Fichera, *Italy on the Pacific: San Francisco's Italian Americans* (New York: Palgrave Macmillan, 2012), and for a more general picture, *The Italian American Experience: An Encyclopedia*, ed. by Salvatore J. LaGumina et al. (New York: Garland Publishing, 2000); *Storia dell'Emigrazione Italiana*, 2 voll., ed. by Pietro Bevilacqua, Andreina De Clementi, and Emilio Franzina (Rome: Donzelli, 2001–02); *The Routledge History of Italian Americans*, ed. by William J. Connell and Stanislao G. Pugliese (New York and London: Routledge, 2018).

24 *Relazione del R. Commissario Generale Italiano* 1916, 50.

25 Ibid., 50–52.

26 Ibid., 54–55.

27 See the volume written by the editor of *L'Italia* himself, Ettore Patrizi: *Gl'Italiani in California, Stati Uniti d'America* (San Francisco: *L'Italia*'s own printers, 1911).

28 On Giannini, see Gerald D. Nash, *A. P. Giannini and the Bank of America* (Norman: University of Oklahoma Press, 1992); Felice A. Bonadio, *A. P. Giannini. Banker of America* (Berkeley: University of California Press, 1994); Guido Crapanzano, *Amadeo Peter Giannini. Il banchiere che investiva nel futuro* (Rome: Graphofeel, 2017).

29 See Simone Cinotto, *Soft Soil, Black Grapes: The Birth of Italian Winemaking in California* (New York: New York University Press, 2012).

30 *Relazione del R. Commissario Generale Italiano* 1916, 86.

31 Ibid., 88. "Approaching as we did, entering the well circuit provided an unusual spectacle: with uniform, monotonous rhythm, the pistons were raised to pour the oil into the deposits, silently, automatically. The lack of a workforce in the face of the multiplicity of machines was strange; it seemed to be the realm of fairy tales, where the people who owned the machines had been called to Parliament to question each other in whispers. One man was often enough—as explained the overseer, whom we tracked down—for running four or five different wells, with the pumps attached to a single, simple petrol engine."

32 See Arduino Colasanti and Ettore Ferrari, *International Panama-Pacific Exhibition San Francisco California 1915. Italian Fine Art Section* (Rome: Stabilimento di arti grafiche E. Calzone, 1915).

33 See Fulvio Conti, *Storia della massoneria italiana. Dal Risorgimento al fascismo* (Bologna: il Mulino, 2003).

34 *Relazione del R. Commissario Generale Italiano* 1916, 67.

35 Ibid., 72.

Model of the Jacuzzi J-7 monoplane. The multinational was founded in 1917 in Chino Hills (CA) by the Jacuzzi brothers, originally from Casarsa della Delizia in Friuli. The company began by making wooden propellers before designing and manufacturing the first seven-seat, enclosed cabin monoplane, patented in 1920
Courtesy Museo Italo Americano of San Francisco

40

ROSA SESSA

ITALIAN ARCHITECTURAL INFLUENCES IN CALIFORNIA, 1900–1930

ITALIANATE STYLE, MEDITERRANEAN STYLE AND PIACENTINI'S ITALIAN CITADEL IN SAN FRANCISCO

Foreword

Italy is the land of the imagination, but . . . its associations of romance and poetry can be repeated in our own land.[1]

In 1891 a book entitled *Our Italy*[2] was published in New York. The book, specifically aimed at an American audience, portrays the young California state in terms of the characteristics of its landscape, climate, economic production, commerce, technological development, and population. It is a veritable presentation of a region that was annexed to the U.S. only in 1848, and was still virtually unknown to the rest of the American population, especially to the inhabitants of the East Coast.[3] Although *Our Italy* was published as an informative essay with the intention of reporting objectively, the title of the work and that of the first chapter ("How Our Italy Is Made") did not fail in making the most of a series of poetic associations that immediately linked the American "refounding" of California as a magnificent, mythical garden of the United States. First through military and then political control of California, the U.S. completed the conquest of the West and reached the extreme edge of the continent. The encounter between American culture and the horizon of another ocean led the U.S. to seize the opportunity to create a new, idealized link with its European origins. Thus, from the very start of the region's conquest, the mythology of the founding of American California associated the Pacific Ocean with the sea of the dawn of Western civilization: the Mediterranean. The gentle profile of the Californian hills was compared to the picturesque landscapes of central Italy; the coasts covered with luxuriant vegetation brought to mind the fragrant and sensual nature of southern Italy and its islands.

In the decades that followed, the parallel between California and Italy continued to permeate the perception of the region and the way its landscape was experienced. Although the physical and climatic characteristics of California undoubtedly recall the Mediterranean landscape, it is impossible not to notice how the insistence of these comments also served a precise political and cultural intention: by linking the young American California with ancient Italy—the cradle of civilization and place of origin—the United States attempted to erase the recent Spanish colonial past and

subsequent Mexican control of the region and instead guarantee it a direct Mediterranean descent. And if it's true that cultural, linguistic, or architectural elements of Mexican derivation resisted this conquest, the American establishment endeavored to seize California from the influence of the Latinos and to appropriate it definitively by assigning the new state an image as fascinating as it was irresistible: that of Mediterranean Italy. In a highly skilled cultural and political operation, the United States completed the process of "Americanizing" California by "Italianizing" it.

Italian references in California architecture: the Italianate Style and the Mediterranean Style

The use of a model always implies a choice . . . the transfer of anything from one place to another requires a certain adaptation.[4]

From the 1880s on, the idealized ties between California and Italy became formalized in urban plans and architectural projects with a clear reference to Italy, whether to its classical and monumental forms, or to its minor vernacular expressions.[5] During the early decades of the twentieth century, the process of interpreting and assimilating Italian features became rooted and complete: in a continuation of the foundation myth, Italian architecture became the inescapable model for the construction of buildings linked to cultural and political institutions, but perhaps above all, Italy became seen by the local elites as a symbol of intellectual refinement and economic power. For this reason Italian-style villas were commissioned by politicians, business people, and exponents of the artistic and cultural world of the Pacific coast, and, obviously, by the rising stars of the new Hollywood film industry.

"Italianate Style" describes buildings characterized by a "classical," often monumental aspect, a reference to the architecture that developed along the whole length of the Italian peninsula in very different periods of its history. Design in this style is based in particular on the free re-elaboration of elements borrowed from Roman, Romanesque, and Tuscan Gothic architecture, from Renaissance and Baroque palaces, and from Palladian and

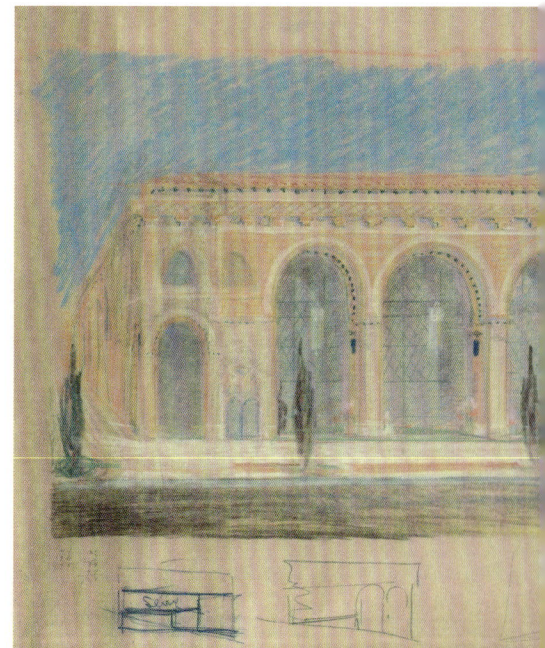

Neoclassical villas. Focusing on the allure of the association and not on historical accuracy in the interpretation of the reference, the new Californian buildings were required to recall in a generic way the refinement of the arts and excellence of craftsmanship that America associated with Italian culture. Needless to say, the empirical accuracy of these architectural borrowings was neither guaranteed nor even demanded: the designers' task was to construct buildings with a format that evoked an Italian, or vaguely European atmosphere, without posing problems of authenticity. Whether cinema sets or architecture, in California a credible similarity could be more real than the real itself.[6]

For these reasons it was not uncommon to find lavish mosaics inspired by Pompeian art in a villa with a typically Tuscan exterior, or baroque decorations in Renaissance-inspired public buildings. It was above all in the design of residences that elements and spaces of Italian derivation coexisted with reinterpretations of other cultures, in particular the neo-Greek revival from England, the French Classicism developed in the ateliers of the École des Beaux-Arts in Paris, or the true Hispanic-Mexican origins of the region with the formal choices of the Mission Style. In California at the beginning of the twentieth century, the fusion between arts from different contexts was accepted and perhaps even encouraged as a tangible transposition of the democratic pluralism at the basis of American society. This actualization of the concept of freedom of choice, an intrinsic and inalienable American value, was translated into architecture as stylistic eclecticism, which to varying degrees characterized all the buildings of the period, including those in Italian style.[7]

If in the collective imagination Italy represented the nation of arts, history, and beauty, then the Renaissance style, particularly in its Palladian forms, was definitely the main reference for the design of Californian cultural buildings, such as auditoriums, libraries, and universities. Among the most outstanding examples is the Hearst Memorial Gymnasium,[8] the women's gym on the Berkeley campus of the University of California, stunning in its systematic classical structure and elegance. Designed by Bernard Maybeck and Julia Morgan, both graduates from the École des Beaux-Arts in Paris, and financed by press mogul William Randolph Hearst, the building was made in reinforced concrete between 1922 and 1927 and incorporates rooms for dance and athletics, outdoor training areas and three swimming pools, all harmonized in a symmetrical composition embellished with

Studies by Bernard Maybeck for the Bank of Santa Barbara (*Santa Barbara Bank*, pastel on heavy paper), the Packard Dealership in Oakland (*Oakland Earle C. Anthony Packard Dealership*, pastel), and the pool of the Women's Gym at the University of California, Berkeley (*Hearst Gymnasium: Perspective of North Pool*, color lithograph) Berkeley, University of California, Environmental Design Archives, Bernard Maybeck Collection, Earle C. Anthony Packard Dealership 1927–1931

Actor Harold Lloyd's Tuscan-style villa with cypress-lined driveway (called "Greenacres") at Beverly Hills, late 1920s

The exterior and vestibule of one of the guest houses (called "B") of William Hearst's estate at San Simeon
San Luis Obispo (CA), California Polytechnic State University, Julia Morgan Papers

neo-Renaissance decorations and completed by gardens and terraces defined by marble balustrades and Roman-inspired sculptures.[9] During construction of the gym, Morgan continued her collaboration with Hearst and designed the latter's residence in San Simeon (1919–47), Hearst Castle, a masterpiece of American residential eclecticism. Julia Morgan, the first female graduate from the Parisian academy and the first woman to obtain an architect's license in California, was one of the most sought-after and prolific designers on the West Coast. She was the author of over seven hundred projects, most of which were villas along the Pacific coast, including the neo-Renaissance Casino on Belvedere Island for the San Francisco prosecutor Gordon Blanding (1914). Hollywood actors and directors the likes of Charlie Chaplin, Clark Gable, John Gilbert, and Rudolph Valentino also decided to live in Italianate villas built along the hills surrounding the film studios and the city of Los Angeles. The home of silent movie star Harold Lloyd, designed in 1928 in Beverly Hills by the famous architect Sumner Spaulding, was a faithful reproduction of a Tuscan villa transplanted to the golden hills of California. It was based on the fourteenth-century Villa Palmieri near Florence, whose garden is described by Boccaccio in his *Decameron*. Cognizant of this literary reference, Lloyd's estate was surrounded by porticos, marble fountains and rows of cypress trees: an atmosphere both charming and uplifting, and one in which the owner often chose to be immortalized.

Thanks to the favorable climatic conditions and landscape, the

Views of Gordon Blanding's residence on Belvedere Island, San Francisco Bay San Luis Obispo (CA), California Polytechnic State University, Julia Morgan Papers and Julia Morgan-Sara Holmes Boutelle Collection

The inner courtyard of the
building housing the chapel and
music room of the Occidental
College Campus in Los Angeles,
designed by Myron Hunt in
1929, and the west facade of the
Bertha Harton Orr Hall,
the first female college
residence, designed by Hunt
and built in 1925
Los Angeles, Occidental College
Library

possibility of merging outdoor and interior spaces was the basis for the success of a new stylistic influence that arrived from Italy in the early twentieth century and was labeled "Mediterranean Style." In total opposition to monumental classicism and historicist eclecticism, this style based its references on minor Italian architecture, also known as "vernacular" or "rustic," which was linked to the practical business of daily life and rural activities. The buildings taken as a model were therefore not found in the historic towns or major centers, but were traditional rural constructions of various types, such as the cottages and farmhouses located in the inland areas of the peninsula, or the small fishermen's houses found along the coasts and on the islands of southern Italy, the simple white volumes that face the panoramic view along the Amalfi coast, or the hanging gardens and pergolas of the houses on Capri. An important vehicle for cultivating awareness of this hidden Italy were the photographs and descriptions by Americans whose curiosity and courage led them to abandon the traditional Grand Tour itineraries and venture into the unknown hidden landscapes of the most visited country in Europe. The publication that had the greatest impact on California architecture in the 1920s and 30s was a book of photographs by Marian Hooker entitled *Farmhouses and Small Provincial Buildings in Southern Italy*.[10] Between 1896 and 1922, Hooker, a scientist and explorer from San Francisco, made five trips to Italy, Europe, and along the Mediterranean coasts with her mother, Katharine,[11] collecting a large number of photographs. Encouraged

The gardens of the Gurdon Wattles residence, built in Hollywood in 1912 on a design by architects Myron Hunt and Elmer Gray, 1917 Sacramento, California State Library

Pola Negri in the garden of her Hollywood home, 1927

The pergola of a garden in Ravello, published in the photography book by Marian Hooker *Farmhouses and Small Provincial Buildings in Southern Italy* (New York: Architectural Book Publishing Company, 1925), plate 86. With texts by her mother Katharine Hooker and architect Myron Hunt, the book became a source of inspiration for many villa gardens along the Californian coast

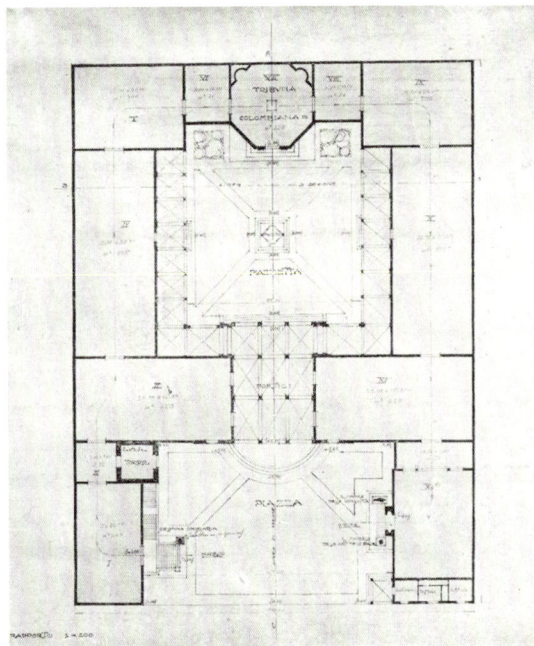

by the celebrated architect Myron Hunt, her friend and an admirer of her art, in 1925 Marian Hooker published more than 120 images of minor architecture and unknown urban views of Abruzzo, Basilicata, Campania, Lazio, and Puglia, which represented an incredible catalogue of architectural forms and compositions that could be interpreted and reformulated along the California coast. In the introduction to the book, Myron Hunt was the first to claim that he had always been inspired by his friend's photographs, a private collection of which he kept in his professional studio. His architectural projects confirm this interest in Italian minor art—indeed, they constituted an important channel for the spread of the Mediterranean Style in California. Whereas Hunt's public buildings draw on a restrained Romanesque vocabulary (as seen in the chapel and music room at the Occidental College of Los Angeles, 1929) or a neo-Palladian style reduced to its essential elements (as seen in the Occidental College auditorium, 1937), for his residential projects Hunt worked creatively, inspired by Hooker's photographs, creating simple stuccoed volumes that open onto the surrounding landscape. His Mediterranean-style houses are characterized by a dynamic composition and a direct connection to nature via porticoes, loggias, and courtyards. The gardens, often defined by rows of trees, avenues of brick and small walls covered with vegetation, were as much part of domestic life as the interior rooms. This is true of the home of wealthy financier Gurdon Wattles, built in Hollywood in 1912, or the villa Hunt designed for himself and his family in Pasadena in 1925.

Fascinated by the Mediterranean Style's pure, romantic architecture, a number of California architects reproduced traditional Italian houses along the Pacific coast. The revival of the original model was so honest and passionate that when looking at a photo of the actress Pola Negri posing under the pergola at her home in Beverly Hills,[12] we no longer care whether the building actually respects the laws underpinning the original Italian model, because we are already enchanted by the woman's delicate pose: a modern nymph whose grace invites us to immerse ourselves in the perennial spring of her classical garden.

Piacentini in California: the Italian Citadel at the 1915 San Francisco Expo

The pavilion is beautiful; it is a real little heart of Italianness (in other words, discernment and taste) transported so very far away.[13]

The paradox of Italian-style architecture built in California in the decades before World War II is that it was never designed by Italians. Firmly convinced that the artists and artisans from the peninsula produced work of excellent quality,[14] the Californians sought the expertise of Italian craftsmen for the defining look of the "skin" of their most important buildings—wood or stone inlays, mosaics, marbles, wall coverings, stuccoes, carved stones, and in general all the decorations, ornaments, finishes, and even pieces of furniture, which often came directly from Italy. But not for the architectural design. Enjoying respect, admiration, and professional success, a peaceful and hardworking Italian army composed of painters, decorators, plasterers, cabinet-makers and, later, Hollywood set designers and decorators, lived in California at the beginning of the century and redesigned its richest and most scintillating surface: the public face that the West Coast chose from that moment

Cover of the book *Della Cittadella Italiana alla Esposizione di San Francisco*, edited by the Royal Italian Commission for the San Francisco International Exposition (Rome: Stabilimento Tipografico "Aternum" di Enrico Sabucchi, 1915) Florence, Museo Salvatore Ferragamo

Marcello Piacentini's first project for the Citadel on the Esplanade area (plan and sketch), published in *Della Cittadella Italiana alla Esposizione di San Francisco* (Rome: Stabilimento Tipografico "Aternum" di Enrico Sabucchi, 1915), 10

on as its identity when presenting itself to the rest of the world, along with postcards of a coast punctuated by thin and elegant palm trees, the kinetic brightness of cars speeding along the city highways or crossing the desert, and the perfect and imperturbable whiteness of the smiles of Hollywood stars.

The architects who undertook the design of buildings, interiors or Italianate gardens were always, inescapably, American. But the most sought-after designers of all were those who, even for a very brief time, had breathed authentic European air: as a matter of fact, their wealthy American clients were convinced of the transforming aura that derived from a direct experience of art in the old continent. The most prominent architects were therefore those who had completed a period of study in Europe, in particular at the prestigious École des Beaux-Arts in Paris,[15] or those who had followed the tradition of the Grand Tour by taking a long training period visiting the major European cultural capitals (London, Paris, and Rome) and remaining in Italy for a while to make a thorough inspection of the architecture of the historic towns and cities, the picturesque hilltop towns of central Italy, the Palladian masterpieces in the Veneto, the majestic archaeological sites in Rome, and those of Magna Graecia in the south.[16]

In this context of total fascination with Italian art—which, we repeat, also coincided with the total absence of the professional figure of the Italian architect—it is important to consider Marcello Piacentini's presence in San Francisco in 1915, a significant event despite lasting just a few months and involving only a temporary exhibition project.

Marcello Piacentini[17] (Rome, 1881–1960) was a prominent figure in the world of twentieth-century Italian architecture and the author of celebrated works during the fascist period (he was project leader for the

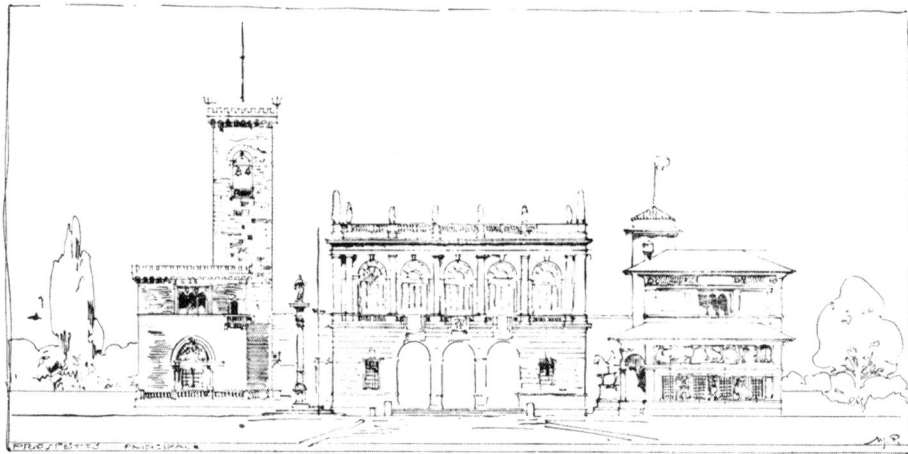

(fig. 10) Prima idea – Schizzo d'insieme.

Il primo progetto, sull'area della " Esplanade ,,.

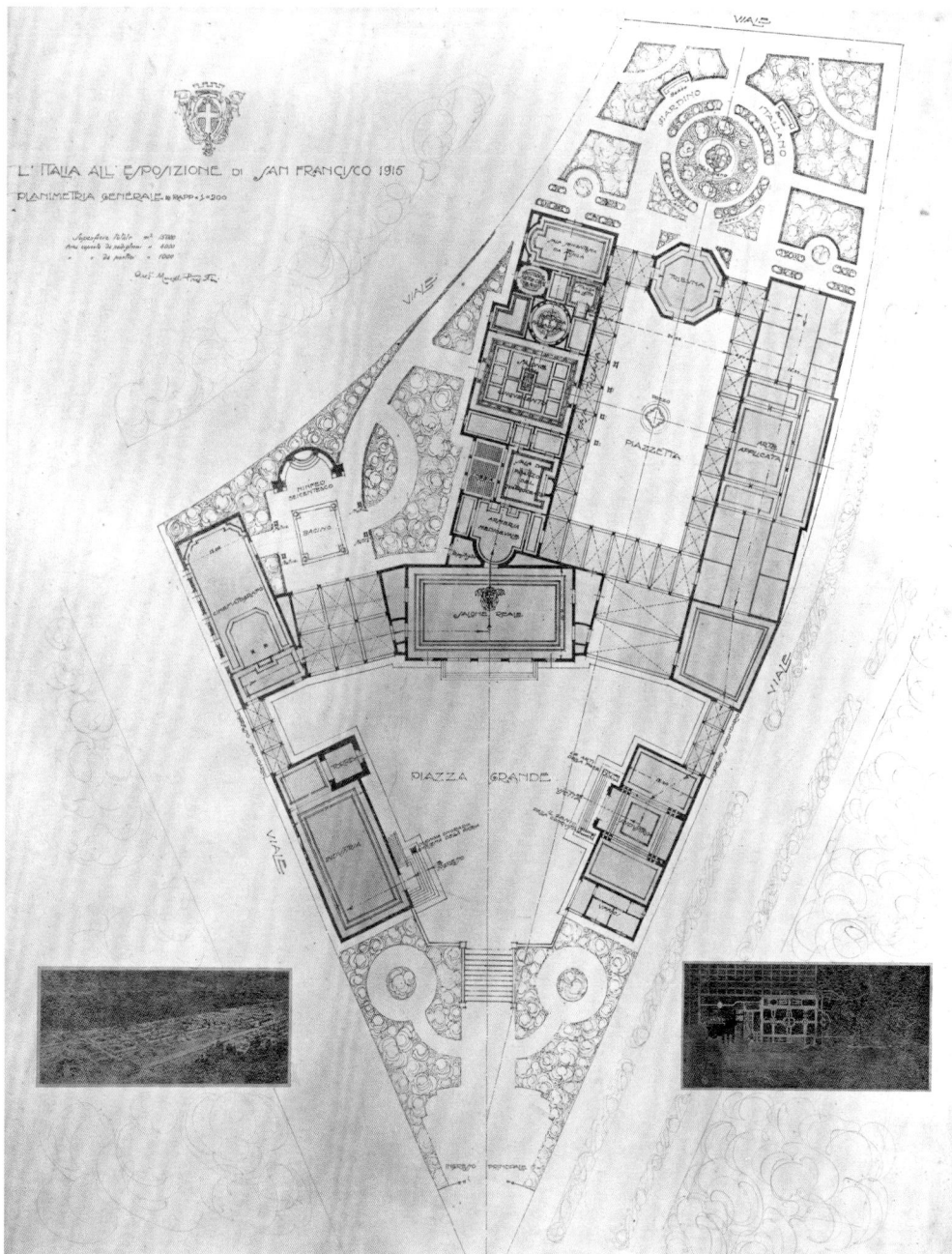

Plan of the Italian Pavilion at the San Francisco Exposition
Engraved print, 36.2 x 29 cm
Florence, Università degli Studi, Department of Architecture, Piacentini Archive

EUR complex and for La Sapienza University campus, among others). He was the son of architect Pio Piacentini (1846–1928), the famous designer of classicist and eclectic works in Rome, such as the Palazzo delle Esposizioni on Via Nazionale and the completion of the Vittoriano in Piazza Venezia. During Marcello's youth, his father ensured he received the best possible architectural training, supplementing his official study courses with private lessons in the fields of drawing and history, as well as frequent visits to his own construction sites and the unlimited availability of the well-stocked family library, which Marcello himself defined as being filled with "huge, heavy tomes, folders of large engravings of ancient and recent architecture . . . and copious French publications on Neoclassicism."[18] The international literature to which he had access, together with his frequent travels in Europe, made Marcello Piacentini an intellectual architect from an early age, interested in the critical analysis and theory of not only Italian architecture. The numerous books he wrote should be considered in this context, since they encompass a comparison of contemporary architecture from various foreign countries, in particular *Il momento architettonico all'estero* (1921) and *Architettura d'oggi* (1930). In both these works Piacentini carefully examines the architecture of major European countries,[19] but he also adds thoughts on Russian[20] and North American architecture. References to American architecture often occur in Piacentini's books, and perhaps due to his awareness of having been one of the few Italian architects to have made a trip overseas, in 1922 he wrote *Influssi d'arte italiana nel Nord-*

America, an entire article dedicated to the U.S. that was specifically intended to outline the relationship American architects had established with architectural references in Italy.[21] In the article, Piacentini reveals all the appeal that Italy was exerting on American architecture, and even before vernacular Italian architecture[22] had been fully recognized in its country, he underlined how it was in fact minor Italian architecture that was inspiring the very modern United States: "American architects have begun studying our beautiful art of the past centuries *in situ*, precisely limiting their field of study to *minor architecture*, to architecture that is not monumental but practical . . . With infinite love, they have drawn the designs of a great number of country villas and houses, especially in Tuscany. They have photographed views of a thousand porticoes, a thousand fountains, every doorway, every little window in Val di Pesa, every railing, and every overhanging roof in the Chianti valley."[23] For Piacentini it was indeed California, "a country so similar in nature and climate to our own,"[24] that had most subtly understood and skillfully interpreted "our humblest and freshest things, happy within the surrounding nature."[25]

Piacentini's interest in American architecture is confirmed by the volumes in his library; notable among these is the catalogue of the 1876 Philadelphia Centennial Exhibition and the volume entitled *The American Vitruvius*[26] from 1922. He also took part in the 1923 design competition for the *Chicago Tribune* headquarters, producing a plan for a rather squat skyscraper covered with baroque decorations. This stylistic decision is surprising, especially when compared with Piacentini's enthusiastic tone as he described only two years earlier the "new trend" in the design of American skyscrapers, praising their "more rational appearance, free from any reminiscences" and the "bare and restful simplicity of a clear investigation of these experiments in modernization."[27] Piacentini's general fascination for tall American buildings spans all his writing on the subject.[28] In *Architettura d'oggi* he argues that "American architecture is especially focused on skyscrapers"[29] and, choosing only four images[30] to illustrate modern America (three skyscrapers and Paul Cret's futuristic bridge over the Delaware River in Philadelphia), he asks himself: "What other staggering achievements is the new world preparing for us?"[31]

Surprisingly, this avid curiosity and confident enthusiasm for the American continent are not directly reflected in the letters that Marcello Piacentini and his wife, the painter Matilde Festa, sent to their relatives during their first trip across the United States. The journey was also the young couple's honeymoon and took place between February and May 1915 so that Piacentini could oversee completion work on the Italian Pavilion at the Panama-Pacific International Exposition in San Francisco.[32] Arriving in New York by sea, the couple reached Chicago by train and from there went by bus to San Francisco. During the long journey, the landscape is described as "squalid, monotonous countryside . . . all burnt and black (like everything in America) . . . Small houses like barracks . . . all of them the same."[33] Chicago is defined as "all the same, dirty, black and unbelievably stupid"[34] and a sole hint of admiration is addressed to New York skyscrapers, "bold and impressive, especially at night, all lit up, even externally."[35]

Even San Francisco, which welcomed the architect and his team of Italian professionals[36] with all honors, is not described in flattering tones. In a letter to his family, Piacentini writes: "This country is too, too empty; all they think about is dancing! . . . [San Francisco] hasn't the slightest

General sketch of the Italian Citadel, published in *Della Cittadella Italiana alla Esposizione di San Francisco* (Rome: Stabilimento Tipografico "Aternum" di Enrico Sabucchi, 1915), 12

Construction site of the Italian Citadel
in November 1914
Florence, Università degli Studi,
Department of Architecture,
Piacentini Archive

25 Novembre 1914

25 Novembre 1914

thing of interest."[37] And in the same missive his wife concludes: "If it weren't for the Pavilion, in which we feel at home, everything else . . . is quite irritating and boring."[38]

In March 1914, Ernesto Nathan, minister plenipotentiary of the Italian government, directly assigned the project for the Italian Pavilion at the Panama-Pacific International Exposition to Marcello Piacentini. The architect, just thirty-two years old, possessed a portfolio full of important projects, but what interested the minister most of all was Piacentini's earlier success in representing Italy: the national pavilion he had designed for the 1910 World's Fair in Brussels had earned Italy first prize in the international competition.

Initially, Piacentini was allocated a rectangular site on which he developed his design: respecting the axis of longitudinal symmetry, the project opened onto a square surrounded by buildings in different architectural styles, and then continued, via a portico, to a cloister with a central garden. Completely unexpectedly during the course of construction, the exhibition commission changed the lot assigned to Italy to one with a larger surface area, about 15,000 square meters, located in a privileged position behind the grandiose Palace of Fine Arts designed by Bernard Maybeck. However, unlike the first site, the new one was extremely irregular in shape, similar to a triangle with a truncated vertex, accommodating on one side the curve of the exedra attached to the Palace of Fine Arts. Piacentini worked masterfully on the irregularity of the site by exploiting this apparent disadvantage and using it to the full benefit of his project. The result was even more convincing: Piacentini returned to his original intention in the first design of working with a variety of historical styles and developing an exhibition route that balanced enclosed and open spaces; moreover, the very nature of the new site allowed him to create an asymmetrical arrangement of the various composition elements, thus obtaining a result that recalled the picturesque, the spontaneity, and the layering of history of a typical Italian town. Piacentini described his goal as follows: "I did not intend to create the usual exhibition-style pavilion for San Francisco. I wanted the Italian vision . . . to be something more complex and characteristic. Therefore not a single building, but a number of harmoniously linked elements that would resemble a corner, a little nook of Italy. Not the ostentation of a great frontage . . . but the intimacy of a congenial atmosphere, like that of a town square, with various buildings erected around its sides inspired by the most beautiful styles that Italy has produced. So that from there . . . visitors do not have to 'pass in front' of Italy, as if passing in

The Medieval Palace,
inspired by the Palazzo
dei Priori in Perugia,
published in *L'Edilizia
Moderna*, XXIV, fasc. XI
(November 1915): plate L
Florence, Università
degli Studi, Department
of Architecture,
Piacentini Archive

The Courtyard with the two copies
after Andrea del Verrocchio, *David*
(Museo del Bargello) and *Putto with
Dolphin* (courtyard of Palazzo Vecchio),
published in *Della Cittadella Italiana
alla Esposizione di San Francisco* (Rome:
Stabilimento Tipografico "Aternum"
di Enrico Sabucchi, 1915), 53

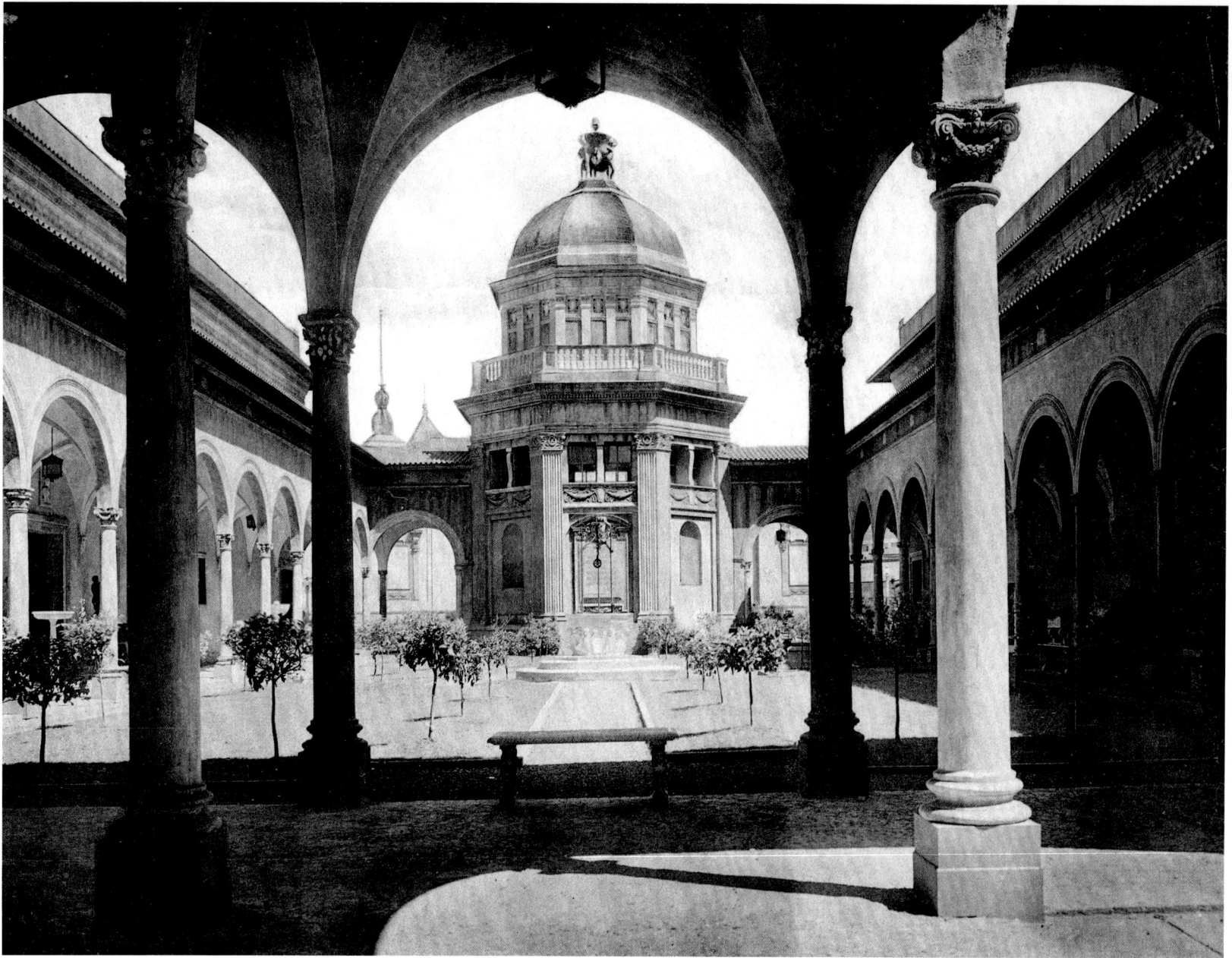

The Piazzetta and the Tribune,
published in *L'Edilizia
Moderna*, XXIV, fasc. XI
(November 1915): plate LIV
Florence, Università degli Studi,
Department of Architecture,
Piacentini Archive

front of a shop window, but have to 'enter' Italy and . . . savor all the marvelous beauty with which Italian art has illuminated the world."[39]

The Citadel was inspired by the two-square system typical of Italian towns. The main entrance opened onto Piazza Grande, surrounded by three built elements and reached by a flight of steps. In its general composition, this space recalled Piazza del Campidoglio in Rome, but the buildings resembled architecture belonging to different historical periods and to different central and northern Italian locations: on the left was the Medieval Palace with a staircase and a square-based tower, reminiscent of Umbrian architecture, in particular the Palazzo dei Priori in Perugia; in the center was the Royal Hall, also called "Casa Italiana": a building in the style of the Venetian Renaissance, characterized by an open facade with a loggia; and on the right was the Quattrocento Palace with its symmetrical, polychrome facade surmounted by a storiated tower, a reference to Lombard architecture. These three main buildings were connected by porticoes and other lower constructions so as to create a "unity of built elements and environment,"[40] in which the prevailing principle was the harmony between the various parts. The archway to the right of the Royal Hall led first to a small Courtyard inspired by the late Tuscan Quattrocento, and from there to the Piazzetta, a true Italian monastic cloister: a spacious rectangle surrounded by a portico with semicircular arches and, in the center, a garden laid out with pathways leading to a well. To crown this scene, already in itself idyllic

Siena's yellow marble well in front of the Tribune
Florence, Università degli Studi, Department of Architecture, Piacentini Archive

The Quattrocento Palace, also called "Palazzo Lombardo," published in *L'Edilizia Moderna*, XXIV, fasc. XI (November 1915): plate LII
Florence, Università degli Studi, Department of Architecture, Piacentini Archive

and evocative of many illustrious pages by poets and travelers, was the Tribune, or Pantheon, in Roman Renaissance style. On leaving the Piazzetta via the rear of the Tribune, one came to a last poetic space: the Italianate Garden, divided by paths and squares and with seats surrounded by low boxwood bushes from where the view ended at a baroque nymphaeum.

In San Francisco, Piacentini's intention was not simply to create a national pavilion—his goal was vastly more ambitious: what the Roman architect wanted to do was to recreate overseas the atmosphere of an Italian town, the life that goes on among the alleyways and covered passages of villages, and even the air breathed in the country most dreamed of by Americans. All the senses were to be involved during a visit to the Citadel: great attention was paid to the layout of the fountains that enlivened the various areas with the sound of water, and to the choice of Mediterranean herbs that recalled the scent of gardens, and even to the perfect simulation of the patina of time on stones, marbles, and bricks. In fact, Piacentini succeeded in designing and actualizing the experience—not real, but deliberately "authentic"—of an Italian town. To achieve this, the architect knew he had to have maximum control over every detail of the construction site in order to "guide" the visitors' perception: their emotions, their desire for Italy, and perhaps their memories related to that country. It is no coincidence that the theme of nostalgia felt by Italian immigrants in California was often mentioned by Piacentini and by the national press that followed the event. "I wanted to recreate the illusion of being in Italy,"[41] he said, aware that with his project he had created "a reflection of the divine beauty of the Great Mother far away,"[42] "a source of legitimate pride for her many children scattered abroad."[43]

The Court of Palms at the 1915 Expo
Fresno (CA), California State University,
Donald G. Larson Collection on
International Expositions and Fairs

The Palace of Liberal Arts facade
at the 1915 Expo
Fresno (CA), California State University,
Donald G. Larson Collection on
International Expositions and Fairs

The dome of the Philosophy Palace
of Education and Social Economy
at the 1915 Expo
Fresno (CA), California State University,
Donald G. Larson Collection on
International Expositions and Fairs

The colonnade along the east wall of the
Palace of Agriculture at the 1915 Expo
Fresno (CA), California State University,
Donald G. Larson Collection on
International Expositions and Fairs

Many other exhibition pavilions were built in a classical style and often included Italian motifs:[44] Neoclassicism was the preferred style of all the event's main buildings, such as the Palace of Liberal Arts, the Palace of Fine Arts, the Palace of Education, and the Tower of Jewels, the symbol of the event. Statues, columns, arches, loggias, domes, entrances framed by fluted pilasters, as well as courtyards, porticoes, pergolas, and nymphaea populated and embellished every corner of the exhibition. But the emotion of the encounter with the Italian Citadel was perceptible and felt by everyone: to the eyes of the visitors, the classical forms of the other pavilions must have seemed a mere grotesque imitation of a distant myth, yet a myth that could still be glimpsed, since it had providentially materialized on the West Coast through the efforts of a Roman architect.

It must have seemed like a dream—for an American, for an Italian immigrant, for every foreign visitor—to ascend the stairway, to stand in the square, to walk in the shadow of the porticoes, or to find refuge in the garden that echoed with the jets of water from the nymphaeum. This was Italy, it could only be Italy, and it did not matter that everything was made of ephemeral structures of American wood covered with papier-mâché and decorated to imitate Medieval bricks or sixteenth-century embellishments.

Captivated by the "allure of wondrous beauty" offered by the Italian Citadel, the international jury awarded it the sole Grand Prize out of 110 competing pavilions. It was one further confirmation of American interest in Italy. In 1915 the Citadel determined the success of the Italian formula for architecture, art, and craftsmanship on the West Coast: it took root even more deeply and symbolically, opening the way for the artistic and entrepreneurial endorsement of another illustrious Italian, Salvatore Ferragamo, who would shortly move to California.

[1] Charles Dudley Warner, *Our Italy* (New York: Harper & Brothers, 1891), 2.

[2] In writing this essay, publications and unpublished documents were consulted from the Fondo Piacentini (Library of the Department of Architecture at the University of Florence) and the American Academy library in Rome. The research was also supported by consulting material available at the following digital archives: Calisphere, University of California; Hathi Trust; and Pasadena Digital History Collaboration.

[3] An earlier book by the same publishing house laments the lack of knowledge the rest of the United States' inhabitants had about California: Charles Nordhoff, *California: for Health, Pleasure, and Residence* (New York: Harper & Brothers, 1872). In the preface (11), Nordhoff dwells on the contradiction whereby many Americans felt the need to visit Europe, but not the beauties of their own country: "There have been Americans who saw Rome before they saw Niagara . . . Now, I have no objections to Europe; but I would like to induce Americans, when they contemplate a journey for health, pleasure, or instruction, or all three, to think also of their own country, and particularly of California, which has so many delights in store for the tourists, and so many attractions for the farmer or settler looking for a mild and healthful climate, and a productive country."

[4] Christian Norberg-Schulz, *Architettura del Nuovo Mondo* (Rome: Officina Edizioni, 1988), 15.

[5] For more on this topic, see *Architecture in California, 1868–1968*, ed. by David Gebhard and Harriette Von Breton (Santa Barbara: University of California, 1968); Peter Holliday, *American Arcadia: California and the Classical Tradition* (Oxford: Oxford University Press, 2016); *Housing the New Roman: Architectural Reception and Classical Style in the Modern World*, ed. by Katharine Von Stackelberg and Elizabeth Macaulay-Lewis (Oxford: Oxford University Press, 2017); Sam Watters, *Houses of Los Angeles 1920–1935* (New York: Acanthus Press, 2007). Also of particular interest is a publication from the period: Josephine Clifford McCrackin, "Villa Montalvo," in *Overland Monthly*, April 1915.

[6] Here, Baudrillard's reflections on the concept of the simulacrum come to mind: Jean Baudrillard, *Amerique* (Paris: Grasset & Fasquelle, 1986).

[7] "One obvious result [of the transfer of forms] is the fragmentation and relativization. The New World, in fact, no longer consists in integrated systems based on definite values, but has become a chaotic aggregate of scattered 'fragments' that in this way manifest freedom of choice," Norberg-Schulz, *Architettura del Nuovo Mondo* 1988, 11.

[8] Michael Corbett, *Hearst Memorial Gymnasium* (San Francisco: SMWM, 2005).

[9] The client expressly asked the architects for a building that recalled the atmosphere of the Palace of Fine Arts built for the 1915 Panama-Pacific International Exposition of San Francisco, a Neoclassical structure designed by Bernard Maybeck (1862–1957).

[10] Katharine Hooker, Marian Osgood Hooker, and Myron Hunt, *Farmhouses and Small Provincial Buildings in Southern Italy* (New York: Architectural Book Publishing Co., 1925).

[11] Katharine Putnam Hooker (1849–1935) is the author of travel books, particularly ones on Italy; among them *Wayfarers in Italy* (1891), *Byways in Southern Tuscany* (1918), and *Through the Heel of Italy* (1927).

[12] The Polish actress's residence was finished in the mid-1920s in a variety of architectural styles: specifically, the main part in colonial style, contrasted by gardens and outdoor spaces in Italian style.

[13] Letter from Matilde Festa Piacentini to her mother, San Francisco, March 20, 1915, Archivio Piacentini, University of Florence. Sincere thanks to archive director Gianna Frosali for her valuable assistance during the archival research.

[14] On the role of artists and Italian craftsmen in America, see Regina Soria, *Fratelli lontani. Il contributo degli artisti italiani all'identità degli Stati Uniti (1776–1945)* (Naples: Liguori, 1997).

[15] On this theme, see Jean Paul Carlhian and Margot M. Ellis, *Americans in Paris* (New York: Rizzoli, 2014).

[16] A vast amount of literature has been written on the theme of the Grand Tour. Despite this, few texts have dealt in depth on the effect that visiting Italy had on the work of foreign architects; see Denise Costanzo, "Travel Architects and the Postwar Grand Tour," in *University of Toronto Art Journal* 1, 2008; Andrea Maglio,

L'Arcadia è una terra straniera: gli architetti tedeschi e il mito dell'Italia nell'Ottocento (Naples: Clean, 2009); Fabio Mangone, Viaggi a Sud: gli architetti nordici e l'Italia, 1850–1925 (Naples: Electa, 2006).

[17] A victim of damnatio memoriae because of his relationship with the fascist regime, only recently did the work of Marcello Piacentini receive a critical reinterpretation. Among the major texts are: Christine Beese, Marcello Piacentini. Moderner Städtebau in Italien (Berlin: Reimer, 2015); Marcello Piacentini architetto, 1881–1960, Conference Papers (Rome, December 16–17, 2010), ed. by Giorgio Ciucci, Simonetta Lux, and Franco Purini (Rome: Gangemi, 2015); Arianna Sara De Rose, Marcello Piacentini. Opere 1903–1926 (Modena: Franco Cosimo Panini, 1995); Architettura moderna di Marcello Piacentini, ed. by Mario Pisani (Venice: Marsilio, 1996); Francesco Tentori, "Marcello Piacentini a cinquanta anni dalla scomparsa," in Rassegna di architettura e urbanistica 130/131 (September–December 2010). See also two recent doctoral dissertations: Guia Baratelli, Dalla trasformazione di un paesaggio alla costruzione di un modello, La Città Universitaria di Roma, tutor F. Cellini (Ph.D. diss., Università degli Studi Roma Tre, 2017); Alessandra Ciacciofera, Inter urbes et colles. Via Bissolati, Roma. Ragioni della forma di una strada dell'architetto Marcello Piacentini, tutor F. Cellini (Ph.D. diss., Università degli Studi Roma Tre, 2017).

[18] Marcello Piacentini, "Confidenze di un architetto," in Scienza e tecnica, February 2, 1943: 56. The quotation is repeated by Clementina Barucci in "La biblioteca di Marcello Piacentini," in Marcello Piacentini architetto 2015, 73.

[19] Piacentini seems to be particularly up to date on the contemporary building output of France and Germany, which he visited for the first time in 1910 and 1913 respectively. This experience was fundamental in his development and sensitivity as an architect.

[20] His knowledge of Russian architecture was probably also the fruit of his association with Boris Iofan in Rome: Marcello Piacentini, "I grattacieli a tavolone," in Il Globo, November 23, 1952: 3, now in Architettura moderna di Marcello Piacentini 1996, 278.

[21] The title of the present contribution, "Italian Architectural Influences in California," pays homage to Piacentini's essay Influssi d'arte italiana nel Nord-America, the first piece written from an Italian perspective to address the topic of Italian references in early twentieth-century American architecture.

[22] Together with a few other Italian architects, such as Gustavo Giovannoni, Piacentini was among the supporters of the interest in "spontaneous" and regional Italian architecture. A first important recognition of the minor arts of the various national areas was the Ethnographic Exhibition at the 1911 Rome International Expo. To mark the first fifty years of the Unification of Italy, pavilions representing the various regional architectural features were built on Piazza d'Armi. Piacentini took part in this exhibition with the design for the Palazzo delle Feste. The theme of spontaneous architecture and its specific regional features later became one of the main topics of the post-war architectural debate, in particular due to the cultural current of Neorealism which, together with architecture, influenced many others of the nation's forms of artistic expression.

[23] Marcello Piacentini, "Influssi d'arte italiana nel Nord-America," in Architettura e arti decorative I, 6 (January–February 1922): 536–55, now in Architettura moderna di Marcello Piacentini 1996, 110.

[24] Ibid., 111.

[25] Ibid.

[26] Werner Hegermann, Elbert Peets, and Alan J. Plattus, The American Vitruvius: An Architect's Handbook of Civic Art (New York: The Architectural Book Publishing Co., 1922).

[27] Marcello Piacentini, "Il momento architettonico all'estero," in Architettura e Arti decorative I, 1 (May–June 1921): 32–76, now in Architettura moderna di Marcello Piacentini 1996, 91.

[28] See also Piacentini, "I grattacieli a tavolone" 1952, 3, now in Architettura moderna di Marcello Piacentini 1996, 277–280.

[29] Marcello Piacentini, Architettura d'oggi (Rome: Cremonese, 1930), 40.

[30] This is a rather small number of images compared to the 29 German, 21 French and 36 Italian projects selected by Piacentini for the same book.

[31] Piacentini, Architettura d'oggi 1930, 41.

[32] For further information on Marcello Piacentini's experience in California, see also Rosa Sessa, "Marcello Piacentini e il mito della città italiana in America. La Cittadella Italiana all'Esposizione internazionale di San Francisco del 1915," in Il segno delle esposizioni nazionali e internazionali nella memoria storica delle città, ed. by Stefania Aldini, Carla Benocci, Stefania Ricci, and Ettore Sessa (Rome: Edizioni Kappa, 2014), 493–511.

[33] Letter from Marcello Piacentini to Maria Piacentini, Chicago, March 12, 1915, Archivio Piacentini, University of Florence.

[34] Ibid.

[35] Ibid.

[36] In addition to Piacentini and Matilde Festa, who created the portico paintings, others involved in work on the Citadel were the engineer Giacomo Giobbe, the painters Pieretto Bianco and Bruno Ferrari, the sculptor Giovan Battista Portanova, and Cesare Formilli and his building firm.

[37] Letter from Marcello Piacentini and Matilde Festa to Pio Piacentini, San Francisco, March 26, 1915 Archivio Piacentini, University of Florence.

[38] Ibid.

[39] Inaugural speech by Piacentini, in "L'Italia all'Esposizione di San Francisco," in Emporium XLII, no. 274 (July 1915): 78.

[40] Della Cittadella Italiana all'Esposizione di San Francisco, ed. by the Royal Italian Commission for the San Francisco International Exposition (Rome: Stabilimento Tipografico "Aternum" di Enrico Sabucchi, 1915), 28.

[41] Ibid., 27.

[42] Inaugural speech by Arduino Colasanti, in "L'Italia all'Esposizione di San Francisco" 1915, 79.

[43] John Arturo Rusconi, "L'Italia all'Esposizione di San Francisco," in Emporium XL, no. 235 (1914): 76.

[44] Official Guide of the Panama-Pacific International Exposition – 1915 (San Francisco: The Walgreen Company, 1915).

STEFANIA RICCI

ITALIAN ARTISTS AT THE PANAMA-PACIFIC INTERNATIONAL EXPOSITION IN SAN FRANCISCO

The 1915 Panama-Pacific International Exposition in San Francisco was the largest fair to be held in the United States between those of St. Louis (1904) and Chicago (1933–34); it received nineteen million visitors and came just nine years after the violent earthquake that had almost completely destroyed the city. The event was organized to celebrate the opening of the Panama Canal (August 1914), which was to provide new commercial outlets for California and the entire country. The exhibition included thirty-two American states and territories and twenty-eight foreign nations, including Italy.[1]

The Italian presence at the American fair was focused on creating new economic relationships with America, and above all on maintaining strong ties—albeit at a distance—with the two and a half million fellow Italians who were living on American soil at the time and whose success in commercial enterprises, especially in California, had distinguished them from other immigrant communities. In the pamphlet written by Vittorio Zeggio in 1914 on preparations for the event, he examined the new profile of the typical visitor to the universal expositions; no longer was it a qualified visitor but a consumer interested in a country's specialties and original products on sale during the event.[2] The world fair thus became a large showcase providing an opportunity to present the best of each country's goods. In the variously themed pavilions, Italian products certainly did not go unnoticed, for instance the clothes and fabrics of Maria Monaci Gallenga. The Italian fashion designer and entrepreneur received the Grand Prize for her garments made of velvet, silk crepe and crêpe de chine, printed with her own designs taken from antique sources (from "a fresco by Pinturicchio," from "a Florentine design," from "the cope of Pope Boniface VIII"). Thanks to the San Francisco event, her creations soon made her famous in the American market.[3]

Among the personalities populating the Expo was Maria Montessori, who in 1907 had opened her first Children's Houses in Rome, also attended by American kids living in Italy. In 1909, with the assistance of Baron Leopoldo Franchetti and his American wife, Alice Hallgarten Franchetti, she had published her book *The Montessori Method: Scientific Pedagogy as Applied to Child Education in the Children's Houses*. It was noblewoman Franchetti who had personally organized Montessori's first American trip in 1913, during which she was received by American president Thomas Woodrow Wilson. Her educational method spread, giving rise in North America to a hundred schools organized according to her teachings.[4] Following the success of this first tour, Montessori was invited to introduce and demonstrate her method at the San Francisco Exposition, since education was one of its most important themes. The Montessori lessons were held for four months, from August to November, in the Palace of Education and Social Economy in a classroom surrounded by glass, which allowed

The Canessa exhibition staged in the Italian Citadel's Medieval Palace, published in *Della Cittadella Italiana alla Esposizione di San Francisco* (Rome: Stabilimento Tipografico "Aternum" di Enrico Sabucchi, 1915), 34

The Casa Italiana: The Museum, published in *Della Cittadella Italiana alla Esposizione di San Francisco* (Rome: Stabilimento Tipografico "Aternum" di Enrico Sabucchi, 1915), 39. In the centre, the bronze sculpture made by the Chiurazzi foundry in Naples, with the replica of *Mercury at Rest*, the Roman sculpture conserved in the Archaeological Museum of Naples

Cover of the catalogue for the Italian section at the exhibition installed in the Palace of Fine Arts, edited by Ettore Ferrari and Arduino Colasanti Florence, Museo Salvatore Ferragamo

ITALIA

VITTORIO GRASSI

INTERNATIO: NAL PANAMA-PACIFIC EXHI: BITION SAN FRANCISCO CALIFORNIA 1915

E. CALZONE · ROMA

Ettore Tito, *La perla*
[The Pearl], 1914
Oil on canvas, 88.5 x 66 cm
Private collection

Plinio Nomellini, *Baci di sole*
[Kisses of the Sun], [1908]
Oil on canvas, 93 x 119 cm
Novara, Galleria d'Arte Moderna
Paolo e Adele Giannoni

Giuseppe Graziosi,
Susanna, 1910
Bronze, 46 x 42 x 30 cm
Piacenza, Galleria d'Arte
Moderna Ricci Oddi, inv. 264

Eugenio Pellini,
L'idolo [The Idol], [1906]
Bronze, 74 x 73 x 66 cm
Bologna, Fondazione Lercaro

the twenty American children, aged between three and six, to be seen by visitors without being disturbed or distracted by their presence. Since the Italian educator did not speak English, she assisted in the activities as an observer. The live demonstrations were held by Helen Parkhurst, an American student of Montessori's who had attended the teacher training courses in Rome, which were started in 1913. When Montessori was called back to Italy at the end of November due to the death of her father, her son, Mario, who had accompanied her on the trip, decided to stay on in California. In 1917 he opened a class in Los Angeles based on the Montessori method, which became so widely known that it was attended by the children of celebrities such as actors Mary Pickford and Douglas Fairbanks.

The construction of the Italian Pavilion at the San Francisco fair was commissioned from the Roman architect Marcello Piacentini, who delegated the decorative part of the architectural project to his trusted collaborators: his wife Matilde Festa, who painted the portico lunettes with episodes form the Crusades in neo-fifteenth-century style; Pieretto Bianco and Bruno Ferrari (the son of Ettore Ferrari), who undertook the pictorial part; and Giovan Battista Portanuova, who made the sculptures. The project also included two exhibitions: one held at the Medieval Palace and the other at the Quattrocento Palace, both inside the Italian Citadel that Piacentini had created for the Exposition. The Medieval Palace hosted the Canessa art show, which included a considerable number of ancient, original, and very valuable works of art from the collection of the famous Neapolitan merchant

and collector Ercole Canessa: furniture, sculptures, bronzes, majolica and classical antiquities. The exhibition was particularly noteworthy for its fifteenth- and early sixteenth-century sculpture, which served to increase many American collectors' appreciation of the Renaissance, and opened the way to subsequent sales from the collection itself, which were held in New York in 1919 and then in 1924.[5]

The Quattrocento Palace, located to the right of the Piazza Grande, housed the Italian Commission's offices and reception rooms, richly decorated by the Monti firm from Milan. From the palace hall one entered the Casa Italiana, a vast building located on the smaller Piazzetta. More than an exhibition, it was a reproduction of a sumptuous, princely apartment, with walls covered in brocades and damasks and coffered wooden ceilings richly decorated in various styles. The work was of the highest quality and had been carried out by a number of specialized Italian firms; among them, the Neapolitan Chiurazzi foundry, famous for their reproductions of Classical masterpieces, and that of Antonio and Umberto Frilli from Via dei Fossi in Florence, already famous in the United States for their woodcarvings and replications of Renaissance sculptures. The firm's founder Antonio Frilli had in fact received an important commission in California from Sir Leland Stanford to make the gigantic sculptures destined for the Palo Alto University located on San Francisco Bay.[6]

The presence of Italian artists in San Francisco is recorded not only in the Citadel. As part of the exhibition route, Bernard Ralph Maybeck designed an imposing Palace of Fine Arts, which was destined to house 11,400 paintings, sculptures, and drawings from the countries taking part in the event. John E. D. Trask, former director of the Pennsylvania Academy of Fine Arts, was appointed coordinator of the Department of Fine Arts, while Captain John Asher C. Baker was given the task of visiting the participant countries to direct the sending of the artworks to San Francisco. The organizers intended to show international contemporary art produced during the last ten years, although in the end a historical part was also included in the American art section, with information on the works and trends that had most influenced its development.[7]

Italian art occupied five galleries (number 21 to 25) on the ground floor of the Palazzo, with the presence of 122 artists and 159 works that offered a broad overview of current Italian pictorial and sculptural production. It included works by Ettore Tito, Camillo Innocenti, Antonio Mancini and Plinio Nomellini, Giuseppe Graziosi, Vincenzo Gemito, and Arturo

Dazzi. The organizers of the Italian art display were Ettore Ferrari, president of the Third Section of the Superior Council of Antiquities and Fine Arts, assisted by art historian Arduino Colasanti.[8]

Italian artists were praised and won a number of prizes. The Grand Prize for Painting was assigned to Ettore Tito, who showed five works. Gold medals were won by Onorato Carlandi, Camillo Innocenti, Plinio Nomellini, Giuseppe Graziosi for *Susanna* and Arturo Dazzi for *Moderna Diana*.[9] All in all, the exhibition at the Palace of Fine Arts received the approval of visitors and collectors, who had the opportunity to buy works at "studio prices," certified by a committee of experts.[10]

Italy's participation at the PPIE (as Americans called the San Francisco exposition) was enthusiastically commented on in the Italian press: it had provided an opportunity to demonstrate that Italian products were able to compete with those of other nations. For a long time Italy's success remained a reason for legitimate pride for Italians residing in America, who saw the artistic values of ancient and modern Italy reaffirmed, in addition to the fascination Italian architecture and art had always held for the United States. However, there was also negative criticism from those who denounced the anachronistic repetition of architectural models of the past and artisanal products that harked back to traditional styles, compared to the modernity and practicality of buildings designed by other countries, such as Austria, Hungary or Belgium, which were able to incorporate the achievements of modern industry and art.[11]

No mention was made of the Futurist works exhibited in San Francisco: forty-two paintings and two sculptures. They were displayed on the second floor of a building adjoining the Palace of Fine Arts, where Norwegian critic J. N. Laurvik, a long-time North American resident, had been commissioned by the Expo organizing committee to gather a large number of modern European artworks intended for the discernment of a more elite public.[12] In May 1916, almost at the end of the event, Umberto Boccioni had a quarrel with the Italian press, which in its commitment to praising the success of the "official, commercial, and academic Italian art" had failed to mention the participation of the Futurists.[13]

The works selected for display were the same as those presented in the rooms of the Doré Galleries in London in April 1914, except "some drawings by Boccioni, a self-portrait by Marinetti, *Mademoiselle Flicflic Chapchap* by Marinetti and Cangiullo, *Spessori di un'atmosfera* by Giacomo Balla (which had been sold to a woman from Munich) and the paintings by Soffici, who was probably absent due to his split from the group, conclusively confirmed in the article 'Futurismo e Marinettismo,' published in *Lacerba* on February 14, 1915, a few days before the Expo opened."[14]

The Futurists had disregarded the important 1913 appointment at the Armory Show in New York, which introduced new art forms that had influenced American artistic trends and collectors' taste. They had preferred to take part in the First Roman Secession exhibition, which was to be held during the same period. For this reason, they did not want to miss the opportunity to enter the American market afforded by the Panama-Pacific event.

The Italian avant-garde was not entirely unknown in the United States: there were photographs of their works, English translations of their manifestos published by various newspapers and magazines, and reports of Filippo Tommaso Marinetti's often explosive public statements. However, it was the first time that Futurist works were to be shown in the United States. None

Amleto Cataldi, *La spiga*
[Wheat], [1909]
Bronze, 52 x 19 x 15 cm
Rome, Galleria d'Arte Moderna
di Roma Capitale, inv. AM247

Gabriel Moulin, *Gallery
141 with the works by the
Futurists displayed at
the 1915 Panama-Pacific
International Exposition*
On the left can be seen
Giacomo Balla's work
*Disgregazione X velocità
Penetrazioni dinamiche
di automobile* [Disintegration
X speed, Dynamic penetrations
of an automobile]
San Francisco, San Francisco
History Center, Public Library

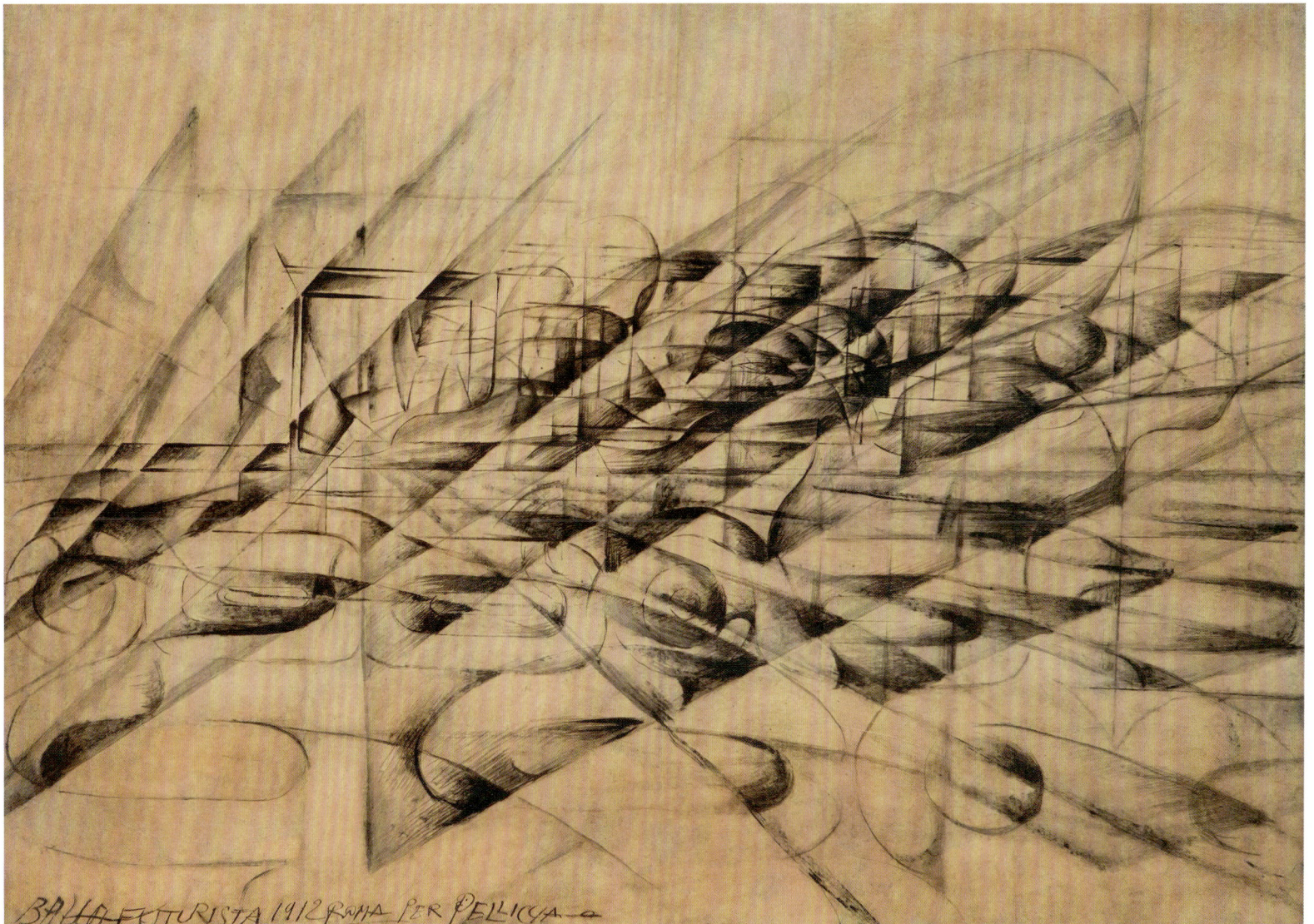

Giacomo Balla,
Disgregazione X velocità
Penetrazioni dinamiche
di automobile [Disintegration
X speed, Dynamic
penetrations of an
automobile], 1913
Tempera, watercolor, and
Indian ink on paper,
67.7 x 95.7 cm
The work was shown with
no. 1131 in Gallery 141 at
the San Francisco Expo
Bologna, Fondazione
Massimo e Sonia Cirulli

Luigi Russolo,
Case e fanali [Houses
and Lights], 1911
Oil on canvas, 40 x 70 cm
Bologna, Fondazione
Massimo e Sonia Cirulli

of the works on display was published in the official catalogue, although Boccioni's essay written for the other European exhibitions was reprinted.[15] "There can be no doubt that the selection of contemporary art that was shown in the annex of the Palace of Fine Arts at the PPIE confirmed the new awareness of an evolution in art, now no longer solely European, which aside from its provocative character was positively influencing American art. Although only two years had passed since 1913, in San Francisco there were none of the street demonstrations that had accompanied the Armory Show, whose artworks many people had deemed scandalously immoral. We believe this to be the reason for the limited show of surprise—disappointingly inferior to Italian expectations—that the Futurists received in San Francisco.[16]

Despite Boccioni's impression, all the American guidebooks to the art sections did in fact record the presence of the Futurists. In his 1916 account of the San Francisco Expo, Christian Brinton shows appreciation for these novel forms of expression that seemed to be pouring new and vital sap into American art: "It is futile to expend one's energies debating whether such tentative manifestations as those under discussion have, or have not, any rightful place in art. The fact remains that they are here, hanging upon our walls, and that alone must go far toward justifying their existence. There is scant doubt but that much of this work is predominantly occult, or even at times positively hieratic. And still, despite what may be termed its over-individualization, it presages a profound spiritual rebirth in the province of aesthetic endeavour . . . Great things were freely predicted for American art following the initial influx of these stimulating and progressive foreign ideas."[17]

[1] For more on this subject, see Lucia Masina, "Panama-Pacific International Exposition San Francisco 1915," in *Vedere l'Italia nelle esposizioni universali del XX secolo: 1900–1958. Atti della Summer School Esposizioni* (Milan: EDUCatt, 2016), 123–62, and James A. Ganz, *Jewel City: Art from San Francisco's Panama-Pacific International Exposition*, catalogue of the exhibition held to mark the centennial of the PPIE at De Young Museum, San Francisco (San Francisco: University of California Press, 2015).

[2] Vittorio Zeggio, *L'Italia all'Esposizione di San Francisco: Osservazioni e proposte* (Florence: Tipografia del Nuovo Giornale, 1914).

[3] Roberta Orsi Landini, "Alle origini della grande moda italiana. Maria Monaci Gallenga," in *Moda femminile tra le due guerre*, ed. by Caterina Chiarelli (Florence: Sillabe, 2000), 30–41: 31–32.

[4] Paola Giovetti, *Maria Montessori. Una biografia* (Rome: Edizioni Mediterranee, 2009).

[5] *Illustrated Catalogue of the Canessa Collection of Rare and Valuable Objects of Art of the Egyptian, Greek, Roman, Gothic and Renaissance Periods. Descriptive matter by Mr. Ernest Govett, Greek and Roman objects; Miss Stella Rubinstein, Gothic and Renaissance objects; Prof. Arduino Colasanti, Renaissance objects*, privately printed for C. & E., Canessa, New York, 1919; *Illustrated Catalogue of the Art Collection of the Expert Antiquarians C. & E. Canessa of New York, Paris, Naples . . . gathered from important collections of Europe: to be sold at the American Art Galleries on Jan 25–26, 1924*, privately printed for C. & E., Canessa, New York, 1924.

[6] *Della Cittadella Italiana all'Esposizione di San Francisco*, ed. by the Royal Italian Commission for the San Francisco International Exposition (Rome: Stabilimento tipografico "Aternum" di Enrico Sabucchi, 1915), 33–42.

[7] Masina, "Panama-Pacific" 2016, 135–37.

[8] See Arduino Colasanti and Ettore Ferrari, *International Panama-Pacific Exhibition San Francisco California 1915. Italian Fine Art Section* (Rome: Stabilimento di arti grafiche E. Calzone, 1915).

[9] "L'Italia all'Esposizione di San Francisco," in *Emporium* 247: 77–80; John Ellingwood Donnell Trask and J. Nilsen Laurvik, *Catalogue de luxe of the Department of Fine Arts Panama-Pacific International Exposition in Two Volumes: Volume Two* (San Francisco: Paul Elder and Company, 1915), 92–95, 156–59.

[10] Sheldon Cheney, *An Art-Lover's Guide to the Exposition* (Berkeley: At the Sign of the Berkeley Oak: 1915); Masina, "Panama-Pacific" 2016, 138.

[11] Giulio U. Arata, "I padiglioni dell'Italia all'Esposizione di San Francisco," in *Pagine d'Arte* 2, no. 11 (June 5, 1914): 149–50. The article also refers to a text by Diego Angeli for the *Giornale d'Italia* newspaper. See also Masina, "Panama-Pacific" 2016, 133–34.

[12] Trask and Laurvik, *Catalogue de luxe* 1915, 123–27, 273–74; Masina, "Panama-Pacific" 2016, 139–43.

[13] Umberto Boccioni, "Le Arti Plastiche (Il monumento a Missori. L'arte italiana all'Esposizione di San Francisco, La mostra di Sarzana)," in *Gli Avvenimenti*, May 14–21, 1916: 5.

[14] Silvia Bignami, "Futurismo, nazionalismo, massoneria. L'Italia alla Panama-Pacific International Exposition di San Francisco, 1915," in *L'Uomo Nero* I, no. 1 (June 2003): 114–18.

[15] John Oliver Hand, "Futurism in America: 1909–14," in *Art Journal* 41, no. 4 (1981): 337–42.

[16] Masina, "Panama-Pacific" 2016, 141.

[17] Christian Brinton, *Impressions of the Art of the Panama-Pacific Exposition* (New York: John Lane Company, 1916), 25.

ROBERTA FERRAZZA

ITALIAN KNOW-HOW IN HOLLYWOOD

In 1907, the Selig Polyscope Company decided to shoot the exteriors of the film *The Count of Monte Cristo*, directed by Francis Boggs, in Southern California instead of Chicago. This marked the beginning of a period that would culminate in the recognition of Los Angeles as the permanent and most popular center of the young cinema industry. In 1908, Selig opened a studio in Olive Street, downtown, closely followed by other entrepreneurs and independent producers.[1]

The varied scenery, wide open spaces and mild year-round climate, combined with favorable laws, encouraged those wishing to invest in film production and distribution to move their businesses to the City of Angels, or set up new ones there. Apropos of this Philip E. Rosen, then president of the American Society of Cinematographers which had moved to Los Angeles two years previously, wrote in 1920: "There is every evidence that the charms and alluring nature-settings of Los Angeles, San Bernardino, Riverside, Redlands, the mountains and foothill districts tributary, and famed Catalina Island, which are embodied in moving pictures, are popular throughout the world. Through the great variety of scenery, plains, forests . . . mountains and marine perspectives, this country offers unusual advantages for the settings of moving picture scenarios, especially in the radiant days of the almost continuous summer months—and nearly all the year is summer in Southland . . . These great advantages have led to a new industrialism. In Southern California, moving pictures studios . . . have been erected in many places, and what the neighborhood has to give to the pictures in perfect surroundings will be returned in commercial profits."[2]

Growth was so rapid that in 1920 around 80 percent of all the films made in the United States were already being produced in the Los Angeles area. "Motion Picture Making Attracts Notable People to Los Angeles and Southern California. Important Developments in Evidence in All Studios. Los Angeles is steadily forging ahead as the greatest of all motion picture producing centers of the world. Millions of dollars are being paid out annually in salaries and operating expenses by companies located in this city."[3]

Between 1910 and 1920 enterprising and visionary impresarios, who would bring international fame to Hollywood through film production and the creation of the "star system," built their studios here with all the necessary technical and logistical apparatuses.[4] In 1920, according to statistics provided by *The American Cinematographer*, there were ninety production companies and the number of stars and actors who had chosen Los Angeles as their "home city" and owned "cozy, some costly and elaborate, homes and estates" topped one hundred, "all adding to the financial importance of the city and creating an atmosphere of permanency for the motion picture industry that is far reaching and valuable." More than eighty-five major directors lived in palatial homes.[5]

Between 1910 and 1930 many theaters, housed in elaborate buildings in diverse architectural styles, sprang up in various parts of Los Angeles. They were designed to enable the public to enjoy the "Dream Factory," which was associated with glamour and luxury, with scandal and extravagance; the evening's entertainment, which could last as long as three hours, featured the movie that was being promoted, as well as short films and live shows. In 1930 Los Angeles had over 1,500 theaters in which films were projected, with the highest concentration downtown, between 3rd Street and Olympic Boulevard in South Broadway. One of the first to be built, in 1910, solely for the purpose of screening movies, was Clune's Broadway Theatre, which was initially owned by William H. Clune, who used it to promote the films that he himself produced. The Palace Theatre, originally known as the Orpheum Theater, was erected in 1911 for staging live shows and converted into a movie theater in 1926. The remodeling was designed by the architect G. Albert Lansburgh, who drew inspiration from the Casino in Venice. Polychrome terracotta was used, for the first time in Los Angeles, to decorate its facade. 1927 saw the building of the Tower Theater, the first to be fitted with sound equipment combining the Movietone and Vitaphone systems; the United Artists Theatre was built the same year. In 1922 Grauman's Egyptian Theatre, the first movie palace constructed in the actual Hollywood area, was inaugurated with a screening of *Robin Hood* starring Douglas Fairbanks: the first gala premiere ever held in Hollywood.

The junction between Olive Street and 7th Street, Los Angeles, 1920
Los Angeles, Los Angeles Public Library, Security Pacific National Bank Collection

On the set of *The Woman Racket* at Metro Goldwyn Mayer Studios, Los Angeles, early 1930s
Los Angeles, Los Angeles Public Library, Security Pacific National Bank Collection

At the various premieres, hundreds of spectators would gather outside and inside the theaters, waiting for their favorite screen idols who would be immortalized by an army of photographers and reporters; images and stories that shed light on their professional and private lives were published in newspapers and magazines.[6]

Alberto Rabagliati arrived in Los Angeles in 1927 as the winner of a competition to find new faces held by Fox in Italy, and stayed in Hollywood until 1931. In his autobiography *Quattro anni fra le "Stelle,"* he describes these social events in detail and comments on the socio-cultural phenomenon they represented: "This first screening is a real gala event. The prices are exorbitant: from 10 to 15 dollars . . . Not only is the entire Hollywood colony in attendance, but also the wealthy families of Los Angeles. The 'boulevard' . . . is lit by powerful spotlights all the way up to the entrance of the movie theater. The public throngs at either side . . . and when the limousines conveying the leading actors glide by, there is thunderous applause and flowers rain down on them. The stars smile and wave, visibly gratified by this wild enthusiasm that accompanies every screening and seems . . . to suggest that the public is always looking for new ways to show its affection, and how much the American masses worship their Hollywood idols. It's a slight form of collective madness, whose transmission to the rest of the world has once again meant 'business' for the Americans, since it has been the making of their second industry. In the auditorium, the gowns and jewels paraded for the occasion create a fabulous show . . . Outside, the crowd, which has waited hours for its idols to come out, call for them, want to see them, acclaim them. Amidst the crowd there are many who have long dreamed of receiving such applause, but as they admire the opulence of the others, they forget their envy and poverty, they forget their own—possibly superior—beauty and worship that which has triumphed, they forget their own intelligence and celebrate that of the luckier ones."[7] Movie stars became testimonials on all kinds of public occasions, from the opening of a bridge to the inauguration of a new railroad track, and their highly-publicized life style had a considerable influence on fashion and lifestyle, but also domestic habits and behavior. The magical, seductive images on the screen, which enabled audiences to escape, if only momentarily, from the everyday and fooled them into thinking that they could realize their dreams, became a unique cultural phenomenon that pervaded all aspects of daily life in America and the world.

Many new hotels were constructed, some of which particularly sophisticated from an architectural and decorative standpoint. They were frequented by the leading lights of the movie world, which made them popular places for holding public events connected with prize givings and celebrations in the business.

The Ambassador Hotel was built in the style of an Italian villa and opened on New Year's Eve in 1921. It was the first grand resort hotel in Los Angeles and many movie stars lived there on a long-term basis. It was a vast complex with gardens, tennis courts, inner courts with beautiful fountains and a swimming pool complete with sandy beach. The Cocoanut Grove, located inside the hotel, was considered the most fashionable nightclub in Los Angeles. The first big event held at the Ambassador after its inauguration was the Annual Ball

The opening of Grauman's
Egyptian Theatre in Los
Angeles with Douglas
Fairbanks as the guest of
honor, October 18, 1922
Los Angeles, Los Angeles
Public Library, Security Pacific
National Bank Collection

Marion Davies with Lawrence
Gray and Charlie Chaplin
for the premiere of the film
The Florodora Girl, directed by
Harry Beaumont, June 4, 1930
Los Angeles, Los Angeles
Public Library, Herald
Examiner Photograph
Collection

Marion Davies and Mrs.
Adolphus Busch with
a group of little orphans
at a benefit day, 1927
Los Angeles, Los Angeles
Public Library, Herald
Examiner Photograph
Collection

Marion Davies with
American football star
Harold "Red" Grange,
January 19, 1926
Los Angeles, Los Angeles
Public Library, Herald
Examiner Photograph
Collection

Marion Davies with
tennis champion
Suzanne Lenglen,
December 23, 1926
Los Angeles, Los Angeles
Public Library, Herald
Examiner Photograph
Collection

of the American Society of Cinematographers, which took place on January 29, 1921. No expense was spared in organizing the ball and the entire movie world, high society, and institutional big shots attended. The write-up in the Society's in-house organ expressed its complete satisfaction and described the decoration of the rooms and the various forms of entertainment that followed one after the other during the evening. It also listed the most important personalities who were there and gave a detailed description of what the ladies wore. The idea had been to recreate "a miniature motion picture land in the beautiful ball and assembly room of the new Ambassador Hotel . . . Attended by the Elite of the Screen World . . . was the first function in the new hotel in which the industry has been directly interested, and it was most enthusiastically supported. During the dancing, lights were lowered and colored rays played on the gliding couples, with the witchery that always comes with shifting color." Obviously there was dance music, followed by jazz after a certain hour, which was played by the Max Fisher Orchestra.[8]

In 1924, the film director Harry L. Fraser, who lived and worked in New York but wanted to move to California, arrived in Hollywood together with his girlfriend Shirley Kellogg, who had made a career for herself as an actress in England, to help her break into Hollywood through his contacts. They stayed at the Hotel Ambassador because, according to Fraser, "in those days, if you needed a showcase to present new talent, there was no better place than the Ambassador Hotel."[9] Between 1930 and 1943, the Academy Awards were presented at the hotel six times.

The Biltmore Hotel, which opened in 1923, was designed by architects Schultze & Weaver who drew inspiration from the Italian Renaissance, interpreted in a Spanish key: the extraordinarily rich interior decoration, with painted murals and polychrome stuccowork, was mostly executed by the Italian artist Giovanni Smeraldi, who also worked on New York's Grand Central Station and the Blue Room in the White House. In 1927, the Academy of Motion Picture Arts and Sciences was founded at an official dinner held at the Biltmore and attended by many important personages in the film industry: the story goes that the first sketch for the statuette that is still presented to Oscar winners was made on one of the hotel napkins. Rabagliati also describes, not without a touch of bitter irony, the sumptuous and

Marion Davies with Gloria Swanson,
Charlie Chaplin, Harold Lloyd,
Norma Shearer, and other friends
in the French Room of the Ambassador
Hotel, October 31, 1928
Los Angeles, Los Angeles Public Library,
Herald Examiner Photograph Collection

extravagant parties that were held regularly in the swankiest hotels: "It was in these hotels that events known as 'Moving Pictures Nights' were organized regularly, once a week, for the Hollywood community, which was a veritable elite. They competed with each other in dreaming up and throwing the best parties, always seeking to go one better, and only succeeding thanks to the amount of dollars that organizers and attendees contributed. It is a nonstop carnival, where you see the wildest costumes and the most comical parodies of life, in which Poverty is the most mocked."[10]

The Roosevelt Hotel was built in 1927 on behalf of a group of actors including Douglas Fairbanks and Mary Pickford. One of its aims was to provide reasonably priced accommodation for film directors, actors, and workers who, due to their professional engagements, had to stay in Hollywood for a certain period but did not live in the Los Angeles area. The first Academy Awards ceremony was held in this hotel on May 16, 1929.

The many clubs and the numerous leisure spots and sporting facilities that opened during the same period, both in the city and on the beaches, were also impressive.

In 1900 the Automobile Club of Southern California was inaugurated in Los Angeles. In the space of a few years the number of inhabitants using private automobiles increased exponentially: between 1920 and 1930 the number of vehicles registered in the Los Angeles area rose from 160,000 to 840,000, since a car was not only useful but became an indispensable status symbol. Rabagliati noticed this as soon as he arrived: "The amount of cars in Los Angeles is incredible. It is said that it is the North American city with the largest number . . . Everyone owns an automobile, from the superb Isotta Fraschini, Rolls-Royce, and Cadillac to the small Ford: all the automobile industry brands are here. Everybody uses a car, from the big star, who has more than one, to the extra and the 'girl'. . ."[11]

Another characterizing element of social life in general, and especially that in the movie business, was body care and the daily practice of one sport or another, either in the city's clubs or outdoors—preferably on the beach. The Hollywood Athletic Club and Women's Athletic Club opened around 1920. Rabagliati describes the former as follows: "it is a huge building with stores that sell every kind of sporting goods and equipment for practicing any type

Interior view of the Biltmore Hotel, 1926
Los Angeles, Los Angeles Public
Library, Security Pacific National
Bank Collection

The Italian racing driver Nina Vitagliano in a photograph of 1918. Vitagliano belonged to a group of women racing drivers called "The Speederettes." She died in a tragic accident while racing her Stutz on a dirt track in 1918 Stockton, University of the Pacific Library, Holt-Atherton Special Collections

of sport. It is frequented by practically all the actors, who go there before and after work to play tennis or Tommy golf, to take a Turkish bath or to do Swedish gymnastics; in other words, to practice the physical education necessary to keep their bodies as slim and lithe as their art requires."[12]

The style of many of the buildings that housed clubs was indebted to the Italian Renaissance. One of the most exclusive was the stunning palace that, as of 1924 (the year it was built), became the seat of the Jonathan Club: it was twelve storeys high, located between Figueroa Street and 7th Street, and designed by the same architects who had conceived the Biltmore Hotel, which, instead, housed the Mayfair Club whose members were almost exclusively "heads of production companies and big stars. The annual membership fee was around one thousand dollars."[13] In 1927, the Jonathan Beach Club would open its doors in Santa Monica.

In 1924, the Friday Morning Club opened on Figueroa Street, downtown. Designed by Allison & Allison, it was in the Renaissance style, like the Casa del Mar Beach Club, with its painted ceilings and bronze statuary, inaugurated in Santa Monica in 1926.

Built in 1904, Venice was a favorite with actors and many other movie people, who often chose to live there;[14] St. Mark's Hotel, with its Casino and Dance Pavilion, had immediately become an irresistible attraction for the Hollywood stars. Social life was very intense and many sporting, promotional, and entertaining events were held at the various venues along the ocean shore.

Luxury apartment blocks were designed by architects who were already famous in other parts of the country. Huge sums of money went into their construction and they were rented or sold to major figures in the movie business or leading personalities in the city that was still being built. Also in this case, the interiors and exteriors of the housing units often drew from Renaissance models. These

The Jonathan Club's Tuscan Terrace, 1910; in 1924 the club moved to the new premises on Figueroa Street Los Angeles, Los Angeles Public Library, Security Pacific National Bank Collection

The exterior of the Casa del Mar Beach Club in Santa Monica, 1926 Los Angeles, Los Angeles Public Library

N-002-762 6   4x5

The Living Checkers
Game played on Venice
Beach, 1930
Los Angeles, Los Angeles
Public Library, Security
Pacific National Bank
Collection

new apartment blocks include the Firenze Gardens Apartments (1922) on Sunset Boulevard, Hollywood Residence (1923), and The Langham Apartments, a residential complex that opened in 1927 and received much publicity because "its foyer was a replica of that of Davanzati Palace in Florence." The Gaylord Apartments, a fine fourteen-storey building right opposite the Ambassador Hotel, were completed in 1924. The prices of the apartments started at $7,850, half of which was given as a down payment, with the rest spread over a period of seventeen years. A large panel on the facade advertised the housing units, which were fully furnished and equipped with all the accessories essential to modern living: "select your own apartment—take possession immediately and save high rents."[15]

Thanks to the film industry, the urban structure of Los Angeles changed completely in the space of a few years: major public works were carried out and the population increased exponentially.

The arrival of motion pictures attracted everyone who wanted to work in the business, which seemed to offer excellent opportunities because it was growing fast and evolving technically, thus requiring the collaboration of many different professional categories. Aside from those directly involved in film-making, many others worked in the hospitality sector, engaging in commercial activities concerning logistics, catering and entertainment, to meet the needs of the countless new arrivals who needed to be housed, fed, and amused.

This resulted in numerous new structures being built. Some of these were patronized mainly by famous movie personalities, and hence only within their financial reach, while others were more moderately priced and accessible to those who had to live on wages that were often

A greyhound race in California, late 1920s
Los Angeles, Los Angeles Public Library, Security Pacific National Bank Collection

The Venice–Los Angeles dance marathon, 1927. Over 300 couples competed for the first prize of 1,000 dollars
Los Angeles, Los Angeles Public Library, Security Pacific National Bank Collection

irregular and precarious. The cheaper structures consisted in small hotels, boarding houses, restaurants, and places where music was played, whose owners tried to make their customers feel at home by offering them the food and atmosphere of their homeland, full catering, and laundry services. The majority of these small hotels and boarding houses were family-run.[16]

Rabagliati describes some of the restaurants and haunts frequented by the rich and famous, where dance competitions were organized for the Hollywood stars. These included the Montmartre, the Plantation Cafe where you could listen to the top jazz orchestras and see fashionable variety shows, and the Paris Inn, owned by a former Italian swimming champion, where the program included Italian, and especially Neapolitan, regional songs.[17] There were other watering holes located in different parts of the city: Sardi's restaurant and night club; Mona Lisa Restaurant; Casanova, which offered "Dining & Dancing" on Sunset Boulevard; and Hammond Steak House, with a sign on the facade that read, "Food the stars eat." Little Joe's Restaurant was opened by two Italians, John Gadeschi and Joe Vivalda, at 900 North Broadway Street, where they enlarged the existing Italian American Grocery and created Joe's Grocery and Joe's Restaurant on the ground floor of the building. The walls of the main room of the restaurant were

The courtyard of Firenze Gardens Apartments in Hollywood, 1922
Los Angeles, Los Angeles Public Library, Security Pacific National Bank Collection

The interior of Little Joe's Restaurant on North Broadway
Los Angeles, Los Angeles Public Library

completely covered with images of monuments and works of art that Gadeschi had photographed during a trip to Italy.[18] Among the eateries patronized by the Hollywood stars was Yolanda's Restaurant, which was opened at the Farmers Market in Los Angeles by "Editor Assistant" Iolanda Magliaro.[19]

As the city developed the Italian community grew proportionately, reaching high numbers: In 1900 there were 2,000 Italians, in 1910 the number had risen to 3,800, but in 1930 it had skyrocketed to 12,700. Most of the Italians who settled in Los Angeles and its surrounding districts during those decades were attracted by the new possibilities offered by the growth of the film industry. After arriving in America as immigrants, they had already lived in other parts of the country, doing the most diverse jobs. They came mainly from New York, Chicago and Boston, from New Jersey, New Mexico, Connecticut, Massachusetts, and Colorado.

The sons and daughters of immigrants also arrived in the city. Some had been born and gone to school in the United States, so at least they did not have a language problem like their fathers, whose inability to speak English made it difficult for them to find qualified jobs.[20]

Another point in favor of the second generation was that they had nearly always become American citizens (the term was "naturalized") and were less likely to be discriminated against for their Italian origin. By contrast, only some of those who had been born in Italy and arrived many years previously managed to obtain naturalization, and then only by taking part in World War I. They all had to Americanize their names and surnames to facilitate their integration into society as well as the labor market.[21]

Some of the Italians who worked in the film industry in Los Angeles in the 1920s and 1930s succeeded in leaving their mark in diverse sectors. This was also due to their ability to switch professions and their excellent artisanal skills, often acquired in a previous activity and, in some cases, complemented by the training received from older members of their family in Italy.[22]

Apart from the famous personalities, we know very little about the large group of professionals—actors and actresses, photographers, cameramen, film editors, musicians, set designers, wardrobe mistresses, makeup

A boarding house near Ord Street in Los Angeles and its Italian residents, 1911
Los Angeles, Los Angeles Public Library

Immigrant children wearing their traditional costumes, 1928. The signs specify their native language, showing how many different races emigrated to California
Los Angeles, Los Angeles Public Library

artists, property men, painters, sculptors and plasterers—whose work made it possible to shoot films that conquered the world. The names of these people get lost among the official documents, unless, of course, their heirs have conserved documentation with a view to sharing it with local institutions or international portals concerned with the recovery and preservation of the historical memory of that period and of the people who experienced it firsthand.[23]

It should be noted that, with the exception of the director and leading actors, the names of the various professionals, not to mention the technicians, did not appear in the credits in the days of silent cinema and at the beginning of the sound era. This means that even the names of important crew members have been irredeemably lost, along with many actual films. Furthermore, in the early years, the leading actors and actresses were listed with stage names instead of their real names, and as an integral part of the production company with which they had an exclusive long-term contract, which simply made them "employees." It is Rabagliati who once again enlightens us about the salaries earned by the stars of the moment, who with "three-year contracts could live in the lap of luxury."[24] But he also mentions "the case of Charles Farrell and Janet Gaynor who, engaged by Fox with a contract of fifty dollars per week for three years, achieved fame after six months and, despite the fact that Fox had made millions on their movies, were obliged to stay on their initial salary for another two and a half years."[25] Of course, those who had a contract with a production company had to consider themselves lucky, because temporary jobs were governed by a variety of factors and often did not provide enough money to live on and keep a family. Rabagliati identifies some of the categories of workers employed on a daily basis, who could certainly not permit themselves a ritzy life that was a continuous round of parties and amusements: "There are the high-class extras—namely those who possess their own wardrobe of high-society clothes which, if they are women, include elegant gowns—who are paid an average of twelve dollars a day. Among them it is not uncommon to find former gentry, grandes dames from Tsarist Russia and aristocrats who have fallen on hard times from every nation . . . There are also extras who have to wear a uniform (fireman's, policeman's, chauffeur's) who are paid an average of seven dollars a day, and, lastly, extras who get five dollars a day and make up the colorful crowds."[26]

To recover, at least in part, the statistics regarding the Italian "artisans" of Hollywood cinema, various types of official documents were consulted. These provided some general data that helps us understand their stories and the milieu in which they lived and worked.

The research concerned a sample of around 250 people. They were examined through the 1920 and 1930 U.S. Federal Censuses of citizens born in Italy (or with Italian parents) and residing in Los Angeles and the surrounding districts. The study was limited to those who, possessing the aforesaid basic characteristics, declared that they practiced a profession or trade in the film industry. To obtain more information or confirmation, the Censuses of 1910 and 1940 were also taken into account. In the majority of cases

we also consulted family histories, marriage registers, applications for naturalization, passenger lists of ships that brought the immigrants from Italy to the United States, registration cards for World War I and II, alphabetical lists specifying addresses and business activities in various cities in different years, passport applications, and death certificates.[27]

Apart from the objective difficulty in obtaining correct information, especially in cases where names were misspelled or partially modified, the data provided by the interested parties concerning their work, their addresses, date of birth, and year of immigration to the United States offers an interesting picture of who our fellow Italians who worked in the film industry actually were.[28]

Italians went to Los Angeles to take advantage of the new opportunities offered by the film industry's rapid growth. Undoubtedly, they benefited from the fact that the first-generation immigrants who had made their home in California had encountered more favorable conditions for settling there and less racial prejudice than they would have in other parts of the country.[29] Many of the Italians who had arrived in the last decades of the nineteenth century had set up profitable businesses and become well-heeled citizens, who were both respected and admired for their intelligence and enterprising spirit, to the extent that they were often a resource for the entire Italian community.

Never forgetting their origins, they promoted mutual aid and recreational societies to help their less fortunate compatriots. A Mutual Aid Society, based on and inspired by the ideas of Giuseppe Mazzini and the actions of Giuseppe Garibaldi, was also set up in Los Angeles—and everywhere else in the world where Italian immigrants had settled, following the Unification of Italy. In 1878 the Società Italiana di Mutua Beneficenza (Italian Mutual Aid Society) was founded, which later became the Società Garibaldina di Mutua Beneficenza (Garibaldina Mutual Aid Society) and subsequently incorporated the Circolo Operaio Italiano (Italian Workers Club). The principal aim was to help families in the community in a time of need, illness or death, but also to give practical assistance to the unemployed in finding work through the network of family and friends in the Italian colony. Nor did the society forget its distant homeland, organizing fundraisers every time there was a natural disaster in Italy, as in the case of the earthquake in Messina and Reggio Calabria in 1908. One of its main tasks was to help the new arrivals, providing them with information about where to stay and how to find work and organize their leisure time. Initially the society's headquarters were at Sepulveda House, the building from which the Spineglio family operated their sausage manufacturing and retail business.

One of the founders of the Società Italiana di Mutua Beneficenza, Ambrogio Vignolo worked hard to set up schools where immigrants could learn English.[30]

In 1904 Amadeo Peter Giannini had founded the Bank of Italy in San Francisco. Convinced that working with small savers was the right thing, he truly became a banker of the people, introducing modern ideas based on an ethical and supportive concept that was extremely

The Italian Workers Club
in Los Angeles, 1920s
Los Angeles, Italian American
Museum of Los Angeles

Members of the Garibaldina Society
with their families at Griffith Park
in Los Angeles, 1920s
Los Angeles, Italian American
Museum of Los Angeles

interesting and innovative. After the major earthquake in 1906, which destroyed most of the city, his granting loans also to people who, having lost everything, had no personal documents, was crucial to restarting the local economy. In 1923, he opened a branch of the bank in Los Angeles, overcoming a series of major obstacles. It grew rapidly, accumulating a vast capital through savings books, which could also be opened by pupils in every kind of school and at all levels. He also managed to create a "Women's Banking Division" with seventeen female employees, where any woman could take out a loan to set up her own business. Giannini also invested in the nascent film industry and financed several productions, especially in the sound era.[31]

Secondo Guasti was another Italian who, after achieving personal success through his ingenuity and enterprise, worked untiringly for the Italian community. He had arrived in Los Angeles in 1883 with three dollars in his pocket and had found employment as a cook at the Hotel Italia Unita. After seventeen years, however, he had built up the Italian Vineyard Company in the Cucamonga area, sixty miles east of Los Angeles, where he actually created a utopian town founded on the values of work and family, complete with houses for the workers, a school, church, post office, and even a branch railroad. Guasti's estate became the largest in the world and made him one of the richest men on earth: his home, built in the early twentieth century on the lines of an Italian villa, cost $500,000. He remained a benefactor of the Italian community until his death in 1927. In 1909 he organized and financed a train to bring 1,200 guests to a fundraiser for building a school to teach Italian immigrants English.[32]

As the community grew steadily, an increasing need was felt for a venue where celebratory events and gatherings could be held. The Italian Hall, whose facade overlooks Main Street, was erected for this purpose in 1907 by the Italian company Pozzo Construction (who also built the oldest parts of the University of California in Los Angeles) using highly-skilled specialized workers for both the exterior and interior. The first floor was rented to commercial and recreational businesses run by Italians, which were useful to the community. These included a tailor and Martinelli's Billiard and Cigar Parlor. The Paggi & Issoglio Saloon, a sophisticated establishment that was well-known in the city, was opened on the ground floor and welcomed its patrons

The Women's Banking
Department of the Bank
of America, 1925
San Francisco, San Francisco
Public Library

from 1908 to 1920, when Prohibition and its restrictive laws on the consumption of alcohol obliged it to close, at least officially. In actual fact, the bar and restaurant moved to the floor above and became one of the many speakeasies, the illicit establishments where liquor could be bought and consumed during the Prohibition era, which sprang up like mushrooms in Los Angeles and other cities, generally located in the back rooms of innocent-looking businesses, from pharmacies to laundries. The second floor was assigned to the Società Garibaldina di Mutua Beneficenza and also housed the Italian Workers Club. It was here that celebrations linked to official Italian holidays were organized, such as the Feast of the Albertine Statute, Labor Day on May 1, the Grape Harvest Festival and other holidays traditionally celebrated in the immigrants' native areas. The Italian Hall also hosted cultural events—shows, concerts, literary presentations—and several illustrious Italian personalities were received there to meet the people when they were in town. Weekly dances were organized, where many met their future bride or husband. Weddings were also celebrated, with lashings of Italian food and traditional music from the various regions. The Italian Hall must be given the credit for unifying the community and for preserving the culture and traditions of the cherished homeland, but also laying the foundations for the necessary integration process in the American context. Although a large part of the area in which it stands was destroyed in 1953, the hall survived and was restored and reopened in 2009. It is now home to the Italian American Museum of Los Angeles.[33]

It can therefore be said that the Italians who worked in the film industry and lived in Los Angeles in 1920, when the General Census was carried out, had found upon their arrival a community that was growing in number and expanding to other areas. Hence they already had at their disposal a useful network of contacts and support at various levels. We know that in 1920 many of them resided downtown, in the streets around the Plaza, where the Italian community had lived for several decades. They shared the area, which bordered on Chinatown and was reserved almost entirely for immigrants, with more than twenty other ethnic groups, including the French, Germans, Filipinos, and Slavs. We may therefore suppose that they frequented places where their countrymen gathered and maybe had their portraits taken in the Ricci and Del Beato photographic studios; however, we do not have any documentary evidence of their belonging to the various societies that the community had created for itself.[34]

At the beginning of the twentieth century, Italians and Mexicans made up 75 percent of the population in this area, and around a third of the commercial enterprises were Italian owned. The more affluent families gradually began to settle in the area to the south and east of the Plaza, creating a new Little Italy in the North Broadway District. In 1910 Italians made up one third of the residents in this area, which was delimited by the streets near the Italian church of St. Peter's, Ord Street, San Fernando Street (now North Spring Street), and Casanova Street. The Italians played cards—Scopa and Briscola—at the Italian Club on San Fernando Street and received their mail at Tognetti's Cigar Factory. The many grocery stores, such as the one owned by the Peluso family on Ord Street, together with the bakeries, churches, and clubs, made the North Broadway District the largest commercial area in Little Italy. Little Joe's started as a grocery store in 1895 and later became famous as one of the oldest restaurants in the city.[35]

The family played an important part both in the domestic and work environment: Italians often lived as an extended family group, whose members were sometimes employed in various capacities in the film industry.

The Chiarigone family came from Colorado and is documented in 1920 as residing in Los Angeles. The father, Hector, was a film director, his wife and eleven-year-old daughter were actresses, and his brother-in-law worked as a "Cutter." Hector was a second-generation immigrant born in 1886 in Colorado, where his parents had arrived in 1880 from Alba in the province of Cuneo. His wife Grace was born in Kansas.

Peter Mule and his wife Mary had emigrated with their small children from Serradifalco, a small village in the province of Caltanissetta, Sicily in 1905. In 1920 the whole family lived on South Vermont Avenue in Los Angeles; the sons Joseph and Philip, who had been born in Italy, the daughter-in-law Jesta, and the five-year-old niece Frances were all actors.[36]

Vincent Russo emigrated to the United States in 1880 and in 1920 is documented as living in Los Angeles, with his wife Concetta and their five children, in the house he owned on Sunset Boulevard. He worked as a "Proprietor Printer" in the film industry, as did his son Charles, aged 22, who was born in Maryland.

Frank Baffa, the head of the family, arrived in the United States in 1892; he was an "Exhibiter" and his two sons—Don, born in New Jersey in 1902 and Emil, born in Pennsylvania in 1905—were musicians. In 1920 the family lived at Redondo, near Los Angeles, while in 1930 they resided, still all together, on West 82nd Street in Los Angeles.[37]

Single people who moved to Los Angeles often lived in small hotels or boarding houses, or co-rented apartments with other people working in the entertainment business. But as soon as they could, they brought the family members they had left behind to America, paying their parents' upkeep and often finding employment in their own sector for the relatives who lived with them.

View of the Italian Hall, 1920s.
It now houses the Italian
American Museum of Los Angeles
Los Angeles, Los Angeles Public
Library

The brothers Frank and Luigi Yaconelli—the former was born in Italy in 1898 and emigrated with his parents at the age of one year and the second was born in Boston in 1903—came from a large family and had worked as street musicians to bring in some money. In 1920 they were already in Los Angeles, domiciled in Figueroa Street, downtown; they described themselves as movie actors and shared an apartment with two other actors, Jack Etri and Peter Momondo. In 1930 they were still living in Los Angeles, but with their mother (who had been widowed in the meantime), their brothers and sisters, their respective spouses, and a cousin. They both had film careers, and Luigi changed his name to Earl Douglas.[38]

Actresses of Italian origin, born either in Italy or the United States, were often married to American citizens, who sometimes also worked in the film industry; they frequently lived with the husband's family. Some of them were shown to be divorced but "naturalized," precisely thanks to their marriage. In the 1920 Census Tina Modotti was registered under the name Tina Richey, since she had married the painter Roubaix de l'Abrie Richey in 1918. She was listed as twenty-three years old, having arrived in 1914, naturalized, and living with her husband's family on 11th Street; she stated that she worked as an actress for La Moderna Dramatte Co.[39]

It is interesting to note how the places of residence changed over the years: in 1930 many Italian film workers had moved from downtown to other areas of Los Angeles, and those

The old road, the main thoroughfare and the square in the new Little Italy that sprang up in the North Broadway District Los Angeles, Los Angeles Public Library

The Italian community of Los Angeles outside St. Peter's Italian Church Los Angeles, Italian American Museum of Los Angeles

Lucy Pugliese poses as Rudolph
Valentino at the Ricci Studio
in Los Angeles, 1928
Los Angeles, Los Angeles
Public Library

The Pelanconi Market
on Broadway, 1910
Los Angeles, Los Angeles
Public Library

who were lucky enough to have steady work had also
managed to buy the house in which they lived.

John Impolito was born in Taranto in 1876 and
emigrated in 1905. In the 1920 Census he was recorded
as married to Millie Impolito, who was born in New
York in 1898. They were both actors who worked on
big productions but in minor roles. They lived on South
Figueroa Street, downtown. In 1930 John was shown to be
married to a different woman and living with her in Gail
Apartments, one of the recently constructed blocks that
symbolized modernity and affluence in Los Angeles.[40]

In 1930, we still find many people in the same sector
of the film industry sharing living accommodation. For
example, three artisans, who described themselves as
"Plasterers," were living together at 957 Herbert Street,
in the Belvedere area. Pellegrino Piacenza, the oldest of
the three and the owner of the house, was born in Lucca
in 1895 and arrived in New York in 1913 from Genoa on the
ocean liner *Berlin*; he was already living in Los Angeles
in 1923. Ubaldo Caprioli, born in 1904 in Petrella Salto, a
small village in the province of Rieti, had emigrated in
1920, sailing from Naples to New York on the *Patria*. And
Joseph Cosenza, the youngest, was born in 1907 in New
York, where his grandparents had emigrated in 1888, when
his father Ralph was only ten.

A large percentage of the Italians working as artists,
sculptors and painters, professional artisans, "Molders,"
"Plasterers," and "Ornamental Plasterers" played an
important part in the creation of film sets. Apart from the
declarations concerning their profession in the General
Censuses, there is very little surviving evidence of their
work in the film industry. One interesting exception is Leon
Tosi, who was born in Rome in 1879, emigrated in 1905,
and resided in Los Angeles in 1920 at 4015 Marston Street
with his wife and five children. Until 1912 he had lived in
New Haven, Connecticut, where he worked as a sculptor
and executed architectural ornaments in various kinds of
stone, first in partnership with another Italian, Mansueto
Rigali, and later as his own boss, after setting up the
Architectural Works Co. We know that he worked on at
least one movie in 1923, *Ashes of Vengeance*, directed by
Frank Lloyd, where he was listed in the credits as "Head

Sculptor" in the Art Department.[41] Tony Gaudio was the "Cinematographer" on this film, and the cast included the Italian actor Hector V. Sarno.[42]

The artist John Patriarca, born in Lecco in 1878, had emigrated in 1905 to New York, where he is still shown to be living in 1910. A few years later he moved to California and in 1918 was already working as a "Painter" for the Triangle Film Co. in Culver City. He must have been on a good salary because in 1920 he already owned the apartment where he lived with his family.[43] Another painter who can be said to have been successful, because we know he was employed by the Paramount Pictures Co. for many years, was Cesar Auda, who was born in Vistrorio, in the province of Turin, in 1885 and emigrated in 1921.

Italian artists and artisans who worked in film were often linked by some kind of relationship between their respective families, who came from the same area and, in some cases, the very same village.

Concezio Santillo was shown to be resident in Los Angeles in 1925, when he described himself as an actor. He was born in San Polo Matese, province of Campobasso, like his wife Teresina Iezza, and had emigrated in 1911. The Santillo and Iezza families were in contact with that of Antonio Campanaro, who hailed from the same village and, in 1920, described himself as a "Laborer" in the film industry and his profession as "Animal Trainer": in fact, he worked in this capacity on various productions, also with leading actors.[44]

We also find a fair number of Italians registered as "Proprietors," or "Property Men," between 1920 and 1930. We know that their tasks were important and varied. Indeed, they were responsible for organizing and maintaining the film props that every production company kept in storerooms according to type, as well as for procuring them when necessary. But they also had to be able to construct any object that was required for the scenery or set, or for use by the actors during filming. Obviously, there is no documentation specifying the work they did on motion pictures. All we have are the images, mainly from the 1930s, in the above-mentioned photographic archives, which show the storerooms where the props were kept, or the proprietors making the necessary objects. Rabagliati explains how the combined skills of the camera crew, lighting technicians, artists, and craftsmen produced thrilling special effects at a modest price: "The spectators are horrified when they see ocean monsters swallowed up by the waves like twigs, and their hearts bleed to see all that money sinking to the sea bed. But there's no complex structure, no colossus, and hardly any expense. All it takes is a six- or seven-meter tank. A special machine creates the artificial waves, spots produce the right lighting, the stormy sky is painted, and devices regulate the force of the rain. The colossi of steel, the magnificent caravels, the brigs with enormous sails are from 25 to 100 centimeters tall, and manipulated by invisible strings. The camera films the scene at a distance of a few meters and then reproduces the images at the appropriate size."[45]

In many cases, the profession stated in the Census forms and other official documents varies through the years. This is obviously because the situations in which the interviewees found themselves changed; some of them actually enhanced their technical expertise by combining it with creative, organizational, and managerial talents.

Rudolph Cusumano was born in Florence in 1904. He emigrated to Boston with his family in 1911 and in 1930 he was living in Los Angeles where he worked as a "Microphone Technician." Later, however, he collaborated on several movies in different capacities, namely "Editor," "Writer," and "Producer."[46]

Augusto Delfino Galli was born in Mantua in 1903, emigrated in 1922, and is registered as an actor in at least three movies between 1917 and 1930. In actual fact, he was active in other sectors of the film industry as well, describing himself in various official documents as "Designer," "Assistant Director," and "Set designer." In 1930 he is shown to have been married to the actress Rosina Galli, born in Venice in 1906, who also worked as a dubber in Hollywood from 1936 to 1950, especially on the Italian versions of several films produced in America.[47]

The advent of sound brought with it many changes, which meant that certain specific new categories of specialized professionals were hired, since they were the ones who could meet the new technical requirements of a production. Rosina Galli is a case in point; in fact, many actors became the dubbers of Hollywood stars, creating a profession in which Italy has always been, and still is, a leader.

Francesca Braggiotti was born in Florence in 1902 and emigrated in 1919. A ballerina and choreographer, she lived in Massachusetts and in New York where she was employed at the Metropolitan Opera. In 1932, at the height of the Great Depression, she was hired by Metro Goldwyn Mayer to dub Greta Garbo in the films made with the new sound technology that were to be distributed in Italy. This was a very important job and Francesca left her family in New York and moved to the MGM studios in Culver City.[48]

Alberto Rabagliati and Marcella Battellini, who won the competition for new faces held by Fox in Italy in 1927, also lived in Hollywood until 1930, thus finding themselves in the middle of the transition from the silent to the sound era. In 1929 Battellini, who had meanwhile changed her name to Lola Salvi, was given voice coaching and acting lessons by Fox and played the part of a young Italian woman who speaks in dialect in the film *In Old Arizona* (1928), which also featured the Italian actor Henry Armetta. The movie was advertised as one of the first made using the Fox Movietone sound system. It also won an Oscar, after receiving four nominations.[49]

In 1930 Rabagliati played a part in *Sei tu l'amore?* directed by the Italian Alfred Sabato and featuring various Italian actors: Luisa Caselotti (actress and singer, and sister of the dubber Adriana Caselotti, who worked at length for Walt Disney and became famous for being the voice of Snow White), Henry Armetta, Mario Dominici, Augusto Galli, and Luigi Colombo. Advertised as the first musical completely in Italian, the film was produced by Georgette & Company, shot entirely in Hollywood at the Tree Art Studio, and presented in the United States before being distributed in Italy.[50]

Rabagliati describes this transition to sound in his memoirs: "All the big Hollywood studios started producing talkies like nobody's business, without bothering too much about the story or settings. Everything was geared to sound. And to achieve their goal, the various directors descended on Broadway and secured the services, at exorbitant prices, of the best opera singers and variety performers, male and female."[51]

In the 1930 Federal Census Tito Schipa, considered one of the greatest tenors in the history of opera, is recorded as residing at North Alpine Drive in Beverly Hills. Born in Lecce in 1889, he had moved to the United States in 1919, the year he debuted in *Rigoletto* in Chicago. He stayed in America for over fifteen years, acting in various films, before returning to Italy and continuing his career as both a tenor and an actor. In 1930 he was living with his wife, the French soubrette Antoinette Michel d'Ogoy, his two daughters and his younger brother Carlo, an actor, who had emigrated in 1921. The fact that he employed three domestics and owned his house confirms that Tito Schipa was already quite successful.[52]

Most of the musicians in the film industry in Hollywood, for whom

Actors Alberto Rabagliati and
Marcella Battellini, winners
of the competition for new faces
held by Fox in Italy in 1927

The tenor Tito Schipa with
Marion Davies, February 1, 1929
Los Angeles, Los Angeles Public
Library, Herald Examiner
Photograph Collection

Bebe Daniels during the
production of the film *Rio Rita*,
directed by Luther Reed in 1929.
Left to right, Russell Mack,
Victor Baravalle, Luther Reed,
and P. H. Townsend

the arrival of sound opened up many
possibilities regarding employment,
worked in "Music Departments," without
receiving any mention in the movies in
which they participated. Yet some of
those in the group under consideration
succeeded in leaving more of a mark
than others.

Victor Baravalle was born in Italy
in 1886 and arrived in America in 1894.
After living in New York, first with his
family of origin (one of his brothers
was also a musician) and then with
his wife and two children, he is shown
as resident at Fareholm Drive in Los
Angeles in 1930, and as the owner
of the apartment in which he lived.
From 1929 to 1939, the year he died,
he gave many live performances as
an orchestra conductor and worked
on numerous films, in at least twenty
of which he appears in the credits
as "Musical Director," "Conductor,"
and "Orchestra Conductor." He also
collaborated on various movies starring
Fred Astaire and Ginger Rogers. For one
of them, *Carefree*, he received an Oscar
nomination for "Best Music, Scoring"
in 1938."[53]

Peter Brunelli (Pietro Giovanni
Maria Brunelli) was born in Rome in
1889 and emigrated in 1923. After
living in Connecticut for a few years,
in 1930 he was recorded as residing
in Glendale, Los Angeles, with his wife
and three children. From 1929 to 1946
he worked as a composer on at least
fifty-six films, and as a member of the
"Music Department" on thirty-two.[54]
On various occasions he collaborated
with Louis De Francesco, a Sardinian by
birth but resident in the United States
from 1910 to 1974, the year he died. De
Francesco had entered the film world as
a composer and arranger in 1930, after
touring the country as the conductor

of an orchestra that performed operatic arias. The two musicians also worked together on the score for the film *Cavalcade* (1933), which won three Oscars and was nominated for another.[55]

Camera technicians, namely "Cameramen" and "Cinematographers," also played a fundamental part in the transition from the silent to the sound era, and Italian "know-how" was crucial in this respect.

The development of the film industry clearly had positive effects on the professions linked to clothing and fashion. The number of tailors and shoemakers who were either self-employed or worked for stores and factories increased considerably during the period we are analyzing. From the Federal Censuses we know that 150 Italian tailors and 64 shoemakers were registered in Los Angeles in 1920 and that these numbers had risen to 310 and 110 respectively in 1930. Many of them must have worked privately for the movie stars at the beginning, then later for the studios. It is worth mentioning the company owned by the six Tartaglia brothers, who had arrived in America between 1902 and 1912 (five of them had emigrated each at the age of fifteen) from Sant'Elia a Pianisi, a small village in the province of Campobasso. Charles was the first to set sail for America, alone, from Naples. In 1907 he had started his business Charles Tartaglia & Bros. Tailors; brothers Joseph and Michael arrived in 1905 and 1906 respectively. That same year they joined the Journeymen Tailors Union of America and advertised their services thus: "UNION Tailors for Men and Women . . . We have the reputation of being the only reliable

Union Tailors in the city at popular prices." They opened their shop on the second floor of a large building, "above [the] American Theatre" in South Broadway, right in the theater district, where a large part of the Italian community was gradually settling. John and Angelo arrived in 1909; the last brother, Otto, in 1912. This is when they changed their promotional slogan to "Six Brothers, Six Reasons." Their policy of producing quality clothes at prices within everyone's pocket worked a treat and they became more and more famous and sought after, also in the movie world. Today, creations by Tartaglia are much in demand by collectors of vintage clothing.[56] In the early years of silent cinema, actors and actresses wore their own clothes on the set—indeed players (especially women) were often chosen also for their excellent dress sense. However, the studios soon realized that clothes, like makeup, made a huge contribution to the success of a film, whether in costume or not, and that the audiences were increasingly following the fashions that the stars promoted through what they wore on screen and in their private life.[57]

"Costume Houses," which rented out or reproduced clothing from all periods, began to spring up on the West Coast from 1912 onward, and the leading studios soon set up their own costume departments with workrooms that employed milliners and tailors, and storerooms where they steadily built up a collection of costumes that could either be used as they were, or adapted and altered.[58]

Cinema and the celebrity of its stars triggered new developments in the fashion world, including major runway shows and the birth of an industry designed to satisfy also the needs and demands of the general public.

Clothes, footwear, and accessories inspired by the models worn by the stars and publicized in magazines increasingly became "objects of desire" and set the style standard, also for the general public. In 1930 Elsa Schiaparelli said: "What Hollywood designs today, you will be wearing tomorrow."[59]

The success enjoyed by Salvatore Ferragamo in his Hollywood years and following his return to Italy certainly derived from his creative flair and extraordinary professionalism, but it was also brought about by the above trend, which soon spread internationally.

Cinema also played a big part in making cosmetics, hair care, and styling essential and innovative at the same time, changing the perception and reality of entire social groups in both the family and work environment. In this regard, in 1910 the *New York World* reported "the widespread adoption of makeup in the workplace, encouraged by employers who wished staff to look vivacious and actively engaged."[60] In 1908 Max Factor opened its first store in Los Angeles, working mainly with the theaters. The company immediately saw the potential of cinema in the makeup sector, developing products that gave the actors' faces a more appealing, softer look that was ideal for the lighting used to shoot scenes in black and white.

Two young women suspended
above the Hollywood sign,
1924
Los Angeles, Los Angeles
Public Library, Security Pacific
National Bank Collection

Cinema was truly one of the biggest revolutions from a technical, cultural, artistic, and sociological standpoint, and all those who contributed at various levels to this epoch-making change and paved the way for modernity deserve to be remembered and honored.

Our hope, therefore, is that the research will continue, so that we might trace and reconstruct history and give a name and face to the many Italians who, with their "know-how," made this cultural revolution possible through the seventh art.

[1] The Selig Polyscope Company built the studio between 7th and 8th Street, where a Chinese laundry had previously stood, and produced *The Heart of a Race Tout* at the studio in 1909. It was the first film shot entirely in California.

[2] "Southern California Ideal for Pictures," in *The American Cinematographer* 1, no. 1 (November 1, 1920): 1. The periodical, published in Los Angeles, was the in-house organ of the newly founded American Society of Cinematographers. In the years that followed it played a major role in promoting cinema and highlighting the contribution made by those behind the camera by regularly covering films on release and providing the names of the cinematographers who had lit them.

[3] "Our Billion Dollar Film Industry," in *The American Cinematographer* 1, no. 1 (November 1, 1920). The same article also provides information concerning the percentage of American movies produced in Los Angeles.

[4] Starting in 1910, the following companies set up in the Los Angeles area: the Biograph Company in 1910, Nestor Film Company in 1911, Keystone Studios and Kalem Studios in 1912, Clune Studios and Triangle Pictures Studios in 1915, and Fox Studios in 1916, just to mention a few. Many small independent companies also arrived, but over the years they were destined to disappear or to be taken over by the future giants of the movie industry, such as Paramount Studios and Warner Bros. Studios. On this, see E. J. Stephens and Marc Wanamaker, *Early Warner Bros. Studios* (Charleston, SC: Arcadia Publishing, 2010); E. J. Stephens, Michael Christaldi, and Marc Wanamaker, *Early Paramount Studios* (Charleston: Arcadia Publishing, 2013). It should be mentioned that World War I destroyed film production in France, Italy, and Germany, thus completely eliminating Europe from international competition. This virtually gave the United States a monopoly on the sector, and after the war it became the leader in film production, thus attracting eminent directors and leading actors. In 1919, Mary Pickford, Douglas Fairbanks, Charlie Chaplin, and David W. Griffith founded the famous United Artists, which had idealistic as well as economic aims, since it was concerned with protecting actors and workers in the entertainment industry in general from the big production companies that completely controlled the market. For further information, see Tino Balio, *United Artists. The Company Built by the Stars*, vol. 1, 1919–1950 (Madison: The University of Wisconsin Press, 2009). On the birth of the star system, see Richard deCordova, *Picture Personalities: The Emergence of the Star System in America* (Urbana: University of Illinois Press, 1990).

[5] The article gives the complete list of the companies and the names of stars and directors: "Motion Pictures Companies and Directors. An Almost Complete List of Leading Organizations and Directors Recognizing Los Angeles as the Film Producing Center of the World," in *The American Cinematographer* 1, no. 1 (November 1, 1920): 3.

[6] With the creation of the star system, the press began to publish more and more articles on the world of cinema. The *Los Angeles Times* was the first daily paper to devote space to it, and *The Preview* the first to dish the gossip about the most popular personalities. The first specialist film magazine was *Photoplay*, which was launched in 1911, creating a new sector in the publishing industry that would soon flourish. In May 1919, the first issue of the weekly *Cinema Chat* came out; in 1925 another important magazine, *Movie Monthly*, began publication.

[7] Alberto Rabagliati, *Quattro anni fra le "Stelle". Aneddoti e impressioni*, ed. by Denis Lotti (Cuneo: Nerosubianco edizioni, 2017), 67–68. The considerations expressed toward the end of the quote almost seem autobiographical, since after four years of sharing the experiences of the successful and cultivating the hope of becoming part of their world, Rabagliati was not considered talented enough: his contract with Fox was not renewed and he was therefore obliged to return to Italy. The Federal Census carried out in 1930 shows that in that year he was still living in Los Angeles, in a boarding house on North Main Street, which was run by an Italian family named Rizzo and whose occupants were mainly Mexicans.

[8] Among the organizers of the evening event was the Italian Tony Gaudio, who attended the ball with his wife and was fêted by everyone. Tony Gaudio and his brother Eugene were among the founders of the American Society of Cinematographers. See "Second Annual Ball Brilliant Success. American Society of Cinematographers Sponsor Notable Event at the Ambassador Hotel, Attended by the Elite of the Screen World," in *The American Cinematographer* 2, no. 3 (1921): 1.

[9] Wheeler W. Dixon and Audrey Brown Fraser, *I Went That-A-Way: The Memoirs of a Western Film Director. Harry L. Fraser* (Metuchen, NJ and London: The Scarecrow Press, Inc., 1990), 86. Fraser was the father-in-law of the Italian actor Frank Yaconelli, who married his actress daughter Ruth Findlay.

[10] Rabagliati, *Quattro anni fra le "Stelle"* 2017, 33. Judging by the photographs consulted at the Los Angeles Public Library (LAPL), the costume parties were definitely the most frequent and popular. In the Biltmore Hotel (now The Millennium Biltmore Hotel), there is the Smeraldi Restaurant, named after the Italian artist who created the stunning decoration inside the building.

[11] Rabagliati, *Quattro anni fra le "Stelle"* 2017, 27. Later in his memoirs Rabagliati returns to this topic, emphasizing that the "very modest Ford . . . was owned by countless students and shop attendants, who mostly built it themselves, assembling the various parts that they purchased one by one from retail outlets" (37).

[12] Rabagliati, *Quattro anni fra le "Stelle"* 2017, 35.

[13] Ibid.

[14] In 1920, a certain number of Italian photographers were already living there. They probably found the house prices affordable, at least at the start, and also appreciated the beauty of the views. Then there was the possibility of work offered by the busy social life on the beach in which the glamorous stars would participate, as well as the competitions and promotional events in which the famous were often involved; but there were also the many "girls" looking for the right break to make it in the movies.

[15] The quotes are taken from the descriptions that accompany the images of the buildings, which are held in the photographic archive of the Los Angeles Public Library. This archive contains some remarkable documentation on the architectural and cultural history of Los Angeles.

[16] Luigi Terrile's Cosmopolitan Bakery on North Spring Street and Agostino Cerrina's Cavour Restaurant on Los Angeles Street offered Italian immigrants the dishes and traditional culture of their homeland. Among the boarding houses and small hotels run and frequented by Italians were Teresa Turchinetto's Plaza Hotel on North Main Street, the Hotel Roma on Alameda Street, Hotel Italia Unita on Olvera Street, run by the Armillo family, and Hotel d'Italia on San Fernando Street, managed from 1904 to 1917 by the Guerrini family, who had emigrated from Piedmont. The husband, Giovanni, registered the guests and did the buying and bookkeeping, while his wife, Emilia Verna, was in charge of the kitchen and the laundry and ironing services for the guests. For documentation on Italian commercial activities concerned with the hospitality of immigrants in the downtown area, see *Settlement – Part I*, in http://iamla.org/permanent-exhibition/. This is the website of the Italian American Museum of Los Angeles (IAMLA), where you can find very interesting and useful information about the Italian community in the city and surrounding area from the time of its origins. I wish to thank the director of the museum, Marianna Gatto, and her collaborators, especially Francesca Guerrini, for their willingness, competence, and courtesy, as well as all for the help they gave me during my research.

[17] Rabagliati, *Quattro anni fra le "Stelle"* 2017, 34–35.

[18] For vintage photographs and information concerning both the historical buildings that have been destroyed and those that have been preserved and converted to different uses, see, in addition to the two above-mentioned sources, the IAMLA website and LAPL archive, as well as Rosemary Lord, *Los Angeles Then & Now* (San Diego: Thunder Bay Press, 2002) and Ead., *Hollywood Then & Now* (London: Pavilion Books, 2013).

[19] Iolanda Magliaro was born in Rome in 1902. She had met Louis R. Loeffler, a film editor with some experience as a director and in special effects, while he was working on a film in Rome. They got married and in 1926 Iolanda emigrated to the United States. In the Federal Census of 1930 she is recorded with her husband's surname, shown to be "naturalized," and states that she works as an "Editor Assistant." The information about the Italian restaurant that she opened during the same period in Los Angeles is provided by the Internet Movie Database (IMDb) entry for Louis R. Loeffler.

[20] The language barrier was a serious problem for Italian immigrants, who mostly only spoke their local dialect, and it forced them to accept any kind of work. Their children, who often emigrated at a tender age, also experienced a feeling of insecurity, partly due to the confusion and overlapping of languages. They were definitely the first generation to go to school, to do their military service, and to secure jobs in America, but also the first to become familiar with "the American manifestations of prejudice and contempt that discriminated against non-natives. For that generation, the biggest dilemma was not knowing how to appreciate the older generation and its peculiarities, or how to reconcile themselves with their culture, so evident in the family, that the older generation had, by definition, rejected in coming to America": Angelo Bartlett Giamatti, "Prefazione," in Allon Schoener, *The Italian Americans. . . per terre assai lontane* (Milan: Rizzoli, 1988).

[21] It became increasingly necessary to disguise one's origins as from 1917, following the Bolshevik Revolution in Russia, the years of intense patriotism during World War I, and the development of anarchist and trade union movements in which countless immigrants from Europe were involved. There was an anti-radical national reaction called the First Red Scare, to distinguish it from the Second Red Scare during the Cold War, after which the fear of an imminent communist revolution, which would have completely changed the founding principles of society and the lifestyle of the whole country, also spread through America. Requests from unions and strikes organized to support workers' rights were condemned and judged to be actual attacks on government and crimes against society committed by foreign agents. So these were years in which being Italian did not help, and obtaining citizenship became a huge problem. In the Census entries we find the terms "naturalized" and "alien." Unless one had been born in America, had married an American citizen or had participated in World War I, it was extremely difficult to obtain naturalization. The application had to be submitted several times over the years and it had to be signed by at least two American citizens acting as guarantors. There was even a space where race had to be stated, which required Italians to specify whether they belonged to the race of "Northern Italy" or "Southern Italy." When submitting the application they had to declare their name and surname at birth, the ones used to enter the United States, and those that were currently used and by which they wished to be identified as an American citizen: the first name, and very often also the surname, were completely Americanized.

[22] This applied above all to technical professions linked to photography or to the creation of materials for a film set, from backdrops to props, which required the skills of various specialized artists and artisans. An obvious example is Tony Gaudio and his brother Eugene, who served as assistants to their photographer father in Cosenza before working in the movies in Rome and then moving to Los Angeles, where the former became a cinematographer, famous for his technical

innovations. Sadly, Eugene died in 1920, shortly after contributing to the birth of the American Society of Cinematographers in 1919.

[23] Part of this documentation (regarding Los Angeles and the surrounding districts) concerning Italian families, whose heirs are striving to gather as much material as possible on their forebears, is held by the Italian American Museum of Los Angeles and accessible on their website http://iamla.org/permanent-exhibition/. Much photographic material is to be found in a file in the Los Angeles Public Library's digital and paper archive Shades of L. A., which contains images from family photo albums.

[24] Rabagliati, *Quattro anni fra le "Stelle"* 2017, 36.

[25] Ibid., 37.

[26] Ibid., 36. Most of the Italians who worked in the movies did not have a permanent contract with a production company, no matter what job they did. In fact, in the Federal Censuses we find that the majority responded to "Class of Worker" with "Wage or salary worker," meaning that they worked on a daily or, at any rate, temporary basis, according to the company's needs.

[27] All the documentation was analyzed by cross-referencing the data to ascertain identities, which were often vague and confused because of conflicting personal information. This enabled us to define the immigrants' profiles and trajectory over the years. For example, the exact date and place of birth (often a small village in the provinces) could only be obtained from an application for naturalization or a ship's passenger list.

[28] For further information about the Italians in California, see Maddalena Tirabassi, "California, The New Promised Land," in *1927 The Return to Italy. Salvatore Ferragamo and Twentieth-century Visual Culture,* ed. by Stefania Ricci and Carlo Sisi (Milan: Skira, 2017), 19–35.

[29] They had arrived in a land with large areas to colonize; moreover, Los Angeles was part of Mexico then, and the similar language and Latin culture had helped them to integrate.

[30] Ambrogio Vignolo had emigrated from Rapallo at the age of twenty, settling first in Boston and then moving to San Francisco in 1849: a journey that, prior to the opening of the Panama Canal and the construction of the railroad network, took around three months. Together with Domenico Ghirardelli he had created the Ghirardelli Chocolate Company, which is still one of the most famous and highly-rated in the United States. In 1872 he had moved to Los Angeles and opened a large grocery, La Esperanza Store, at the junction between Main and Commercial Street. A strenuous champion of the need for education and literacy for all, he used his contacts to facilitate the donation of thousands of books to the Los Angeles Public Library, built between 1922 and 1926. On Ambrogio Vignolo, see *Pioneers*, http://iamla.org/permanent-exhibition/.

[31] Giannini financed the creation of the United Artists Studio and various productions, including *Snow White and the Seven Dwarfs* for Walt Disney and *Gone with the Wind* for MGM. For further information about Giannini, see "The Giannini Success Story," in Schoener, *The Italian Americans* 1988, 154–55; "A. P. Giannini – The People's Banker and Founder of Modern Banking," in *Settlement II*, http://iamla.org/permanent-exhibition/.

[32] Guasti survived the Prohibition years by obtaining a permit to produce cooking wine, and inventing all kinds of recipes that included liquor, which were published in a small volume. For more information on Guasti, see *Pioneers*, http://iamla.org/permanent-exhibition/.

[33] The history of the Italian Hall, its significance and the use the Italian community made of it, as well as its subsequent decline and recent restoration and conversion to the actual museum, are exhaustively documented at *Italian Hall*, http://iamla.org/permanent-exhibition/ and in the designated subsection in the Permanent Exhibition section.

[34] Unfortunately there do not exist, regarding the period that interests us, consultable documents concerning lists of members, minutes of the members' assemblies or even detailed information about the celebrations, gatherings and cultural events held. Italian Mutual Aid Societies constituted an extremely interesting phenomenon that, from the Unification of Italy onward, involved all Italian communities abroad. Surviving documentation enables us, in many cases, to reconstruct the history of these societies and to identify the names of those who were part of them over the years, as well as their role within the community of the city in which they were located. For further information on this topic, see, for example, the case of the Italian community in Istanbul: Roberta Ferrazza, "Introduzione" and "La Società Operaia Italiana di Mutuo Soccorso di Costantinopoli 1863-1913," in *Italiani di Istanbul. Figure, Comunità e Istituzioni dalle riforme alla Repubblica,* ed. by Attilio De Gasperis and Roberta Ferrazza, Collana Centro Altre Italie sulle Migrazioni Italiane (Turin: Edizioni della Fondazione Agnelli, 2007), 1–14 and 121–46 respectively.

[35] The area corresponds to what is today the center of Chinatown. The building that housed Little Joe's was demolished in 2014. For further information, see *Settlement Part I*, http://iamla.org/permanent-exhibition/.

[36] Private lessons with teachers were organized for children who worked on the various productions, so that the young actors might continue their education, given that their film commitments made it impossible for them to attend school. Photographic documentation regarding this is to be found in the archive of the Los Angeles Public Library.

[37] The examples cited represent but a small part of the material gathered and analyzed, which could only be minimally quoted here.

[38] The two Yaconelli brothers also set up their own small production company, which went bankrupt during the years of the Great Depression and the advent of sound. For further information on their professional activity, see their respective IMDb entries.

[39] For Tina Modotti, see the information presented in the exhibition and in other sections of this catalogue. See also her IMDb entry.

[40] In 1918 John Impolito was living in New Mexico and working as a "Proprietor" for a company called Shooting Gallery. For further information, see the relative IMDb entries.

[41] See IMDb entry.

[42] Sarno was born in Salerno 1880 and arrived in New York in 1905, sailing from Genoa on the *König Albert*. In 1920 he was already living in Los Angeles. From 1912 to 1950 he acted in at least 212 movies and was also a scenario writer and director. See IMDb entry.

[43] From 1915 on, Culver City attracted many studios, and MGM, Triangle Studios, Selznick International, and Hal Roach Studios set up there more or less at the same time. Between 1930 and 1940, nearly half the movies made in America were produced in Culver City. 1924 saw the opening of the Culver City Hotel, which became a temporary home for many stars. This was followed, in 1919, by the Culver Studios, where many famous pictures were shot, especially from the 1930s on, as well as various popular TV series. Numerous workers in the industry moved there, including Italians, and some of them are buried in the Culver City cemetery; one of these is Antonio D'Elia, "Artist" in the film industry, who was born in Pescina (province of L'Aquila) in 1897 and emigrated in 1920.

[44] For information about Antonio Campanaro, see *Italians in Hollywood*, http://iamla.org/permanent-exhibition/.

[45] Rabagliati, *Quattro anni fra le "Stelle"* 2017, 40.

[46] Cf. IMDb entry.

[47] From 1914 to 1929 Rosina Galli was the prima ballerina at the Metropolitan Opera in New York, where the Italian Giulio Gatti Casazza was general manager from 1908 to 1935. See IMDb entries.

[48] In the summer of the same year her husband John Lodge, who was an attorney with offices on Wall Street, came to Culver City to spend time with her. But, as fate would have it, a talent scout spotted him while he was playing in a famous tennis tournament at Santa Monica, and suggested he did a film test, on the basis of which Paramount Pictures offered him a six-month contract at 75 dollars a week. Seeing that John hesitated and considering him ideal for the new cinema, Paramount upped their offer to 275 dollars per week, and the contract was signed. He and his wife stayed in Hollywood for several years, also making some films together. John Lodge then became an important politician, and was also made Ambassador to Spain. See IMDb entry. In the Braggiotti family there were two other artists who worked in Hollywood, Francesca's two younger brothers. Herbert, an actor known to have made at least three films between 1930 and 1932, and Mario, a pianist and solo performer, who made his American debut at Carnegie Hall, had a radio program for six years, and played the part of a musician in a number of films in the 1930s. See IMDb entries.

[49] See IMDb entry. In August 1928 the first issue of *Sound Waves – Sound Motion Pictures Periodical* came out.

[50] With the arrival of sound, which coincided with the years of the Great Depression, many small production companies went bankrupt, like the one owned by the Yaconelli brothers (see note 38) who were unable to meet costs that had skyrocketed. The Italian banker Amadeo Peter Giannini, who had opened a branch of his Bank of Italy in Los Angeles in 1923, financed Walt Disney's production of *Snow White and the Seven Dwarfs*.

[51] Rabagliati, *Quattro anni fra le "Stelle"* 2017, 38.

[52] Carlo Schipa acted in various films, especially after 1925, when he made his name with his performance in *Little Annie Rooney*, which starred and was produced by Mary Pickford. His brother's contacts certainly helped Carlo, who lived in Los Angeles until his death in 1988. For Tito and Carlo Schipa, see IMDb entries.

[53] See IMDb entry.

[54] See IMDb entry.

[55] See IMDb entry.

[56] The Tartaglia brothers' story was the subject of the lecture "Six Brothers, Six Reasons: Charles Tartaglia & Bros. Tailors" given by Geraldine Knatz at the Los Angeles City Historical Society on October 15, 2017, as part of the Marie Northrop Lecture Series. Very few of the people who took part in the Federal Census specified that they worked as tailors in the film industry. One of them was Laura Mariotti, "Dressmaker," who was born in Monsummano in the province of Pistoia in 1875, emigrated in 1913, and was married to the actor Anacleto Lazzeroni. They were resident in Los Angeles in 1930, but had previously lived in Chicago. Emilia Grella, whose profession was "Tailoring," was born in Italy in 1881, arrived in the United States in 1898, and was living in Los Angeles in 1930. Paul M. St George, "Dressmaker," born into an Italian family in New York in 1899, was resident in Los Angeles in 1930.

[57] "Cinema emerged just as fashion was shifting from an exclusive costumer base into a large retail market. Early Hollywood films provided an unprecedented opportunity to view new clothing as fashion because the movie industry's newly anointed stars initially wore their own clothes on set, often couture they had purchased themselves if they could afford it. As film costuming, no less than the actors who wore it, became vital to the studio system and the stories that films told by the late teens, American fashion and film costume design began to enter into a world economy together"; Drake Stutesman, "The Silent Screen, 1895–1927," in *Costume, Makeup and Hair*, ed. by Adrienne L. McLean (New Brunswick, NJ: Rutgers University Press, 2016), 23.

[58] Around 1920, Paramount, MGM, and Fox created their own costume departments, which housed a vast permanent collection. Indeed, Paramount had a collection of 50,000 items in its storerooms. See Stutesman, "The Silent Screen" 2016, 30.

[59] Ibid., 28.

[60] Aileen Ribeiro, *Facing Beauty: Painted Women and Cosmetic Art* (New Haven: Yale University Press, 2011), 298.

GIULIANA MUSCIO

ITALIANS IN HOLLYWOOD

"In America there are many Italians and their offspring. The children of immigrants or immigrants themselves, who left Italy at a very young age . . . Other Italians were invited to Hollywood . . . after reaching fame in Italy and elsewhere: actors or directors, musicians or skilled artisans . . . The dynamic gifts of the Italians—their incredible ability to adapt immediately, their lively imagination, and their natural agility—seemed to be designed to help them prosper in the film industry.

Then there are other Italian qualities—constancy, a sense of order, the spontaneous creativity of a glorious heritage. Italians were always able to give a structure or a form to whatever they were doing. Their instinctive panache was spurred on by the more impulsive and hurried spirits that the new countries, with their fresh and recent blood, could only translate as disorder. The Italian, on the other hand, gritted his teeth and brought his panache, ardor, and vibrancy to a higher level of clarity . . . he never lost the sense of harmony."[1]

The fine essay by Gianni Puccini, published in 1937, gives a rare picture of the work of Italians in the world of American cinema before World War II. A reticent silence has long surrounded these figures, hiding the relations between the world of Italian spectacle and Hollywood in the era of silent film. In the 1930s, when Puccini was writing, it was still possible to sense a certain snobbery in the attitude of Italian critics toward American films, accused of being commercial and popular: an attitude inherited from the international supremacy of European and Italian cinema, which was interrupted by the outbreak of World War I.[2] Even when American filmmakers came to shoot films in Italy, thus paying homage to cultural traditions that they had decided to explore, the Italian critics seemed not to notice. This happened with the pioneer of early American cinema Edwin Porter, who in 1914 arrived in Rome to direct *The Eternal City*, one of the first American feature films, based on the socialist novel by Hall Caine. Ten years later, little space was devoted in the specialized press (and even in the local press) to the presence of Lillian Gish in Florence on the set of Henry King's *Romola*.

Still in the following decades there was little understanding of the depth and duration of Italian participation in early American cinema, while the impact of Italian Americans on contemporary cinematography is today clear to everybody.

Prejudices on both sides have contributed to this historical gap. American attitudes toward Italy were contradictory: on the one hand Italy was seen as the cradle of art and craftsmanship, while on the other WASP society viewed Italian immigrants with scorn, seeing them as almost primitive, excessively instinctive, passionate, and too sentimental.[3] In Italian culture, still today, the centuries-old phenomenon of emigration is largely judged as negative; it is seen as significant in scale but also, wrongly, as a consequence of poverty and backwardness, entirely unrelated to the artistic and cultural developments of the twentieth century.[4]

The procession of names that emerge from this story shows that the presence of Italians in American cinema between the two wars was much more substantial than is commonly thought. Often they are figures halfway between international artists and immigrants in search of better lives, and not exiles or luxury travelers like the European stars of Hollywood.[5] They were not only actors but also directors, cinematographers, and set designers, above all from the south of Italy and with little propensity for cultural assimilation, to the extent that most of them chose to Americanize their names but to keep their Italian surnames, proudly preserving the identity of their family and origins. Very few opted for a totally American name, such as Mario Bianchi who became Monty Banks, or Lido Manetti who was briefly known as Arnold Kent. There were, however, many American actresses who assumed an Italian name: Virginia McSweeney became Virginia Valli and Mary Dooley became Nita Naldi—proof that an Italian surname in show business must have been an advantage. But the desire of the Italian community in the United States and in Hollywood to keep their cultural traditions alive had to reckon with the anti-Italian prejudice among Americans.[6] Actually, in early American cinema there were no Italian actors, and the few Italian characters in the short films of the period were always "bad guys," or followed the classic stereotypes: the impoverished aristocrat, the pathetic orphan girl, or the Black Hand gangster.[7] Italian participation subsequently grew, and the characters portrayed became less negative, although still largely stereotypic.[8] In any case, the roles were hardly ever assigned to Italian actors. The discrepancy between the nationality of the actor and that of the character persisted throughout the entire history of American silent cinema, and once again masked the general hostility toward immigrants from Italy, avoiding any association between that "race," considered to be problematic and not entirely "white," and that of the character; the same thing happened with the African Americans and Native Indians.[9]

Many Italian actors active in American silent film came directly from the world of performing arts in Italy. In the second half of the nineteenth century, Italian theater had already established itself as a model in America through the tours of Adelaide Ristori, Ernesto Rossi, and Tommaso Salvini, and later of Eleonora Duse and Giovanni Grasso. These companies often performed Shakespeare and the classics in Italian for audiences that, as with opera music, were already familiar with the plays and appreciated their naturalistic performances, considering the Italians to be the masters of modern acting. It was by studying their performances that Konstantin Stanislavski developed his "Method," an highly influential system of dramatic training that is still practiced today at the Actors Studio in New York.[10] Some of the Italian actors who appeared in American silent film had performed with Duse or had visited the United States for the first time on tour with her. This was the case with the actor and aristocrat Tullio Carminati, who was invited to Hollywood by Joseph Schenck in 1925 to play romantic roles thanks to his elegance, blue eyes, and light hair. The Venice-born Agostino Borgato had also begun his career with the great Italian actress before making his debut in Italian silent film in 1913, while Antonio Maiori had become famous in New York for his intense performance of the classics, which drew members of Upper West Side high society to a small theater in the Bowery despite the fact that he acted in Italian and the sets of his productions were somewhat ramshackle.[11] With her sensual acting style and her intense Mediterranean beauty, Mimì Aguglia even attracted the attention of the English royal family and of the Mexicans in the full throes of revolution, who rushed to see her shows. Aguglia shunned silent film, however, with just a cameo appearance in *The Last Man on Earth*.

As well as the great stars of the stage, there were also Italian touring companies, which reached the remotest corners of America with their performances—both classic plays and variety shows. They were the heirs

The actress Mimì Aguglia
in costume photographed by
Mario Nunes Vais, c. 1910

Tullio Carminati in the movie
The Bat, directed by Roland
West in 1926

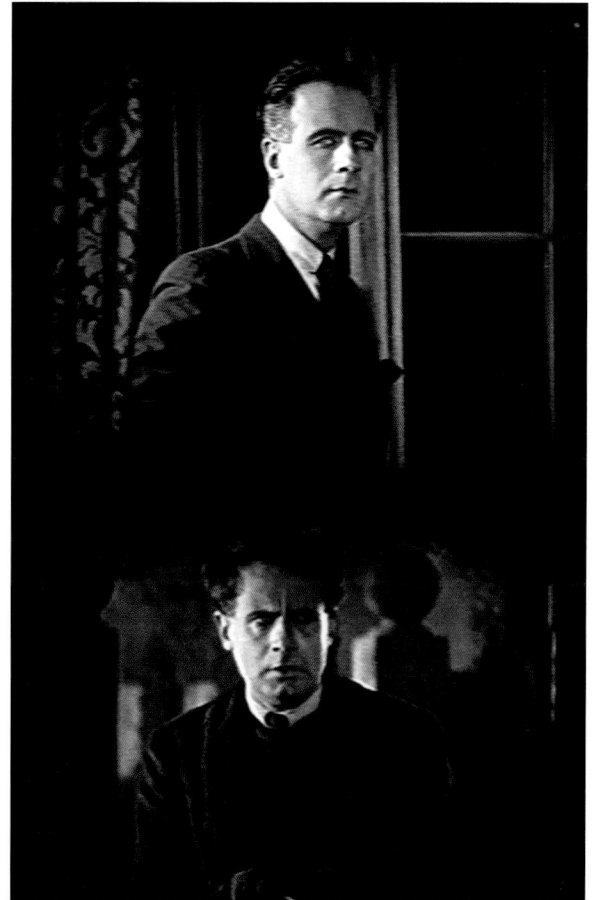

of Commedia dell'Arte and of comic opera, that is of an Italian tradition characterized by the ability to improvise around plot outlines and to condense the most important scenes of a classic text or an opera. The actor thus had to be able to act, sing, play music, and perhaps even perform acrobatics; when too old to do all this, he could reinvent himself as a director or a set designer, or manage the company. These groups of artists performed both tragic and comic works, passing from one genre to another and one show to another every night, while their American colleagues usually offered the same shows and specialized in a single repertoire on their tours. Versatility was a typical characteristic of Italian performers, something that soon became a precious commodity in the new world of American cinema, popular, commercial, and rapidly produced.

The fact that Italian actors and Italian theater were well-known and appreciated in the United States at the very beginning of the twentieth century is confirmed not only by the articles published in important daily newspapers, like *The New York Times*, but also by the popularity of several plays in Italian, such as Sem Benelli's *La cena delle beffe*, written in 1909.

In the 1910s the popularity of Italian theater began to wane, while variety shows gradually gained ground. An artist like Antonio Maiori, who had featured largely in the theater seasons in the Lower East Side, agreed on his return from a tour to San Francisco in 1915 to play the role of a Mafia butler in *Poor Little Peppina* (Sidney Olcott, 1916), starring Mary Pickford. Set on the Amalfi Coast but shot on location in America, the film featured several Italians, including the actor and musician Cesare Gravina, who played the part of another *mafioso*. Gravina had already acted with Mary Pickford and would go on to have a successful career in silent movies in Hollywood. The names of the two Italian actors were included in the opening credits, underlining their supposed fame. The production was accurate and Italy was presented as the "Bel Paese," although the film still reflected the prejudices of contemporary American culture, struggling with the waves of migration from southern Europe, by describing the Italians

as "bad guys." However, compared to other productions of the time, the representation of the Italian landscape and way of life is realistic; Maiori himself may have contributed, perhaps teaching Mary Pickford to dance the tarantella and to use typically Italian gestures. The close-ups of Maiori and Gravina allow us to appreciate their style of acting: Maiori's performance is emphatic and theatrical, while Gravina is made even more menacing by his irregular features, emphasized by his evil expressions. Having said that, it is saddening to see American cinema using a Shakespearian actor like Maiori in the role of a *mafioso*, especially considering that this seems to have been his only film appearance in the United States. His star soon began to wane, also on the stage.

In San Francisco Italian theater was much appreciated by immigrants (and not only by immigrants) and was supported by all the local Italian press. On the West Coast most of the immigrants came from northern Italy and Tuscany, so it sometimes happened that the Florentine mask of Stenterello appeared on stage, commenting ironically on current news stories.[12]

This San Francisco of the cultural elite loved the theater and all forms of spectacle. It was inhabited by well-integrated Italians who had often achieved considerable financial well-being, as was recorded by Frank Capra, one of the most successful Italians in American cinema, who in 1921 made his first film, *La visita dell'incrociatore italiano Libia a San Francisco*, a documentary sponsored by the Italia-Virtus Athletic Club. The arrival of the cruiser is greeted enthusiastically by the Italian community in San Francisco: from the Virtus athletes, who play soccer with the sailors from the *Libia*, to the children in the Italian schools and the crowd in Washington Square, the heart of the community and the home of one of the most important Italian theaters. Capra also shows the magnificent Bank of Italy building[13] and the elegant offices of the newspapers *La Voce del Popolo* and *L'Italia*, whose editor Ettore Patrizi acted as master of ceremonies at the dinner for the Italian sailors. The film presents a class of eminent figures who dress with sober elegance, attend mass, and play soccer as if they were in Italy. And, above all, love the Fatherland. The film ends with the caption "Viva l'Italia!" and the image of the Italian flag fluttering in the wind. There are also appearances by Livia Maggiora, "winner of the beauty contest organized by the *Motion Picture Magazine* of New York," and the film star Dorothy Revier, born Doris Valerga, a third-generation Italian who featured in around ninety films: proof that the community was already immersed in the new world of the silver screen, to the extent that it offered the young Capra, pictured on the pier of Fisherman's Wharf, his first professional job. For an Italian, California was thus a dynamic, welcoming land. Santa Barbara was the home of the Flying "A" Studios of the American Film Manufacturing Co., active from 1910 to 1922, the largest production center in early American cinema.

Mary Pickford and Antonio Maiori (wearing a white shirt) in *Poor Little Peppina*, directed by Sidney Olcott in 1916

Frames from Frank Capra's documentary *La visita dell'incrociatore italiano Libia a San Francisco*, 1921

The cinema industry was, however, still in its pioneering phase. Most films were made in Chicago and New York, which were the homes of theater and publishing and thus of a supply of actors and screenwriters, but which were also dominated by the Edison Trust, a cluster of production companies that used Edison's patents, shutting out smaller producers.[14] It was the independent producers, in order to avoid the (sometimes armed) Trust agents, who were the first to leave the East Coast to relocate in California, where union rules were less strict and the sun always shone. Making silent films with the low sensitivity emulsions then in use required a large amount of light, so studios with glass ceilings and open-air stages were used.

The films made by the Edison Trust were of poor artistic quality. Actually, it was almost an "assembly line" operation, aimed at the market of the nickelodeons, foul-smelling theaters for working-class audiences, who could enjoy themselves indoors for 5 cents. In Italy, on the other hand, the cinema grew out of the great tradition of theater, from opera to Commedia dell'Arte, and thus attracted performers and artisans from the world of high culture.

Some prestigious Italian silent films, such as *Gli ultimi giorni di Pompei* (Ambrosio, 1908), *Inferno* (Milano Films, 1911) based on Dante, and the various *Quo Vadis* movies (Guazzoni, 1913), made a great impact in the United States.[15] They were costume films that contained art, archaeology, and the iconographic traditions of antiquity, and for this reason were also appreciated by the American middle classes, which yearned for cultural emancipation, and in particular by female audiences: those women who in WASP culture were responsible for the education and entertainment of the family while their husbands focused on their jobs, as the sociologist Max Weber maintained.

Italian cinema made people dream of the Grand Tour, which many of those watching these films could certainly not afford. But they could still dream watching these images and feel the emotions, the thrilling excitement aroused by adaptations of Gabriele d'Annunzio's novels starring languid divas like Francesca Bertini, Lyda Borelli, and Rina De Liguoro.

Cinema taught fashion, make-up, and manners; but while Italian cinema aimed to show the luxury of the wealthy aristocrats who often produced the films, American cinema soon presented luxury as an aspiration of the middle classes: it was no coincidence that the dresses worn by the great divas were copied and sold at the department stores.

It was above all *Cabiria* (Giovanni Pastrone, 1914), one of the most celebrated epic films in the history of cinema, produced in Turin by Itala Film with intertitles by Gabriele d'Annunzio, which became a model around the world for popular cinema that was at the same time of undeniable artistic quality. Particularly memorable are the spectacular sets, the accuracy of the historical details (founded on archaeological discoveries of Phoenician artifacts made just a few years earlier), the duration, comparable to that of a lyric opera, and also the figure of Maciste, the muscular slave who added an element of circus arts that certainly appealed to audiences.[16] The great master of American silent David W. Griffith—whom the Biograph Company, one of the pillars of the Edison Trust, did not allow to make feature films—was very impressed by *Cabiria*. In an article in *Photoplay* about the film's intertitles, his trusted screenwriter Anita Loos confessed that she had admired and studied d'Annunzio's literary writings.[17]

The influence of *Cabiria* is evident in Griffith's most magnificent film, *Intolerance* (1916), for which he engaged Italian artisans to construct Babylon in California, as the Taviani brothers recounted in *Good Morning Babilonia* (1987). *Cabiria* is an example of the social and cultural impact of Italian cinema on American cinema, whose audience it transformed by creating a demand for a more highbrow form of entertainment and spurring film-makers to tackle more complex stories, which the feature film format now allowed. The influence of Italian cinema on American cinema before the war has, however, been entirely forgotten—or rather, cancelled.

While there is no doubt that the Americans were enchanted by the Italian arts, to the extent that John Paul Russo coined the term "Italomania,"[18] and that the preferred destination of Americans on their Grand Tours was the Bel Paese, we should not forget the ambivalence of WASP culture, the contemporary phobia, the scornful attitude toward lower-class Italians and toward immigrants in general.

The WASP prejudice easily led to irritation with other aspects that were conventionally attributed to the Italians, in particular to southern Italians: their over-exuberant, almost dangerous nature, represented by the image of Naples with the gulf shining in the sunlight but surmounted by the menacing volcano. Therefore, a powerful ideological need was felt to reconcile this Nature, of men and things, with Italian Culture: art, crafts, physical disciplines—from boxing to dance and circus acrobatics—and finally with the magic of voices that were naturally expressive yet at the same time trained to reach the heights of bel canto, as in the case of Enrico Caruso.

For Italy opera music was one of the most popular cultural exports: Italian singers have always been welcomed warmly in the United States. It is no coincidence that among the first Italian artists signed up by American cinema, still produced on the East Coast, were the opera singers Lina Cavalieri and Enrico Caruso.[19] Though this might seem a bizarre choice for silent films, there were, in fact, several reasons behind it: the use of artists who were famous all over the world, the legitimizing prestige of the lyrical music (in other words, of high culture), and their great personal appeal and charisma. Both had great natural gifts—the face and the poise of Lina Cavalieri, the muse of many painters, and Caruso's clear, powerful voice. Both were able to charm and seduce the audience with their performances, characterized by the natural grace of the "world's most beautiful woman," as Lina was known, and the perfection of Caruso's seemingly effortless musical performances. As well as their exceptional talents, however, both brought an element of modernity, well aware of the value of their image: Cavalieri through the shrewd use of her sophisticated wardrobe and her subsequent entrepreneurial activity in cosmetic and perfume business, Caruso through the way he managed to exploit the new media industry for his own ends. Special natural gifts, sensuality, modernity, and awareness of their own image also characterized two other Italians who conquered Hollywood a few years later: Tina Modotti and Rudolph Valentino.

Four icons who immediately convey the happy harmony between Nature and Art and the desire to

Lina Cavalieri in a dance scene from *Sposa nella morte!* (*The Shadow of Her Past*), directed by Emilio Ghione in 1915

improve continually by making best use of their physical gifts. A body displayed, as in the nude photos of Tina Modotti or in the sensual exuberance of Lina Cavalieri, or in the vests that show off the sculpted (rather than beefcake) muscles of Rudolph Valentino, who in his films was dressed, undressed, disguised, whipped and caressed lovingly, providing women all over the world with the thrill of a masculine sensuality that had previously been hidden and forbidden. A body used as an instrument of expression as well as of seduction, as when Valentino, filmed from behind, bows his head and drops his shoulders to convey his despair. A body tamed by Art and Culture: a magic that emerges powerfully in dance scenes.

Valentino dances the tango in his unforgettable entrance in *The Four Horsemen of the Apocalypse* (Rex Ingram, 1921), and Cavalieri dances in a sequence of *Sposa nella morte!* (released in the United States as *The Shadow of Her Past*); Modotti dances a Mexican dance and as Salomè, veiled and bare-bellied, in *The Tiger's Coat* (Roy Clements, 1920). Dance, the harmony between nature and art, between passion and technique, transforms a body of "impure blood" into an object of desire for the American public.

Caruso did not dance. And he was not handsome in the classical sense. However, he was endowed

Tina Modotti in Hollywood, 1920-21
Pordenone, Cinemazero, Archivio fotografico Zeroimage

Rudolph Valentino and Alice Terry photographed for the advertising of His Master's Voice gramophone, 1921

Rudolph Valentino and Beatrice Dominguez in *The Four Horsemen of the Apocalypse*, directed by Rex Ingram in 1921 Turin, Collection Museo Nazionale del Cinema

Rudolph Valentino and Gloria Swanson photographed by Henry Waxman on the set of *Beyond the Rocks*, adapted from the novel by Elinor Glyn and directed by Sam Wood in 1922

with appeal and expressivity and was capable of a modern and extremely naturalistic style of acting.[20]

The bodies of Caruso and Rudolph Valentino were worshipped even after their death: their funerals were followed by hundreds of thousands of people, anticipating the media appeal of these ceremonies in more recent times.

The first to appear on the silver screen was Lina Cavalieri, who had an intense international career including several long stays in the United States. As early as 1914 she starred in an American film version of *Manon Lescaut* (Herbert Hall Winslow), almost a year before Geraldine Farrar (usually thought to be the first female opera singer to appear in a movie) performed in Cecil B. DeMille's *Carmen*.

The following year Cavalieri appeared in two Italian films, the above-mentioned *Sposa nella morte!* and *La rosa di granata* (distributed in the United States by Paramount Pictures with the title *The Rose of Granada*), both directed by Emilio Ghione. Between 1917 and 1918 she signed a contract with the Famous Players-Lasky to make *The Eternal Temptress* (Émile Chautard, 1917), *Love's Conquest*, *A Woman of Impulse* (1918) and *The Two Brides* (1919), all three directed by

Edward José. These were not the usual film versions of operas offered to lyrical singers, but were modern dramas, for which she was engaged as an actress and not only as a celebrated star of musical theater.

Although she did have a beautiful voice, Lina Cavalieri was famous in particular for her delicate features, her natural elegance, her sensitive performances and her uncommon exuberance. She and Tina Modotti were the only Italian actresses to play starring roles in American silent cinema. It's interesting to note that while most of the famous actresses in silent film played the role of an Italian woman at least once in their careers—an orphan girl (Lillian Gish, Mary Pickford) or a dangerous vamp (Theda Bara, Greta Garbo)—the roles of Italian characters were not normally assigned to actors of Italian origin, as was mentioned above. But as an international star, Cavalieri—like Caruso—was able to evade this unwritten rule. Her film career, however, passed almost unobserved, while her beauty remains, immortalized by the many artists who portrayed her almost obsessively in the attempt to fix on canvas the mystery of her extraordinary grace.

Enrico Caruso was the tenor who brought the new, more modern naturalistic or realistic style of opera singing to the United States. Always attracted by the media and by modern technologies, he was among the first to record his voice (in Milan, in 1902). The company who signed him was called Gramophone & Typewriter Limited and the recoding of the voice was associated more with the office dimaphone than with entertainment for the general public. It was his recordings made in Italy

Crowds along the streets of New York on the occasion of Rudolph Valentino's funeral, 1926. Another funeral would be held in Hollywood, where his body was brought to be buried in the Memorial Park Cemetery

Enrico Caruso in a 1910 photograph

Paolo Troubetzkoy,
*Enrico Caruso performing
in* La Fanciulla del West, 1912
Bronze, 55 x 32 x 37 cm
Lastra a Signa (Florence),
Museo Internazionale Enrico
Caruso, inv. 8074

Enrico Caruso, *Self-portrait
as Canio in* Pagliacci *by
R. Leoncavallo with dedication
to soprano Carmen Melis*, 1913
Indian ink on paper, 21 x 17 cm
Lastra a Signa (Florence), Museo
Internazionale Enrico Caruso,
inv. 15Bbis

Enrico Caruso, *Self-portrait
as Canio in* Pagliacci *by
R. Leoncavallo*, 1913
Pencil on paper, 27 x 22 cm
Lastra a Signa (Florence), Museo
Internazionale Enrico Caruso,
inv. 1453

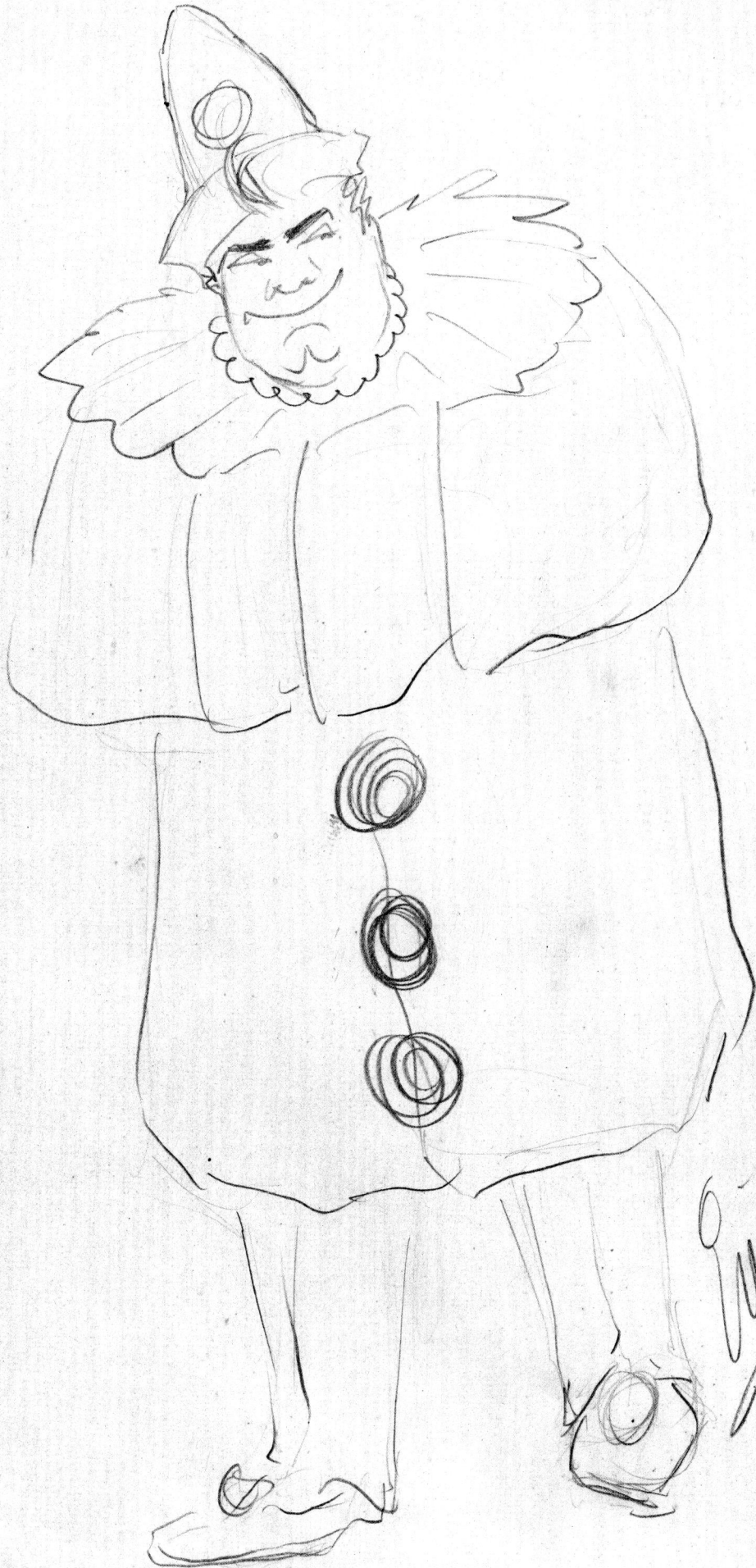

Emil Braun
Hamburg
1913

that drew the attention of American theaters, and not the other way around. And it was with his voice that Victor made its name, changing the recording industry forever by shifting the focus toward music.

Caruso was the first singer to sell a million copies of a single record ("Vesti la giubba"). Between 1903, when he arrived in New York, and his death in 1921 he earned the incredible sum of 1,825,000 dollars from his phonograph recordings alone. He was used for promotional purposes by Victor, which presented him in carefully designed color pictures in the costumes he wore in his various roles at the Metropolitan Opera. The aim was to convince people that a recording could replace the experience of theater-going and thus could bring the enjoyment of culture to a much wider public.

Caruso played a crucial role in the development of modern entertainment and media, in the birth of the record industry, as we have seen, in the relationship between the press and celebrities, and in the very creation of the star system. He was constantly present in the newspapers all over the world as a result of his frequent tours. His daily life had also become a subject of interest for the press, which was beginning to break down the barriers between public and private life. He appeared in the first newsreels and even made some home movies. His

Woolen cloth and felt costume Enrico Caruso wore as Canio in the opera *Pagliacci* by Ruggero Leoncavallo, early twentieth century
Lastra a Signa (Florence), Museo Internazionale Enrico Caruso, inv. 7904

Silk embroidered costume Enrico Caruso wore as Osaka in the opera *Iris* by Pietro Mascagni, staged at the Metropolitan Opera House in New York, 1907
Lastra a Signa (Florence), Museo Internazionale Enrico Caruso, inv. 2070

Waldorf Luggage touring trunk, early twentieth century
This traveling trunk with two compartments, in galvanized iron and wood, and lined with fabric, belonged to Enrico Caruso who used it on his American tours
102 x 56 x 56 cm
Lastra a Signa (Florence), Museo Internazionale Enrico Caruso, inv. 2052

133

Enrico Caruso seated at
the piano in his New York
apartment, c. 1915

Enrico Caruso in Sorrento,
c. 1920

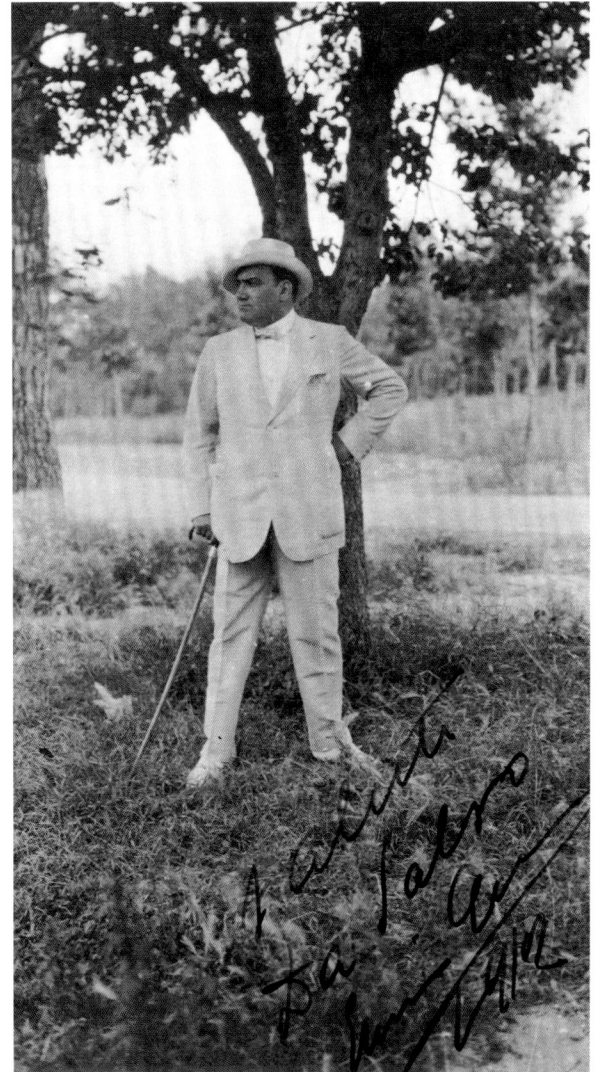

Enrico Caruso in a photo
from 1912 with a hand-
written dedication: "Saluti da
Salso[maggiore] Enrico Caruso
1912." The photo is part of an
album purchased in 1973 from
Giuseppe Carfagna in Rome
Naples, Biblioteca Lucchesi
Palli, section of the Biblioteca
Nazionale di Napoli,
inv. 1414821

Enrico Caruso, *Self-portrait as Alfredo in* La Traviata *by G. Verdi*,
Hamburg, 1912
Pencil on paper, 21.5 x 14.5 cm
Lastra a Signa (Florence), Museo
Internazionale Enrico Caruso,
inv. 1448

Enrico Caruso, *Self-portrait as the Duke of Mantua in* Rigoletto *by G. Verdi*, Hamburg, 1906
Pencil on paper, 21 x 13 cm
Lastra a Signa (Florence),
Museo Internazionale Enrico
Caruso, inv. 1450

image was known everywhere: the number of photographs portraying him, both posed and spontaneous, is truly incredible and demonstrates his growing awareness of the power of this medium.

The image of the celebrated singer was exploited not only by his recording company but also for products of all kinds, including cigarettes. Furthermore, newspapers often published his brilliant caricatures: he drew in a very personal style and also knew how to sculpt, as shown by the caricature self-portrait busts he made for friends and colleagues.

His decision to record various Neapolitan songs, which brought together lovers of both opera and popular music, was also of great cultural significance. He was not the first opera singer to record songs but, more importantly, his songs were drawn from the Neapolitan tradition and thus helped to champion the culture of southern Italy and consequently the immigrant community in the United States.

In 1918, Famous Players-Lasky offered Caruso, then at the peak of his career, 200,000 dollars for two films directed by Edward José, *My Cousin* (1918) and *The Splendid Romance* (1919), shot at the Artcraft Studios in New York in order not to interfere with his recording activities. Some newspaper photos from the period show Cesare Gravina on the set, working as Caruso's "personal film trainer." Another immigrant actor, William Ricciardi, played one of the main roles in *My Cousin*, proof of the synergy within the community of Italian performers and the driving role played by Caruso.

In *My Cousin*, set in Little Italy, Caruso plays a double role: he is Tommasso [sic], a poor Italian immigrant who makes his living modeling plaster casts, and his cousin, the great tenor Caroli. The story revolves around Tommasso's love for Rosa, the daughter of an Italian restaurant owner (who would prefer to see her married to a greengrocer, he too Italian, rather than to a poor artist), and on his desire to be recognized by his famous cousin.

The description of the plot in the American press[21] contained several baffling errors: the names of the characters are different from those that appear in the film, and the story seems to be a drama of jealousy, characterized by highly unpleasant anti-Italian stereotypes. "Tommasso brandishes a knife with the ferocity of the Black Hand," reads one of these articles, and Rosa's hand is described as "dark." Given the discrepancies in the names and the plot, the postponement of the premiere and the fact that in some of the publicity materials the cousin's moustache seems to have been

Portrait of Enrico Caruso, c. 1915. The photo was taken for Bain News Service, New York

Enrico Caruso, *Self-caricature with humorous caption in Neapolitan*, New York, 1909 Pencil on paper, 40 x 53 cm Caruso depicts himself while smoking a pipe featuring the face of the baritone Eduardo Missiano. The caption reads: "Statte sore Missiá/ I me t'aggia sfeziá/ Tu te crire' e pazziá/ I à pipp' aggiá fumā/ Enrico Caruso/ NY 1909" (Don't worry, Missiano/ I've got to have some fun with you/ You think you're the joker/ But I'm the pipe smoker/ Enrico Caruso/ NY 1909) Lastra a Signa (Florence), Museo Internazionale Enrico Caruso, inv. 1776

added later, we would be justified in thinking that the version in circulation today is a new edit with extra sequences. It could well have been Caruso himself, unhappy with a film full of the stereotypes presented by the anti-Italian press, who suggested shooting several scenes again. He played the emigrant cousin as a good-natured character, turning the melodrama of jealousy into a story of everyday life in Little Italy. Rather than showing off his dramatic gifts he adopted a naturalistic style, his most characteristic and innovative feature as an opera singer. He also gave more space to the figure of the immigrant, abandoning the violent gestures of the first version in favor of humorous touches, which allowed him to highlight the comic side of the character, something which was not possible in opera. Caruso's performance in the film is remarkably modern, especially when compared to the style not only of opera but also of silent film at the time. He plays the two characters in different ways, using different facets of his own personality: while the sculptor is shy and capable of humor, the tenor is powerful, elegant, bored with his own fame and capable of making fun of himself. Almost a parody of Caruso himself. Despite the many positive, even enthusiastic reviews, the film was considered a flop. As a matter of fact, the production and release remained something of a mystery, but it suffices to watch it to realize that Caruso was a great actor. On the surface, therefore, his cinema career seems to have been a failure; but we should examine the reasons for its lack of commercial success more closely. We need only read the publicity material for *My Cousin* to discover the misleading deceit that probably put audiences off: the expectation that the film would feature Caruso and his voice. On the contrary, the scenes in which he performs *Pagliacci* were not shot and edited to allow syncing with a record. The mistake, therefore,

Article on the scenes that do not appear in the final version of *My Cousin*, 1918 Baltimore, Johns Hopkins University, Archives of the Peabody Institute, Caruso Collection

Enrico Caruso in *My Cousin*, directed by Edward José in 1918

Enrico Caruso in some frames from *The Splendid Romance*, directed by Edward José in 1919 Baltimore, Johns Hopkins University, Archives of the Peabody Institute, Caruso Collection

lay entirely with Famous Players-Lasky, who publicized the tenor but gave audiences something different: an immigrant Caruso.

With her sensibility and restless nature, Tina Modotti already belonged to the Jazz Age. An interesting, controversial figure, in 1913 she had left the Italian region of Friuli, where she was born at the end of the nineteenth century, to join her Socialist father, who had some experience of photography, in San Francisco.[22]

Employed like many immigrant girls in the local textile industry, she was soon hired as a model at the I. Magnin department store. She was, in fact, a great beauty, with an elegant bearing, dark hair and eyes, and very sensual lips—the perfect Latin look.

In the stimulating atmosphere of the Panama-Pacific International Exposition she met the painter Roubaix de l'Abrie Richey, known as Robo; their relationship was a mixture of mutual seduction, transgression, and artistic aspirations. Robo introduced her to a different side of San Francisco, inhabited by a community of intellectuals who preached the values of peace and art. And revolution.

In 1917 she began to act regularly in the local Italian theater with the Città di Firenze company, earning several positive reviews in *L'Italia*, one of the Italian newspapers of San Francisco.[23]

Enrico Caruso in London, n.d.

In the meantime, the Friuli girl had cut her hair short and developed a new look, more in keeping with the fashion of the time, as she had begun to think about a career in motion pictures. She moved to Los Angeles with Robo, and while touring the studios with her portfolio she began to frequent the city's bohemian circles, permeated by Oriental mysticism, revolutionary excitement, anti-bourgeois attitudes, and ideas of free love.

In 1920 she obtained the leading role in the above-mentioned movie *The Tiger's Coat*, a melodramatic story of mistaken identity: the rich WASP Alexander believes that the Mexican Maria (played by Modotti) is Jean, a rich Scottish girl, and falls in love with her; soon, however, her dark hair, her sensual lips, and the way she performs traditional Mexican dances betray her identity and he leaves her. When a political rival tells him that Maria is not only Mexican, but also a waitress, Alexander exclaims: "I thought I had given my love to one with blood as pure as my own. Instead of that I find myself yoked to a low-born peon, one of a race loathed and despised." (Their explicit use in a Hollywood production shows that issues of race and class were not a background theme but a real subject of conflict in 1920s America.) Maria leaves, but returns to the city as an actress, dancing in a modern, sensual way dressed as Salomè, a costume that highlights her figure.

The audience applauds enthusiastically and Alexander seeks her out, but at first Maria rejects him, before joining him at his home and accepting his love. The Mexican girl "of impure blood" thus becomes socially acceptable after becoming a successful actress. Modotti's performance is free of the mannerisms one might expect from a young actress who had started out in émigré theater.

While she was working in Hollywood, Tina frequented artists who were very distant, in terms of culture and values, from the world of cinema. Among them was the photographer Edward Weston, with whom she began an intense romance and professional relationship after first working as a model for him. Weston portrayed her in close-ups that brought out her expressiveness and in poses that enhanced the sensuous beauty of her naked body: these are photos of surprising modernity.

Unsatisfied with her film career, especially the ways she was used in Hollywood, and experiencing problems in her relationship with Weston, Modotti decided to follow Robo to Mexico but the painter died suddenly while she was on her way to Mexico City.

Her life from then on changed radically. Having previously acted and posed for the cameras, she became a fine photographer, expressing her great social and artistic sensibility through her work.

She chose to document the social unrest in Mexico, often focusing on the intense figures of Mexican women. While anticipating the realist photography of the Great Depression, at the same time she managed to maintain a unique aesthetic taste and a thorough attention to the composition of the image that make her photographs formidable visual messages.[24]

Among the Italian actors in Hollywood in the era of silent film, Rudolph Valentino is undoubtedly the most famous. A mythical aura has developed around his figure, turning him into a timeless star. The actor was launched by June Mathis, an intelligent and influential woman in the motion picture industry who felt a particular attraction to Italy (it was she who had decided to shoot *Ben-Hur* in the country). Mathis was a brilliant screenwriter and producer, who discovered Valentino when he was still playing minor roles, usually as a "seducer."[25] It was Mathis who insisted that Valentino should play the role of Julio in *The Four Horsemen of the Apocalypse*, building the adaptation of Blasco Ibáñez's bestseller around his character. The almost brutal tango in his first entrance, his passionate gaze, veiled in melancholy or shining ironically, his sensual grace, his elegant movements and his richly nuanced performance made Rudolph Valentino an overnight success: the ultimate star. As an actor he knew how to use every little expression of his

Tina Modotti in
San Francisco, 1915

Edward Weston, *Tina*, 1921

Tina Modotti in San Francisco,
1920
Pordenone, Cinemazero,
Archivio Fotografico Zeroimage

William Frederick Seely,
Tina and Robo painting batiks,
Los Angeles, 1921

Tina Modotti with her family
in Los Angeles, 1921

Publicity poster for
The Tiger's Coat, directed
by Roy Clements in 1920
Pordenone, Cinemazero,
Archivio Fotografico Zeroimage

Portrait of Tina Modotti at the
time when she performed in
The Tiger's Coat, 1920

Tina Modotti in a scene from
The Tiger's Coat, 1920
Pordenone, Cinemazero,
Archivio Fotografico Zeroimage

Edward Weston, *The White
Iris*, Los Angeles, 1921

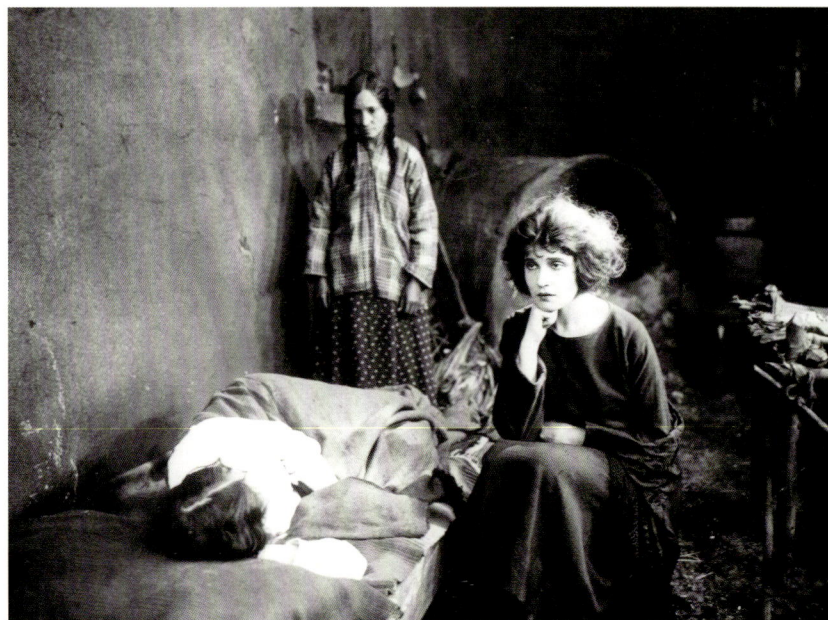

Edward Weston,
Tina Modotti, 1924

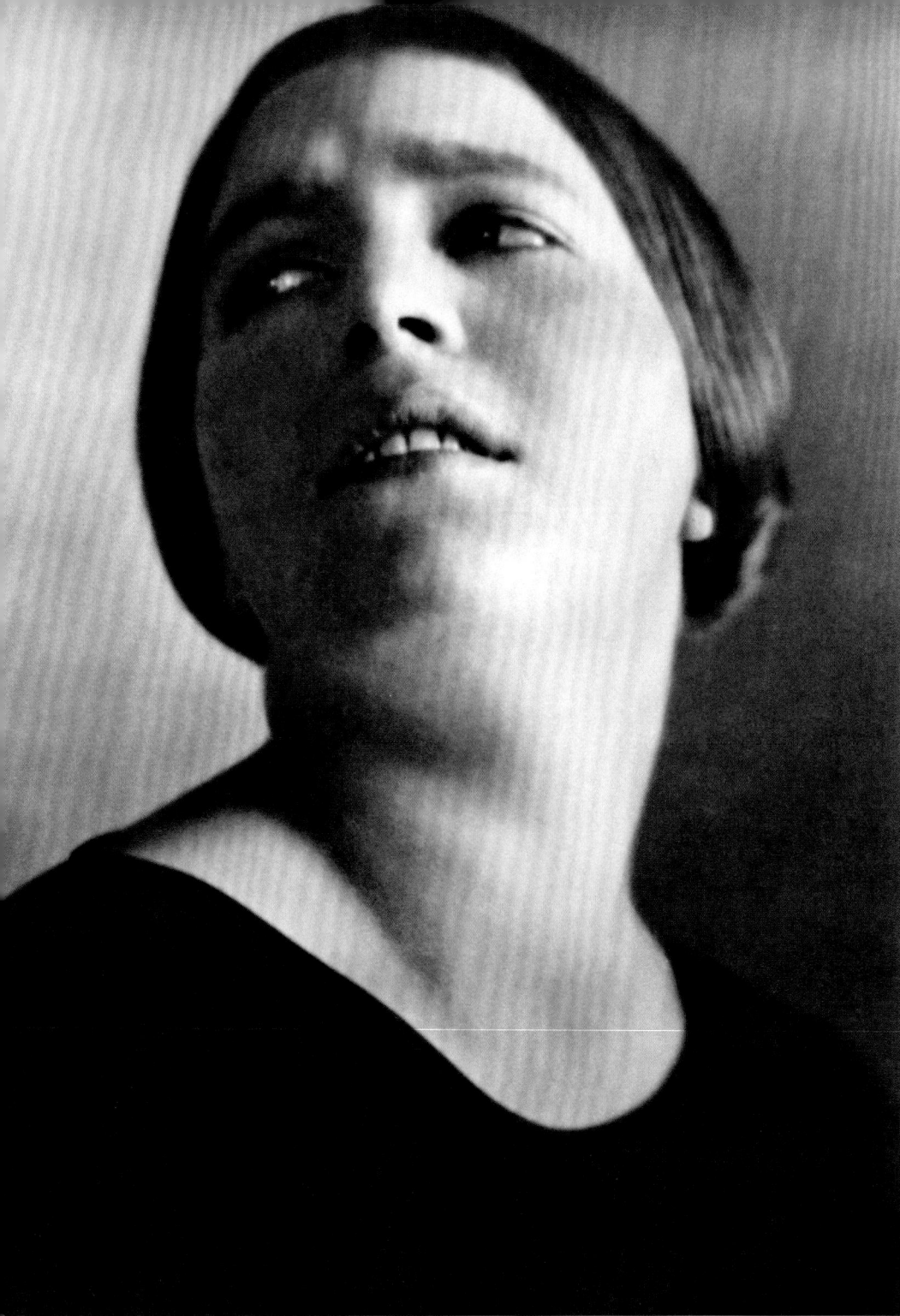

Johan Hagemayer, *Tina*,
San Francisco, 1921

Following pages
Edward Weston, *Tina*,
Mexico, 1924

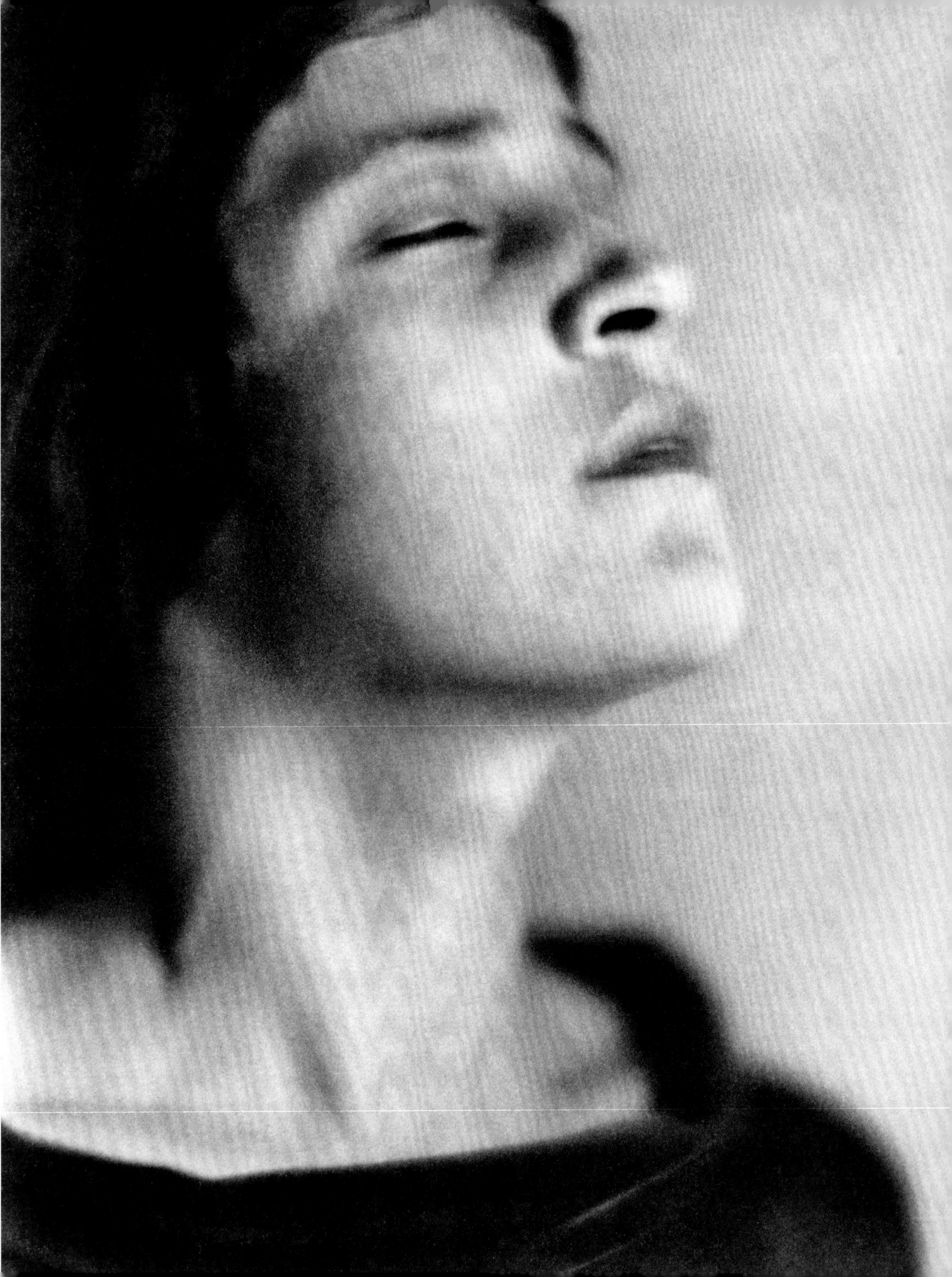

M. Geely, *Tina Modotti*,
Los Angeles, 1921

Edward Weston, *Tina*,
Tacubaya, 1923

Edward Weston, *Tina
on the Azotea*, Mexico, 1924

Edward Weston, *Tina Modotti*, Mexico, 1924

Edward Weston, *Tina on the Azotea*, Mexico, 1924

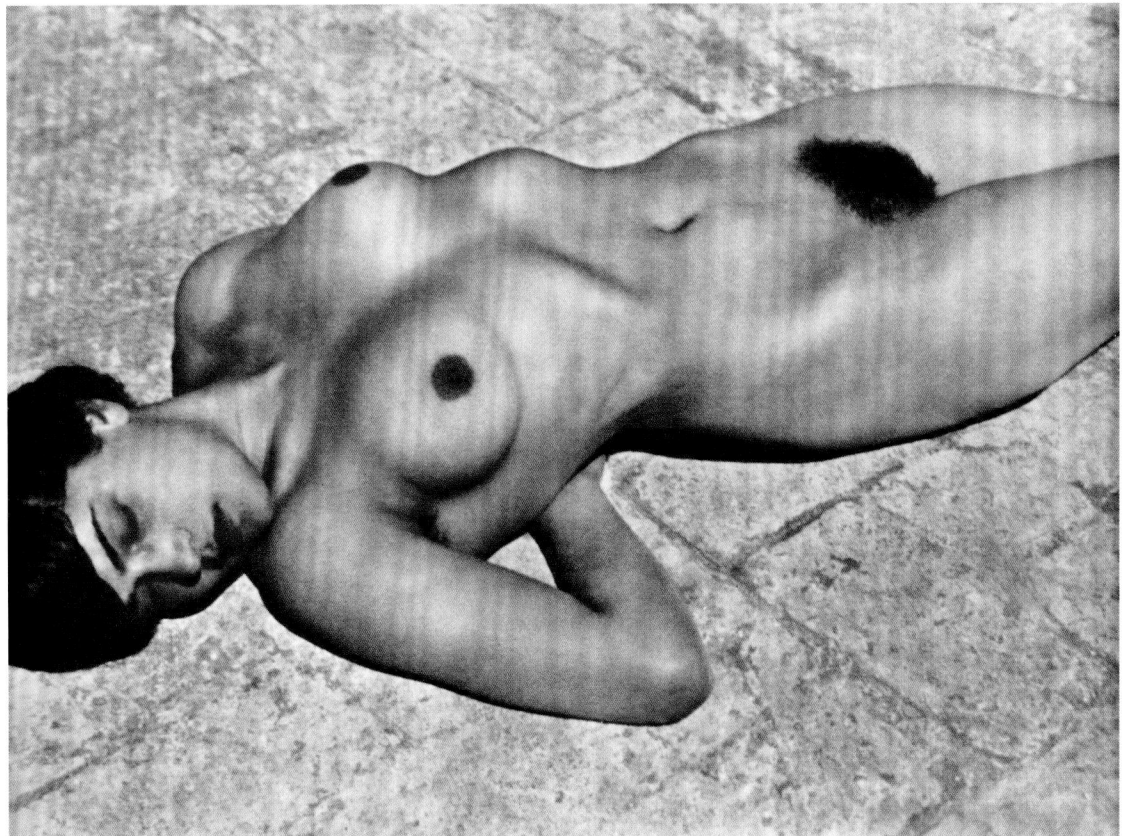

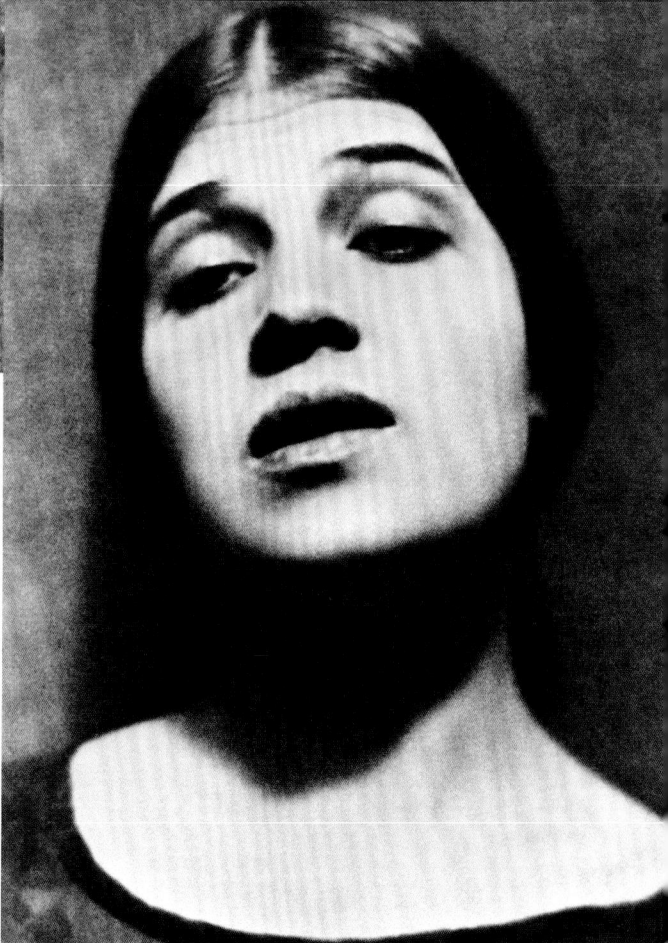

Edward Weston, *Tina Acting*,
Mexico, 1925

Edward Weston, *Tina*, 1925

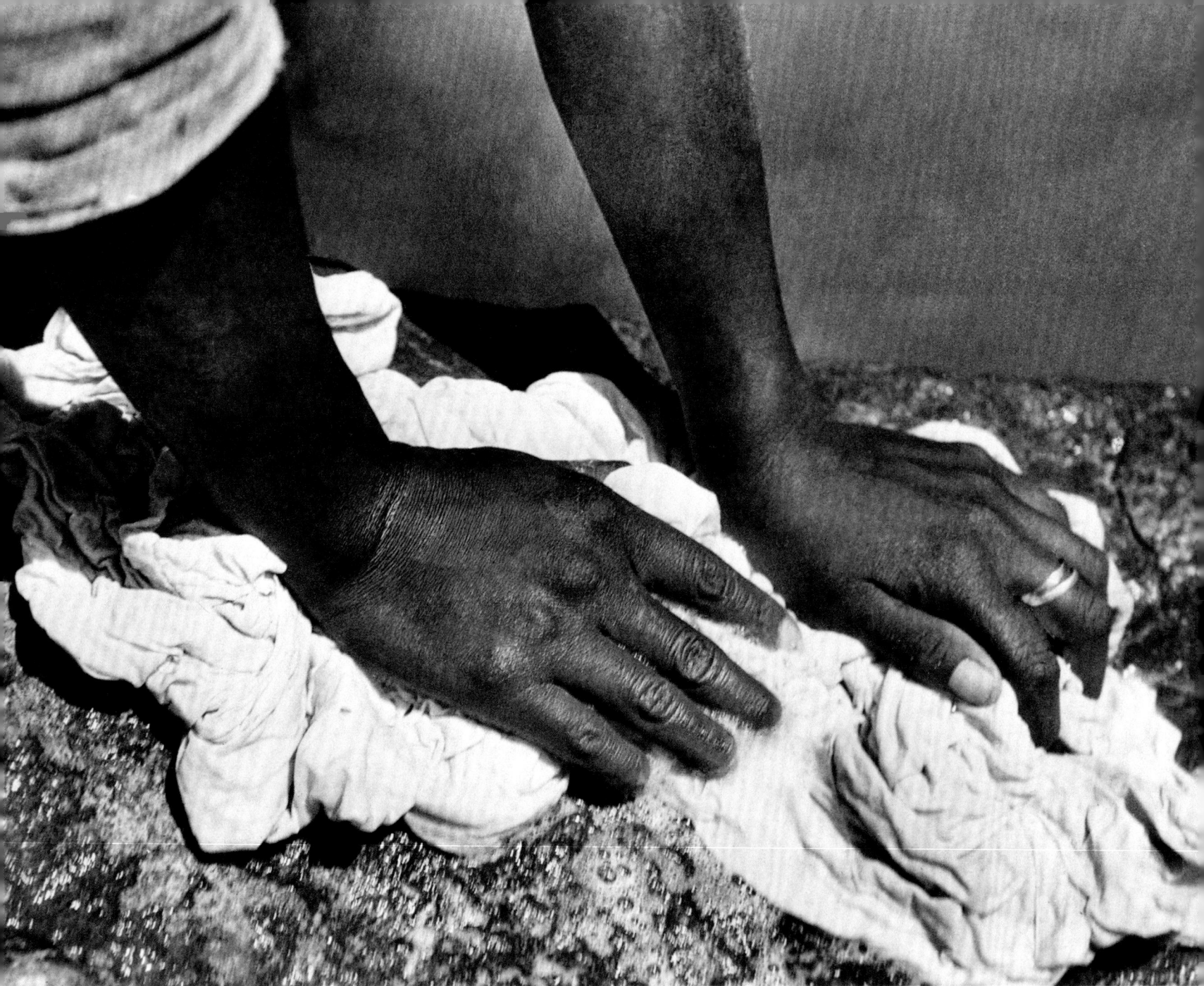

Tina Modotti, *Hands Washing
Laundry*, Mexico, 1927
Pordenone, Cinemazero,
Archivio Fotografico
Zeroimage

Tina Modotti, *The Hands
of Assunta Modotti*,
California, 1926
Pordenone, Cinemazero,
Archivio Fotografico
Zeroimage

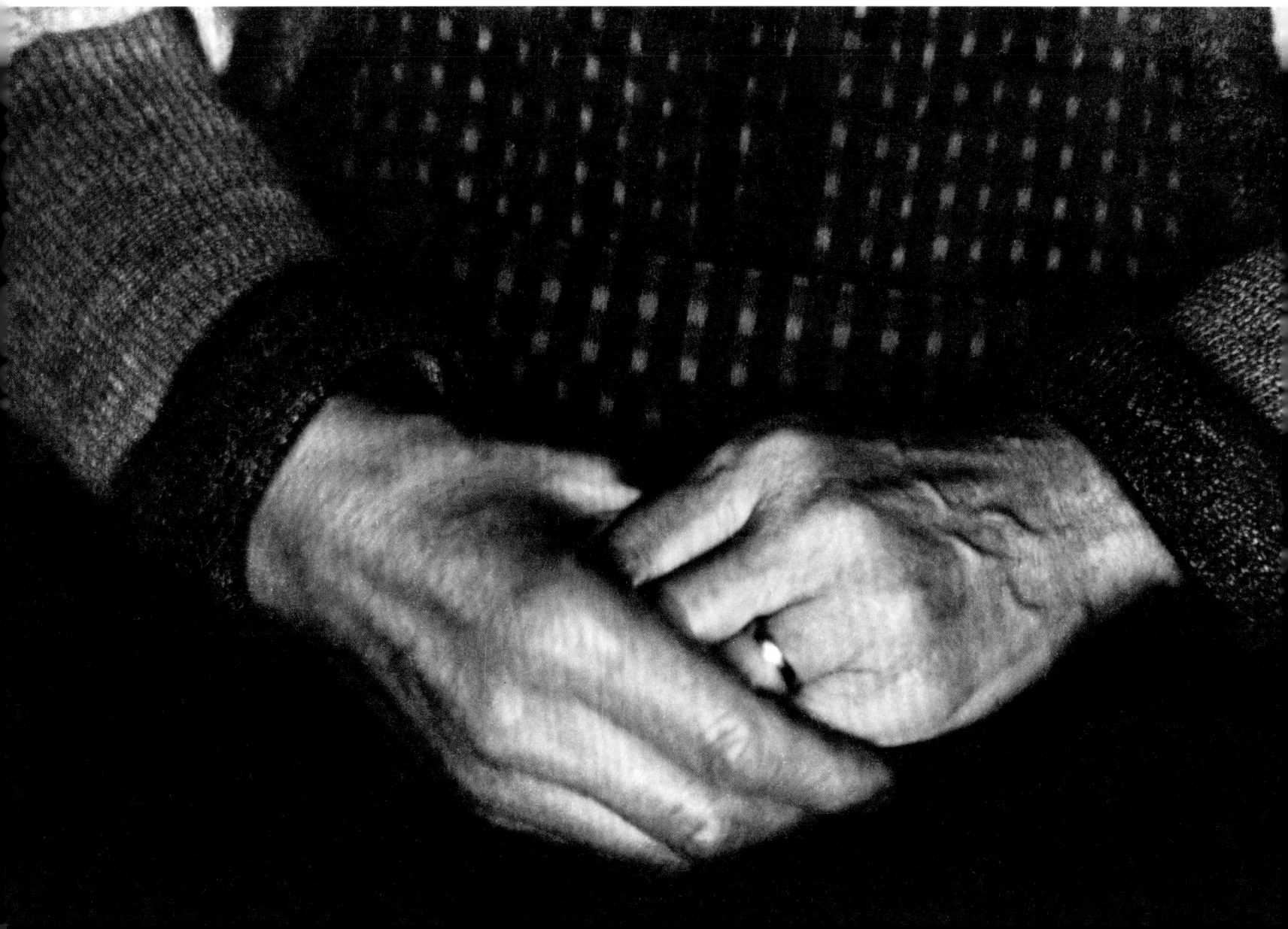

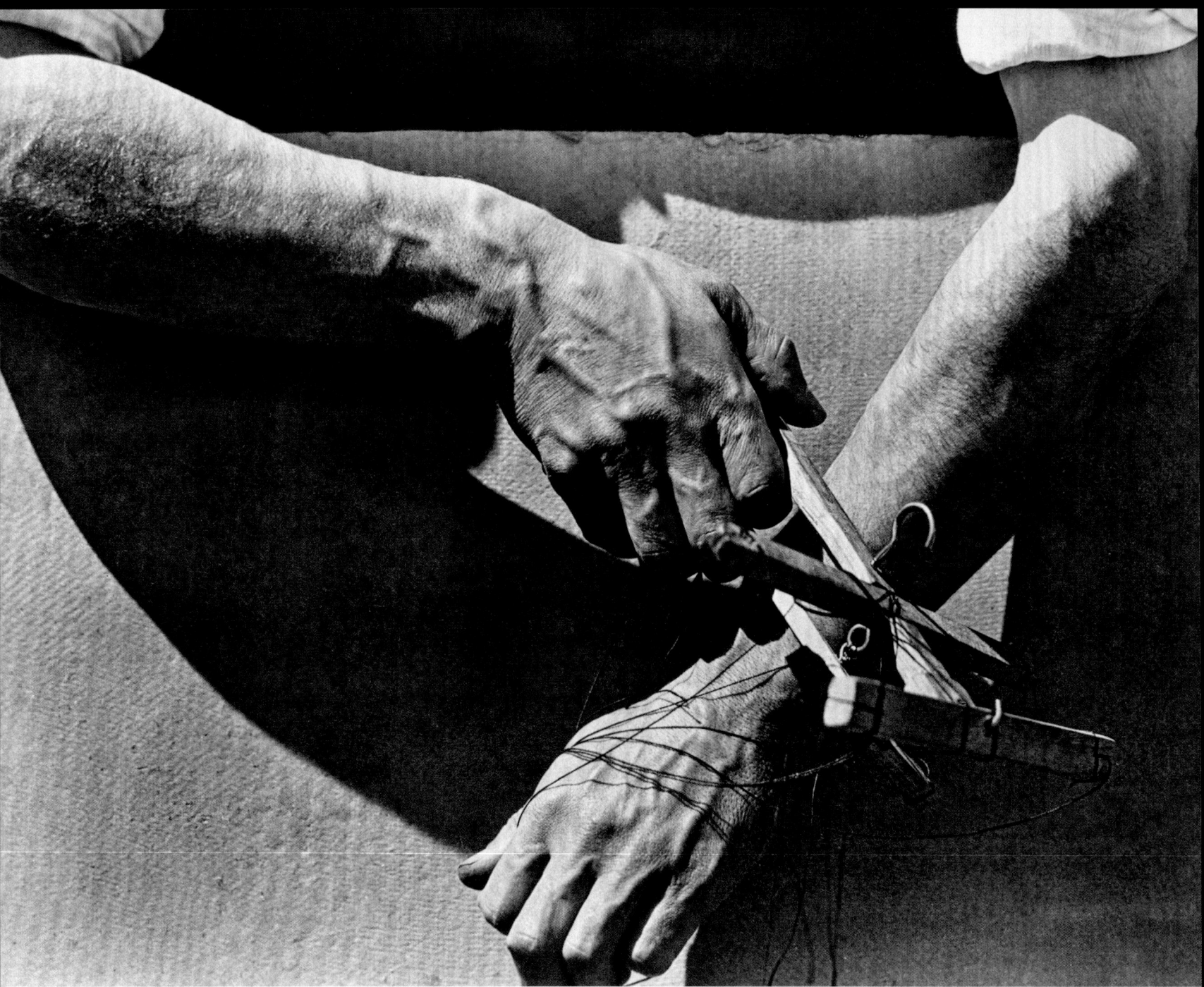

Tina Modotti, *Hands of the Puppeteer*, Mexico, 1929
Pordenone, Cinemazero,
Archivio Fotografico
Zeroimage

Tina Modotti, *Hands on Shovel*, Mexico, 1927
Pordenone, Cinemazero,
Archivio Fotografico
Zeroimage

face and his eyes, every posture or gesture to express complex moods and feelings: truly a perfect style for silent film.

His fame grew with *The Conquering Power* (Rex Ingram, 1921), based on Balzac's *Eugénie Grandet*, in which he played the sentimental victim of the economic interests and greed of bourgeois society. This theme was partly repeated in the adaptation of *Camille* (Ray Smallwood, 1921), featuring Alla Nazimova. As an actor Valentino was very different from the typical heroes of American cinema, generally men of action: he managed to combine seduction with a romantic ethos that was never amoral. This transformation in some way attenuated the feeling of "erotic" danger that American society might feel in a seducer belonging to a different race and nationality. It was the same form of "spiritualization" that Hollywood tried to apply at the time to foreign female stars, especially to Greta Garbo, with the aim of toning down her vampish sensuality to make her an icon of spiritual eroticism. In the 1920s the American star system

French poster for the film
A Sainted Devil, directed
by Joseph Henabery
in 1924
Lithographic print,
162.3 x 122.6 cm
Turin, Collection Museo
Nazionale del Cinema,
inv. P30034

Poster for the film *The
Eagle*, directed by Clarence
Brown in 1925
Offset print, 140 x 100 cm
Turin, Collection Museo
Nazionale del Cinema,
inv. P00980

French poster for the
film *The Son of the Sheik*,
directed by George
Fitzmaurice in 1926
Lithographic print,
160 x 120 cm
Turin, Collection Museo
Nazionale del Cinema,
inv. P01475-001

Silkscreen poster (printed
in the 1980s) for *The Son
of the Sheik*, 1926
Los Angeles, Academy
of Motion Pictures

required passion to be associated with romanticism: the seducing body had to contain a romantic soul to appeal to an audience that could not be afflicted by the sense of guilt brought about by pure sexual desire.

Before the war, it had been Italian and European cinema that had attracted more cultured audiences in the United States. In order to establish itself, therefore, American cinema had observed these models and adopted their directors, actors, and professionals who were faced after the war with a serious economic crisis that encouraged emigration to the New World. In the meantime, moreover, Hollywood had become a lively, attractive cosmopolitan center.

Between 1919 and 1925, at a time of expansion and success for U.S. culture and cinema in Europe, coinciding with the decline of Italian silent film, the Americans came to shoot around a dozen films in Italy. As would happen in the aftermath of World War II, the decision stemmed partly from the opportunity to take advantage of cheaper labor costs. What is significant here, however, is that these productions led to a great deal of interaction between the two cultures. Another factor in the choice to film in Italy was the awareness that it was a perfect location, with its magnificent art and landscapes, inhabited by a people, as was often mentioned in interviews, who lived life as if on stage. The publicity material about these films also shows how the American producers scrupulously researched iconographic sources in order to create costumes and sets, an evident homage to the history of Italian art and Italian cinema, which led the world in terms of the development of artisanship. Like the American artists and writers who traveled to Italy in the nineteenth century on their Grand Tour, the film-makers also followed an essential itinerary, usually taking in Venice, Florence, Rome, Naples, and more rarely Sicily. The records of their experiences in Italy often contain warm praise for the local craftsmen for their ability to build sets, to work long hours and to find imaginative technical solutions to problems and inconveniences of all kinds.[26] As a matter of fact, Italian craftsmanship had numerous ardent admirers in America: a synthesis of art, as embodied in the country's unique, unparalleled monuments, and the consumer production of the modern world, it maintained recognizable features of Italy's cultural heritage and adapted them to the present day. The Americans also made use of research conducted in loco by art specialists to ensure the accuracy of their historical reconstructions in the face of audiences all over the world. In the film *Romola*, shot in Florence in 1923 by Henry King, a crucial role was played by the then director of the Biblioteca Laurenziana, Guido Biagi, and by Tito Neri, the founder of the Neri Shipyard in Livorno, who was assigned with the task of building the historical vessels both for *Romola* and for the above-mentioned *Ben-Hur* (Fred Niblo, 1925), another Hollywood silent kolossal shot in Italy. Without going into the rollercoaster adventure of the production of *Ben-Hur*, full of unlikely twists, the collaboration between the Neri Shipyard and the American art directors is proof not only of professional but also of personal

Rudolph Valentino relaxing in his Los Angeles home, 1922

One of the last official portraits of Rudolph Valentino, 1926

relations. They were called on to reconstruct the fleet of ships, with the trireme flagship, in record time; built initially according to the design of the Americans, the ships sank almost as soon as they were put in the water. "That was the beginning of one of the most rewarding relationships in my entire life," recalled Arnold Gillespie, assistant to art director Horace Jackson, who described how he and Neri supervised the feverish activity of the shipyard sleeping on a straw mattress in a shed; in just two weeks they managed to refloat the ships, thanks to the sense of responsibility and sacrifice and to the professional pride of Neri and his four hundred workers who sang opera songs as they toiled.[27]

In the context of this complex back-and-forth movement between the United States and Italy we would imagine that there was a great exodus of Italian actors leaving the dying world of Italian cinema for Hollywood. But this was not the case. As well as the anti-Italian sentiments of the Americans during the great wave of migration, we must also consider the nationalistic prejudices of the Italians toward the United States and Hollywood.[28]

The small number of Italian film actors who moved to California included Luciano Albertini, Guido Trento, Lido Manettti, and Agostino Borgato, who all set out in the mid-1920s, when Italian film-making all but came to a halt. Their professional careers give a good measure of the uneven relations that were being established at the time between Italian cinema and Hollywood.

Luciano Albertini came from the world of the circus and had been the star of several films characterized by athletic and acrobatic feats shot in the wake of the unbelievable popularity of Maciste, the powerful slave in *Cabiria*[29]. Statuesque and athletic, in 1924 Albertini signed a contract with Universal for *The Iron Man*, but on arriving in Hollywood he discovered that it was not a film but a series, in which he was not even the main actor. Annoyed, he returned to Berlin, where he had worked previously and where he resumed his career successfully. The legend of the Mecca of the film world was still not firmly established, and in the eyes of some in the Italian film industry it lacked the creative splendor of German cinema.

Before going to Hollywood, Lido Manetti had had a highly successful career in Italian silent film, working with stars like Francesca Bertini, Italia Almirante Manzini, and Rina De Liguoro in forty or so pictures. He set out for the United States in 1925, following his friend Agostino Borgato, another Italian film actor who had recently emigrated (again a confirmation of the phenomenon of chain migration). Tall and handsome, he was offered a contract with Paramount and made seven films between 1926 and 1928, alongside American actresses of the caliber of Virginia Valli, Louise Brooks, Clara Bow, Pola Negri, Florence Vidor, and Norma Talmadge. These were prestigious films, made by leading directors, in which he generally played the role of the rival and only rarely the romantic lover. In 1927 Manetti changed his name to Arnold Kent, not because he wanted to "become American" but because he hated the embarrassing English pronunciation of his name, which sounded like the Italian word "laido" (foul or filthy), although the word obviously meant nothing to Americans.

In 1928 he began work on *The Four Feathers*—which would become *Beau Sabreur*—by John Waters, with Gary Cooper and William Powell, but he never managed to complete the film. He died in a car accident, which remains one of the unsolved mysteries of Hollywood.[30]

Agostino Borgato had arrived in Hollywood in the mid-1920s, when he acted with his fellow countryman Monty Banks (Mario Bianchi) in *Horse Shoes* (Clyde Bruckman, 1927) and *A Perfect Gentleman* (Clyde Bruckman, 1928). With his prominent nose, spiky hair and strong features, he played roles of varying importance in several major films. He also appeared in *Woman of Affairs* and *Romance*, both by Clarence Brown, with Greta Garbo; it is said

Rudolph Valentino kissing his wife Natacha Rambova, 1920s Turin, Collection Museo Nazionale del Cinema

that Garbo appreciated his presence on the set, because he reminded her of her mentor, the director Mauritz Stiller.

One Italian film actor in Hollywood about whom little has been written, although he played an important role in this story, is the Neapolitan Guido Trento. With his regular features and natural elegance, he was the young actor in the Neapolitan company Polifilms. With seventy Italian silent films as second lead to his name, he acted alongside many great actresses in films made by important directors. With Francesca Bertini, for example, he featured in *Frou-Frou* (Alfredo De Antoni, 1918) and in the series of films on the seven deadly sins.

In 1922 new professional opportunities arose when he was hired to take part in the two spectacular costume films made in Rome by the American director Gordon Edwards, *The Shepherd King* and *Nero*, in the roles of Saul and the Christian Tullius respectively. When shooting was over, Edwards invited him to Hollywood and directed him in *It Is the Law* (1924). However, his mentor's sudden death left him without support, so he moved to San Francisco to work in the Italian immigrant theater. In 1928 he returned to Hollywood and joined the cast of *Street Angel*, a silent masterpiece directed by the sensitive Italian American director Frank Borzage. The film was set in Naples and starred Charles Farrell and Janet Gaynor, Fox's greatest stars at the time. As well as Trento, the film also featured other Italian actors such as Henry Armetta, Gino Corrado, and Alberto Rabagliati. In *Street Angel* the narrow streets of the capital of southern Italy did not have the falsely picturesque atmosphere of similar Hollywood productions, as if the numerous Italian actors had suggested a more truthful representation of the city. Trento played an important role, that of a *carabiniere*, and was often filmed in close-up. The Italian censors, however, could not accept this gritty portrait of Naples, nor the fact that the film makes fun of the *carabinieri*. Many of the scenes featuring Trento were cut, which explains why the actor never received much attention in Italy for his fine performance in this famous film.

With the advent of sound, Trento performed an epic feat: the making in Hollywood of the first sound picture in Italian. Traveling around California in a battered old car with Alberto Rabagliati, he contacted the many Italian vinedressers and managed to raise the funds necessary for the production, for which he also wrote the screenplay. Entitled *Sei tu l'amore?*, the film starred Rabagliati alongside Luisa Caselotti.[31] Distributed in the United States and reviewed favorably by the American press, it arrived in Italy and was shown in theaters before *La canzone dell'amore*, officially considered to be the first Italian sound picture. It is not even mentioned in film histories, perhaps because it was made by emigrant actors.

Sei tu l'amore? was brought to Italy by Rabagliati, a strapping young actor who in 1926 had won the contest organized by Twentieth Century Fox to find actors for Hollywood.[32] The director and intellectual Alessandro Blasetti, a key figure in the subsequent rebirth of Italian cinema, expressed his bitter disapproval of the contest in an article entitled "Il nostro oro."[33] In his opinion, by attracting Italian actors Hollywood was stealing artistic and financial resources from the Italian film industry, thus preventing its rebirth. He went on to mention in particular Valentino, Carminati, and Manetti, who

The ships built by
Tito Neri for the film
Ben-Hur, 1925

were making vast amounts of money for Hollywood with their art. He called on the fascist government to take suitable measures against this unfair competition by halting the contest. However, his appeal fell on deaf ears and it went ahead as planned.

The contest regulations required competitors to send two photos, one close-up and one full figure, in "simple, tight-fitting clothes, or even better in swimming trunks, to highlight the contours of the body." With his photos and a screen test, Rabagliati won the contest and boarded a steamer for America. In Hollywood, however, he spent most of his time doing the social rounds and his acting career never really took off, apart from his role as another *carabiniere* in *Street Angel*, through which he got to know Frank Borzage and above all Guido Trento. After Fox changed his name to Gino Conti, because Rabagliati was practically impossible for Americans to pronounce, he obtained small parts in *Making the Grade* (Alfred Green, 1929) and in the musical *Let's Go Native* (Leo McCarey, 1930) with Jeanette MacDonald: three brief appearances on the silver screen in four years. Help eventually came from Trento, who, as

we have seen, involved him in the project for *Sei tu l'amore?* As his Hollywood career came to an end, he embarked on a new adventure as a swing singer. Of his Hollywood years there remains an entertaining account, published a year after his return to Italy, in which he describes the vices and virtues of the world of American cinema at the time.[34]

The mystery of why so few Italian film actors, and not a single actress, moved to Hollywood during the era of silent film cannot be entirely explained and has probably contributed to the fact that the memory of this chapter of film history has been erased both in Italy and in the United States. Many more Italian actors, on the other hand, were recruited by American silent film from the world of immigrant theater, or directly from Broadway. Theater, in fact, remained at the heart of the activity of Italian life in the United States, where immigrant or Italian American actors had already begun to carve out their own space and soon started to move nonchalantly between the stage, the set, the screen, and the radio. They had often arrived at a very young age, or had toured the Americas with operetta or classical theater companies; they called themselves musicians or singers, but they could also act, and they learned very quickly: to the extent that they could later boast of careers comprising hundreds of titles. It is possible to retrace briefly the gallery of these true show business workers, who shared the lively gestural expressiveness of the Italian people and the physicality of the Italian theater tradition. The Italian actor was able to exploit fully gestures and facial expressions (and not only in silent film), turning them into a universal language.

The biographies of many of these performers are full of holes, but the fact that they should have deserved much greater attention in the homeland, and not only in the United States, where they have been the subject of study, is proven by the hundreds of films in which they appeared.

The Neapolitan Cesare Gravina toured the Americas with his operetta company and moved to the United States in 1914, when many of his companions set off to take part in the war. Too old to enlist (he was born in 1858), he joined the theater world of Little Italy. His previous musical experience emerged in many films, as often happened with many of his

Fred Niblo studying the battle scene for *Ben-Hur*, 1925 Courtesy Kevin Brownlow Collection, UK

colleagues; he made his debut with Mary Pickford in an adaptation of *Madame Butterfly* (Sidney Olcott, 1915); again with Pickford, he then took part, as we have seen, in *Poor Little Peppina* (Sidney Olcott, 1916) and *Less Than the Dust* (John Emerson, 1916), in which Erich von Stroheim was one of the assistant directors. He subsequently became von Stroheim's favorite actor, playing roles of varying importance in all his films.

His haggard, deeply-lined face—at times menacing, at times ironic—and his effective use of gestures made him an ideal actor for silent film, and above all for Stroheim's extreme realism. Gravina was able to use his irregular, mobile features to move in the space of a few seconds from pathos to comedy. In several films his performances were moving, as in the role of the father forced to defend his daughter's honor (*The Wedding March*, Erich von Stroheim, 1926) or in that of the kind old man who protects poor kids like Jackie Coogan, the star of Chaplin's *The Kid*. He was often a victim, less often a murderer, as when he kills the evil count (played by Stroheim himself) who is about to seduce his "backward" daughter in *Foolish Wives* (Erich von Stroheim, 1922). One of his best performances came in the role of Ursus, the mountebank who looks after the disfigured boy in *The Man Who Laughs* (Paul Leni, 1928). Gravina's filmography includes sixty or so titles, all silent and mostly dramatic, among which *The Man in Blue* (Edward Laemmle, 1925), set in Little Italy, stands out.[35]

Black hair, dark eyes, regular features and a refined style of acting made Frank Puglia an ideal actor in the 1920s. Sicilian by birth, he had emigrated as a young boy with his father's operetta company, with which he had already toured the Americas before settling in the United States. In 1915 he had joined the Compagnia La Moderna in San Francisco, where he met Tina Modotti. On the suggestion of Lillian Gish, David W. Griffith went to see him in an Italian-language performance of *The Two Orphans* and immediately offered him a part in the film adaptation of the well-known play, which he was about to make with the Gish sisters under the title *Orphans of the Storm*. Puglia played the role of the good brother who protects his blind little sister (Dorothy Gish) from her scoundrel mother.

The 1920–21 season was an important turning point in this story, because it marked the official debut of Rudolph Valentino and the arrival in Hollywood of both Puglia and Modotti. Puglia's career in silent film continued in Griffith's wake: he acted in *Fascination* (Robert Leonard, 1922) with Mae Murray, in Florence he played the role of the Machiavellian Adolpho Spini in *Romola* (Henry King, 1924), starring Lillian Gish, and

The final scene of
Ben-Hur, 1925

Laurel wreath, 1925
Gilded metal trimmed
with gold lamé ribbon,
worn by Ramón Novarro
as Judah in *Ben-Hur*
Courtesy of The Collection
of Motion Picture Costume
Design: Larry McQueen,
Los Angeles

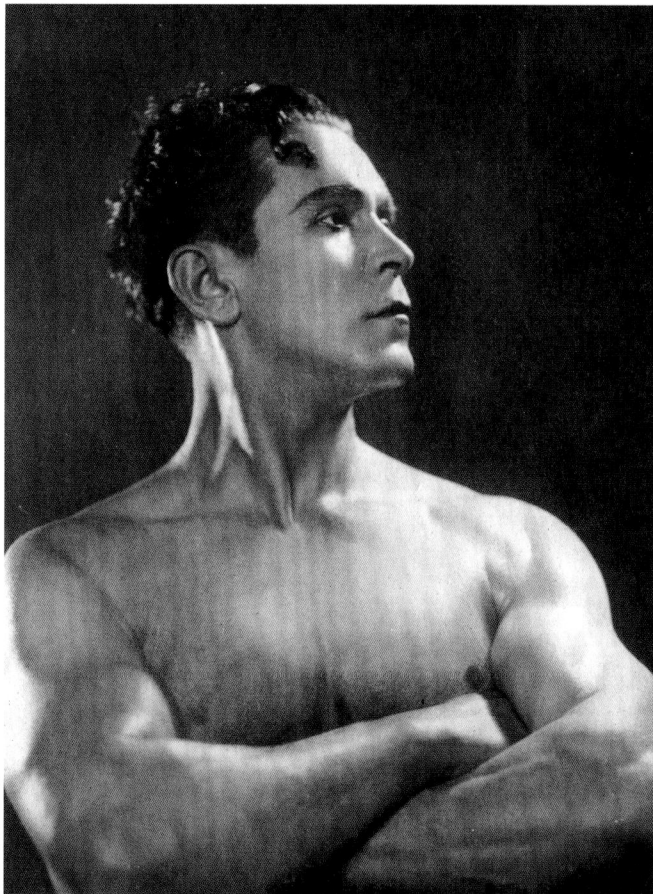

The actor Alberto Rabagliati, winner of the competition organized by Fox, in a 1928 photograph

Luciano Albertini in the title role of *Sansone contro i filistei*, directed by Domenico Gaido in 1918 Bologna, Cineteca di Bologna

Lido Manetti in the 1920s

Paul Porcasi in *Broadway*, directed by Paul Fejos in 1929

Agostino Borgato in *The Street of Forgotten Men*, directed by Herbert Brenon in 1925

Cesare Gravina in *Merry-Go-Round*, directed by Erich von Stroheim in 1923

Guido Trento in a frame from
Street Angel, directed by Frank
Borzage in 1928

Frank Puglia in *Orphans
of the Storm*, directed by David
W. Griffith in 1921

Albert Conti in *The Eagle*,
directed by Clarence Brown in
1925; Rudolph Valentino was
part of the cast

Monty Banks (Mario Bianchi)
in a photo from the 1920s

William Ricciardi
in the 1920s

immediately afterwards he joined Griffith in Germany to play the part of the Polish refugee Theodor in *Isn't Life Wonderful* (1924). He then acted alongside Dorothy Gish and Richard Barthelmess in *The Beautiful City* (Kenneth Webb, 1925), playing the part of an Italian American gangster in Little Italy. The film is the prototype of melodramas set in the Italian American community, with a mother torn between a good son and an evil son who stand on opposite sides of the law. This narrative model, recurrent in films about Italian American criminals, highlights the role of the family in the Italian community, but at the same time shows that there were honest, law-abiding people among the Italians. Puglia's career in silent film seemed to have taken off, but he never achieved star status.

Another successful Sicilian in the last years of the silent film era was Paolo (Paul) Porcasi, who also had a musical background and started his career as a tenor in Italy to subsequently tour Europe and the Americas. In 1917, during one of these tours, he decided to stay in the United States. He worked on Broadway for around ten years, achieving success in the role of Nick Verdis, the main character in the magnificent gangster-musical *Broadway*. In silent film he played the role of a diplomat in *Say It Again* (1926), a comedy set in the imaginary kingdom of Spezonia, directed by the Italian American Gregory La Cava and featuring another interesting actor from immigrant theater, William Ricciardi, as Prime Minister Stemmler. Soon afterwards Porcasi was lucky enough to play his signature role, Nick Verdis, in Paul Fejos's spectacular and visionary version of *Broadway* (1929), one of the first sound pictures. In an elegant double-breasted jacket and two-tone shoes, with his Mediterranean looks, his moustache, and his inevitable cigar, Porcasi offered a leaner, more versatile variant of the Italian. He had a long and successful career in sound pictures, with over 140 titles, including *Footlight Parade*, *Morocco*, and *Casablanca.*

Albert Conti was "a tall, handsome man, very dignified, with a permanent line of sadness on his forehead," as Puccini described him, noting that "he wasted his whole fortune on a brilliant cosmopolitan life."[36] An aristocrat from Trieste, he arrived in New York in 1919 and was obliged to take many manual labor jobs before moving to California, where he was chosen by Erich von Stroheim as a consultant on military uniforms for *Merry-Go-Round* (1923). He went on to act in many films alongside Stroheim, Cesare Gravina, Rudolph Valentino in *The Eagle*, and Charlie Chaplin and Marion Davies in *Show People* (King Vidor, 1928), one of the films from the silent era that best conveys the carefree atmosphere of Hollywood. The roles he played were always linked to his refined and aristocratic appearance.

Conti was undoubtedly a better actor than most of his fellow Hapsburg Empire expatriates, as reported by the American press, since his filmography includes as many as 112 titles, silent and sound, mostly in dignified roles even if never as the leading character. With his elegant bearing and his air of magnificent decadence, he seemed to have come out of a Joseph Roth story. He played himself, an affable skeptic or a lady's man, as in the sound adaptation of Pirandello's *As You Desire Me* (1932), in the role of a captain who has the good fortune to seduce Maria, played by Greta Garbo.

Monty Banks (or Mario Bianchi, from Cesena) was a comedian, short in stature but attractive, with a round face and elegant moustache. As an actor, he was extremely versatile, capable of performing his own acrobatic stunts. After working in Europe, in 1914 he had set out for the Americas, where he had performed in variety shows as a dancer. Three years later he made his film debut with Mack Sennett, the master of slapstick, playing the straight man to Roscoe "Fatty" Arbuckle.

After this excellent apprenticeship, Abe Warner, the youngest of the Warner Brothers, offered him a series of eight shorts. He thus began to write, direct, and act in his films. The series was so successful that he was able to set up his own independent company, the Monty Banks Pictures Corporation. His first feature film as a director, *Racing Luck* (1924), was set in the Italian American community. Banks played a character with his own name, Mario Bianchi, who arrives in New York to work in his uncle's restaurant. The gangster Tony is his rival in love, but he wins out and conquers the girl's heart by winning an automobile race.

"Rollicking hair, black and glossy, parted in the center," wrote Dorothy Spensley in the magazine *Photoplay*. "It's a symbol of character, that hair. Of the spontaneity of his Latin temperament, through which runs a clear, sharp line of business ingeniousness. Monty is a comedian, but Monty is also a business man. He would not have his own producing unit with Pathé if he were not. He would still be a dancing dandy at Dominguez Cafe, in New York, as he was ten years ago, or a stunt man, doing other people's hazards."[37] Although recognizing his abilities, the article ends by defining him a "natural" performer, as often happened with Italian actors, whose naturalistic style was mistaken for spontaneity, ignoring the hard work and the long apprenticeship, together with an exceptional sense of rhythm and balance, needed to master the art of slapstick (in this case): in short, a controlled use of the body that was anything but "spontaneous."

Bianchi was one of the greatest comedians of the silent film era, but the fact that his films are so hard to find makes it difficult to analyze his work. Of all the "Italians in Hollywood," he was the only one to have his own production company and to move easily between Europe and America, making films in many different places.

According to his own account, Henry Armetta left Palermo in 1902 when he was still a young boy, a stowaway on a ship bound for America. Having reached the United States, he was about to be repatriated when an Italian barber offered to adopt him. After doing all the normal immigrant jobs, he was taken on as a valet in a club frequented by actors such as Raymond Hitchcock, who helped him to make his stage debut. After learning his trade with the company of William Farnum, he took part with him in several films still made on the East Coast, appeared in a few comic shorts, and played the part of the jester in *The Eternal Sin* (Herbert Brenon, 1917) based on Victor Hugo's *Lucrezia Borgia*. His character really emerged, however, in the silent films directed by Frank Borzage, who appreciated the way he had played the army cook in *Seventh Heaven* (1927) so much that he offered him the part of Mascetto, the kind-hearted but easily-angered circus owner in *Street Angel*.

Famous for his funny walk and his way of slapping his forehead when he was irritated or baffled, Armetta embodied the image of the good-natured and warm Italian to perfection, and was blessed with such natural comic timing that he even stole the show from Laurel and Hardy in *The Devil's Brother*.

The tall, dark-haired Fred Malatesta made around ninety films, silent and sound, of varying quality, playing many different roles including musician, aristocrat, soldier, and even cowboy. He played French or Spanish characters more often than Italians, as he had acted in his youth on stages all over Europe and the Americas and spoke both languages fluently. Among his most memorable performances are his roles as the shoeshiner friend of Mary Pickford in *Little Lord Fauntleroy* (Alfred Green, 1921) and as the French ambassador who consoles the Czarina (Pola Negri) in *Forbidden Paradise* (Ernst Lubitsch, 1924).

Albert Roccardi was one of the first Italian theater actors to emigrate to the United States, in 1884, working on Broadway in important companies like those of John Drew and the Barrymores, and was also one of the first to work in American cinema, in 1911, when New York was still the home of film production. A small man with a lively expression, Roccardi was also highly knowledgeable and cultured, as is clear from several interviews he gave at the time.[38] He made about thirty films, including *The Passionate Pilgrim* (Robert Vignola, 1921) and *The Love Parade* (Ernst Lubitsch, 1929).

Although it is difficult to fill the gaps in these patchy biographies, the continuous exchange between Italian and American spectacle, as outlined here, confirms the great adaptability as well as the talent of the Italian actors.

The Italian American actress Miriam Battista also came from Broadway theater: she had, in fact, been a child prodigy, first on stage and later in silent film, with a notable filmography that included Miriam, the main character's best friend, in the highly popular *Humoresque*, directed by Frank Borzage (1920). She then appeared in other outstanding films alongside Billie Dove, Norma Talmadge, and Lionel Barrymore. However, the careers of child prodigies are always rather uneven; she later became a dancer with the Ziegfeld Follies, but with typical Italian versatility also made best use of her beautiful black curls and dark eyes taking part in some of the films that the American Italians made in New York in the early 1930s, thus rejoining the lively immigrant theater world.

The Tuscan actor Gino Corrado is a strange character in the history of cinema, with 253 titles to his credit, stretching from 1916, with his uncredited role as a marathon runner in Griffith's *Intolerance* and with *Gretchen the Greenhorn* (Sidney Franklin), a film about emigration with Lillian Gish, right up to 1954, with *Three Coins in the Fountain*. Outstanding in the silent film era is his performance as Aramis, alongside Douglas Fairbanks as D'Artagnan, in the crepuscular *Iron Mask* (Allan Dwan, 1929).

Some Italians reached Hollywood through roundabout routes. Bull Montana, born as Luigi Montagna, was one example. After working in quarries and mines he used his muscles to become a boxer and wrestler, eventually working as Douglas Fairbanks's personal trainer. He then began a film career as a comic character actor, with some hilarious performances such as the parody of the three musketeers directed by and featuring Max Linder (*The Three Must-Get-Theres*, 1923) in which he plays Li'l Cardinal Richie-Loo. Montagna was not the only Italian boxer to act in American films. Primo Carnera is another notable example. What is interesting, however, is that in American films about boxing the fighter is often of Italian origin—a further confirmation of the fact that when a technique or art tames the body and turns it into a celebrity, even an Italian emigrant, with calluses on his hands

Bull Montana (Luigi
Montagna) in 1922

The director Frank Capra with
Clark Gable and Claudette
Colbert on the set of *It
Happened One Night*, 1923

Henry Armetta in *Street
Angel*, directed by Frank
Borzage in 1928

Portrait of the director
Frank Borzage, 1923

Albert Roccardi playing in
The Virtuous Model, directed
by Albert Capellani in 1919

Fred Malatesta playing in
Forbidden Paradise, directed by
Ernst Lubitsch, 1924

Mario Carillo (Mario Caracciolo)
playing in *The Only Thing*, directed
by Jack Conway in 1925

Miriam Battista and Frank
Borzage on the set of
Humoresque, 1920

The director Gregory La Cava with Bebe Daniels during shooting of *Feel My Pulse*, 1927 (released in 1928)

Sol Polito and Bette Davies together on the set in a rare photograph from 1942

The director Robert Vignola

Cinematographer Tony Gaudio (left) with the director Fred Niblo on the set of *The Temptress*, 1926

Gino Corrado playing in *La Bohème*, directed by King Vidor in 1926

after so much digging and fighting, becomes something acceptable and admissible.

Another actor who used his sporting talents, in this case as a horseman and swordsman blessed with aristocratic charm, was the Neapolitan Count Mario Caracciolo, known as Mario Carillo. His most memorable roles include the King of Spain seduced by Greta Garbo in *The Torrent* (Monta Bell, 1926) and the French tutor whose identity is used by Valentino in *The Eagle* (Clarence Brown, 1925).

As well as actors, there were also Italian or Italian American directors in American silent film: Frank Capra, the famous Sicily-born director who was the first in movie history to have his name above the title of his films, above those of the producers; the Italian American Frank Borzage, whose successful films dominated the last years of the silent era, reaching new heights in the direction of dramatic silent actors; the less well-known (at least to the general public) Gregory La Cava, who began as a cartoon producer with *Happy Hooligan* and *The Katzenjammer Kids*, continued as a director with W. C. Fields, and in the sound film era directed Katharine Hepburn in the enchanting *Stage Door* and William Powell in the brilliant social comedy *My Man Godfrey*. Robert Vignola, born in Trivigno in the province of Potenza, should be remembered as the co-author of a film on the life of Christ shot on location in Palestine in 1912, *From the Manger to the Cross*, and as the director chosen by the publishing magnate William R. Hearst to launch his beloved mistress Marion Davies. For her he directed spectacular pictures such as *When Knighthood Was in Flower*, defined in the publicity material as the most expensive film of the time, and the delightful *Enchantment*, in which he played with the theater in the cinema—a reflection of mirrors of all the forms of spectacle.

Then there were the cinematographers, another "Italian specialty": Tony Gaudio, Sol Polito, Nick Musuraca, Al Liguori, Silvano Balboni, Joe Valentino, Arthur Martinelli, and Gaetano Ventimiglia, who enhanced many a film with their sophisticated use of light and composition. And set designers such as Gabriele Scognamillo and Albert D'Agostino. And artisans, dressmakers, and hairdressers, in other words all those figures without whom the glamor of Hollywood would never have existed, but whose names have been forgotten.

The Italians managed to carve out their own space in Hollywood (and not only in film) with their skills, intelligence and determination, in a continuous search for a balance between artisanship and art. After all, that sun-baked California reminded them of the land they had left behind.

[1] Gianni Puccini, "Italiani nel mondo del cinema," in *Cinema* 20 (1937).

[2] On the pre-eminence of Italian and French cinema on the American market, see Richard Abel, *The Red Rooster Scare. Making Cinema American 1900–1910* (Berkeley: University of California Press, 1999).

[3] In particular Richard H. Broadhead, "Strangers on a Train: The Double Dream of Italy in the American Gilded Age," in *Modernism/Modernity* 1, no. 2 (1994) and Joseph P. Cosco, *Imagining Italians: The Clash of Romance and Race in American Perceptions, 1880/1910* (Albany: State University of New York Press, 2003).

[4] "The government . . . tried to intervene to halt or reduce the phenomenon of migration. The Italian parliament condemned emigration as 'evil and immoral' and defined the peasants and workers who emigrated as 'deserters' who were abandoning their villages, their homes and their families to plunge into the 'unknown'"; Pellegrino Nazzaro, "The Mezzogiorno and the Questione Meridionale," in *Italian Americans. Bridges to Italy, Bonds to America*, ed. by Luciano Iorizzo and Ernest Rossi (Youngstown: Teneo Press, 2010), 241.

[5] On Europeans in Hollywood see *Journeys of Desire. European Actors in Hollywood*, ed. by Alastair Phillips and Ginette Vincendeau (London: BFI, 2006); *Hollywood Les Fictions de l'exil*, ed. by Irène Bessière (Paris: Nouveau Monde éditions, 2007); *Les Européens dans le cinema Américain, emigration et exil*, ed. by Irène Bessière and Roger Odin (Paris: Presses Sorbonne Nouvelle, 2004); Graham Petrie, *Hollywood Destinies, European Directors in America, 1922–1931* (London: Routledge & Kegan Paul, 1985); John Baxter, *The Hollywood Exiles* (New York: Taplinger, 1976), and Giuliana Muscio, "European Actors in Classical Hollywood Cinema," in *The Place of Europe in American History*, ed. by Maurizio Vaudagna (Turin: Otto, 2007).

[6] On anti-Italian prejudice see *Anti-Italianism. Essays on a Prejudice*, ed. by William J. Connell and Fred Gardaphé (New York: Palgrave, 2010); John Dickie, *Darkest Italy: The Nation and Stereotypes of the Mezzogiorno 1860–1900* (New York: St. Martin's Press, 1999).

[7] The Black Hand was a criminal organization formed of immigrants from the south of Italy that operated in Chicago and New York. Its main activities were extortion and kidnapping, and its victims were generally fellow Italians. It is considered the cradle of Mafia gangster culture in America. This hypothesis is called into question by Robert M. Lombardo, *Organized Crime in Chicago: Beyond the Mafia* (Urbana: University of Illinois Press, 2012). See also Francesco Benigno, *La mala setta. Alle origini di mafia e camorra 1859–1878* (Turin: Einaudi, 2015).

[8] On the representation of Italians in American cinema see Peter Bondanella, *Hollywood Italians* (New York: Continuum, 2004); Ilaria Serra, *The Imagined Immigrant* (Madison, NJ: Fairleigh Dickinson, 2009); Giorgio Bertellini, "Black Hands and White Hearts. Immigrants as Urban Racial Types in Early Twentieth-Century American Cinema," in *Urban History* 31, no. 3 (2004); Flaminio Di Biagi, *Italoamericani: tra Hollywood e Cinecittà* (Milan: Le Mani, 2010).

[9] On the intense debate on the "race" of the Italians, see *Gli Italiani sono bianchi?*, ed. by Jennifer Guglielmo and Salvatore Salerno (Milan: Il Saggiatore, 2003); *Parlare di razza*, ed. by Tatiana Petrovich Njegosh and Anna Scacchi (Verona: Ombre corte, 2012); David Richards, *Italian American: The Racializing of an Ethnic Identity* (New York: New York University Press, 1999); *The Invention of Ethnicity*, ed. by Werner Sollors (New York: Oxford University Press, 1989); Thomas A. Guglielmo, *White on Arrival:*

Italians, Race, Color, and Power in Chicago, 1890–1940 (New York: Oxford University Press, 2004); David R. Roediger, *Working Toward Whiteness: How America's Immigrants Became White* (New York: Perseus Books Group, 2005).

[10] Konstantin Stanislavski, *An Actor's Work: A Student Diary, 1938* (London: Routledge, 2008).

[11] Emelise Aleandri, *The Italian-American Immigrant Theater of New York City* (Charleston, SC: Arcadia, 1999); Maiori's show at the Bowery is described by John Corbin, "Shakspere [sic] in the Bowery," in *Harper's Weekly*, March 12, 1898: 244–46 (Maiori Clipping Files, Rose Library, New York).

[12] Lawrence Estavan, *The Italian Theater in San Francisco* (San Bernardino, CA: Borgo Press, 1991).

[13] The Bank of Italy, founded by Amadeo Peter Giannini in 1904, would become the Bank of America in 1919. It was his brother Attilio Giannini who established the first relations with the new-born film industry (in 1918), opening a special office for the cinema in Los Angeles in 1923 and building several branches of the bank close to the studios. Janet Wasko, *Movies and Money: Financing the American Film Industry* (Norwood, NJ: Ablex, 1982), 123.

[14] For a cultural history of American cinema, see Robert Sklar, *Cinemamerica* (Milan: Feltrinelli, 1975).

[15] Giuliana Muscio, "In Hoc Signo Vinces: Historical Films," in *Italian Silent Cinema: A Reader*, ed. by Giorgio Bertellini (New Barnet, England: John Libbey Publishing, 2013).

[16] Jacqueline Reich, *The Maciste Films of Italian Silent Cinema* (Bloomington: Indiana University Press, 2015).

[17] "Photoplay Writing," in *Photoplay*, April 1918: 88–89, 121. See also Giuliana Muscio, "Le didascalie di Anita Loos," in *Scrittura e immagine: Le didascalie nel cinema muto*, ed. by Francesco Pitassio and Leonardo Quaresima (Udine: La Tipografica, 1998).

[18] John Paul Russo, "From Italophilia to Italophobia: Representations of Italian Americans in the Early Gilded Age," in *Differentia* 6/7 (Spring–Autumn 1994).

[19] Paul Fryer, *The Opera Singer and The Silent Film* (Jefferson, NC: McFarland & Co., 2006).

[20] See Pietro Gargano, Gianni Cesarini, and Michael Aspinali, *Caruso* (Milan: Longanesi, 1990); Dorothy Caruso, *Enrico Caruso: His Life and Death* (New York: Simon and Schuster, 1945); Enrico Jr. Caruso and Andrew Farkas, *Enrico Caruso: My Father and My Family* (Portland, OR: Amadeus, 1990); Michael Scott, *The Great Caruso* (London: Hamilton, 1988); Francis Robinson, *Caruso: His Life in Pictures* (New York: Studio Pub., 1957); and Howard Greenfield, *Caruso* (New York: Putnam's, 1983).

[21] For my research on Caruso's cinema work I made use of the collection that his American wife, Dorothy Park Benjamin, left to the Arthur Friedheim Library, in the Peabody Institute, Johns Hopkins University.

[22] On Modotti see Pino Cacucci, *Tina* (Milan: Feltrinelli, 2007); Margaret Hooks, *Tina Modotti: Photographer and Revolutionary* (London: First Glance Books, 1993); *Tina Modotti: Gli anni luminosi*, ed. by Valentina Agostinis (Pordenone: Cinemazero, 1992).

[23] Estavan, *The Italian Theater in San Francisco* 1991, 60.

[24] On realist photography, see Carl Flieschauer and Beverly Brannan, *Documenting America, 1935–1943* (Berkeley: University of California Press, 1988); on Modotti as a photographer, see Laura Mulvey and Peter Wollen, "Radici e movimenti," in *Tina Modotti: Gli anni luminosi* 1992, 91–94.

[25] Giuliana Muscio, "Rudy e June," in *Valentino. Lo schermo della passione*, ed. by Paola Cristalli (Ancona: Transeuropa, 1996).

[26] In an interview Lillian Gish stated: "I will never be able to praise enough the Italian workers who managed to create the exact setting of the story in minute detail," in *Motion Picture Magazine*, October 1924 (Kevin Brownlow Collection).

[27] Arnold Gillespie in "Remembrances of Ben-Hur. Part II," in *Classic Images* 162 (December 1988): 25–26.

[28] On the Great Italian Emigration, see *Storia dell'Emigrazione Italiana*, 2 vols., ed. by Piero Bevilacqua, Andreina De Clementi, and Emilio Franzina, (Rome: Donzelli, 2001–02); Stefano Luconi and Matteo Pretelli, *L'immigrazione negli Stati Uniti* (Bologna: il Mulino, 2008); Donna Gabaccia, *Emigranti* (Turin: Einaudi, 2003); Mark Choate, *Emigrant Nation: The Making of Italy Abroad* (Cambridge, MA: Harvard University Press, 2008); Richard Alba, *Italian Americans into the Twilight of Ethnicity* (New York: Prentice Hall, 1985; Donna R. Gabaccia, *Italy's Many Diasporas* (London: University College of London Press, 2000).

[29] On Albertini see Mario Quargnolo, *Luciano Albertini. Un divo degli anni venti* (Udine: CSU editrice, 1976).

[30] Interview with Sergio Leone in Diego Gabutti, *C'era una volta in America* (Milan: Rizzoli, 1984).

[31] On the production of *Sei tu l'amore?* see Mario Quargnolo, *La parola ripudiata* (Gemona: Cineteca del Friuli, 1986).

[32] Denis Lotti, "Milano-Babilonia e ritorno," the introduction to the reprint of the diary of Alberto Rabagliati, *Quattro anni fra le "Stelle". Aneddoti e impressioni*, ed. by Denis Lotti (Cuneo: Nerosubianco edizioni, 2017).

[33] Alessandro Blasetti, "Il nostro oro," in *Lo Schermo* 2 (August 28, 1926): 3.

[34] Rabagliati, *Quattro anni fra le "Stelle"* 2017.

[35] *The Man in Blue* is set in Little Italy in the passage from the Old to the New World, as we read in the opening intertitles, with an early representation of a Mafia boss and also of a democratic Italian newspaper editor who opposes him. *The Man in Blue* pits the Italians and the Irish against each other, portraying the Irish in a more positive light: the main Italian characters, Tony (Gravina) and Carlo, are street traders, the former a florist and the latter a figurine seller, but both are incapable of protecting Tita, "the flower of Naples" (played by Madge Bellamy), while the Irish policeman in Little Italy not only saves some Italian children who are playing in the street, but also rescues Tita from the clutches of the Mafia boss. Gravina is, however, the only Italian in the cast.

[36] Puccini, *Italiani nel mondo del cinema* 1937, 330.

[37] Dorothy Spensley, "And Monty Banks' Home Town Turned Out," in *Photoplay*, August 1927; Monty Banks clipping files, Academy Library, Los Angeles.

[38] Albert Roccardi in *Moving Picture World*, December 12, 1914.

SILVIO ALOVISIO

"WHERE SHALL WE FIND THE ELEPHANTS, MISTER GRIFFITH?"
CABIRIA, INTOLERANCE AND THE ITALIAN HISTORICAL EPIC IN HOLLYWOOD

"A new definition of the possibilities of cinematographic art."[1] With these words, the leading film magazine *Motion Picture News* gave American approval to the nascent myth of the 1914 epic movie *Cabiria*. The review was published the day after the film's press screening held in the huge ballroom of the Astor Hotel in New York on May 9, 1914, organized by the enterprising director of the Itala Film Co. of America, Harry R. Raver. A few days later, on June 1, the Italian film held its continental premiere at the Knickerbocker Theatre in New York, a venue not usually employed for showing movies and refitted for the solemn occasion with Egyptian-theme sets and decorations.

As Giorgio Bertellini reports, "the galleries of the theater were adorned on the one side by American flags and on the other by Italian flags"[2]: a tangible celebration of an embrace between cultures, united also by their mutual fascination for Orientalism, although this was based on very different ideological premises as I shall shortly explain. The 1,500 spectators that congregated among the stuccos and ornamental plants of the vast auditorium (including Sir Arthur Conan Doyle, the "father" of Sherlock Holmes, and some of the richest Hollywood producers, from Sigmund Lubin to Adolph Zukor) were immediately aware they were attending an unprecedented event. It was, in fact, from this prestigious

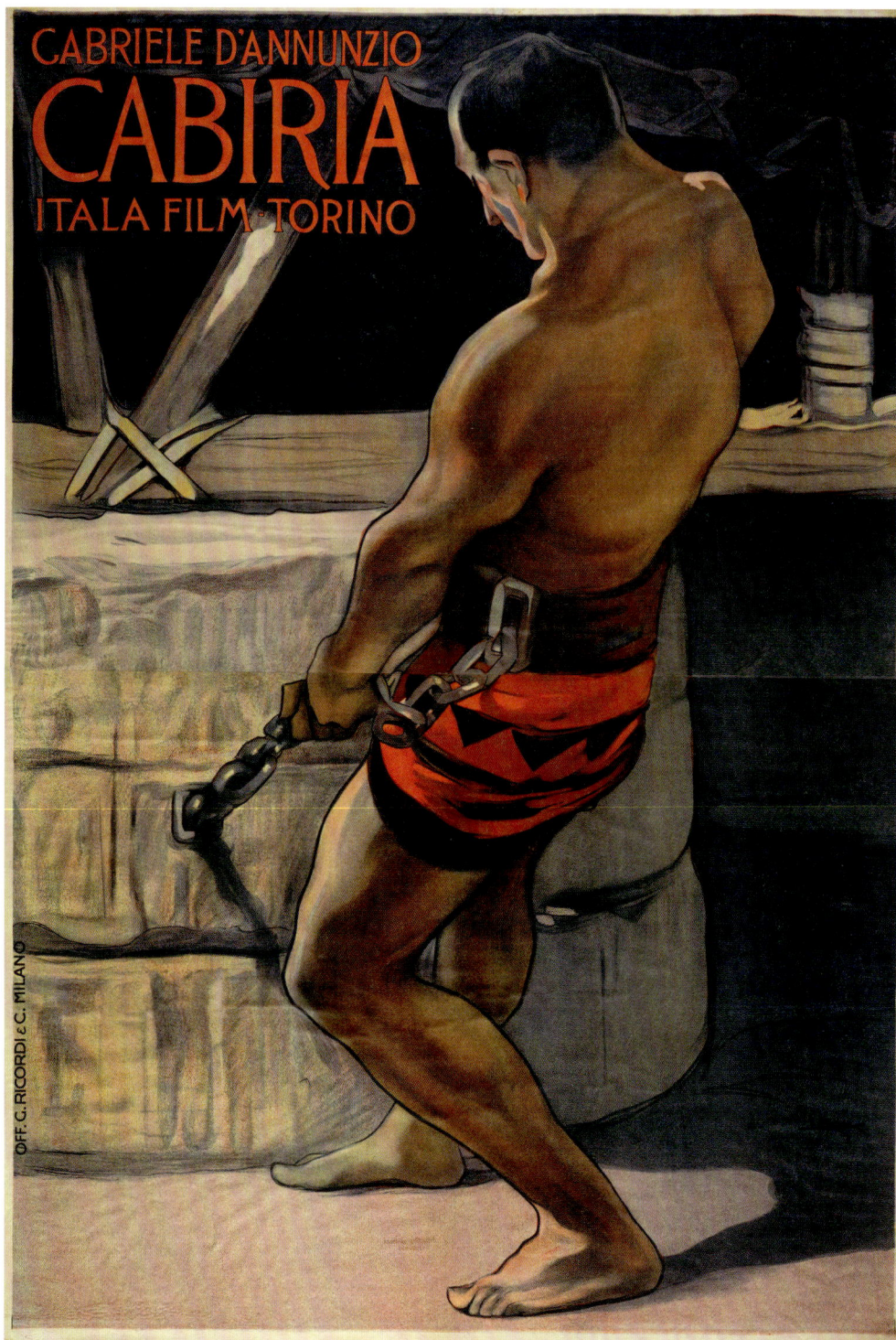

Leopoldo Metlicovitz, *Maciste*, [1914] Lithographic poster for *Cabiria* (1914), directed by Giovanni Pastrone and produced by Itala Film, 207 x 144.5 cm Turin, Collection Museo Nazionale del Cinema, inv. P30034

Leopoldo Metlicovitz,
Fiamme [Flames], [1914]
Lithographic poster for *Cabiria*
(1914), directed by Giovanni
Pastrone and produced by Itala
Film, 206 x 145 cm
Turin, Collection Museo Nazionale
del Cinema, inv. P30008

Cecchetto, *L'appuntamento*
[The appointment], 1932
Lithographic poster for the
French sound version of *Cabiria*
(1932), 157.5 x 118 cm
Turin, Collection Museo Nazionale
del Cinema, inv. P01327

The facade of the
Knickerbocker Theatre,
New York, where the
American premiere of *Cabiria*
was held on June 1, 1914
Turin, Collection Museo
Nazionale del Cinema

Program for the screening of
Cabiria at the Knickerbocker
Theatre, New York
Turin, Roberto Devalle
Collection

Broadway theater that *Cabiria* began its sensational triumphal march to conquer the profitable U.S. markets: a journey that would far exceed any previous record held by a film, and which continued with unwavering success for over seven months.

Apart from certain reservations about the weakness of the storyline, positive North American reviews accompanied the widespread diffusion of this triumph of Italian cinema and reiterated with a generous dose of hyperbole the comment from the *Motion Picture News* quoted at the start. Even intellectuals did not shy away from the irresistible allure of the Italian epic. From Harvard, a young Eugene O'Neill wrote to his girlfriend, *"Cabiria* is simply stupendous,"[3] whereas in *The Art of the Moving Picture*, the first book on film theory published in the United States, the poet Vachel Lindsay defined Giovanni Pastrone's masterpiece as "the pioneering work of a genius."[4] Excitement over *Cabiria* even justified a special screening at the White House in June 1914 for the benefit of President Thomas Woodrow Wilson and his closest associates.

In a poster that Raver printed for the American launch of the film, *Cabiria* was described as "the daddy of spectacles." In addition to their role as advertising, these words recognized the film's birthright as a new, exceptional, and aesthetically

Cover of a U.S. brochure for *Cabiria*, 1910s Turin, Roberto Devalle Collection

Gabriele d'Annunzio (referred to as "The Italian Shakespeare") is presented as the author of *Cabiria* in a U.S. 1914 brochure Turin, Roberto Devalle Collection

187

rich model for future productions. Before Pastrone, no one had ever dared to propose such an ambitious project. Almost every aspect of its creation set a new record or was an innovation. There was the running time of almost three hours, a disconcerting length of time, especially for an American public still partially conditioned by the declining dominance of the "one-reel" film,[5] imposed by Edison's powerful trust the MPPC (Motion Picture Patents Company); then there was the exorbitant budget, and there was the film's ennobling association with poet Gabriele d'Annunzio, well known among the Italian American communities[6] and described in an Itala Film Co. of America brochure as "The Italian Shakespeare." And then there were the monumental three-dimensional sets, expressly designed for the filming; the suggestive special effects created by the talented Catalan technician Segundo de Chomón; the innovative movements of the camera crane and lights; and the presence of a choir and orchestra in the auditorium, at least for the most prestigious screenings.

In the eyes of the critics, but especially the American public (including the vast immigrant communities), *Cabiria* enhanced all the attractions of the mise-en-scène: the camera lens roams from snow-covered Alps to Etna's fire, history is reinvented between the two Mediterranean shores, and, in a narrative that unwinds over ten years, personal and collective destinies intertwine, not only due to war but also due to love. Architecture, painting, archaeology, lyric and prose theater, high literature and feuilleton, cultured music and ideology merge together in this stunning, colossal project that experimented with all the expressive resources of the new medium.

It would be a mistake, however, to explain the good fortune of Pastrone's masterpiece in America as due only to its exceptional nature, as if it were an isolated case in the history of relations between early Italian cinema and the United States. If *Cabiria*'s success was so great as to influence Hollywood moviemaking itself, this happened

Picture postcard sent from
St. Louis on September 1, 1914,
showing Vitale De Stefano
in the role of Massinissa
in *Cabiria*
Turin, Roberto Devalle
Collection

Itala Film brochure promoting *Cabiria* in the United States with captions by Gabriele d'Annunzio Turin, Roberto Devalle Collection

precisely because at the time of its release, in the late spring of 1914, the Italian film industry's ability to produce historical epics had long been internationally recognized.[7] For a brief but intense phase between 1908 and the eve of World War I, the worldwide success of Italian cinema was in fact primarily guaranteed by its historical films, frequently set in the ancient world.

While much of this costume drama naturally evoked ancient Rome— the republican and, more often, the imperial Rome—the imaginary revisiting of the past also involved biblical inspired subjects, stories set in Assyria and Babylon, Greek epics and tragedies, Punic themes, or tales that reinvented ancient Egypt and often included the use of opera.

However, it would be simplistic to assume that the importance of this body of work is proportionate to its size, given that Italian silent movies set in antiquity are not as numerous as one might expect: they actually amount to no more than 150, very few compared to the ten thousand titles produced in Italy between 1905 and 1931. On the contrary, the importance of the so-called Italian *peplum*, or "sword and sandal film," was expressed in qualitative terms: on the one hand due to the peculiarity of the cultural, spectacular, and ideological notions underpinning the genre; on the other, due to its prodigious ability to circulate the

Series of stills on hand-colored slides. The slides were displayed inside the movie theaters and were also used in 1931 to launch the sound version of *Cabiria*. The shots are the ones taken for the original version of 1914 Turin, Collection Museo Nazionale del Cinema

The eruption of Etna and consequent destruction of Catana

Batto's house in Catana, where the story begins

The monumental gate of the
huge Temple of Moloch

A multitude of believers attend
the religious rite officiated in
the Temple of Moloch

After breaking into the Temple
of Moloch with Fulvio Axilla
(Umberto Mozzato), Maciste
(Bartolomeo Pagano) saves
Cabiria from sacrifice

Fulvio Axilla and Maciste
in Bodastoret's tavern

results on international markets, in particular in the United States, where the Italian historical epic contributed decisively to the success of feature-length films. What especially drew North American audiences was their long-held fascination since the eighteenth century for a representation of antiquity that combined the typical Anglophone cultural world's attraction toward classical culture with a generalized desire for the spectacular, rekindled by new visual media technologies. What's interesting, however, is that antiquity as portrayed on screen in these films was the product of a fanciful reworking that hybridized the most diverse artisanal and artistic components: the long Italian tradition of applied arts, pre-Raphaelite painting, nineteenth-century architectural historicism, Verdi's melodrama, the most renowned historical novels (paradoxically, almost always non-Italian), pyrotechnic and circus shows, Pietro Cossa's plays focusing on ancient Rome, and the somewhat exotic style of Art Nouveau, which imposed itself in Italy beginning with the 1902 World Exposition in Turin.

In its transfer from Italy to the United States, however, this imagined antiquity assumed different ideological facets. In the Italian context, films on ancient Rome

Maciste chained
to the millstone

Sofonisba (Italia Almirante Manzini) in her room

Sofonisba returns to Carthage palace after a secret meeting with Massinissa (Vitale De Stefano). The maidservant brings with her little Cabiria

supported an ideological project intended to boost national identity, promoted by the ruling classes of post-unification Italy and interpreted by recalling the myths of *mare nostrum* ("our sea," the Latin appellation for the Mediterranean) and the so-called "fourth shore" (the conversion of Libya into an Italian colony). In the American context, the idea of Romanity, set at the center of a cultural, political, and aesthetic mythology whose origins date back to well before the birth of cinema, was not connected to contemporary Italy at all. In among the stereotypes that forged the American image of a weak and backward Italy, burdened by inertia, poor and uneducated just like the thousands of immigrants that crowded the Ellis Island pier, there was no place for the historic image of a nation rising from the ashes of its glorious past. Which is why the nationalism that pervaded Italian historical movies was acknowledged only within the Italian American communities and generally discarded by the WASP public, who replaced it with a different reading, whereby the myth of Rome became the root and metaphor for the American nation and its capacity to realize the democratic virtues of republican Rome, the political-military power of the Empire, and the link between civil ethics and religious vocation hinted at by the early spread of Christianity.

Sofonisba in her room at Carthage palace

Sofonisba, Karthalo, Siface, and Cabiria/Elissa in the great hall at Cirta palace

Maciste, Fulvio Axilla, and a multitude of refugees and prisoners reach Cirta's walls

Film still from *Cabiria*, 1914.
At the center, Vitale De Stefano
as Massinissa
Turin, Collection Museo Nazionale
del Cinema

Costume for Hannibal in *Cabiria*, 1914
Moleskin cuirass with studs. The fur has
been added, in keeping with the images
of the scene in which Hannibal crosses
the Alps to descend into Italy
Turin, Roberto Devalle Collection

Costume for Fulvio
Axilla in *Cabiria*, 1914
Metal breastplate with
studs and shoulder pieces.
The helmet indicated the
soldier's rank
Turin, Roberto Devalle
Collection

Costume for Massinissa
in *Cabiria*, 1914
Leather cuirass with
decorated metal scales.
Helmet with decoration
and black pigtail
reminiscent of a horse's
mane. The cloak has
been remade
Turin, Roberto Devalle
Collection

Costume for centurion
in *Cabiria*, 1914
Metal helmet and
breastplate with studs and
shoulder pieces
Turin, Roberto Devalle
Collection

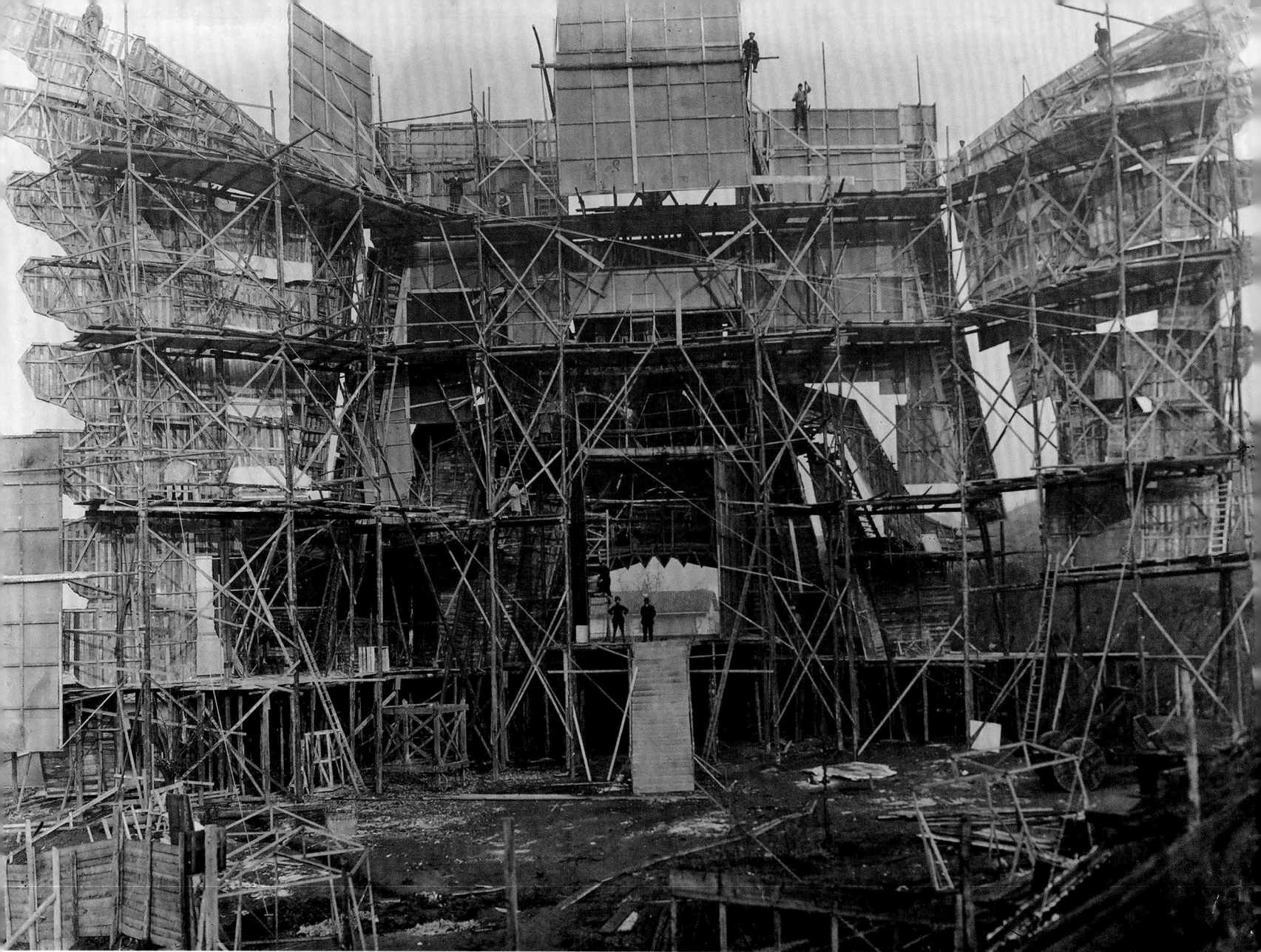

Despite America's increasingly dense unawareness of the nationalistic link between ancient Rome and contemporary Italy, U.S. audiences perceived Italian historical films at least to some degree as "Italian," but for different reasons, which can be ascertained by examining the press of the period. In the aforementioned eulogy to *Cabiria* published in the *Motion Picture News*, the quality of the "most highly skilled Italian filmmakers" is greatly appreciated.[8] A similar evaluation of the film was expressed in the magazine *The New York Dramatic Mirror*: "for those who know about cameras and gels," *Cabiria* confirms "the superiority of Italian art."[9] Thus, the "Italianness" of historical films was guaranteed by the technical and creative excellence of Italian artisan/artists: painters, set designers, architects, decorators, carpenters, and costume designers, who were perceived—and not only in their homeland—as the heirs of a thousand-year tradition of accomplishments and taste and, in perhaps rhetorical but effective words, declared themselves to be the "sons of the sons of the sons of Michelangelo and Leonardo." This proud statement, drawn from the 1987 film *Good Morning Babilonia* by the Taviani brothers, is uttered by the character of Andrea Bonanno, a talented restorer of Tuscan churches seeking his fortune in the Hollywood of the first decade of the 1920s.

The success of the Italian epic movie in the United States was so great that it even influenced the contents and style of Hollywood's historical films. The most sensitive to such influences was the top American director working in those days: David W. Griffith. His film *Intolerance* was a bold opportunity for revival and experimentation, also due to its similarity to contemporary Italian historical films.

Primary sources do not offer certitudes about the parallels between *Cabiria* and *Intolerance*. The only certain fact is that when Griffith started filming *Intolerance* in July 1914, *Cabiria* was showing in San Francisco. It is said that Karl Brown, the assistant to *Intolerance*'s director of photography Billy Bitzer, was

Hebrew pectoral, part of one of the costumes for *Intolerance*, 1916 Gilded bronze set with glass gems Courtesy of The Collection of Motion Picture Costume Design: Larry McQueen, Los Angeles

Construction of the *Cabiria* set, 1914 Turin, Collection Museo Nazionale del Cinema

Construction of the Babylonian Temple in *Intolerance*, directed by David W. Griffith in 1916

The Temple of Moloch in a
scene from *Cabiria*, 1914
Turin, Collection Museo
Nazionale del Cinema

convinced that Griffith saw Pastrone's movie at that time.[10] However, since Brown himself was not present at this hypothetical screening, his recollection should be evaluated with caution. Nonetheless, it cannot be ruled out that things happened just as they are presented in the aforementioned *Good Morning Babilonia*, that is, Griffith has *Cabiria* screened in a cinema in San Francisco, remains speechless, and immediately dictates a telegram to Pastrone: "I don't know if I should be grateful to you or hate you," but then tears it up, convinced that the only sensible reaction to a film of such power is to respond with an even more stunning film.

The Taviani brothers' reconstruction proves how the absence of sources has fueled the spread of almost legendary anecdotes. One of these, a success since the early 1930s, especially on Italian soil (and one can understand why), presents Griffith as obsessed with *Cabiria*'s greatness. In this totally imaginary version of events, the celebrated director even degrades himself with the crime of theft, as Pastrone claimed (with ill-concealed pride) in interviews with Georges Sadoul and Mario Verdone: "The films were not sold but rented. I sent a copy of *Cabiria* to America, and I was told it had got burnt. I think some emissary of Griffith made up the fire in order to keep the copy and study it."[11]

This episode of plagiarism invented by Pastrone reveals wider tendencies on the part of criticism and historiography, both Italian and American, sometimes aimed at denying Griffith's debts to the Italian director, and other times to excessively emphasize them. In reality, as Paolo Cherchi Usai has written so well, "to speak of *Cabiria*'s influence on *Intolerance* is undoubtedly legitimate, provided that the word 'influence' is understood in its less strict meaning: a visceral, instinctive resonance, which arouses wonder even before becoming thought."[12]

As Bitzer recalls, the success of *The Birth of a Nation* (1915) led Griffith to redesign what was to be his next film, *The Mother and the Law*, as a more complex project centered on intolerance in the history of mankind and articulated through the interweaving of four stories that take place in different eras. One of the episodes is set in Babylon, and Griffith absolutely wanted a herd of elephants to appear in it. Bitzer

The Babylonian sequence in *Intolerance*, directed by David W. Griffith in 1916

Film still from *The Ten Commandments*, directed by Cecil B. DeMille in 1923

was rather disconcerted by the request: war had broken out in Europe and long sea transport was increasingly difficult. "Where shall we find the elephants, Mister Griffith?" he asked, perturbed. In the end, as the film testifies, the director managed to get hold of real elephants—very similar to those used by Pastrone in *Cabiria*—for the sequence when Hannibal crosses the Alps. The famous elephants of *Intolerance*, however, those very elephants that will leave an indelible mark in the history of cinema, are the eight giant papier-mâché specimens sculpted by skilled artisans (Italians, according to *Good Morning Babilonia*, but the truth remains unknown) and mounted on top of the columns of the colossal Belshazzar palace. According to quite a few scholars,[13] these sculptures are an explicit allusion to *Cabiria*, in particular to the imposing elephant statues (definitely made by Italian artists) that adorn the column bases of the Temple of Moloch and the palace of Asdrubale in Carthage. The presence of elephant statues in *Intolerance* is, in fact, rather incongruous since there is no such evidence in Babylonian artistic tradition, and thus highly surprising, given that the film was nurtured by aspirations of historical fidelity and archaeological rigor.

The hypothesis of an explicit allusion to *Cabiria* is therefore more than founded, but cannot exclude the perhaps even more obvious influence of the film *Salambò*, a sumptuous epic directed by Domenico Gaido in Turin in the same year as *Cabiria*, which also has a Punic setting and was released in the United States in 1915. The similarities between the two films have never been studied with due attention, but they do exist, and not only in the numerous and stately elephant statues that adorn the semicircular Carthaginian assembly room: in actual fact, in terms of majesty and architectural style, *Salambò*'s set designs for the walls of Carthage are much closer to Babylon's walls in *Intolerance* than to those of Cirta in *Cabiria*. Moreover, the gigantic arched doorway in *Salambò* is very similar to the entranceway to Babylon, designed by Frank "Huck" Wortman for the Griffith film.

However, aside from the elephant statues and other minor similarities punctually recorded in the studies,[14] it is perhaps more fruitful to question the deeper influences that link the two films. Some of these have still to be verified and merit further investigation (for example, d'Annunzio's intertitles for *Cabiria*, admired by screenwriter Anita Loos who authored those for *Intolerance*[15]), whereas others are easily verifiable. There are two particularly innovative aspects of *Cabiria* that exerted a "visceral" influence on *Intolerance*, to use Cherchi Usai's adjective: the monumental nature of the set and the moving-camera shots. These two aspects are interrelated, because the famous "traveling" shots used by Pastrone and Griffith serve to visualize and enhance the set design.

Just like the sets for the Guazzoni, Gaido, and Pastrone films, those for *Intolerance* were also no longer two-dimensional perspectives but real architectural constructions—an actual space that dominated human events, the movements of multitudes, and individual destinies, enclosing them within a vastness of volumes that were capable of synthesizing the most diverse styles. Both in *Cabiria* and in *Intolerance*, the meticulous antiquarian realism and archaeological fidelity were transcended by an Orientalist-inspired eclectic taste, in which Greco-

Roman, Punic, Assyrian-Babylonian, Egyptian, and even Indian decorative elements were hybridized. In the case of *Intolerance*, the tendency toward monumentality became further radicalized. Only the statue of Ishtar seems less gigantic than that of the ferocious god Moloch, while all the other spaces, in many ways similar, have become swollen, almost hypertrophic: the royal atrium of the palace of Asdrubale has expanded into monstrously colossal proportions in the court of the Belshazzar palace, whereas in the transition from Cirta to Babylon, the walls have grown dizzily in height and power, and the Persian siege weapons multiply to ten times the number, some of them similar to those used by Massinissa's troops in the final battle of *Cabiria* (from mobile towers to the pouring of boiling oil).

As mentioned above, the moving-camera shots contribute to this triumph. It is well known that the recurring use of the crane is one of *Cabiria*'s most innovative and famous solutions. Pastrone moved the camera about sixty times, as though it were a routine procedure for the period—but it was not like that at all. In *Cabiria*, the crane assumed a dual function: on the one hand it explored and expanded the scenic vastness of a given environment, and on the other it established narrative connections between characters and elements within the scene. If we consider Griffith's decisive contribution between 1908 and 1912 to the birth and development of film narration centered on editing, it would be reasonable to expect the prolonged camera moves of *Intolerance* (in particular those shot using a mobile tower equipped with a lift during the enormous banquet of the Babylonian court) to be a further enhancement of the narrative function heralded by the cranes used in *Cabiria*. Actually, this is not so but indeed quite the opposite. In fact, Pastrone's cranes inspired Griffith to use camera moves as a means of discovering and displaying a monumental environment.

The implausible vastness of the set, both amplified and made almost disproportionate by an "excessive and alienating"[16] depth of field, diminishes the decipherability of the events taking place, weakening the storyline and partially interrupting the fluidity of the links between frames. According to a number of scholars, *Cabiria*'s camera movements invite the spectator to follow the camera into the world of fiction,[17] while according to other interpretations it is the very space of the story that advances toward the spectator seated in the audience.[18] Whichever the case, the crane serves to explore the storyline of the fictional world and demonstrate its habitability. In *Intolerance* instead, as Giulia Carluccio pointed out, the camera movements generate "an alienating and illusionary effect rather than the physiological crossing of a tangible, lifelike space."[19]

Hence, the assumed influence of *Cabiria* on *Intolerance* produces an unexpected result: in the transition from Turin to Hollywood, from an Italian cinematic language of framing and staging to the American practice of montage and narration, the problem of establishing a harmonious balance between an "excessive" vision and an organic narration of history—a problem Pastrone intelligently posited but did not resolve—becomes further complicated. If *Cabiria* was received in its time by both Italians and Americans as a film in which "the plot is no more than a pretext for the unrelieved presentation of immense, picturesque images,"[20] then *Intolerance* (defined by its author as "a suggestion of a story") deepens the gap between the vision and the plot. Whereas *Cabiria* broadens its power of suggestion through the monumentality of the scenes, *Intolerance* abandons the possibility of relying on a main character and slackens its pace. As Carluccio has acutely observed, Griffith's Babylon, built on the foundations of the Punic cities in *Cabiria*, raises and questions "an idea of autonomy of vision that disturbs the growing conviction about the necessity of directing the range of visual effects toward enhancing the story."[21] In the move from short films made until 1913 to the great structured systems that produced the Historical Spectacular, Cecil B. DeMille, another great director of historical films who considered himself Griffith's student, criticized the latter's approach as greatly lacking in "dramatic construction."[22] And therefore *Cabiria* and *Intolerance*, from opposite sides of the ocean, propose a refined and visionary spectacle, ambitious and all encompassing, enchanting but totally unbalanced. Between 1914, before Sarajevo, and 1916, before the U.S. entered the war, this model seemed to promise further development. "Who can tell us what the next four years will bring?"[23] Stephen Bush asked in the pages of *Moving Picture World* after admiring *Cabiria*. Unfortunately, the answer did not reward the projects of either Pastrone or Griffith. After 1914, due to the decline in exports caused by the outbreak of war and the emergence of new and more effective models of visual storytelling, the Italian historical epic entered a phase of inexorable decline, while the Hollywood version, then on a trajectory toward the blockbusters of the 1920s, sought new directions that were ever more distant from Griffith's visionary model. But that's another story.

[1] *Motion Picture News* 9, no. 20 (May 23, 1914).

[2] Giorgio Bertellini, "Risuscitare la storia: Cabiria e gli Stati Uniti," in *Cabiria & Cabiria*, ed. by Silvio Alovisio and Alberto Barbera (Turin: Museo Nazionale del Cinema and Milan: Il Castoro, 2006), 174.

[3] *Letter from Eugene O'Neill to Beatrice Ashe*, October 7, 1914, cited in Ian Christie, "Ancient Rome in London," in *The Ancient World in Silent Cinema*, ed. by Pantelis Michelakis and Maria Wyke (Cambridge: Cambridge University Press, 2013), 110.

[4] Vachel Lindsay, *The Art of the Moving Picture* (New York: Macmillan, 1915).

[5] The standard one-reel film was approximately 15 minutes long.

[6] Concerning Gabriele d'Annunzio's reputation among the Italian American communities, see the in-depth study by Luca Scarlini, *D'Annunzio a Little Italy: avventure del Vate nel mondo dell'emigrazione* (Rome: Donzelli, 2008).

[7] For an overall assessment of the phenomenon, see Giuliana Muscio, "In Hoc Signo Vinces: Historical Films," in *Italian Silent Cinema: A Reader*, ed. by Giorgio Bertellini (New Barnet, England: John Libbey Publishing, 2013), 161–70; Irmbert Schenk, "The Creation of the Epic: Italian Silent Film to 1915," in *A Companion to Ancient Greece and Rome on Screen*, ed. by Arthur J. Pomeroy (Hoboken, NJ: Wiley, 2017), 37–60; Andrea Meneghelli, "Cabiria e il film storico italiano," in *Cabiria & Cabiria* 2006, 285–98; Gian Piero Brunetta, "L'evocation du passé dans le film historique italien," in *Cinéma italien 1905–1945*, ed. by Aldo Bernardini and Jean-Antoine Gili (Paris: Centre Pompidou, 1986); Giovanni Calendoli, "Cabiria e il film storico della romanità," in Id., *Materiali per una storia del cinema italiano* (Parma: Maccari, 1967), 61–108; Giorgio De Vincenti, "Il kolossal storico-romano nell'immaginario del primo Novecento," in *Bianco e Nero* XLIX, no. 1 (1988): 7–26.

[8] *Motion Picture News* IX, no. 20 (May 23, 1914), in *Cabiria & Cabiria* 2006, 401.

[9] *The New York Dramatic Mirror* LXXI, no. 1847 (May 13, 1914): 40.

[10] Kevin Brownlow, *Hollywood. L'era del muto* (Milan: Garzanti, 1980), 71.

[11] Mario Verdone, "Pastrone, ultimo incontro," in *Bianco e Nero*, January 1, 1961: 90.

[12] Paolo Cherchi Usai, *David Wark Griffith* (Milan: Il Castoro, 2008), 266.

[13] See for example Eileen Bowser, "Griffith e la struttura circolare in alcuni film Biograph," in *Bianco e Nero* XXXVI, 5–8 (1975): 51.

[14] See also Bernard Hanson, "D. W. Griffith: Some Sources," in *The Art Bulletin* 4 (December 1972): 493–515.

[15] Anita Loos and John Emerson, "Photoplay Writing (VI)," in *Photoplay*, April 1918. My thanks to Giuliana Muscio for pointing out the article.

[16] Giulia Carluccio, *Scritture della visione. Percorsi nel cinema muto* (Turin: Kaplan, 2006), 107.

[17] Cherchi Usai, *David Wark Griffith* 2008, 276.

[18] See Elena Dagrada, André Gaudreault, and Tom Gunning, "Lo spazio mobile. Del montaggio e del carrello in Cabiria," in *Cabiria e il suo tempo*, ed. by Paolo Bertetto and Gianni Rondolino (Turin: Museo Nazionale del Cinema and Milan: Il Castoro, 1998), 150–83.

[19] Carluccio, *Scritture della visione* 2006, 109.

[20] *Corriere della Sera*, April 19, 1914, now in *Cabiria & Cabiria* 2006, 384.

[21] Carluccio, *Scritture della visione* 2006, 40.

[22] *The Autobiography of Cecil B. DeMille* (Englewood Cliffs, NJ: Prentice Hall, 1959), 126.

[23] *Moving Picture World* XX, no. 8 (May 23, 1914): 1090–91, in Davide Turconi, "G.P. e D.W.G., il dare e l'avere," in *Bianco e Nero* XXXVI, 5–8 (1975): 35.

ELENA MOSCONI

LINA CAVALIERI ON THE SILVER SCREEN

Since the 1950s, the close-up of a woman gazing enigmatically with two big round eyes as she hints at a smile, printed on dishes and decorative objects, has become an absolute icon, the hallmark of the designer Piero Fornasetti. Looking straight into the eyes of the viewer is an archaic Mona Lisa with regular facial features, traced with a black line and offered in a multiplicity of *Themes and Variations*, as the name of the series suggests: with a Dalí moustache, with one patched eye, while sipping a saucer filled with milk, wearing an astronaut's headgear, and in a number of other disguises. For over six decades the image of this woman has been printed on dishes, scarves, coasters, cups, and sugar bowls, wallpaper and objects for the interior in hundreds of variations, according to an intuitively postmodern and almost anti-Warholian project that seems to have only recently revealed, in hindsight, its aesthetic meaning. Warhol chose to use a photograph of Marilyn Monroe taken in 1953 by Gene Kornman to advertise Henry Hathaway's movie *Niagara*. The artist worked on it right after the actress's death, isolating the face in order to emphasize the eyes and the lips that had won over millions of people thanks to the power of the Hollywood movie industry. The procedure Warhol used was silk screening, multiplying Marilyn's image to excess and accepting only chromatic, loud, and vulgarized combinations as variants. The actress's large face, crystallized in its fixity, becomes the emblem of Pop art and culture. Answering the ingenious provocation by the American artist is the talented Milanese decorator and designer Fornasetti, who discovers the photograph of a classical, timeless, archetypal, and Mediterranean beauty, whom he reinvents in a host of variations that bring her back to life in incongruous and at times ironic and playful contexts. Fornasetti redesigns her in the most heterogeneous transfigurations and, using innovative lithographic techniques, transfers her image to porcelain plates. Thus the woman's face relives in everyday objects, beautifying them, making them more captivating, more aesthetic. Fornasetti's obscure and archaic muse and the more recognizable and contemporary Marilyn do have one thing in common, however: that of having been famous in their day as "the most beautiful woman in the world." For Fornasetti, that woman was Lina Cavalieri.

Only recently has light been cast on a woman so beautiful that Gabriele d'Annunzio described her as "the utmost proof of Venus on Earth," associating the reconstruction of her artistic activity with numerous affirmations of her charm.[1] Needless to say, "beauty was always the focus of the attention in every field she tried her hand at"[2]—from cabaret artist to opera singer, movie star, and, lastly, writer and manager of beauty salons. In each of her professions, Lina Cavalieri seemed to pursue an ideal of artistic perfection where beauty played a crucial role. In 1890, not much older than a child, she performed in the theater in Piazza Navona to earn something for her family who had fallen into poverty, as well as to pursue her own artistic vocation; at the time, all she had was her ingenuous air, sublime grace, and modest attire as she sang her allusive words. But the young Lina was determined to make the best

Piero Fornasetti,
Theme and Variations
Lithograph and serigraph
on porcelain, diameter
26 cm each plate
Lina Cavalieri's face as
a motif was used for the
first time in 1952; in 1966
the number of plates
had grown to 288, today
there are over 350
Milan, Archivio
Fornasetti

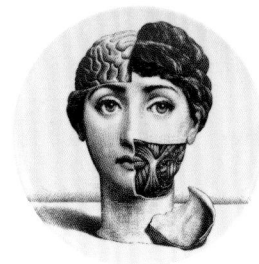

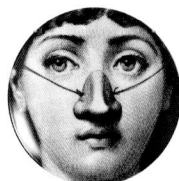

of the situation: she bought some new clothes and, thanks also to the help of Roman princes and other notables, she began performing at Naples' Salone Margherita and *café chantants*, adding to her repertoire a good number of Neapolitan songs. She debuted at the Folies Bergère in Paris in 1896. A young woman who had once sold flowers in Rome now saw her name in lights alongside those of the most famous artists (and often *demi-mondaines*) on the international scene—names like Loïe Fuller, Cléo de Mérode, Liane de Pougy, and Carolina Otero. The international scene in Paris contributed greatly to the creation of the glamour of this "petite italienne." Despite this, Lina continued to perform accompanied by an orchestra of mandolins, guitars, and violins (at times using a tambourine to play and dance bits and pieces of a tarantella), singing folkloristic Italian songs that resounded from the variety shows in London, Berlin, and especially Saint Petersburg, where the renown of the "beautiful Italian" preceded her arrival there in 1897. In the paper "Sankt-Peterburgskie Vedomosti," Lina Cavalieri was introduced with these words: "She is very elegant and graceful, dressed with fine taste. I have traveled a lot in Italy but I have never seen an Italian woman more refined than Cavalieri. She is an Italian from Paris, capable of combining Italian simplicity and French elegance. So great is her beauty she could inspire a painter to make her portrait on canvas, a poet to glorify her fascinating figure, and the aesthete of a pleasure garden to fall in love with her."[3] Lina's beauty grew even more fascinating thanks to the elegance she honed in the Paris maisons, with which she had a close relationship:

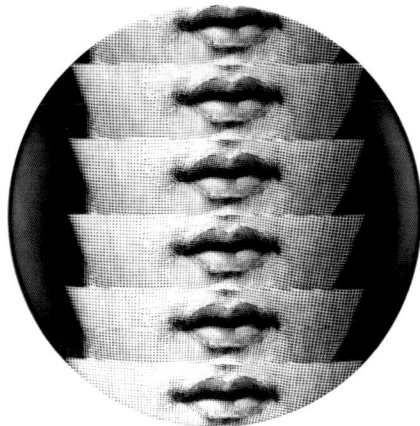

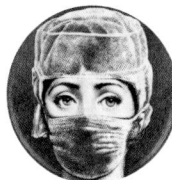

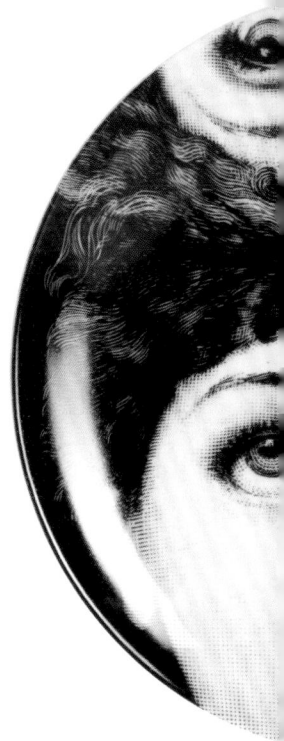

"The fashion houses vied over my beauty so that they could show their models to theater audiences and spectators at the races. I was a regular customer of Paquin and Doucet, and quite honestly a thorn in the side for the dressmakers," she confessed in her memoirs.[4] The singer went from artist to diva: her presence was noted by the media and she would always arouse the enthusiasm of her admirers, who saw her at high society events in Moscow and Saint Petersburg, or in Paris, at the opera, in the company of the painter Giovanni Boldini. Always wearing expensive jewelry—especially pearls and diamonds, at times set in fabulous dresses that earned her the nickname "queen of diamonds"—Lina Cavalieri offered herself to the eyes of the public just as she did to the snapshots of the photographers, who immortalized her image in an endless number of poses. Postcards of her by Reutlinger and other photography studios filled the shop windows of the major European cities and inflamed the desire of more than one generation of men. Student Emilio Ravaglia, for example, described how in the dead of night, inside his dimly lit bedroom, he would find himself contemplating Lina's portrait, which would distract him from his studies: "her large eyes, which alone lit up that beautiful long oval face, seemed to envelop me in a voluptuous, indefinite gaze, and her slender neck, the provocative arch of her hip, her tapered hand, all that sculptural purity of lines and forms that make her as straight and flexible as a reed, emanated irresistibly powerful vibrations."[5] If we look back over the numerous postcards in which she is portrayed wearing elegant

Lina Cavalieri in two Reutlinger postcards from the late nineteenth century. Her classical beauty emerges in many promotional photographs emphasizing the harmony of her nakedness, which is never vulgar

dresses or soft veils that leave her shoulders, arms, neck, and décolleté bare, we can see how Lina, well aware of her beauty, used it to create her persona as a diva. Her exceptional appeal and fascination have been highlighted by some of the most authoritative names in the fashion world such as Erté (born Romain de Tirtoff, a costume designer and painter *par excellence* of art deco), and by the English photographer and costume designer Cecil Beaton. When asked by reporters who was the most beautiful woman he had ever met, Erté answered, without hesitation, Lina Cavalieri, while Beaton, in his memoirs, offered an in-depth description of the beautiful singer's physical features with emphasis on her Latin origins: "Physically, she was hardly a woman of heroic proportions, being of medium height and slender build. But Cavalieri was undeniably a great classic beauty. Her features were of a blunt, Roman cast, a magnolia complexion that complemented the black, wavy hair, which was parted in the middle like that of a Spanish dancer and gathered in a bun at the nape of the long neck. Even as a young woman

Lina's beauty continued to grow and became increasingly refined thanks to the Paris maisons with which she had a close relationship

Lina Cavalieri photographed by Herman Mishkin in 1916, at the time of her participation in the movie *La rosa di granata*, directed by Emilio Ghione and distributed in America by Paramount Pictures in 1919 as *The Rose of Granada*. In many scenes in the film the focus was on her arms and her ability to make wide movements that were always enjoyable to watch

Following pages
Lina Cavalieri in the garden of her summer residence in Waterford, Connecticut, 1910, published in *Tatler*, October 17, 1917

Italian manufacture,
*Evening gown. Attributed
to Lina Cavalieri*, c. early 1906
Lace and black velvet ribbon on
pink ivory satin base decorated
with sequins and black glass
beads, length 185 cm
Rome, Sorelle Gazzoni,
Fondazione Tirelli Trappetti

Vittorio Corcos, *Portrait
of Lina Cavalieri*, c. 1903
Oil on canvas, 265 x 178 cm
Private collection

Cesare Tallone,
*Portrait of Lina
Cavalieri*, c. 1905
Oil on canvas, 96 x 70 cm
Milan, Archivio Galleria
Campari

Emilio Sommariva, *Portrait
of a Woman. Lyda Borelli in
the Studio of Cesare Tallone*, 1911
To the left the full-length portrait
of Lina Cavalieri by Cesare Tallone
Milano, Biblioteca Nazionale Braidense,
Fondo Sommariva

Cavalieri had the gestures, the bearing and the grace of a woman in her prime. Until the 1914 war women did not seek to appear more youthful, as they do now: on the contrary, maturity was the keynote of feminine beauty, and Cavalieri had the air of sorrow and experience that comes only with years of living. Her Italianate aura of sad perfection was dominated by large eyes, compassionate and somber, set beneath eyebrows raised not in question but in inner sorrow. Her equally somber but sensuous mouth completed features that seemed to have derived from a painting by Murillo."[6] The importance of skin, color, complexion, the figure, as well as the shoulders, the hands, and posture in creating her persona emerges from the book of aesthetic suggestions she wrote and published in 1914 in the United States,[7] within the new climate of professionalism of beauty where the Roman singer found a place for herself with the far-sightedness of the entrepreneur. Here is Beaton again, underscoring her skill at posing in sensual photographs without ever seeming vulgar: "Her arms were employed for flamboyant yet beautiful gestures, which have been immortalized in photographic poses where the right hand is idly fingering a long string of pearls, or where, with arms locked behind her head, she outlaws the vulgarity that such an odalisque gesture would normally imply. Often there might be a picture of her with one arm curved upwards, the palm of the hand with its pointed fingers resting on the crown of her head, while its counterpart was placed on a hip."[8]

The change in status that occurred at the beginning of the new century, when Lina Cavalieri debuted at the opera and had her first successes, undoubtedly further "ennobled" the image of the singer. This could also be seen in portraits by famous artists: for instance, in the two paintings made by Boldini in 1901, a side view and a front view, in which Lina wears an austere black dress and a double

Enrico Caruso and Lina Cavalieri in the opera *Fedora* by Umberto Giordano in Paris. The drawing, by Edward Zier, was published in *The Sketch*, June 14, 1905, 271

Lina Cavalieri in the title role of the courtesan in Jules Massenet's lyric comedy *Thaïs*, published in *The Bystander*, July 13, 1910

A Romance of the Opera

SIGNORINA CAVALIERI MARRIED TO A WEALTHY AMERICAN

Photograph   *Bert*

THE WORLD'S MOST BEAUTIFUL PRIMA DONNA : SIGNORINA LINA CAVALIERI IN "THAIS"

Signorina Cavalieri, who was recently married in Paris to Mr. Chanler, an American millionaire, is one of the most beautiful women on the operatic stage. Her career has been a romantic one. Twelve years ago she worked as a paper folder in a printing office in Rome. Now she is right in the front rank of operatic singers

strand pearl necklace; or in the large portrait by Vittorio Corcos, where Cavalieri is standing and wearing an elegant gray and black dress; or in the one painted by Cesare Tallone in 1906, where the reflections of the singer's blue dress are refracted in the background. In a 1911 photograph by the Milanese Emilio Sommariva, a full-length portrait of Lina Cavalieri, to the left, accompanies that of the Milanese publisher Ettore Baldini, while to the right, next to Tallone, we see Lyda Borelli both in the painter's portrait and in the flesh. Three different symbols of the emerging mass culture in Italy are seen together here: the publisher, the primadonna, and the movie star. Thanks to her beauty and her fame, Lina Cavalieri was immortalized by many Italian painters in Paris, such as Pietro Scoppetta, Antonio de la Gandara, and Antonio

Argnani; and by Francesco Paolo Michetti (who also portrayed her in numerous photographs in 1909), as well as Tito Corbella.

When time was ripe for Lina Cavalieri to cross the Ocean and go to the United States, where she was greeted as "the beautiful Italian," she did so as an opera singer. On December 5, 1906 at the Metropolitan Opera in New York she performed alongside Enrico Caruso in a memorable *Fedora* (by Umberto Giordano). Under pressure from the media, who eagerly awaited her debut, and fully aware of the fact that she needed to get ahead at all costs, at the end of Act II, after the singer's declaration of love, she spontaneously kissed him on the lips. The audience loved her for it and she became known as the "kissing primadonna." Because of her impetuous, passionate Italian temperament that she was able to contain thanks to her refined and elegant manner, the critics spoke favorably of her and forgave her for her voice, which wasn't always perfect. Over the four years during which she performed in New York and Philadelphia, Lina breathed life into a series of characters, expressing herself in affected and sensuous tones enhanced by the intensity of her large eyes. She loved the roles of Fedora, Tosca, and Adriana Lecouvreur for which she could wear fancy costumes and jewelry; she played Margherita in *Mefistopheles* (by Arrigo Boito); she played the role of the courtesan in works like *Manon* by Massenet and Puccini, in *Thaïs* by Massenet, and that of Salomè in Massenet's *Herodiade*.

After a season of concerts and a few recording sessions, it was time for Lina Cavalieri to approach the cinema. Beating her historic rival Geraldine Farrar to it (Farrar would debut a few months later in *Carmen* directed by Cecil B. DeMille), Lina brought to the silver screen her most

A scene from *Sposa nella morte!* (*The Shadow of Her Past*), directed by Emilio Ghione in 1915 and starring Lina Cavalieri and Alberto Collo
Turin, Collection Museo Nazionale del Cinema

Lina Cavalieri portrayed by
Herman Mishkin at the peak
of her acting career, 1916

famous characters, often in narrative contexts inspired by the dramas played by the European movie stars. As Giuliana Muscio notes,[9] unlike the Italian actresses who lost their ethnic identity once employed by the Hollywood movies, Lina Cavalieri safeguarded her Italian nationality in every single role she played, perhaps also owing to her previous career as an opera singer that associated her with the Italian tradition of the bel canto. Lina thus appeared in some of the first "star vehicles" of American cinema, although the roles she was assigned were not always suited to her age, which was no longer young. On the other hand, cinema had the power to resonate her image, safeguarding her from the risks that had to do with her modest vocal capabilities. In 1914 in New York, Lina debuted in Herbert Hall Winslow's *Manon Lescaut* made for the Playgoers Film Co. Filmed in France in the very places where the drama took place and with an abundance of means, it was shown after the start of World War I, when Lina returned to France to be close to her son and husband, Lucien Muratore, both involved in the war effort.[10]

The second film, *Sposa nella morte!* (*The Shadow of Her Past*), directed by Emilio Ghione in 1915, was produced in Italy by Tiber Film and then distributed in the United States.

Francesco Paolo Michetti,
Portrait of Lina Cavalieri
wearing a voluminous hat, 1909
Florence, Archivi Alinari,
Michetti Archive

It is the only film starring Cavalieri of which a fragment has survived. Lina plays the part of a young woman studying piano at Villa Medici whose fiancé is a penniless painter (played by her husband, Lucien Muratore). Seduced and taken to Paris by an elderly count, it is only when she sees a painted image of herself—an image that recalls the numerous portraits that had immortalized her—that she finally understands the generosity of the young man's love and commits suicide. The subsequent *La rosa di granata* (*The Rose of Granada*) of 1916, also directed by Emilio Ghione and distributed in America by Paramount in 1919, is the adaptation of a novella by Rameau that foreshadows the story of Thaïs, the redeemed courtesan.

In 1917, Lina Cavalieri signed a binding contract with Paramount for some films. The first of these, produced by Famous Players, was *The Eternal Temptress*, directed by Émile Chautard and written by Fred de Gresac, wife of the baritone Victor Maurel and a friend of Lina. The actress played the role of a Venetian princess with whom a young American falls in love. In the background a political story of espionage takes place that will lead to the woman's death by suicide in her lover's arms. The film was preceded by a prologue in which the protagonist embodies women's power to seduce, from Eve to Cavalieri herself, by way of some of the most famous "irresistible" ladies. The sequence would later be repeated in *The Most Beautiful Woman in the World*, starring Gina Lollobrigida and directed by Robert Z. Leonard in 1955, a fiction biography of the actress).[11] In 1918, Lina Cavalieri played the main character in *Love's Conquest*, directed by Edward José for Famous Players-Lasky, based on *Gismonda* by Victorien Sardou and set in early sixteenth-century Greece. The main character is a duchess whose son is kidnapped. She sends all her suitors away, promising her hand to the man who will succeed in bringing him back home alive. The most autobiographical movie of them all is *A Woman of Impulse*, again directed by Edward José and produced by Famous Players-Lasky (distributed in 1918 by Paramount), based on a pièce performed in Broadway in which Lina Cavalieri had the chance to perform, together with Lucien Muratore, passages from *Carmen*, accompanied by an entire theater company. The film tells the story of a poor young girl with a beautiful voice who, after being adopted by an American family, becomes a famous opera singer in Paris. The last American movie Lina made is *The Two Brides*, again directed by Edward José and produced by Famous Players-Lasky in 1919. The rather flimsy plot revolves around the daughter of a sculptor who lives with her father on an island and has a complicated love life. This time it is a statue resembling her—and not a painting—that is irresistible to men. But by that time Lina was 44 years old and she could no longer play the roles of young women and *femme fatales*. The last movie we know of, *L'idole brisé*, made in southern France with Lucien Muratore (directed by Maurice Mariaud and distributed in America in 1922, with the title *The Crushed Idol*, by Comptoir Cinelocation Gaumont), marked the end of Lina's movie career. As Fryer and Usova remark, "her farewell to the silver screen also marked the end of her public life."[12]

When her work for the cinema, which had opened up further markets and guaranteed even greater popularity, came to an end, Lina Cavalieri decided that Italy was the place where she wanted to spend the rest of her life. In her memoirs, written when the country was under fascist dictatorship, she confessed her love for her homeland: "I have loved life, men, my Italy and my art!"[13] We don't know for sure whether this tribute was a reflection of the "monumental" rhetoric typical of the autobiographical genre or the expression of a sincere sentiment. Umberto Notari, a brilliant journalist who interviewed her at the start of her career as an opera singer, said that "Lina Cavalieri . . . is an ardent *chauviniste*. Italian by birth, temperament, and beauty, she will not compromise, she will not yield before all that can obfuscate the name

and the fame of her country."[14] Whatever the case may be, Lina Cavalieri succeeded, like few others, to conquer world fame and to draw the attention of intellectuals, musicians, princes, and ordinary folk alike to the prerogatives of beauty and, we might add, to an Italian industriousness that was rare. The notion of "natural" gifts (the attributes of Italianness) nurtured by the "cultural" learning of constantly evolving fashions (elegance, use of jewelry, artistic experience, etc.); the cult of the body as a "device" of beauty and dominance with which to contrast male power; self-entrepreneurship as the key to personal affirmation; and the mindful use of one's own image and of advertising to direct the public's attention were the strategies that this "Italian Woman of Hollywood" used to face the challenges of modernity and especially of mediatization, precociously paving the way for the future of her fellow citizens.

[1] On Lina Cavalieri (1875–1944) see the following monographs: Paul Fryer and Olga Usova, *Lina Cavalieri. The Life of Opera's Greatest Beauty, 1874–1944* (Jefferson, NC: McFarland & Company, 2003); Franco Di Tizio, *Lina Cavalieri, la donna più bella del mondo. La vita 1875–1944* (Chieti: Ianieri, 2004).
[2] Stephen Gundle, *Bellissima. Feminine Beauty and the Idea of Italy* (New Haven: Yale University Press, 2007), 130.
[3] *Sankt-Peterburgskie Vedomosti* 170 (June 24, 1897).
[4] Lina Cavalieri, "Una lingua incomprensibile – La carriera comincia," in *Film* II, no. 52 (December 30, 1939): 4.
[5] Emilio Ravaglia, "Contemplando il ritratto di Lina Cavalieri," in *La Grancassa. Giornale di spettacoli teatrali* II, no. 2 (October 12, 1901): 4.
[6] Cecil Beaton, *The Glass of Fashion* (London: Weidenfeld & Nicolson, 1954), 65–66.
[7] See Lina Cavalieri, *My Secrets of Beauty* (New York: The Circulation Syndicate, 1914).
[8] Beaton, *The Glass of Fashion* 1954, 66.
[9] Giuliana Muscio, *Lina, Tina, Miriam e Mimi: quattro attrici italiane nel cinema muto americano*, forthcoming.
[10] "Cavalieri a War Nurse," in *The Moving Picture World* 21, no. 13 (September 26, 1914): 1790.
[11] Vittorio Martinelli, "L'avventura cinematografica di Lina Cavalieri," in *Il territorio. Quadrimestrale di cultura e studi sabini* II, no. 3 (September–December 1986): 293.
[12] Fryer and Usova, *Lina Cavalieri* 2003, 159.
[13] Lina Cavalieri, *Le mie verità*, ed. by Paolo D'Arvanni (Rome: Società anonima poligrafica italiana, 1939), 7.
[14] Umberto Notari, *Signore sole* (Milan: Amministrazione Notari, n.d. but 1903), 21–22.

GIULIA CARLUCCIO

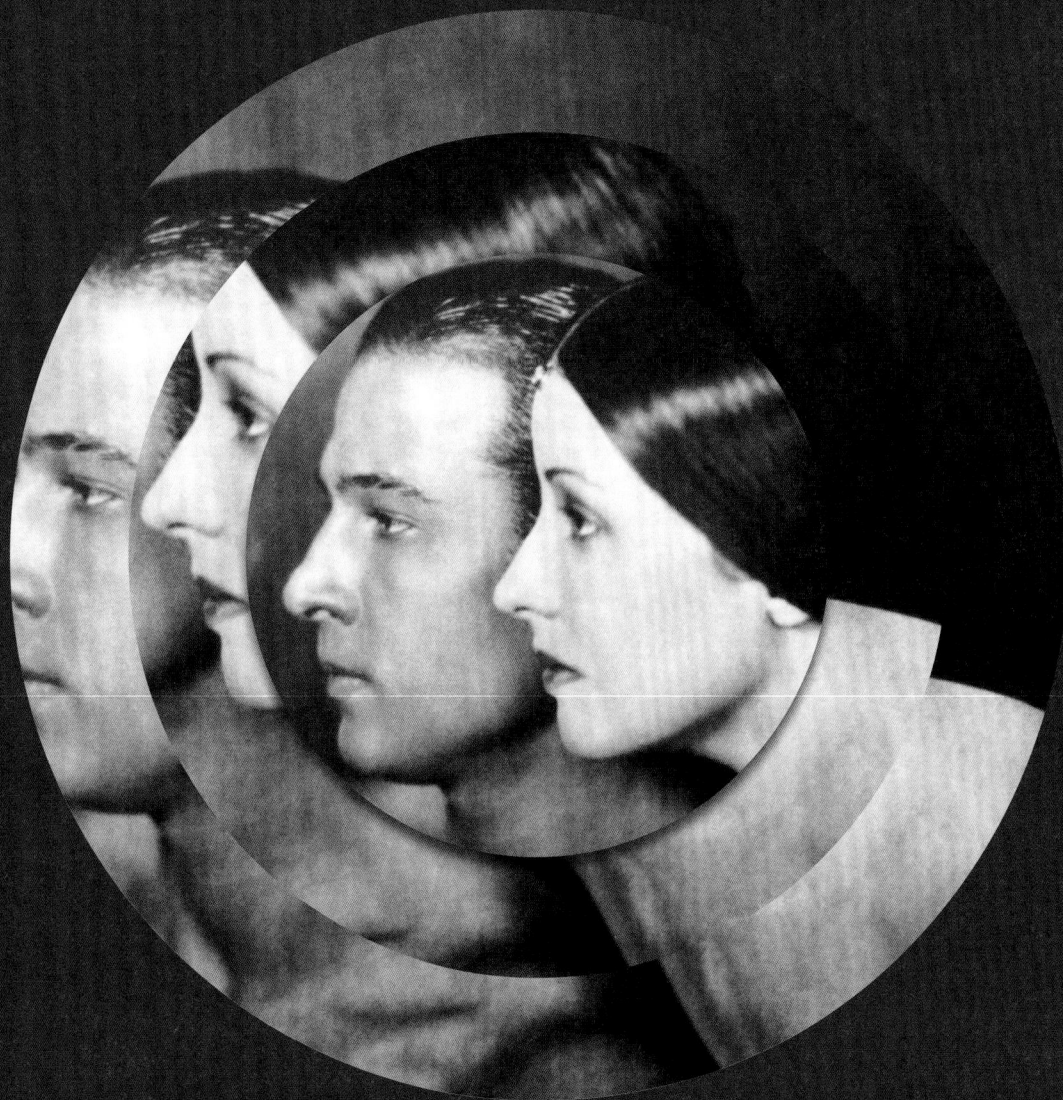

RUDOLPH VALENTINO: AN ITALIAN STAR IN HOLLYWOOD THE MYTH, THE IMMIGRANT, THE ACTOR

The myth

   "Arcane face, exotic splendor, Baudelairian beauty, inaccessible," "theomorphic and hierocratic ultra-face . . ." This is how Roland Barthes defined the face of Rudolph Valentino,[1] ascribing its traits to the domain of myth. For Barthes, the image of Valentino, just like that of Greta Garbo (which the French theorist discusses in a well-known text), "still belongs to that moment in cinema when the apprehension of the human countenance plunged crowds into the greatest perturbation. People literally lost themselves in the human image as if in a philter, where the face constituted a sort of absolute state of the flesh that one could neither attain nor abandon."[2] An era in which, says Barthes, "Valentino's face provoked suicides."[3]

   Later, in one of the most influential theoretical essays on the subject, Edgar Morin, in agreement with Barthes, classified Valentino as the peak of the first embodiment of stardom, a world peopled by Olympic idols, inaccessible and sculptural demigods.[4]

Rudolph Valentino
photographed by Helen
MacGregor as Vaslav
Nijinsky in a faun
costume, 1921

Rudolph Valentino as
an Indian warrior, 1921

Rudolph Valentino as an Indian
chief, 1921

Rudolph Valentino training
with weights in Palisades Park,
Santa Monica, 1922
Turin, Collection Museo
Nazionale del Cinema

Although a careful study of Valentino's stardom parabola and acting performances might today suggest that he belongs in the category of the "typical"—which Morin, however, defers and contrasts with that of the Olympic stars of Valentino's era[5]—it is indisputable that Rudolph Valentino's image during the span of his brief, explosive and uncontested career, not to mention during the course of almost a century that has followed, has achieved and preserved the status of a true icon, as complex as it is absolute.[6] Its is complex due to the many concentrated stratifications that define it, for example in relation to the ethnic and racial identity that at one and the same time nourishes the myth and is transcended by it, or in relation to the peculiar image of manliness and masculinity that the image transmits against the background of American society in the 1920s. It is absolute due to its persistent potency and ability to generate and regenerate contingents of fans who update it to suit the times, desires, and needs of social contexts that are chronologically and geographically different. It is also absolute due to that arcane and inaccessible dimension Barthes emphasized about thirty years after Valentino's death, but which was cultivated by the star himself at the height of his career, just under a year before his death on August 23, 1926: "The situation of a movie star is really curious . . .. The fact that he appears before your eyes in an impalpable form has something

Rudolph Valentino on the set of the film *Moran of the Lady Letty*, directed by George Melford in 1923

of the mysterious that unleashes your imagination."[7]

That the film star Valentino, who came to Hollywood from Castellaneta in the province of Taranto, "unleashed the imagination," and extraordinarily so, is evident to everyone today. The first great cinema star, in his lifetime he already triggered very specific fandom phenomena,[8] while his early death inspired an unprecedented cult and mythicization that has had very few equals in the course of subsequent movie history; the most similar case to Valentino's is that of Marilyn Monroe, another diva-icon.[9] As with Marilyn, long after Valentino's earthly existence generations of people have continued to create fan clubs (increasingly organized and internationally widespread due to the internet), re-elaborating his memory and extending its range to include more extreme interpretations and reinterpretations related to specific communities and categories, such as queer and gay re-readings that involve the stardom mythologies of both.

This phenomenon is even more surprising in Valentino's case because it is totally in inverse proportion to the current circulation of his films, which beyond the festival or art house scene is rather scarce and, in any case, decidedly less than the diffusion of films that feature Marilyn, given that Valentino is essentially linked to the genre of silent movies. Yet in spite of this, Valentino's image has remained fertile and is referred to in countless narratives and portrayals, whether in the pages of literature (such as the

Rudolph Valentino in a publicity shot for *The Young Rajah*, based on a novel by John Ames Mitchell and play by Alethea Luce, and directed by Phil Rosen in 1922

Rudolph Valentino in a publicity shot for *The Young Rajah*, 1922

Rudolph Valentino as Monsieur Beaucaire in the eponymous film, adapted from the novel by Booth Tarkington and directed by Sidney Olcott in 1924

extraordinary *Tango lento* that Dos Passos wrote about Valentino's death and funeral,[10] or Daniel Pennac's evocation in *The Dictator and the Hammock*[11]),musical and theatrical performances (such as Garinei and Giovannini's famous 1966 *Ciao Rudy*, with music by Armando Trovajoli and starring Marcello Mastroianni, to mention the Italian context), cinema, which has dedicated numerous films to the Valentino myth (including the visionary 1977 *Valentino* by Ken Russell, starring Rudolf Nureyev) and even sapid parodies (already being made while the star was still working, from Stan Laurel onwards), and, finally, documentaries.

The star of great films such as *The Four Horsemen of the Apocalypse* (Rex Ingram, 1921), *The Sheik* (George Melford, 1921), *Blood and Sand* (Fred Niblo, 1922), and *The Son of the Sheik* (George Fitzmaurice, 1926, distributed after his death), Valentino has left a deep impression on the history of film stardom, despite the short chronological span of his career. He exceptionally and exemplarily united dynamics and methods that would subsequently define the processes and functioning of the classic "studio system," among them production logics and consumption and reception practices, as well as, in a broad sense, semiotic and symbolic elements, together with others of a sociological and cultural nature.

From this perspective, and aside from reasons more specifically related to the history of cinema (such as the barely studied qualities of Valentino the actor and not just the star, and the narrative genres and direction styles of the films he acted in, which also deserve significant consideration[12]), the characteristics of the cult that arose after his death are open to questions of broader social and cultural history, touching on specific issues of ethnic and racial representation, gender, as well as the bold phenomenon of immigration, which are first and foremost strongly related to (but not only) American ideology and imagination in the 1920s. Not to mention all that was to further affect other contexts and historical configurations during the years of the survival and relaunch of the Valentino myth after his death.

With reference to the context of the 1920s, it should be kept in mind how access routes to the socio-cultural landscape that includes the Valentino phenomenon are made up of an extraordinarily rich body of public and private sources, a corpus that the most recent research on the star has begun to penetrate in a targeted way. However, as Silvio Alovisio emphasizes in an extensive essay on this subject, "within this enormously documented and discursive network, the publicity dedicated to the star from Apulia . . . still awaits a systematic exploration and inventory."[13]

Again it is Alovisio who indicates how within this range of sources and documents, questions and connections emerge as regards "the strategies of promotional control of the four film studios that produced the star's major films; the political and cultural interests that inspired the articles written by the most influential newspapers (not only the *Chicago Tribune* but also, for example, *The New York Times*); the identity of the ghost writers who worked for Valentino; and the ambiguous and decisive role . . . of fan magazines."[14]

And together with all of this, it should be added, are several hundred public and private photos including publicity shots, film stills, portraits or poses taken in private (all of which are also the product of strategic goals of representation or self-representation), poetry, literary images, and so forth.

Studying Valentino's paradigm of stardom and mythological status involves shedding light on the web that was created between films and other media, which in their turn define an often indestructible framework that links the real biography of Valentino the man—the Italian immigrant who disembarked in New York in 1913 and became a Hollywood actor and star, with all the related array of alternating luck, failed marriages, illness and early death—with other, superimposed, official and fictitious biographies (and autobiographies) influenced by the characters he played. These were often,

Rudolph Valentino, 1922

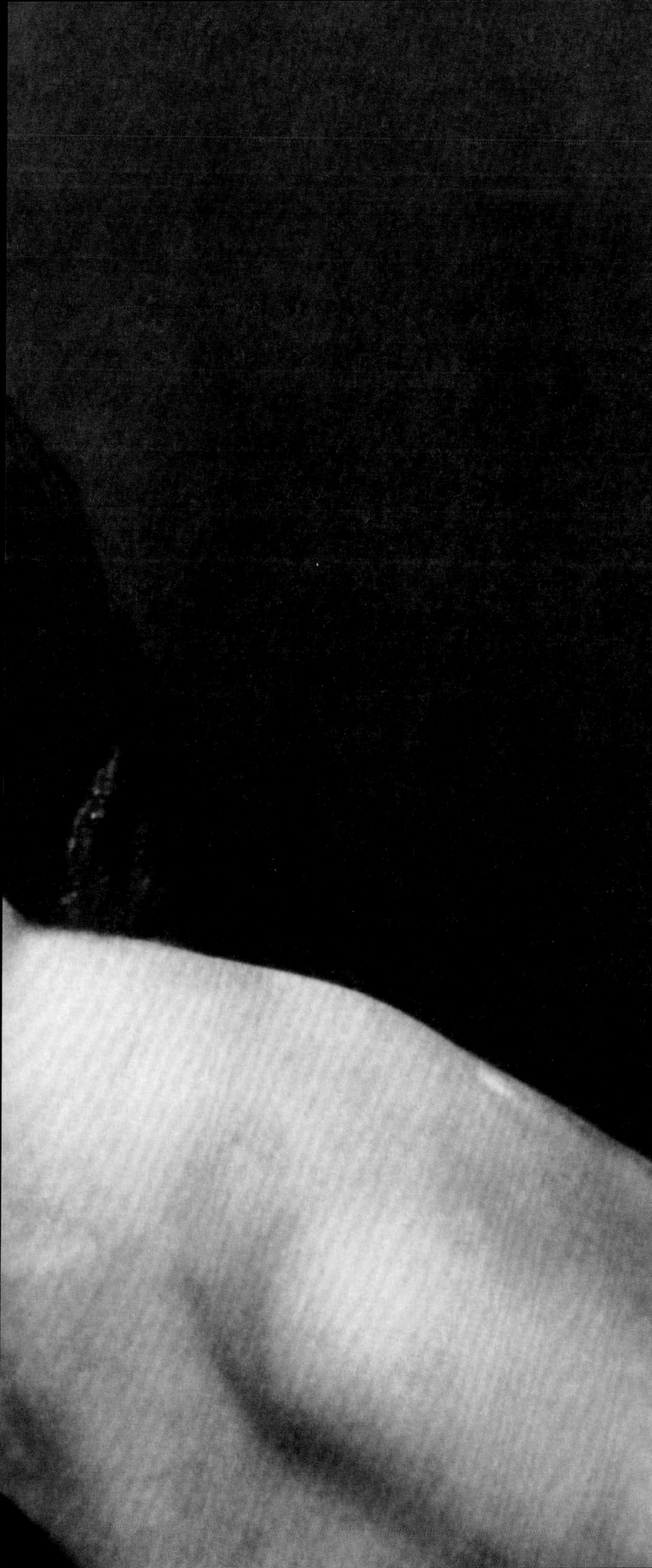

and from the very outset, deliberately mythologized re-elaborations of the young actor's Italian ethnic identity in an exotic guise (an Argentinian roughneck, Spanish bullfighter, Arab sheikh, and so on).

The immigrant

His identities were multiple yet all related to the Italianness of the man and the star. It was perhaps a "representative Italianness," but nevertheless authentic, as Gianni Puccini noted in the late 1930s in a portrait of the actor, by then deceased for about a decade: "It would be difficult to find an Italian more Italian than he was. Like fresh, new lifeblood destined to revitalize stories and characters very far from his sentimental and historical identity, Valentino clearly incorporated the particular characteristics of his race. The Frenchman Beaucaire, the Russian hero of *The Eagle*, the Spanish bullfighter in *Blood and Sand*, the Arab in *The Sheikh*: they all changed their names and latitude but remained Italian. The human empathy that emanated from those eyes and his sad, courageous smile could in no way be applied like makeup under any kolpak or turban."[15]

Aside from a certain degree of rhetoric and Puccini's good-natured paternalism (Italians' "human empathy"),[16] the text captures the ethnic reference that fascist Italy at some point claimed, something that cost the immigrant Valentino dearly in America when he was subjected to xenophobic-based attacks, as Giuliana Muscio and other scholars have emphasized.[17]

From this point of view, one cannot forget the emigrant and immigrant

Rudolph Valentino and his wife
Natacha Rambova, 1922

Half-length portrait
of Rudolph Valentino
in profile, 1920s

Rudolph Valentino and Natacha
Rambova in their house at
Whitley Heights, Los Angeles,
1922

Rudolph Valentino
and Nita Naldi in a
1924 publicity shot
for the film *A Sainted
Devil*, directed
by Joseph Henabery

Rudolph Valentino
reading a fan letter,
New York, 1922

Rudolph Valentino, 1925

Rudolph Valentino, 1922

status of the star from Castellaneta in the United States of the 1920s, a decade in which these topics were all crucial. And, after all, Rudolph Valentino was the first non-all-American Hollywood male star.[18]

It is no longer necessary today to debunk the myth of Valentino the emigrant with the cardboard suitcase. Nonetheless, the journey in first class aboard the *Cleveland*, which brought the eighteen-year-old guy to New York in December 1913, was certainly not painless from the point of view of cultural disorientation and the need to adapt and integrate into the American social context of the 1910s, and then the 1920s. Although a souvenir Valentino sent from aboard the *Cleveland* to his mother, recently found in the family archives, combines an Italian paper flag and an American one with the inscription "Viva l'America" and "Viva l'Italia,"[19] immigrant Rodolfo Guglielmi's initial optimism often had to face the actual difficulty of negotiating his ethnic identity. Moreover, the learning curve that saw the young man with high hopes make ends meet first as a taxi dancer in New York and then as an extra in Hollywood reflects to a degree his progressive capacity to direct the exotic charm of his (handsome) appearance into a quality that could be accepted and appreciated by the American imagination. It was not by chance that, in his first cinema roles, the ethnic quality of his dashing appearance was conveyed through

Rudolph Valentino on the set of the film *The Conquering Power*, based on the novel *Eugénie Grandet* by Honoré de Balzac and directed by Rex Ingram in 1921

the stereotype of the rogue. Only later, through a skillful stylization undertaken by various women (first, the screenwriter June Mathis, who discovered and launched him in 1921 with *The Four Horsemen of the Apocalypse*; then the set designer Natacha Rambova, who became his second wife), did the physical and cultural identity of the Italian immigrant actor achieve the level of star status as the first great Latin Lover. But, as was mentioned earlier, the specificity of his ethnically designated image was marked by complex and intense negotiations. Just over a month before his death, the *Chicago Tribune* published an editorial in which the star was compared to a powder puff and held responsible for the increasing effeminacy of the male, calling into question his own virility.[20] Certainly Valentino's exotic and sophisticated eroticism, which American audiences adored, questioned the American male identity, and this may explain the violence of the attack. But just as certainly, Valentino's diversity was ethnically different—he was an immigrant. Furthermore, as Giuliana Muscio has pointed out, Valentino had triumphed in Hollywood just "when America was in the grip of a fierce xenophobic intolerance, whose primary target was the Italian immigrant community."[21] So, behind the attack by the press was a strong anti-immigration sentiment, which in the case of the star idolized by crowds of female fans, led to an attempt to weaken his erotic charisma by emasculating and ridiculing it, or even by associating it with ideological dangers.[22]

The actor

Of course, all of this also gave rise to a total negation and devaluation of Valentino's acting skills. As a matter of fact, it was precisely his quality as an actor that long paid the price for the escalation of his public and star image, both during his life and after his death. What's more, as Muscio noted, even in Puccini's benevolent commentary on Valentino's Italianness, his talents as an actor appear more closely linked to the human empathy of his Italian

Rudolph Valentino and spaghetti in a photo from the 1920s

traits than to the quality of his performance. For better or worse, the image of Valentino the "exotic Italian" prevailed over that of Valentino the actor—in other words, the icon swallowed the performer. And yet the first great Hollywood star was also a consummate actor: varied, modern, often surprising, equally as complex as his iconic dimension.

A recurring feature of Valentino's critical reception concerns either the ineffable nature of his virtues as an actor or a complete disregard toward them. Whether laudatory or otherwise, the opinion that often emerges is that Valentino's "qualities," whatever they were, in some way transcend his films, which themselves, for the most part, have been subject to strong relativization, even by silent movie historians and specialists.[23] Many commentators and critics from that period spoke instead about the actor's photogenic quality, but without venturing to consider his acting and interpretive ability, except occasionally and in a skeptical way. Even when David W. Griffith recalled an encounter with the young, unknown actor at a "spaghetti dinner," which, of course, Valentino cooked and served, he talked about his photogenic appearance, captured live: "I was immediately struck by the special quality of his perfect features, something that the French would have called *photogénie*," adding that

Rudolph Valentino wearing a fencer outfit outside his home in Los Angeles, 1922

247

"if only the kid's acting had been as good as his profile, I would have found myself in the company of an exciting discovery."[24] This is only one of many other similar comments. In numerous reviews of the time, Valentino's "artistic ability"[25] is sometimes mentioned, even recognized, but only in a generic way. And what this actually consisted of, we are never told. The "star persona" has somehow overtaken the actor, following a trend that is also recognizable in the case of Marilyn Monroe, where the icon of beauty, the sex symbol, the dumb blonde and the girl child have long obscured her qualities as a sensitive and intelligent actress. Moreover, in the case of Valentino, alongside an unbalanced star/actor discussion that persists even in the most advanced and recent studies (in which the methods and approaches focused on the cultural discourse prevail over those based on film analysis), there is also the difficulty of situating the stylistic dimension of his performances in the broader transition from the visual and narrative style of proto-classical silent movies to the one defined as classical, which was to triumph with the advent of sound a few years after his parabola of fame. And yet, Valentino's acting and specific performance qualities have a lot to do with these intense, transitive dynamics. Many of his films constitute force fields where different styles and changing registers come into play, such as melodrama, adventure, and comedy, in which his performing style proves capable of sustaining the shifts in temperature that on the one hand deliver the typical *eloquence* of the silent movie in a dramatic, mediated way, and, on the other, the *sobriety* required by the nascent classical style.[26] In this respect he was a modern actor, open to the changes taking place in American cinema at the time, aware of his acting skills to the point of being able to express a second level of irony, even a touch of parody. An example of this stratification and interpretive ability can be seen in Valentino's extraordinary performance in the 1925 movie *The Black Eagle*, directed by Clarence Brown, in which the opportunity to express himself in various contexts and to play a series of different characters demonstrates what Gianni Rondolino describes in his valuable analysis of the film: "This versatility of Valentino the actor, already partially shown in his previous films and still present in the last, *The Son of the Sheik*, is certainly one of the most important elements, perhaps *the* most important, of his whole film career." And again: "The irony that surrounds his screen performance in its various manifestations is something more than a trait of his personality: it gives his acting a sort of distance from the scene—even from the subject, the story, and the character—which makes it modern."[27]

But where Valentino's performance becomes a true source for reflection on the acting codes and stylistic models of that period and their contradictory nature and dialectic, is a film such as Joseph Henabery's 1925 *Cobra*, in which his awareness of how he is playing the role of the Italian Rodrigo (Rodolfo?) Torriani, who leaves Italy for the New World, acquires an almost metalinguistic (as well as autobiographical) flavor as he modulates his acting style in one way for the Italian part and in another for the American section of the story, as if presenting a comparison of Latin and Anglo-Saxon stylistic models.[28]

Here, of course, Valentino is at the peak of his career, but even in previous roles, from *The Four Horsemen of the Apocalypse* to *The Sheik* and *Blood and Sand*, he offers a very varied repertoire of gestures, expressions, and postures that modulate eloquence and sobriety, drama and melodrama, a serious and lively register, and a kinetic and dancing manner (so important in Valentino, whom Anton Giulio Bragaglia aptly defined as "Maître à danser").[29] At times the use of stereotype is totally deliberate, typical of an actor who is master of his gifts and capable of using facial mimicry to caricature his own exotic Latin features, which at other times become instead a more naturalistic imitative tool, or hieratic mask. Which, in its own turn, can then become an icon.

Rudolph Valentino
photographed by Henry
Waxman on the set of
the film *Beyond the Rocks*,
adapted from the novel by
Elinor Glyn and directed
by Sam Wood in 1922

henry waxman

Rudolph Valentino in *The Eagle*,
directed by Clarence Brown
in 1925

Rudolph Valentino in *The Son
of the Sheik*, directed by George
Fitzmaurice in 1926

Rudolph Valentino in
Cobra, directed by Joseph
Henabery in 1925

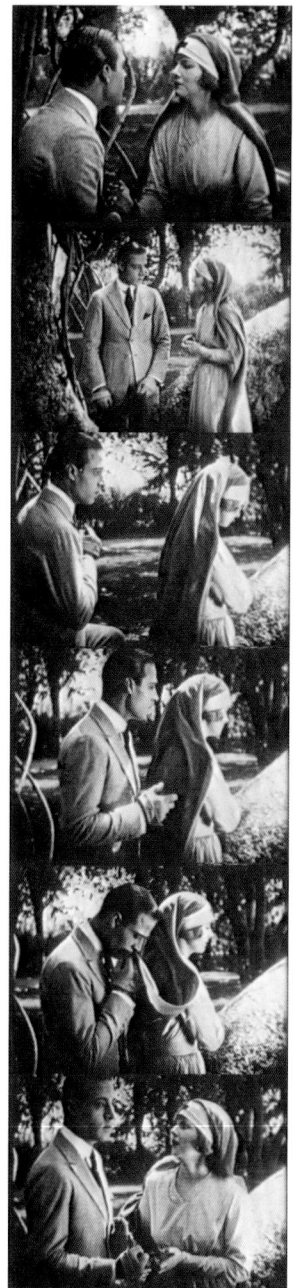

Rudolph Valentino in
*The Four Horsemen of the
Apocalypse*, directed by
Rex Ingram in 1921

[1] Roland Barthes, "Visages et figures," in *Esprit*, July 7, 1953.

[2] Roland Barthes, *Mythologies* (Paris: Éditions du Seuil, 1957).

[3] Ibid.

[4] Edgar Morin, *Les Stars* (Paris: Éditions du Seuil, 1957).

[5] Silvio Alovisio, "Valentino 'divo'. La prospettiva sociale. Fonti e interpretazioni," in *Rodolfo Valentino. Cinema, cultura, società tra Italia e Stati Uniti negli anni Venti*, ed. by Silvio Alovisio and Giulia Carluccio (Turin: Kaplan, 2010), 27 ff.

[6] Chiara Simonigh, "Un'icona della cultura moderna," in *Rodolfo Valentino. Cinema, cultura, società* 2010, 403–18.

[7] Herbert Howe, "A Confession," in *Photoplay*, November 1925; translated in Italian as "Valentino descritto da se stesso," in *Corriere d'America*, August 26, 1926, now in *Intorno a Rodolfo Valentino. Materiali italiani 1923–1933*, ed. by Silvio Alovisio and Giulia Carluccio (Turin: Kaplan, 2009), 226.

[8] These phenomena were studied masterfully by Miriam Hansen in relation to the centrality of the female audience: see "Pleasure, Ambivalence, Identification: Valentino and Female Spectatorship," in *Cinema Journal* XXV, 4 (Summer 1986); extended version in Miriam Hansen, *Babel & Babylon. Spectatorship in American Silent Film* (Cambridge and London: Harvard University Press, 1991). Hansen's essay is the basis of many more recent studies that consider Valentino from the perspective of cultural history.

[9] There is limitless bibliographical material concerning Marilyn. Regarding her specific iconic and fictional dimension and the way her myth functions, see Giulia Carluccio and Mariapaola Pierini, "Miti d'oggi. L'immagine di Marilyn," in *La Valle dell'Eden* 28–29 (Turin: Kaplan, 2015).

[10] John Dos Passos, "Adagio Dancer," in *The Big Money*, 1936.

[11] Daniel Pennac, *Le Dictateur et le Hamac* (Paris: Gallimard, 2003); English trans. *The Dictator and the Hammock* (London: Harvill Secker, 2006).

[12] Among the most recent studies to have prompted a systematic and updated analysis of these issues is *Valentino. Lo schermo della passione*, ed. by Paola Cristalli (Ancona: Transeuropa, 1996), and the aforementioned *Rodolfo Valentino. Cinema, cultura, società* 2010. Within the Italian context but with an international perspective, both books have aimed to focus not only on the sociological dimension of the stardom phenomenon Valentino represents, but also on the actor and his film roles.

[13] Silvio Alovisio, "Valentino divo," in *Rodolfo Valentino. Cinema, cultura, società* 2010, 30–31.

[14] Ibid., 31.

[15] Gianni Puccini, "Italiani nel mondo del cinema," in *Cinema*, April 25, 1937: 329–31.

[16] Pointed out by Giuliana Muscio in her essay on Valentino's Italianness, "L'italianità di Valentino," in *Rodolfo Valentino. Cinema, cultura, società* 2010, 221–29.

[17] On the question of Valentino's Italianness in America, in addition to Muscio's essay, see Amy Lawrence, "Rodolfo Valentino: un italoamericano negli anni Venti," and Giorgio Bertellini, "Divo/Duce: virilità italiane negli anni Venti," both in *Rodolfo Valentino. Cinema, cultura, società* 2010, respectively 229–39 and 244–59.

[18] See the monographic section "Italy In & Out. Migrazioni nel/del cinema italiano," in *Quaderni del CSCI* 8 (2012), and in particular, my own "Rodolfo Valentino, emigrante," 34.

[19] See the essay by Jeanine Villalobos, Valentino's great granddaughter, "Sognando Valentino: lo spettacolo della celebrità nella corrispondenza e negli scritti giovanili inediti di Rodolfo Guglielmi," in *Rodolfo Valentino. Cinema, cultura, società* 2010, 64–65.

[20] "Pink Powder Puff," in the *Chicago Tribune*, July 18, 1926.

[21] Muscio, "L'italianità di Valentino" 2010, 221.

[22] Ibid.

[23] For a more in-depth and detailed analysis, see Giulia Carluccio "Valentino 'actor'," in *Rodolfo Valentino. Cinema, cultura, società* 2010, 49–58, parts of which I refer to in this text.

[24] David W. Griffith, "Recollections of Rudolph Valentino" (1938), in Eva Orbanz, *There is a New Star in Heaven. . . Valentino*, Internationale Filmfestspiele Berlin – Stiftung Deutsche Kinemathek (Berlin: Verlag Volker Spiess, 1979), cited in *Valentino. Lo schermo della passione* 1996, 19.

[25] For example: Pierinetti, "Ecco l'uomo perfetto," in *La tribuna illustrata*, October 2, 1927: 4, now in *Intorno a Rodolfo Valentino* 2009, 262.

[26] Regarding the eloquence/sobriety polarity, see Jaqueline Nacache, *L'Acteur de cinéma* (Paris: Nathan, 2003), 43.

[27] Gianni Rondolino, "The Eagle: Valentino attore-personaggio," in *Rodolfo Valentino. Cinema, cultura, società* 2010, 335.

[28] On Valentino's acting (and the analysis of *Cobra*), see Cristina Jandelli, "Lo stile di recitazione di Valentino," in *Rodolfo Valentino. Cinema, cultura, società* 2010, 339–55.

[29] Anton Giulio Bragaglia, "Valentino Maître à danser," in *L'Ambrosiano*, January 6, 1938, now in *Intorno a Rodolfo Valentino* 2009, 273.

LUCA SCARLINI

ELECTRIC RENAIS-SANCE: THE MEMORY OF ART AT THE CINEMA, FROM EUROPE TO HOLLY-WOOD AND BACK

"This art was born out of a ray of poison."
Guido Gozzano, quoting Arrigo Boito on the invention of photography

The start of the twentieth century, when all the furious gestures of the historical avant-gardes were in the making, was the prerogative of all the eclectic forms of art. The prefix "neo," based on nineteenth-century experiences, had a huge flourishing, freely intersecting the echoes of Art Nouveau and the outcomes of the research carried out by the Nazarenes and the Pre-Raphaelites with reminiscences of Hellenistic statuary, the world of Antonio Canova, the Middle Ages, and the Renaissance. Cinema, the new art that yearned to be constantly renewed, conceived of by looking at contemporary reality from up close, immediately became a vehicle not just of trains leaving from stations or of workers emerging from a factory at the end of their shift, but also of this aesthetic attitude toward witnessing and revisiting the past. The period reconstructions were aimed at seducing the masses, as well as ennobling the new art that in the 1910s was the object of numerous critical attacks by the intellectuals and was still far from being consecrated the seventh art, as it was famously defined by Ricciotto Canudo in 1921. Actually, the severe warning addressed by the playwright William C. DeMille to the younger Cecil B. who was just getting started in his Hollywood adventure, sounds like an exemplary declaration of this critical attitude: "You come from a good family, I don't understand how you would want to identify with a form of entertainment that is miserable, that no one calls art. You are no doubt aware of the scorn with which the movie is considered by all the writers, actors, and producers of Broadway."[1] In a short period of time, this acrimonious judgment faded away and on the wave of his brother's success William too became a filmmaker, directing over fifty movies. In Europe, the suspicion that was felt toward this new art form often became the occasion for a broader philosophical

La·Cena·Delle·Beffe·
Poema·Drammatico·In·IV·Atti·
·Di·Sem·Benelli·
Musica·Di·Umberto
Giordano
Editore
Sonzocno

G.CHINI.M.D.FIRENZE
909-924

MANIFESTI CHAPPUIS BOLOGNA

Galileo Chini, poster for the
theater performance of *La cena
delle beffe* (*The Jester's Supper*)
by Sem Benelli, opera version
by Umberto Giordano
Milan, Museo Teatrale
alla Scala

accusation against the new empire of the machine of creation. This is clearly illustrated by the indictment against the inhumane impact of automation signed by Luigi Pirandello in the brilliant novel *Si gira* (1915), which later became *Quaderni di Serafino Gubbio operatore* (1925).

At the start of the century, the world of entertainment in Europe experienced the strong emotions offered to it by the Gabriele d'Annunzio & Eleonora Duse duo, which borrowed from the Romantic legacy to perfect an important strand of historical-aesthetic eclecticism on stage. They did not, however, receive the praise of the crowds for their effort, praise that d'Annunzio obtained only with *La figlia di Iorio* (*The Daughter of Iorio*, 1904). And yet the golden model of his play *Francesca da Rimini*, staged in 1901 in Rome with gorgeous medieval decor and flashes of Art Nouveau, did resound in the imagination. Furthermore, d'Annunzio's poetic dictate made it possible to allow his erotically charged contents to pass: they would have never been accepted in a contemporary setting, inside a classical sitting room. The 1901 performance brought with it an entire Italian school of fine arts and crafts, committed to offering only the finest to the stage, costumes, accessories, and props: even the most scathing criticism of that adventure never called into question the quality of the costly production. The artisans who created it belonged to the rich world of traditional arts that designed the Italian Pavilion at the 1915 San Francisco International Exposition and found itself collaborating in various roles on film productions in the United States: it was the world celebrated by the Taviani brothers in their 1987 film *Good Morning Babilonia*.

In Italy and elsewhere, cinema made aesthetic eclecticism its own language from the very outset. The revival of plots from remote worlds (from ancient Rome to Greece all the way to the India of the *Mahabharata*) allowed audiences to dream and made it possible to indulge in representations of sensuality that would otherwise have been very much forbidden. All of this originated from the practice of *serate nere*,[2] or black nights, which spread far and wide from the days of the first rudimentary projections in itinerant shacks. These short films were addressed to men only and had titles that were often inspired by the classics, such as *The Birth of Venus* or *The Judgment of Paris*, not to mention *Ladies of the Court Bathing*, set in Versailles in the age of Marie Antoinette. Produced by Pathé, they contained *scènes grivoises* that might seem chaste today, but at the time overcame the senses. And while a film like *Sappho and Priapus* (1921–22), on various occasions attributed to d'Annunzio himself, was excessively explicit and therefore remained clandestine, Rina De Liguoro, the Italian star most suited to performing a strip-tease in front of the camera, appeared almost naked in *Messalina* (1923) and in the lost *Savitri* (1923), said to be the most risqué films of those years.[3]

At the theater and in the other arts, eclecticism in verse triumphed with Sem Benelli, and especially his *La cena delle beffe* (*The Jester's Supper*, 1909). Its murky plot of sex and violence (drawn from the short stories of sixteenth-century poet and playwright Lasca), with the Florence of Lorenzo the Magnificent in the background, caused quite a stir. It was advertised by a beautiful poster made by Galileo Chini, with a streak of blood sullying the hooded figure of Giannetto Malespini. From one success to another, before also becoming a melodrama for music by Umberto Giordano (1924), in Paris in 1910 the text was clamorously retitled *La beffa*, performed by Sarah Bernhardt *en travesti* as Giannetto. Even greater was its triumph on Broadway as *The Jester* in the 1919–20 season: its neo-Renaissance taste immediately conquered the New York ladies, who acquired new styles of apparel and fabric designs. On stage together with the beautiful Maude Hanaford, the histrionic duo John and Lionel Barrymore were especially popular—so much so that, when Sem Benelli passed away, their sister Ethel remarked: "I had never understood John the eccentric, John the madman, John the intelligent, perverted, unhinged, and generous, as I did in his performance as Giannettaccio."[4] In short, this was perfect scenic poetry for the actors of those years and their melodramatic gestures of strong resonance. Antonio Gramsci, with his typical accuracy, had a few years earlier established an exact parallel between the playwright's verses and the famous body of Lyda Borelli: "Borelli prefers Sem Benelli because he is more careful about the musicality of his verses than the strict sense of the words. This way, Borelli could be the star, the artist par excellence of the movie, in which the only language was the flexible and constantly changing expressiveness of the human body."[5] The playwright's elaborate eclectic world was geared toward the celebration of the senses, and everything seemed perfect for him to become the leading figure of sexy period reconstructions for the cinema, which was the protagonist of the new electric celluloid Renaissance. But that is not the way things went. Indeed, many were the Italian movies based on his work. *La gorgona*, directed by Mario Caserini in 1915, was highly successful, a film on which Benelli himself worked closely, overseeing surveys throughout Tuscany together with the screenwriter Arrigo Frusta, which led to filming in Pisa, Tombolo,

and San Gimignano as well as in Piedmont (Saluzzo and the Borgo Medievale of Turin).[6] The movie, starring Madeleine Céliat and Annibale Ninchi, was followed by the relatively good success of *L'arzigogolo*, directed by Mario Almirante (1924). In America there had been lots of discussion about *The Jester's Supper* with Benelli himself, who had asked to direct the movie, requesting an astronomical amount of money and a substantial investment in the scenes and costumes—all of which was to no avail. Finally, the rights were sold in 1928 to Defu Productions, which never made the movie. Benelli, at the height of his popularity, promoted an important exhibition event in Florence, *La Primaverile Fiorentina*, held in 1922 at Parterre, at the time called Palazzo del Parco di San Gallo. Many were the artists whose work was on display: it was a vast panorama of current Italian production, with a specific passion for eclectics and a taste for Neo-Renaissance nuances. The exhibition program strongly stressed the connection between the arts, the stage, and cinema, in accordance with the curator's vision. At that time Benelli had become immensely popular, but it all ended abruptly: in 1924, right after the Matteotti murder, he spoke out against Mussolini in Parliament, which led to his spending the following years under close surveillance. When it came to censorship, the Duce had a rather ambiguous attitude toward him: he authorized several of his productions and two decades later he did nothing to stop the success of the movie version of *La cena delle beffe*, which was finally produced in 1942, directed by Alessandro Blasetti.

In the pioneering era, Italian cinema was often nurtured by explicit references to painting, as well as to theatrical and melodramatic representations, which were the most popular and widespread form of entertainment at the time. As for what was being produced in Turin in the 1910s,[7] the devil who torments the main character in *Come l'ingordigia rovinò il Natale a Cretinetti* was evidently inspired by the Mephistopheles in the melodrama of the same name by Arrigo Boito. In *La figlia di Iorio* (1911), producer S. A. Ambrosio explicitly harks back to the painting of Francesco Paolo Michetti, while in the key scene of *Le tentazioni di San'Antonio* (1911) the famous eponymous painting by Domenico Morelli preserved at the Galleria Nazionale d'Arte Moderna in Rome is quoted. *Teodora* by Leopoldo Carlucci (1922) offers a reproduction of classical Byzantine models that peculiarly intersect with their Art Nouveau revisitation, without overlooking the presence of some scantily-clad young ladies in the retinue of the empress. Giovanni Pastrone's famous *Cabiria* (1914) triumphantly links the eclectic legacy to the destiny of cinema through the sumptuous intertitles by Gabriele d'Annunzio, which seemed to foreshadow the imminent conflict: "the winds of war converted the peoples into a sort of inflamed material."[8] Soon afterwards, and for a short period of time, d'Annunzio was the most famous Italian in the world, especially owing to the two-year experiment of the Free State of Fiume (1919–20), which ended tragically. At the time, people in the United States could read his verses and prose, in syndication, in all the country's major newspapers.[9] The success of *Cabiria* would continue to echo because of this historical coincidence in the years to come, even when, starting in 1921, the crisis of the Italian productive system due to the war, the post-war period, and the advent of fascism suddenly passed the baton for productions of historical films to the United States, where the tried and tested Italian models were revisited and transformed. Italian cities were filled with the survivors of a golden world of celluloid that had vanished in a puff of smoke. No one has ever done a better job at summing up the climate of confusion in Rome's world of cinema in the 1920s than the forgotten writer-reporter Arnaldo Frateili, closely involved in what happened as a screenwriter: "Cleopatra

T.ª 37.

F. B. dis.ᵗ   Lit. Salucci

Riverso......

T.ª 53.

F. B. dis.ᵗ   Lelo Salucci

Spavento.......

T 9.

V. M. dis.ᵗ   Lit. Salucci

Orribil vista!

T.ª 21.

F. Beggi dis.ᵗ   Lit. Salucci

Or del flagel che sanguinoso ei ruota.

continued for a while to have the airs of the Queen of Egypt, passing before the Caffè Aragno in her car without deeming us common mortals to even be worthy of a glance, but then she began looking around for another Antony who would pay for the car. Only Dante and Nero ended up with enough money in their pockets to be able to continue to pay for orgies of poetry and blood . . . until it was time for them too to remain jobless. So it's easy to imagine the cursing in Florentine and Roman dialect that the two of them, who were both ill-natured, abandoned themselves to." Or, "passing by the cafés was a group of young men with long hair and sideburns, third-class actors in a film with a Russian and Spanish setting, interrupted because of the crisis, who vaguely hoped to get work that would keep them from going to the barber's so they could look decent again."[10] In other words, it was truly a disaster: suddenly and drastically the end had come for the first period of Rome as the heart of cinema, which had begun in 1914 and as early as 1921 was being seen as an essential element of the city's identity by Ettore Veo, an expert on the history of the capital who published the curious *Fantasio-film*, a novel that tells the story of a production that wavers between comedies and a project for the impressive adaptation of Pietro Cossa's *Nerone*. In other words, it was the end of what Bruno Barilli called "the cinematographic hour," during which "everywhere you looked [in Rome] there were names, even in Latin sometimes, for the studios that were being built: 'Tespi Film,' 'Lux et Umbra,' 'Silentium,' a hundred houses boiling over with films, and then clamorous examples of the haughty occupation of entire areas, gardens, potato and wheat fields, even the sacred cemeteries around the capital."[11]

Many Italian writers, in spite of the long-lasting diatribe about the art of cinema, soon became fully aware of the immense power of the new medium. So much so that the movie world often became the setting for the fiction that was being written. Edmondo De Amicis, who was always interested in the new metaphors stemming from technology, set this merry-go-round in motion with the lovely story he wrote called "Cinematografo cerebrale," published in *L'Illustrazione Italiana* in 1906, in which he described the morbid meditations of a bored middle-class man. In 1910 Jarro (born Giulio Piccini), a well-known humorist, published *Le novelle del cinematografo* (including titles such as "Cinematografisti tra i cannibali"). Giovanni Papini opened the critical debate with a relevant theoretical article: "La filosofia del cinematografo," which appeared in the May 18, 1907 issue of *La Stampa* newspaper and aroused a great deal of discussion. The following year, the *Gazzetta di Torino* inaugurated the first film section and from that moment on the intellectuals got right down to work—from Giuseppe Prezzolini (who published an enthusiastic "Viva il cinematografo" in *La Stampa* in 1914) to Goffredo Bellonci, the author of pointed notes such as "Estetica del cinematografo," published in the magazine *Apollon* that dedicated a lot of space to the topic. In 1918, in the pages of the magazine *In penombra*, Federigo Tozzi published the short story "Una recita cinematografica," in which a poor troubled soul about to commit suicide changes his mind after seeing a company of actors using a dummy to stage the very same action on the banks of the Tiber. This sophisticated magazine, which was published between 1917 and 1919, regularly commissioned important names to write about cinema: among other things, still in 1918, it published texts by Salvatore Di Giacomo and Alfredo Testoni. Guido Gozzano ended his short life by signing the screenplay for a *San Francesco* that would never be produced. By nature suspicious of the seventh art, Gozzano knew how to capture its evocative powers perfectly, as he summed up in his excellent article "Il nastro di celluloide e i serpi di Laocoonte," combining the new art with the memory of antiquity. Cinema and the world of movies reappeared on several occasions in his short stories. In "Il riflesso delle cesoie," the movie star Albina Albini, who has grown old in spite of her efforts to look young, finds herself playing the part of a nun in the convent where she herself had been educated. The comical sketch "Pamela-Film" is truly enchanting: the ultra-conservative *madamigella* Ottempati finds out that she inherited the studios in Turin that mockingly bear her name. When she arrives there, dressed in nineteenth-century style and looking rather ugly, she is mistaken for a make-up wizard, the ineffable

The classification of facial expressions of affection and emotion in the book by Antonio Morrocchesi *Lezioni di declamazione e d'arte teatrale* (Florence: Tip. All'insegna di Dante, 1832) Florence, Biblioteca Nazionale Centrale di Firenze

Enrico Caruso in the movie
My Cousin, directed by Edward
José in 1918 and produced by
the Famous Players-Lasky
Corporation, where he plays two
roles: the sculptor Tommasso
and his cousin the tenor Cesare
Caroli

Tulipier. Arousing the gentlewoman's anger no doubt.[12] Alfredo Panzini, a successful novelist and lexicographer, had the task of censoring the films' intertitles and this helped him add more and more words to his successful *Dizionario moderno*, which at an early stage already contained the word "borelleggiare." Panzini also wrote the texts for the successful *Gli ultimi giorni di Pompei* (*The Last Days of Pompeii*, 1926) by Carmine Gallone and Amleto Palermi using simpler, everyday language as compared with *Cabiria* to tell one of the most popular classical stories at the cinema.[13]

In parallel with the wealth of references to the arts, the Italian visual lexicon penetrated the cinema of the New World by way of a gestural and expressive language that prose theater and melodrama had disseminated in a capillary way across the world. Proof of this is the success of the Italian handbooks of the stage arts in English-speaking countries. This repertoire was based on that perfect rhetoric of actions symbolizing emotions that in time underwent a merciless condemnation in taste, when in the lexicon the word "melodramatic" took on the negative characteristics of exaggeration and redundancy. In the turbulent century of the Risorgimento, while the notion of creating a national company based on the example of the Comédie-Française (which everyone was hoping would happen) seemed impossible, many prominent figures of the theater scene, almost as a reward for a complex and under-protected professional life, promoted the idea of making a catalogue of facial expressions, in which each gesture corresponded to a specific emotional meaning. This was the intention of two of the main writers of such practical and theoretical books: Antonio Morrocchesi, who wrote *Lezioni di declamazione e d'arte teatrale* (Florence, 1832) and Alamanno Morelli, the author of the popular *Prontuario delle pose sceniche* (Milan, 1854). While Symbolist experimental theater had already undermined this great work of codification, based on a division of roles that had been crucial to the Italian theater companies between the nineteenth and twentieth centuries before the slow advent of directing, this was not the case with melodrama, where the eloquent gesture remained the basis of the representation for a long time. In the 1920s, cinema replaced the opera as a form of popular entertainment, the former often borrowing the plots as well as the actors from the latter. And indeed, melodrama quickly reached cinema: the exploitation of the theatrical repertoire that was in vogue soon produced experiments in which famous actors

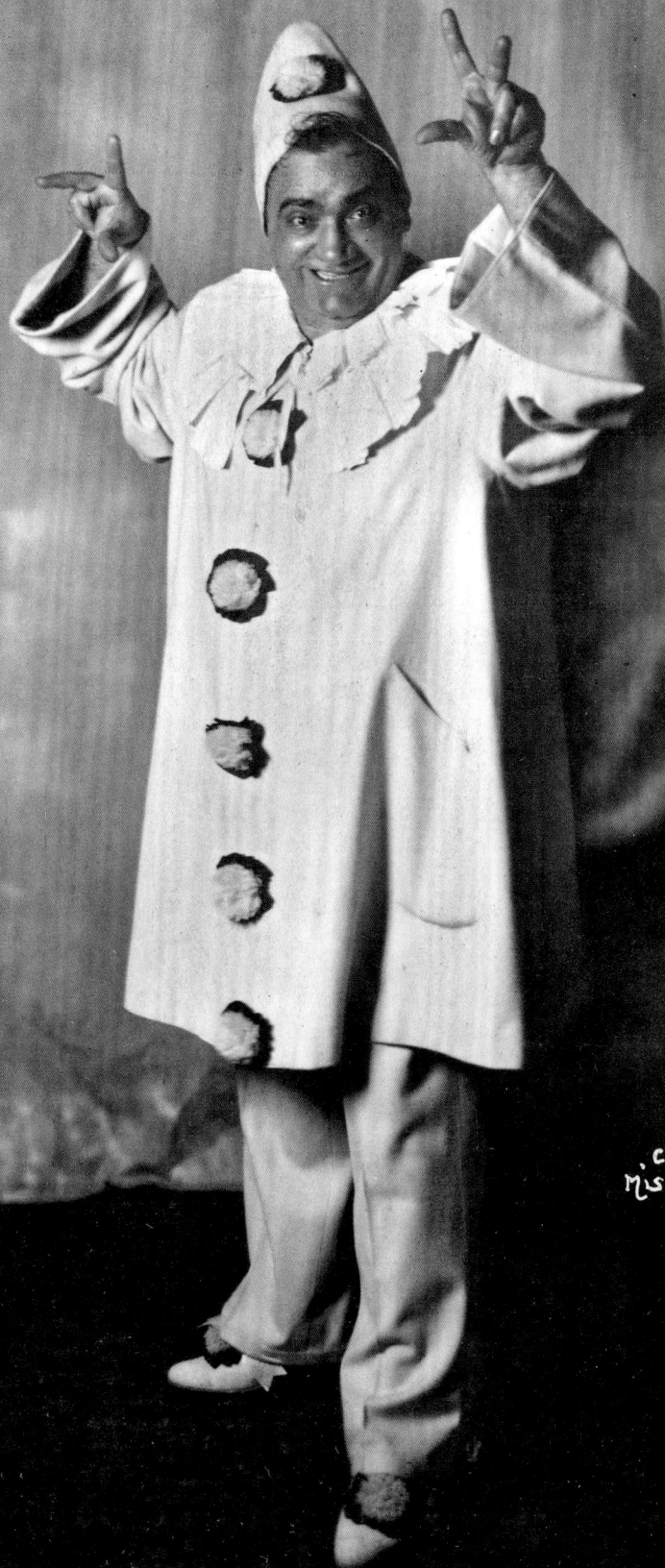

brought classical roles to the silver screen: in 1908 Giovanni Zenatello and Alessandro Bonci were both successful in the films *Traviata* and *Un ballo in maschera*. Behind the screen was a gramophone, which conveyed their interpretation more or less in sync.[14] On the other hand, many were the singers who had a movie career that went beyond the reproduction of their repertoire. All of them in their own manner recalled, via the filter of the stage dictionary, the lexicon of stage poses that reproduced the gestures depicted in Renaissance paintings and Neoclassical statues. In *My Cousin* by Edward José (1918), Enrico Caruso reproduced an entire sampling of sculptural poses from his interpretation of Canio in *Pagliacci*—a fetish-role performed dozens of times at the Metropolitan—and transferred them to the character of the illustrious singer Cesare Caroli, cousin of the poor sculptor Tommasso. Also famous were the films starring Lina Cavalieri (three of them directed by Edward José) who, after a heated scene of passion between her and Caruso in *Fedora* at the Metropolitan, was dubbed "the kissing primadonna." She debuted on the silver screen in *Manon Lescaut* directed by Herbert Hall Winslow, now lost, inspired by Prévost's novel and Puccini's opera, which she had already performed in on the stage. However, the most famous case of an opera singer who

Enrico Caruso
photographed by
Herman Mishkin on
the set of *My Cousin* as
the tenor Cesare Caroli
while performing in
Leoncavallo's *Pagliacci*, one
of his most famous roles
New York, The
Metropolitan Opera

then moved on to cinema in the United States was that of Geraldine Farrar, one of Cecil B. DeMille's stars. If we look at her performance in the film *Carmen* (1915), one of her triumphant roles at the Metropolitan, we can easily identify codes and styles from the theater. Highly regarded was her performance in *Joan the Woman* (1916), also directed by DeMille, in which Joan of Arc, a character of great dramatic strength, appears at the beginning of the film in a crucifixion pose, with the lily of France projected in the background. Equally stylized was her performance in *The World and Its Woman* directed by Frank Lloyd (1919), in which she played a bejeweled Thaïs before the tsar and the applauding Russian aristocracy.

Gemma Bellincioni's career in Italy as a star of musical verismo was particularly significant. The great singer triumphantly abandoned the scene in 1911 after traveling all around Europe as Salomè, her last stage role. In 1916 she was Santuzza in *Cavalleria Rusticana* directed by Ugo Falena, the film she is most famous for. The experience in front of the movie camera led her to establish the production company Biancagemma, for which her young daughter Bianca was a leading actress. In 1917–23 the singer directed twelve films, including *Vita traviata* (1918), which was censored for its orgy scenes, the sumptuous costume movie *Giovanna d'Angiò regina di Napoli* (1920), and a popular melodrama with the curious title *Satanica* (1923). Throughout the entire production, amidst historical reenactments in period costumes and contemporary sketches, Bellincioni reproduced the gestural lexicon that had made her famous on stages around the world.[15]

Among the strategies to ennoble the movies, between 1912 and 1920, on a number of occasions the stars of the silver screen played characters from melodrama with the evident intention to elevate acting on the screen. Suffice to recall the magnetic performance of Francesca Bertini in the engaging and demanding production of *Tosca*, directed by Alfredo De Antoni (1918). Even when she got older she was still very clear-sighted as she recalled the events of her career, explaining in her memoirs how the adoption of the opera imaginary on the silver screen was an explicit way of seeking authority. This is how she summed up the impact of the first private screening, where she was sitting next to Guglielmo Marconi and Victorien Sardou's daughter: "that was the first time I decided I had finally become something in the world of art."[16] In the alluring 1982 documentary *L'ultima diva*, Gianfranco Mingozzi asked her to repeat the farewell to the world of Floria Tosca on the slopes of Castel Sant'Angelo. The elderly actress faithfully reproduced for the camera the gestural rhetoric, clearly inspired by melodrama, that had pervaded all her works.

The theme of the relationship between cinema and literary or melodramatic works was debated at length: the *literati* often cried foul because of film scenes that were too superficial or dismissive with respect to the operas adapted, at times even abusive. In 1920 Italian bookstores sold the volume *L'arte di fare un "soggetto" per cinematografo* by Pasquale Marica, the first of its genre. It was a manual on how to write for the silver screen and the cover rather explicitly showed a writer-marionette whose strings were being pulled by three figures: the director, the producer, and the diva. The historical film, so as to avoid the frequent accusation of excess simplification (in Italy the word "americanata" was coined, which Alfredo Panzini promptly added to his *Dizionario moderno*), in the years of the silent film claimed, using different strategies, the authenticity of reconstruction, calling writers, artists, and scholars to collaborate. Lucio D'Ambra was categorical in his recalling of how absurd things were back then when he was asked by Ugo Falena to write his first screenplay: the director had asked him to reduce *The Betrothed* to a single day, and in reply to his friend's protests he had said: "the less you remember the better it will be; in the movies you have to be concise, use as little as possible, and be very quick."[17] Often the quality of the artistic work was only declared in the titles, for promotional purposes, but the results in no way corresponded to what had been promised. Alberto Savinio wittily summed up the matter: after panning Mario Bonnard's *I promessi sposi* ("that stuff we were forced to see"), he indicated that the pull quotes for *Il corsaro* by Augusto Genina read: "his imagination is Dantesque," while to be honest "it was only Benellian."[18] This tension was especially relevant in the cinematographic representation of Dante. The poet was the central figure of the culture of the Risorgimento—unsurprisingly, the Società di Diffusione della Cultura Italiana was named after him, an association that was strongly supported by a group of intellectuals led by Giosuè Carducci and inaugurated in 1889; it is still active today. The poet's role in modern culture was especially honored in the competitions for the illustration of the *Divine Comedy* held beginning in 1900 by Vittorio Alinari, where all the current trends were summed up.[19] In 1911 there were two different productions of the *Inferno*, the most famous the one by MilanoFilms, directed by the erudite Adolfo Padovan assisted by Francesco Bertolini and Giuseppe De Liguoro. It was a significant production, which also had to come to terms with lengthy time frames that were up to then unknown to Italian standards. The movie led to a radical change in the country's film distribution policies, managing to be disseminated in the United States as well, with presentations for the first time in academic circles. The number of copies sold of the new edition and English translation of the *Inferno* rose sharply. The poster, featuring a classical illustration by Gustave Doré, advertised the film as being "The successor to the Passion Play," thus creating a promotional link to movies on Biblical subjects. The advertising investment was huge and diversified in Italy as well: the Neapolitan poet and journalist Teodoro Rovito was commissioned to write amusing advertising in verse, *La divina visione*, in which Dante finds himself, a bit bewildered by all that light and all those colors, before the movie theater where his work was being shown: "per la gran luce in cui sembrava avvinto/ (luce partente da mille ampolline)/ e per un cartellon tutto dipinto."[20]

In 1921, the six-hundredth anniversary of Dante's death, again it was time for the poet to go to the movies in Italy. Caramba (born Luigi Sapelli), master of costume design and in charge of scenery at La Scala, after the very decadent and highly successful *I Borgia* (1920), was criticized for his ambitious *La mirabile visione*, which came out a year after the celebrations had ended. But among the criticisms, the film was praised for its visual arrangement, in which Caramba the author showed an amazing historical reconstruction as well as his closeness to the work of contemporary sculptors (Leonardo Bistolfi above all, about whom he wrote passionately as a critic for the *Gazzetta di Torino*), while Caramba the director used a number of new technical effects with surprising results especially as regards night-time shooting. Also making an appearance on the set was Benedetto Croce in his role as Minister of Public Education, interested in seeing whether this version of Dante was dignified; but this new art didn't appeal to him at all.[21] In the United States the film

Film stills from *La mirabile visione*, directed by Caramba (pseudonym for Luigi Sapelli), who also designed the costumes, subject by Fausto Salvadori, with Camillo Talamo, Liliana Millanova, and Gustavo Salvini. The movie was produced on the occasion of the sixth centennial of Dante's death

svi luppo

Stampa

ntrale Elit.ca

Proiezione e Montaggio

Teatro

Operatori

was only relatively successful. Across the ocean Caramba was already known for his perfect historical reconstructions and appreciated for his acclaimed installations of Italian operas at the Metropolitan. In 1915, he had staged *Madame Sans-Gêne* by Umberto Giordano and had received enthusiastic reviews for Puccini's *Triptych*, which debuted in New York in 1918—an absolute *tour de force* with three different settings.

It is easy to imagine the impact of the Dante-year on Florence—conferences, performances, celebrations, parties one after another, even a triumphal parade that witnessed the participation of His Majesty the King. In 1920, around this very occasion, the V.I.S. (Visioni Italiane Storiche) studios were established in Rifredi.[22] Promoted by Count Giovanni

Montalbano, they were devoted to the production of "epic films on historical subjects." Montalbano's aim was to valorize the city's great artisanal tradition and also involve the academic community, scholars and researchers, in order to always guarantee the historical authenticity of the films. V.I.S.'s first project was the complex film *Dante nella vita dei tempi suoi*, which was also released late, in 1922, and heralded as "the greatest Italian movie about the rebirth." Domenico Gaido, a painter and the director of the film, had just finished making *Il ponte dei sospiri* (*Bridge of Sighs*, 1921), praised for its perfect reproduction of the Venetian setting and starring the beautiful and scantily-clad Antonietta Calderari, who had become famous in the plots à la Grand-Guignol produced by Aquila Film, specializing in titles like *Sua maestà il sangue* and *Il suicida n. 359*. The text was written by Valentino Soldani, the author of historical dramas in the style of Benelli with a particular focus on the history of Florence. The film was overseen by a prestigious scientific committee, but in spite of the fact that Isidoro Del Lungo—a major Dante scholar in his day, working with Corrado Ricci—and the poet's biographer Giuseppe Lando Passerini were involved in it, it did not achieve the results that had been hoped for. However, the Dantesque city created on site with its entrance on Via delle Panche, designed by the architect Giuseppe Castellucci (to whom was due the reconstruction of the Casa di Dante at Torre della Castagna in 1911), was truly impressive, in that a huge effort had been made to closely adhere to the original models and iconography. Ugo Ojetti discussed the visual impact of that production in his brilliant article "Le case di Dante a Rifredi,"[23] where he describes his descent from the Medici Villa in Careggi and suddenly seeing the enchanted city looming up before him. The painter and art director Carlo Bonafedi gave him a tour of it and emphasized a very important element in the

amministrazione
scenograf[i]

The Rifredi studios in
Via delle Panche in
Florence, 1926

relationship between European and American cinema: Italian homegrown epic film, even during a time of severe crisis in production, could count on a group of artisans whose work was truly amazing. "He praised the ability of the Florentines to build a marble temple in four days, craft a throne in a half an hour, a diadem in fifteen minutes, the wings of an angel in five."[24] It was on the set for the Dante film that Giovanni Del Lungo, Isidoro's son, took his first steps in cinema: he would play an important role as a translator of Hollywood movies into Italian, working for MGM in Rome for many years.

Although the success of Caramba's and Gaido's films was limited, the Americans clearly understood the cinematographic potential of the *Divine Comedy*, which resulted at first in the sumptuous *Dante's*

Inferno directed by Henry Otto (1924). The movie tells the story of a ruthless businessman who is responsible for his rival's suicide and is punished for it in hell. Worthwhile noting in this movie are the hell's circles with many nude or scantily-clad figures moving around in a frenzy in the fiery lakes in the background. The results were so effective that in 1980 Ken Russell borrowed from the movie to create some of the most "altered" scenes in *Altered States*. Ten years later, *Dante's Inferno* (1934) directed by Harry Lachman was set in an amusement park with a Dantesque theme, starring a lovely, triumphant sixteen-year-old Rita Hayworth.

After the Dantesque movie, the American studios began eyeing the Florentine V.I.S. plant that offered highly qualified skilled workers. *Marco Visconti*, V.I.S.'s second production, based on the novel by Tommaso Grossi and directed by Aldo De Benedetti, was started by Montalbano in 1922 but didn't reach the movie theaters until 1926 after a series of problems and complications. All the same, it made clear that in Florence the connection between history and cinema offered a high-level staff. This is why, in 1924, Inspiration Movies was established in the city; it was a production company in MGM's orbit that would ensure the distribution of the movies that were being made. The attitude of the American directors toward Renaissance subjects was ambivalent: what interested them was what could easily be reduced to melodrama, so when the projects had too many complex symbolic implications, they were kindly returned to the sender. Gabriele d'Annunzio sought in vain to sell to David W. Griffith the subject of *L'uomo che rubò la Gioconda*, loosely inspired by the 1911 theft at the Louvre. This highly complex work was actually linked to an intricate metaphysical event focused on Gian Giuseppe Vermeer, "the man who lost his gaze" on a beautiful altar table. D'Annunzio's son Veniero wrote to his brother Gabriellino from New York to inform him of the director's opinion: "he greatly feared that the grotesque could not be avoided; in conclusion, he asked me to leave the story with him another ten days. He said he was studying new photographic procedures that would be of great help in overcoming difficulties." However, the project never got off the ground.[25]

The celebrated *Romola* (1924) starred Lillian Gish along with her sister Dorothy, Ronald Colman and William Powell. Its director Henry King had just enjoyed the success of *The White Sister*, a love and death melodrama based on the novel by the Italian-American Francis Marion Crawford. Shot in Italy and set with a stunning eruption of Vesuvius in the background, it featured Lillian Gish in the main role. Wrapped in the white veils of a nun, she had been a hit. The actress was always identified with the role of the innocent in Griffith's masterpieces, so much so that by 1924 her character was inescapably related to a past, Victorian, moral vision, while by that time Hollywood wanted wild flappers who drank, kissed like the French, and danced the Charleston the way Clara Bow, Joan Crawford, and Viola Dana did on the silver screen. Aware of the need to renew her role, Miss Gish started interpreting romantic heroines, innocent yet intrepid, all the way to *La Bohème* (from Murger and Puccini, 1926), in which King Vidor placed

a special emphasis on her alongside John Gilbert. She arrived in Florence after attempting, to no avail, to make a *Romeo and Juliet* set in Verona: the producers couldn't envision it being a box-office success so they suggested another subject, *Romola*, a magnificent novel by George Eliot set in Renaissance Florence, which Mario Caserini had already brought to silver screen in 1911 (starring Maria Gasparini and Amleto Novelli; only one copy is preserved, at the BFI in London, and little else remains). The V.I.S. studios were perfect for *Romola* because they were so close to the places described in the plot, but most importantly because of the skilled workers who managed to build a parallel Florence, often reusing materials from the Dante film that many of the artisan-builders and stand-ins had also been involved in. Miss Gish, starring in the movie along with her sister Dorothy, who was effective in the comic role of Tessa, arrived in the city with her mother. Though the local press said hardly anything about their presence, contacts with the local artistic environment were numerous. The sisters had rather different

Film stills from *Dante nella vita dei tempi suoi*, directed by Domenico Gaido in 1921 at the V.I.S. studios in Rifredi

Lillian Gish in one of
the final scenes in *The White
Sister*, directed by Henry
King in 1923; the film was
shot in Italy

personalities: Dorothy was a party girl while Lillian was more reserved and devoted to helping their mother who was ill. The last time they had starred together under Griffith's direction was in *Orphans of the Storm* (1921), adapted from Dickens's *Tale of Two Cities*—a high point up to then in their collaboration with their mentor. In the meantime, Griffith had begun a less felicitous work relation with his new discovery, the trained dancer Carol Dempster who, in 1919 in New York, had performed a *Dance of Life and Death* before the first screening of *Broken Blossoms*.[26]

At the very start of *Romola*, a caption stood out categorically stating that "the historical veracity of this production is confirmed by Guido Biagi, director of the Biblioteca Medicea Laurenziana." This prolific scholar and writer, who had close ties to the Florentine English-speaking community, is due a vast historical introduction to the novel in the Fisher Unwin edition of 1907. Biagi wrote many successful books featuring a conspicuous iconography, such as *The Private Life of the Renaissance*

Florentines (1896) and *La Renaissance en Italie* (1913). King used these materials as a basis for the painstaking reconstruction of scenes, costumes, and hairstyles. Miss Gish herself was a museum-goer, with a passion for the clothes designed by Mariano Fortuny (there is a famous picture of her in a *Delphos* dress); furthermore, she carried with her a precious viaticum for her Renaissance adventure: a dried rose blossom from Eleonora Duse's funeral garland preserved in a small box decorated with Botticelli's Graces.[27] The work for the movie was intense and the results were of great aesthetic coherence. Despite the fact that the film was a success both in Europe and the United States, in her memoirs Lillian expressed some reservations, making comparisons with her luminous Griffithian past. In any case, in her book Gish proudly describes the positive opinion of Firmin Gémier, founder of the theater direction in France, and that of the austere Giovanni Poggi, director of the Uffizi, whose words to the press were: "in the movie *Romola*, the main and secondary characters, as well as the choral scenes, were studied as painstakingly as possible."[28] Much later, when he was at the peak of his success thanks to *The Thin Man*, William Powell left a detailed account of the work in Florence[29] as did King himself, referring to the studios with words of great admiration and above all expressing appreciation for the remarkable team of artisans at the service of production under the supervision of the art director Robert Haas. The latter had also overseen, at the Neri construction site in Livorno, the creation of two galleys named *Liliana* and *Dorothea*, in tribute to the actresses. "In *Romola* we tried to reproduce Palazzo Davanzati, we made a perfect plaster replica with all the details, as though it were a mask . . . On the grounds around the studio we reconstructed fifteenth-century Florence. One of the buildings, the Cathedral, was over eighty-three meters in height. I also filmed with the real Cathedral and Campanile in the background and nobody could tell the difference."[30] *Romola*, therefore, from the

Some of the scenes
from *Romola* shot
in Florence and in the
Rifredi film studios
Gemona, La Cineteca
del Friuli

Lillian Gish as Romola
in the eponymous film, 1924

point of view of the reconstruction of a Renaissance setting, is a chapter in what we might refer to as "Davanzatimania," which was so rich in developments in the United States. The famous Palazzo Davanzati, reconstructed by the antiquarian Elia Volpi and inaugurated, after much discussion, in 1910, touched the hearts of those traveling across the ocean, who saw a visit to this refurbished medieval Florentine home as being a cultural necessity. The artisans who had decorated the rooms were called to the United States to reproduce their frescoes. The brothers Alberto and Federigo Angeli, specialized in "copies of primitives," were summoned by the architect and interior decorator Addison Mitzner to reproduce the Davanzati decorations in Palm Beach, at Villa La Guardiola (later named Playa Riente), the residence of the Cosden family, in a triumph of trees, birds, and orchards. The triumphal "parrot room" they created ended up directly in the pages of such prestigious magazines as *Vogue* and *Town & Country*. Traces of this Neo-Renaissance taste, supported by the magazine *Architectural Record*, are frequently seen in the United States: suffice to recall the East Room at the Morgan Library in New York, or the immense Ca' d'Zan of John Ringling in Sarasota, which also contains an illustrious painting gallery. Not to mention William Randolph Hearst and Marion Davies's castle in San Simeon, truly a triumph of eclecticism, with one room borrowed from a castle in Ireland and another one from a Venetian palazzo, with numerous nods to the Renaissance including a copy of Donatello's *David* positioned like a plume atop a fountain.[31] The very idea of a castle with rooms in period style was typical in the United States in the 1920s. In Beverly Hills, Harold Lloyd owned a villa in Renaissance style with many of the rooms decorated to look like movie sets. Alberto Rabagliati, who visited that wonderland after winning the Fox competition, described it as follows: "if the park is marvelous, the inside of the castle is superlative. Although Harold would prefer a lift, his castle has only a small dumbwaiter for domestic use. The inside is a sequence of rooms, inside each of which the ceiling and the floor are a fitting frame to the very precious artistic furniture."[32]

Despite *Romola*'s success, the V.I.S. studios still did not attract American productions—actually, they declined steadily from that moment onwards. However, in the following years Amleto Palermi made two comedies in Rifredi, *L'uomo più allegro di Vienna* (1925) and *Florette e Patapon* (1927); in the meantime, in 1926, the plants had become the property of the I.C.S.A. company. And in 1928, *Boccaccesca* by Alfredo De Antoni was a success starring Elena Sangro, whom d'Annunzio was very fond of and to whom he devoted the erotically-charged cine-poem *Alla piacente*. Also working there, at the height of his mystic fervor, was Giulio Antamoro, director of *Frate Francesco* (1927), which was appreciated for its setting and costumes; many of the staff members had previously worked on *Romola*. Antamoro would also be the tenacious artificer of the box-office flop *Antonio da Padova* (1931), a silent film that for some strange reason was released when sound was all the rage. But it was pitilessly panned by the press and the ten-year history of the Rifredi studios, which had experienced with *Romola* a moment of true glory, came to an end. Henry King returned to Tuscany after the war, in 1948, when on the outskirts of Florence a project (never realized) was announced to relaunch the cinematographic vocation of the city through Studi Sant'Angelo, planned for somewhere between Florence and Prato with a project overseen by architect Italo Gamberini. In San Gimignano, renamed Città del Monte, in 1949 King filmed a part of *Prince of Foxes*.[33] Once again in the interviews he gave he praised the professionalism of the Tuscan artisans involved in making the movie, as well as of the numerous stand-ins. The film was highly successful; Orson Welles's hypnotic performance as Cesare Borgia, also known as "the Valentino," got rave reviews. The outcome was positive, proof of this being that soon afterwards Mitchell Leisen returned to the Borgia subject with the improbable *Bride of Vengeance* (1949).

The philological reconstruction conducted by King had a by-product in the United States: for a certain period of time, Lillian Gish as Romola became the heroine of a Neo-Renaissance line in art. Indeed, her face was on the cover of various new editions of George Eliot's book—either photographs or illustrations. After *Romola*, a number of Slavic émigré artists also asked her to pose for them. They were

Nicolai Fechin, *Lillian Gish as Romola*, 1925
Oil on canvas, 125.1 x 114.9 cm
Private collection

Arturo Martini, *Portrait of Lillian Gish*, 1929
Terracotta, 29 x 31 x 23 cm
Venice, Galleria Internazionale
d'Arte Moderna di Ca' Pesaro,
inv. 2173

Paolo Troubetzkoy,
Mary Pickford, 1919–20
Plaster, 45 x 35 x 26 cm
Verbania, Museo del Paesaggio,
inv. T307

LA DOMENICA DEL CORRIERE

Anno XXVIII — N. 45.   7 Novembre 1926.   Centesimi 30 la copia.

Alla ricerca degli eredi di Rodolfo Valentino e delle rivali di Maria Pickford.
La sfilata dei partecipanti milanesi - giovanotti e signorine - al concorso bandito da una Casa cinematografica
americana, per scegliere bellezze italiane da inviare a Hollywood. Disegno di A. Beltrame.

trying to restore in America some aspects of their work in Russia in the days of *Mir iskusstva* and of the "dekadent" artists, with references to Slavic folklore, to Far Eastern influences, to the eighteenth-century erotic feasts of Catherine of Russia and of Marie Antoinette, and to Italy. Gleb Derujinski portrayed the actress in a bust that was reminiscent of Rossellino; the Lithuanian Boris Lovet-Lorski reinterpreted the Renaissance legacy in an Art Deco key; while Nicolai Fechin, who had become famous for his images of Native Americans, portrayed her on canvas wearing the lavender dress she had worn in the movie (or in any case similar to one of her costumes), with a fresco "in Davanzati style" behind her, a quill pen in her hand, and a large codex in her lap. This "classical" note stands out in the repertoire of the portraits of divas, which are usually more closely related to a "Parisian" key, such as the many paintings by the Polish-American artist Tade Styka who was especially known for his Boldini-inspired portraits of his fellow citizen Pola Negri. In short, as an Italian female viewer categorically declared in a survey conducted by the magazine *Kines* in 1931, "today the world sees feminine beauty through different eyes. If Leonardo were to come back and had to choose a female model, he would not hesitate between Mona Lisa and Bebe Daniels."[34] Lillian Gish, an outsider diva, perfectly embodied this idea, offering herself as the new icon of the electric Renaissance. Although he had never met her personally, in 1929 Arturo Martini created in her honor a magnificent terracotta portrait (later recast in bronze), of which there is a copy in the Ca' Pesaro collection in Venice. Martini, who followed cinema,[35] described the actress (whom he had especially appreciated in *Broken Blossoms*) as "the greatest romantic dream of the cinematographer."[36] Cesare Pavese accurately described the enthusiasm for Hollywood divas in provincial Italy in the 1920s. His early short story "Arcadia," written in 1929, contains

"In search of heirs to Rudolph
Valentino and the rivals of
Mary Pickford," cover of
La Domenica del Corriere,
November 7, 1926

daily excursions to the movies and describes an erotic relationship with the silver screen.[37] The same dynamics can be found in his screenplay for the never realized *Breve libertà*, set in Turin in the 1920s, where the characters "go to the movies, go out (to the amusement park?), and the girls pay."[38] When he was still in secondary school, the young writer fell in love with Lillian Gish: he wrote letters to her (which were probably never sent) in stilted English, declaring his absolute love for her, ending one of them with these words: "if you are fond of art, my dream of speaking about it with you will perhaps become reality."[39]

In the city of cinema, among other things the actors were open to the offers they received from European artists who wanted to portray them in busts and sculptures in classical style. Paolo Troubetzkoy, a talented sculptor who was very close, by way of his family and his art, to international high society, had a studio in Hollywood between 1919 and 1920, at the time when he was creating the impressive monument to General Otis. The Museo del Paesaggio in Verbania, which preserves his casts, owns two stunning portraits, one of Mary Pickford at the peak of her success (by the way, the artist had also made a portrait of Douglas Fairbanks) and the other of the Japanese Sessue Hayakawa wearing a kimono: at the time he was the most popular Far Eastern actor by far, with a huge following in Hollywood.[40] An art enthusiast, Hayakawa enjoyed using the traditional artistic techniques of his native country, which he made known to American movie-goers in the magnificent film *The Dragon Painter* by William Worthington (1919), the lyrical story of a visionary village painter who dreamed about finding his bride turned into a dragon.

With huge investments in propaganda, it didn't take long for the Hollywood stardom to find a way to celebrate its most clamorous feasts in Europe, imposing itself over the course of the 1920s, that is,

before the nationalist regimes began to instead prefer homegrown stars, in some cases explicitly excluding American actors for political reasons. From 1923 onwards in Europe, once the war had ended, the revolutions had been terminated, and the new governments had taken office, the increasingly intensive promotion of Hollywood also took on the aspect, for many of the stars, of a cultural Grand Tour. This was especially the case for promotional tours in Italy, where the artistic cities played a central role, and Rome above them all: with its symbolic charge and the presence of the Pope, the City of Dreams was enchanting the Hollywood people. They were also particularly interested the new dictator, Benito Mussolini, who even had a cameo role in *The Eternal City*, directed by George Fitzmaurice in 1923. During those same years, Rudolph Valentino arrived in Italy on a study trip, which he described in a diary that was published many years after his death. His presence was strictly private: by his side was his wife Natacha Rambova, a highly talented set and costume designer (suffice to see the work she did for *Camille* and *Salomè* with Alla Nazimova); she unfortunately became unpopular after the failure of *Monsieur Beaucaire* (1924) and was forbidden to set foot on the set. The itinerary they chose was based on what they wanted to learn about. Valentino would have loved to visit the Castello di Vincigliata, a place that is in many ways the model for Palazzo Davanzati and very dear to American tourists, as Henry James had explained in *Italian Hours* in 1909. The castle was then the property of Alberto Fassini, an admiral and an entrepreneur in the textile sector who had directed Cines for ten years and had grown into an important figure in public affairs during the fascist regime.[41] For the actor the place was "very, very ancient, built over its original ruins from the eleventh century." Valentino and his wife were very disappointed that they hadn't been able to visit it, and especially that they hadn't been able to admire the collection hosted in it: "Here the eye becomes lost in the painting when it is sublime to such a degree, endowed with lines so pure that they take your breath away. It would have been an orgy of art."[42] In Florence, where the star hoped to return with more time to visit, the couple only stayed a few days. Besides taking walks (also close to Palazzo Spini Feroni: "the famous painting of the meeting between Dante and Beatrice reproduces this very place"[43]), Valentino bought an endless number of books, including a not better identified "sixteenth-century book with models for the Oriental costumes in that period."[44] The two of them were categorical: "in cinema, where we are required to re-evoke periods that are hardly frequented, having

Dolores Del Río
photographed in Venice
during her trip to Italy,
published in *Gazzettino
Illustrato*, September
30, 1928

Douglas Fairbanks and
his wife Mary Pickford
photographed in Rome in
1926 while touring Italy

The cover of the magazine
Piccola dedicated to Greta
Garbo's trip to Milan,
May 12, 1931

ANNO IV - N. 19 - 12 MAGGIO 1931 - IX
CENTESIMI 40 - ARRETRATI IL DOPPIO

PICCOLA

GRETA GARBO È A MILANO ? - VEDI LA NOSTRA INCHIESTA PARTICOLARE A PAGG. 6-7

"... E SI FERMA DINANZI AL DUOMO, ESTATICA ..."

a collection of books of this type is of invaluable importance."[45]

1926 was the year of Hollywood stardom's triumph in Italy. On November 7, on the cover of the *Domenica del Corriere* was a drawing by Achille Beltrame publicizing a contest for new stars organized by an American production company. The caption read: "In search of heirs to Rudolph Valentino and the rivals of Mary Pickford." That same year, in the spring, the lady had gone on a triumphal tour of Italy with her husband, Douglas Fairbanks. The trip, organized in detail by United Artists, began in Genoa, then Montecatini, where they arrived by train on April 13: Renzo Martinelli, a journalist of *La Nazione*, was waiting impatiently at the train station, and when finally the train arrived: "That's Mary Pickford? A child. A plaything. We almost stepped on her and hadn't noticed . . . The filmmaker sure has some tricks up his sleeve."[46] As always, seen from up close, the stars looked more homegrown, even though they arrived with an amazing retinue. If their welcome in Montecatini was lavish, in Florence it turned into a veritable triumph.[47] Indeed, the couple arrived with a procession of cars; the first stop was in Via Magliabechi, at the seat of the ancient Guilds of Florence, alongside the "royal family" (so referred to by the press) and with Odoardo Spadaro doing the translating. The monarchy of the imagination was by that time what Hollywood forced on the world. Reunited all around was a crowd that waited for the epiphany of the golden couple, listening to the music played by a small orchestra that alternated the American national anthem and *Giovinezza*. This was followed by a reception at the Palagio di Parte Guelfa, and then the screening of *Don Q, Son of Zorro* (where Fairbanks had the lead role with Mary Astor) at Supercinema, which was inaugurated for the occasion after the restoration work carried out by Piero Caliterna, Giorgio Neumann, and Ezio Zalaffi on the pre-existing structure designed by architect Luigi Bellincioni. The couple was struck, as reported in many interviews, by the presence of a movie theater in the heart of the medieval city, near the house where Dante had lived.[48] In short, it was the triumph of the modern surrounded by antiquity. In the official speeches that were given there was a constant resounding of "God save the Duce," a repetition motivated by the recent attempt by the Irish woman Violet Gibson to murder Mussolini. The following days, the newspapers were filled with interviews and comments with every single detail about the famous couple's visit. It was the same in Rome on the following days, although the Pope chose not to receive them because they were both divorced. Mussolini, on his part, was hard to get, though he eventually granted them a brief meeting and two signed pictures.[49] This trip established the central role of the Hollywood production system, which had taken hold of the Italian imagination; but this absolute dominion did not last long. As early as 1928, when the regime had reorganized Italy's productive forces and the nation's "renaissance" was about to begin, the welcome that the Mexican actress Dolores Del Río was given at the Supercinema was rather different. The actress was on tour in Italy along with the director of *Ramona* Edwin Carewe, who had launched her in *Joanna* (1925). When they passed through Florence, only a small advertising message was published in *La Nazione* on September 29: "the interpreter and the director of *Resurrezione* will honor the gala show this evening with their presence." In the early 1930s, Gary Cooper often went to Rome for personal reasons—a love affair. The actor bought his clothes at Caraceni and visited the museums and monuments. In 1931 a crowd welcomed Charlie Chaplin in Venice. During the following years, there were many actors on tour to present films or for personal trips; the Mostra del Cinema was, of course, an important runway, but the fascist propaganda continued to insist on homegrown actors. In the final, harsh phase of the fascist regime, the 600 days of the Repubblica di Salò, they decidedly and openly chose to denigrate Hollywood. In 1943 Marco Ramperti published in *Primi Piani* an incredible "Alfabeto delle stelle morte,"[50] where he panned all the Hollywood celebrities—a group of Jews, Communists, and homosexuals, all of them decadent or corrupt. The new fascist guidelines needed to establish an aesthetic canon in which Mussolini's Italy and the country's noble traditions had to be in unison, finding in the past an immediate reflection of the present. Unsurprisingly, many films with sound of these years celebrated the Renaissance, with works of diverse intensity such as *Condottieri* by Luis Trenker (1937) or *Sei bambine e il Perseo* by Giovacchino Forzano (1939).

[1] William C. DeMille, *Letter to Cecil*, September 3, 1913, quoted in Sumiko Higashi, "Cecil B. DeMille and the Lasky Company: Legitimating Feature Film as Art Author(s)," in *Film History* 3 (1990): 181–97: 181.

[2] On the theme of the "black nights" see Sergio Toffetti, "La scena primitiva," in *La fiamma del peccato. L'eros nel cinema muto*, ed. by Elisabetta Bruscolini, Angela Prudenzi, and Sergio Toffetti (Turin: Lindau, 1997), 17 and Gian Piero Brunetta, *Il cinema muto italiano* (Bari and Rome: Laterza, 2008), 110.

[3] See Riccardo Redi, "Film erotici del muto," in *La fiamma del peccato* 1997, 43–46.

[4] Ethel Barrymore, "Un grande poeta del teatro ha lasciato per sempre questa nostra famiglia," in *Il Dramma*, January 15, 1950, 22.

[5] Antonio Gramsci, "In principio era il sesso," originally published in *Ordine Nuovo*, February 16, 1917, then in *Letteratura e vita nazionale* (Turin: Einaudi, 1954), 274.

[6] An analytical reconstruction of the filming of *La gorgona* and of the collaboration between Benelli and the screenwriter Arrigo Frusta is in Silvio Alovisio, *Voci del silenzio. La sceneggiatura nel cinema muto italiano* (Turin: Museo Nazionale del Cinema and Milan: Il Castoro, 2005), 318–27. Arrigo Frusta recalled these events in "I ricordi di uno della pellicola," in *Bianco e Nero*, July–August 1952, 31–39.

[7] For an overview see *Immagini del silenzio. L'avventurosa storia del cinema muto torinese*, ed. by Roberta Basano and Gianna Chiapello (Turin: Museo Nazionale del Cinema, 2006).

[8] Gabriele d'Annunzio, *Cabiria* (Turin: Stabilimento Tipo-Litografico Toffaloni, 1914), 5.

[9] See Luca Scarlini, *D'Annunzio a Little Italy* (Rome: Donzelli, 2008).

[10] Arnaldo Frateili, "Grandezza e decadenza del cinema romano," in *Scenario*, May 1933, now in Eugenio Ferdinando Palmieri, *Vecchio cinema italiano* (Vicenza: Neri Pozza, 1994), 190–92.

[11] Bruno Barilli, "Tempi muti," in *Star*, December 9, 1944, now in *Lo spettatore stralunato* (Parma: Pratiche, 1982), 26–28.

[12] Guido Gozzano's writings on cinema are now in *La sceneggiatura del San Francesco e altri scritti*, ed. by Mauro Sarnelli (Anzio: De Rubeis, 1996); the short stories mentioned are on pages 181–90 and 171–80.

[13] On Panzini see Sergio Raffaelli, "Alfredo Panzini titolista per *Gli ultimi giorni di Pompei*," in Id., *L'italiano nel cinema muto* (Florence: Franco Cesati Editore, 2003), 133–48.

[14] See Palmieri, *Vecchio cinema italiano* 1994, 25.

[15] On Gemma Bellincioni see Giuliana Bruno, *Rovine con vista. Alla ricerca del cinema perduto di Elvira Notari*, ed. by Maria Nadotti (Milan: La Tartaruga, 1995), 120–22. The singer left behind an autobiography offering a great deal of information on gestures and expressions on the stage: Gemma Bellincioni, *Io e il palcoscenico. Trenta e un anno di vita artistica* (Milan: Quintieri, 1920).

[16] Francesca Bertini, *Il resto non conta* (Pisa: Giardini, 1969), 127.

[17] Lucio D'Ambra, *Gli anni della feluca*, ed. by Giovanni Grazzini (Rome: Lucarini, 1987), 166–67. The author remembers how Luigi Pirandello, his neighbor, helped him in the mad dash to write it; Pirandello then had to turn *Le confessioni di un ottuagenario* into a script in a week's time. Buti t was never performed.

[18] Alberto Savinio, "Sul cinematografo" (1924), in Gian Piero Brunetta, *Spari nel buio. La letteratura contro il cinema italiano: settant'anni di stroncature memorabili* (Venice: Marsilio, 1994), 49–52.

[19] See *La Commedia dipinta: i concorsi Alinari e il simbolismo in Toscana*, ed. by Carlo Sisi (Florence: Alinari, 2002).

[20] On Dante in the silent movies see Aldo Bernardini, "I film dall'Inferno dantesco nel cinema muto italiano," in *Dante nel cinema*, ed. by Gianfranco Casadio (Ravenna: Longo Editore, 1996), 29–33. The advertising in verse by Teodoro Rovito, "La divina visione," appeared in *Lux*, October 30, 1905; now in Raffaelli, *L'italiano nel cinema muto* 2003, 191–93.

[21] Vittoria Crespi Morbio, *Caramba Mago del costume* (Milan: Amici della Scala, 2008), 31.

[22] For a reconstruction of the activities of the studios in Rifredi, which went through troubled times, see Gaetano Strazzulla, "Il kolossal negli anni venti. Gli stabilimenti di Rifredi," in *La Toscana e il cinema*, ed. by Luca Giannelli (Florence: Banca Toscana, 1994), 174–87; Stefano Beccastrini, *Una valle sullo schermo* (Florence: Aska, 2015), 94 ff. See also the essay by Gianni Isola, "Alle origini del cinema italiano. L'effimera avventura di Giovanni Faraglia, mancato produttore fiorentino," in *Archivio Fiorentino* 2 (1998): 219–26.

[23] Ugo Ojetti, "Le case di Dante a Rifredi," in *Corriere della Sera*, December 10, 1921, now in *Cose viste* (Florence: Sansoni, 1951), vol. 1, 28–30.

[24] Ibid.

[25] The letter written by Veniero d'Annunzio to his brother Gabriellino is mentioned in Irene Gambacorti, *Storie di cinema e letteratura. Verga, Gozzano, D'Annunzio* (Florence: SEF, 2003), 277. The screenplay for *L'uomo che rubò la Gioconda* is in Valentina Valentini, *Un fanciullo delicato e forte. Il cinema di Gabriele D'Annunzio* (Rome: Biblioteca del Vascello, 1995), 89–118.

[26] For a reconstruction of the complex relationship between Lillian and Dorothy Gish and David W. Griffith see Stuart Oderman, *Lillian Gish: A Life on Stage and Screen* (Jefferson and London: McFarland& Company, 2000), especially chapter 11.

[27] Lillian Gish with Anne Pinchot, *The Movies, Mr Griffith and Me* (London: Columbus Books, 1988), 257.

[28] Ibid., 264.

[29] William Powell, "L'Italia e il successo," in *Cinema*, November 30, 1937, 294–95.

[30] Henry King, *Henry King Director. From Silents to Scope*, based on interviews with David Shepard and Ted Perry, ed. by Frank Thompson (Hollywood: Directors Guild of America, 1996), 59-61.

[31] See Roberta Ferrazza, *The Allure of the Florentine Style in the United States*, in *1927 The Return to Italy. Salvatore Ferragamo and Twentieth-century Visual Culture*, ed. by Stefania Ricci and Carlo Sisi (Milan: Skira, 2017), 37–54; see also *Federigo e la bottega degli Angeli, Palazzo Davanzati tra realtà e sogno*, ed. by Caterina Proto Pisani and Francesca Baldry (Livorno: Sillabe, 2009).

[32] Alberto Rabagliati, *Quattro anni fra le "Stelle." Aneddoti e impressioni*, ed. by Denis Lotti (Cuneo: Nerosubianco edizioni, 2017), 42.

[33] On *Prince of Foxes* starring Tyrone Power and Orson Welles, scenes by Elso Valentini (not credited) and costumes by Vittorio Nino Novarese, see Giovanni Bogani, *Good Morning San Gimignano. Il cinema tra le torri* (Municipality of San Gimignano, 1994), 53–62.

[34] Mentioned in Gian Piero Brunetta, *Il ruggito del leone. Hollywood alla conquista dell'impero dei sogni nell'Italia di Mussolini* (Venice: Marsilio, 2013), 102–03.

[35] In 1919 Martini collaborated with Elettra Raggio on the production of the film with an Oriental subject *San-Zurka-San*. See Elena Pontiggia, *Arturo Martini. La vita in figure* (Monza: Johan & Levi, 2017), 93.

[36] Gino Scarpa, *Colloqui con Arturo Martini*, ed. by Maria and Natale Mazzola, introduction by Guido Piovene (Milan: Rizzoli, 1968), 243.

[37] Cesare Pavese, "Arcadia," in *Lotte di giovani e altri racconti (1925–1930)*, ed. by Mariarosa Masoero (Turin: Einaudi, 1993), 121–54.

[38] Cesare Pavese, "Breve libertà," in *Cinema Nuovo* 141 (1959): 397.

[39] See Brunetta, *Il ruggito del leone* 2013, 215–16.

[40] On Troubetzkoy's period in Hollywood see Federica Rabai and Roberto Troubetzkoy Hahn, *Paolo Troubetzkoy* (Verbania: Museo del Paesaggio, 2017), 184–87.

[41] A description of Alberto Fassini is in Riccardo Redi, *La Cines. Storia di una società di produzione italiana* (Rome: CNC, 1991), 25–29.

[42] Rodolfo Valentino, *Il mio diario privato*, ed. by Paolo Orlandelli (Lindau: Turin, 2004), 135.

[43] Ibid.

[44] Ibid., 139.

[45] Ibid.

[46] Renzo Martinelli, "Mary Pickford e Douglas Fairbanks visti a occhio nudo," in *La Nazione*, April 13, 1926.

[47] "Douglas Fairbanks e Mary Pickford a Firenze," in *La Nazione*, April 23, 1926.

[48] On Supercinema see the entry by Federica Fazzuoli in *Buio in sala. Architettura del cinema in Toscana*, ed. by Maria Adriana Giusti and Susanna Caccia (Florence: Maschietto Editore, 2007), 174.

[49] For a reconstruction of the couple's trip to Italy see Lorenzo Quaglietti, *Ecco i nostri. L'invasione del cinema americano in Italia* (Rome: ERI, 1991), 41–45.

[50] Marco Ramperti, "Alfabeto delle stelle morte," in *Primi Piani* 18 (April 1943), now in Brunetta, *Il ruggito del leone* 2013, 117.

CARLO SISI

ROMOLA. A SET FOR THE IMAGE OF FLORENCE

A photograph from the set of *Romola* offers much food for thought with regard to the context in which the crew of this challenging film found themselves operating in 1924, along the banks of the River Arno. These were years in which the turn made by the avant-garde and by modern spirits was marking a break with revivalist tendencies—in the figurative arts as well as in the development of taste more generally. Yet in Florence these tendencies continued to show a certain endurance, fueled by a desire to keep alive the city's Renaissance matrix and its legendary aura.[1] On the one hand, the drive for progress favored the overcoming of historicism and of the Symbolist legacy that had survived into the post-war period, in an attempt to shape new cultural trends in the city and the very geography of its urban fabric. On the other hand, the old image of Florence, which had "charmed sentimental travelers," proved particularly resilient, as it continued to draw tourists and visitors interested in arts and craftsmanship—the distinctive and sought-for features of a highly evocative city prone to being romantically transfigured.

During her sojourns in Florence, in 1849 and 1861, George Eliot was consciously fulfilling a dream—or even vow—with regard to a destination she had long yearned for. The city not only lived up to her expectations, but conveyed certain civil and religious values that inspired the idea of a historical novel. This focused on the tragic story of Girolamo Savonarola, while at the same time encapsulating Eliot's personal experience of Florence and its monuments, which she visited in search of Giotto and Beato Angelico, Orcagna and Masaccio. In *Romola*, the image of the city, still largely untouched by Savoy building work, intertwines with the atmosphere and leading figures from the Medici period. The novelist had first come across them in the books from the Magliabechiana Library, which her keen husband had consulted for her, spending entire days poring over Rastrelli and Del Migliore's guides, the *Malmantile*, the *Istorie fiorentine* by Cavalcanti and Nerli, the *Mandragola* and *Calandra*, Agostino Ademollo's *Marietta de' Ricci*, Giulio Ferrario's *Costume antico e moderno*, and the more recent *Vita di Savonarola* by Pasquale Villari.[2] This varied and highly significant anthology illustrates the kind of preliminary research that is usually undertaken by a writer of historical novels interested in records of events and descriptions of everyday customs, practices, and linguistic features: elements required in order to evoke settings for the characters to whom George Eliot lends a modern sensibility. The "screenplay" she provided was skillfully adapted by Henry King to a film equally committed to translating available documentary evidence into images, so as to bring the narrative as close to historical reality as possible.[3]

The production process was lengthy and challenging. Supplementary research tasks were assigned to Guido Biagi, the director of the Laurentian Library. He provided a crucial contribution to the weaving of a visual narrative that sought

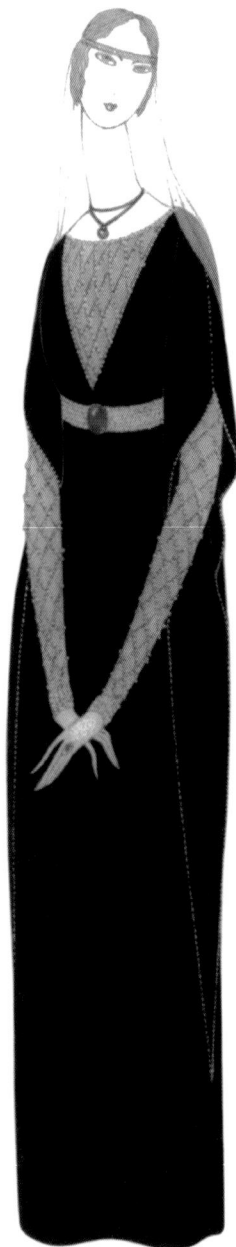

to demonstrate to what great pains the producers had gone to reconstruct buildings and interiors akin to those one could visit in the city—adorned with furniture, tapestries, and paintings purchased from antiquarians, and decorated with frescoes faithfully painted after late-fifteenth century ones.[4] Even the costumes were carefully reproduced by Florentine tailors, and were often matched with original jewelry perfectly in line with the kind of taste developed in the Pre-Raphaelite milieu and further refined through Gabriele d'Annunzio's aesthetic research: a taste that looked to the Renaissance as a period of perfect harmony in which the work of man—in all its forms—had attained excellence. The photograph portraying Lillian Gish against the background of Sandro Botticelli's *Madonna Adoring the Child*, now in the Baltimore Museum of Art, illustrates the endurance of this aesthetic legacy in twentieth-century sensibility by drawing a parallel between the actress's neo-Renaissance attire and the fifteenth-century artist. After his rediscovery through Herbert Horne's studies,[5] Botticelli had awoken an almost feverish interest in that kind of painting, dense with unexpected lyrical and sensuous harmonies and capable of evoking intriguing analogies with the modern aspiration to turn toward the past as a haven for an imagination threatened by the shackles of everyday practical concerns. By comparing another photographic portrait of the actress to one of the famous faux-Renaissance busts by Giovanni Bastianini,[6] we can further appreciate how the historicist taste endured well into the twentieth century, and with it the capacity to create masquerades—with the utmost attention to detail—replete with literary references. These may be regarded as the final expression of an aesthetic sensibility that is rooted in the Symbolist atmosphere of the late nineteenth century and that extended into the following century through the evocative resources made available by the new storytelling industry.

In a loggia brightened up by spring flowers, the actors, sporting fifteenth-century costumes, are having a chat during tea break. Whether consciously or not—but at any rate betraying a visual training based on refined models—the photograph provides a further, elegant illustration of present-day appearances and habits against the backdrop of a magnificent past that is yearned for and relived in all of its valuable expressions, particularly by British ex-pats. The visits to the many local museums and churches celebrated in John Ruskin's *Mornings in Florence*, the villas selected as private dwellings with Boccaccio's *Ninfale fiesolano* in mind, the choice to

Design for a fifteenth-century-style dress created for Henry King's *Romola* and worn by the lead actress Lillian Gish

Copy of Sandro Botticelli's
Madonna of the Magnificat,
first–third decade of the
twentieth century
Oil on canvas,
diameter 106 cm
Private collection, Heirs
Bianca Capoquadri Tommasi

Lillian Gish on the set
of *Romola*, 1924. In the
background, Sandro
Botticelli's *Madonna Adoring
the Child*, now in the
Baltimore Museum of Art
Florence, Museo Salvatore
Ferragamo

embrace an aesthetic lifestyle to keep away from the "Circes of industrialism"—these were all practices and goals that, a few years later, would find a coherent expression in cinematographic fiction, through the use of artistic and historical material that had long become entrenched and was ready to be consigned to the "tenth Muse." In the photograph mentioned, the costumes and the skillfully reconstructed setting bear witness to the integration between the new technique and the know-how of craftsmen recruited in order to faithfully reconstruct the atmosphere featured in George Eliot's novel. In its composition, this photographic "conversation piece" is instead strikingly reminiscent of a 1860 painting by Vincenzo Cabianca, *Tuscan Storytellers of the Fourteenth Century*, which in turn expressed the same aspiration to bring the dream of happy bygone eras back to life.

The Macchiaioli group's revolution springs precisely from a renewed focus on historical painting, with subjects drawn from the Middle Ages and key episodes of the Renaissance. These are portrayed, as in Cabianca's work, through an experimental use of lighting that lends a modern touch to costumed figures by placing them under the sky of a modern Florentine spring. Key episodes from the chronicles of the period of tyranny or of the Republic were also selected, illustrating how history could be used to fuel the patriotic ideology of the Risorgimento,[7] even through painted scenes. What come to mind, in this respect, are the kinds of subjects that enjoyed great popularity at the national expositions organized after the Unification of Italy and that widely circulated on the market, riding on the success of historical novels—including Eliot's *Romola.* These works provided figurative renditions of major events that were deemed an effective way of illustrating the continuity of thought rooted in the ethics of republicanism, with its ideal of liberty, and of lending shape to its protagonists and most significant deeds. I like to imagine here that, during the work on the setting for the film and in the impressive workshop space set up to reconstruct the ancient historical center of Florence almost on a 1:1 scale, some paintings belonging to

Left to right, Ronald Colman,
director Henry King, Dorothy
Gish, and Lillian Gish relaxing
during the shooting of *Romola*
in 1924

Vincenzo Cabianca, *Novellieri toscani del XIV secolo* [Tuscan Storytellers of the Fourteenth Century], 1860
Oil on canvas, 78 x 99 cm
Florence, Gallerie degli Uffizi, Galleria d'Arte Moderna, inv. 300

the historical genre helped inspire the set designers. After all, nineteenth-century painters with an academic background were required to have an in-depth knowledge of historical events and period costumes, so as to make their representations as faithful as possible—not unlike novelists or librettists.

It is easy to imagine the functionality of a painting such as Stefano Ussi's *The Execution of Savonarola*, where the massive scaffold cuts off the horizon of the square, with a striking effect; or Raffaello Sorbi's *Corso Donati Kidnaps His Sister Piccarda from the Convent of Santa Chiara*, which conveys gestures and emotions through a perfect dramatic arrangement, while providing a detailed rendition of the clothing and accessories— the very rendition expected of the many craftsmen recruited for the American production of the film. In the articles celebrating this challenging enterprise, which was accomplished in over a year through the use of a colossal set, the authors emphasized the crucial contribution made by Italian craftsmen who had been born and bred in the historic city and therefore had an almost natural ability to revive the Florentine tradition of manufacturing, which in the second half of the nineteenth century had received a new impulse precisely from the presence of foreigners and their taste for the applied arts. The image of Florence was never dissociated from the Gothic or Brunelleschian settings celebrated by Baedeker and that—in different times and hence with various nuances—had become the object of eager exercises in imitation and artistic and literary transfiguration, thereby nourishing the legend of

Photograph taken on the set of *Romola* during the scene of Girolamo Savonarola's execution, 1924
Gemona, La Cineteca del Friuli

Stefano Ussi, *Il supplizio
di Savonarola* [The Execution
of Savonarola], c. 1850
Oil on glass, 30 x 43.5 cm
Florence, Gallerie degli Uffizi,
Galleria d'Arte Moderna, inv. 66

a city alive in the present almost exclusively by virtue of its most noble past. However, what proved equally enduring was the relation between this image and the creative drive circulating in the many craftsmen's and antiquarians' workshops scattered all over the place.[8]

Already in his *Lions*, William Blundell Spence recalled that in the fifteenth century Florence had been "the cradle of all that was great and enlightened" and that the influence of art "was not only felt . . . in the most trivial and everyday article of jewellery, furniture or pottery that was used by the middle and even poorer classes": a perfect civic example of the combination of functionality and beauty, where "a pair of ear-rings, a chest of drawers, a lock and key, a basin or a knocker of those days, were all stamped with a *cachet* of excellence and taste that we are now trying to revive by schools of design and schools of art, academies and museums."[9] On the other hand, the transfiguring prose of the celebrated Ouida, translated in the pages of the *Nuovo Osservatore Fiorentino* in 1885, almost cinematographically extended the work of Florentine craftsmen to the entire cityscape, the *genius loci* of such beauty: "At last my eyes gazed on her!—the daughter of flowers, the mistress of art, the nursing mother of liberty and of aspiration . . . The shops of the goldsmiths, and mosaic sellers, and alabaster workers gleamed and

Lillian Gish in a scene
from *Romola*, 1924

Raffaello Sorbi, *Corso Donati che rapisce la sorella Piccarda dal convento di Santa Chiara* [Corso Donati Kidnaps His Sister Piccarda from the Convent of Santa Chiara], 1866
Oil on canvas, 175 x 230 cm
Florence, Gallerie degli Uffizi, Galleria d'Arte Moderna, inv. O.d.A. 1911 n. 893

sparkled in the light . . . Florence is never old . . . The past is so close to you in Florence. You touch it at every step . . . [in] some dusky interior of a smith's forge . . . [in] some gigantic mass of blossoms being borne aloft on men's shoulders for a church festivity of roses . . . Buy eggs in the market, and you buy them where Donatello bought those which fell down in a broken heap before the wonder of the crucifix . . . Buy a knot of March anemoni or April arum lilies, and you may bear them with you through the same city ward in which the child Ghirlandajo once played amidst the gold and silver garlands that his father fashioned for the young heads of the Renaissance."10

What emerges is the image of a radiant, Mediterranean Florence, filled with workshops and capable of achieving unprecedented heights— the Florence of which Anglo-Saxon culture was particularly fond. It is evoked in a famous painting by Frederic Leighton, which is just as rich in vivid details and a sense of personal involvement in the events described by medieval art. It shows the *Santa Trinita Maestà* being carried through the city streets

in a procession led by Cimabue and a child Giotto (both displaying the kind of elegance that only a follower of the Pre-Raphaelites could conjure up). The *Maestà* is supported by the finest artists of the time— Arnolfo di Lapo, Gaddo Gaddi, Andrea Tafi, Nicola Pisano, Buffalmacco, and Simon Memmi. A young and nonchalant Dante is seen admiring it from afar.[11] This kind of sequence shot takes us into the Florence which foreigners on the Grand Tour would search for with Ruskin's help and an enthusiasm that led them to accomplish very concrete yet at the same time imaginative feats. Around 1860, John Temple Leader—a scholar and writer of Florentine episodes who shared the taste I have been outlining in relation to the shooting of *Romola* and its possible sources of inspiration— chose to rebuild the ruins of Vincigliata into a castle that stands as one of the best projects developed within the framework of the revivalist culture. With its austere architecture, sprung from the convergence of historical accuracy and fiction, this building is the work of artisans whom Ouida's pen could easily have recast in a brisk and joyful medieval age, and which Leighton's imagination might have dressed in sumptuous fabrics—such as those painted and admired in fourteenth-century frescoes. Indeed, two of the stonecutters engaged in that imposing building work, David Giuntini and Angiolo Marucelli known as Canapino, were seen at the time as modern embodiments of the genius of the ancient masters, who lived on in the quarries and workshops dotting the

Frederic Leighton, *Cimabue's Celebrated Madonna Is Carried in Procession through the Streets of Florence*, 1853–55
Oil on canvas, 222 x 521 cm
London, The National Gallery, inv. L275

Fiesole hills. Similarly, the smith Contri, with his grilles and chandeliers, was seen as a "modern Caparra," whereas Marucelli—who was to craft the new marble decorations for the facade of Santa Maria del Fiore—had the honor of being featured in a small book as the "new Desiderio da Settignano."[12]

At this stage, one is inclined to think that the workshop space set up for the film *Romola* reproduced—by different means yet with the same aim of bringing back to life the city of Savonarola's day—that kind of dynamic craftsmanship that up until the early post-war years had promoted conservation and restoration work in the style favored by the British and American community, starting from Vernon Lee and Henry James. Both were eager to witness the transformation of Florence—which had temporarily become the capital of Italy—into a modern metropolis. On the other hand, with the utmost care these foreigners sought to combine functionality and decoration in their own mansions by drawing upon the antiquarian resources of a city that, with little regret, was stripping itself of ancient masterpieces by

putting them on the market—especially the American market. The myth of the Renaissance, nourished by William Roscoe's studies, by John Ruskin's enthusiastic research, and by the enduring popularity of Walter Scott's novels, had identified Florence as a setting for the aesthetic and literary adventures of foreigners pursuing their own modern utopia in opposition to industrial society. The latter was seen to have produced only wealth and social contrasts, frustrating the aspiration to serenity and beauty. Spiritual resources in this respect were suitably provided by the villas overlooking Florence from the surrounding hills: ideal havens for the seasonal rites of sophisticated idylls, places of freedom in which to create revivalist settings or indulge in study, reading, and conversation—a "quiet manner of life" jealously guarded and readily translated into an aesthetic canon.[13]

Leaving aside the disappointment caused by the "terribly actual Florentine question"—as Henry James defined the debate on the gutting of the historic center—Florence offered the opportunity to trace unconventional itineraries, in line with the escapist yearnings of sentimental travelers. In the city's museums these visitors could find the most notable testimonies to Renaissance civilization; in its buildings they could appreciate a solemness evocative of bygone glories; and in the humblest artifact on sale on the Ponte Vecchio, or on display in the renewed exhibit in the Bargello Museum, they could find a perfect example of the combination of functionality and beauty. After 1896, they

Art critic Bernard
Berenson posing in front
of a painting by Domenico
Veneziano at Villa I Tatti
Florence, Archivio
Villa I Tatti

Roger Fry, *Boccaccio's
Garden of Love*, 1901
Oil and tempera on wood
Artist's wedding gift to his
friend Bernard Berenson
Florence, Archivio
Villa I Tatti

could also rely on a landmark in the rediscovery of the Renaissance: *The Florentine Painters of the Renaissance* by Bernard Berenson. The photograph portraying the art critic in a hall in Villa I Tatti, posing next to a painting by Domenico Veneziano, is a genuine icon of that Renaissance "conquest" that transferred into the twentieth century a model of refined collecting and aesthetic living made possible by an urban and civil context in which theories of historical restoration or even a taste for period costumes could still find a place. As a wedding gift to his friend Bernard, Roger Fry painted a Botticelli-style tondo with an inscription (in Italian) evoking the delights of Settignano, translated as: "This fantasy was conceived and painted by the Englishman Roger and dedicated by him to the Berenson spouses, which like the old vacationers on the banks of the Mensola creek always while the hours away joking and discussing the follies of mankind."[14] This sophisticated masquerade confirms the widespread practice of historical transposition, preferably into the Renaissance age, with the aim of emphasizing the fact that in that period the pursuit of beauty was not limited to poetic abstraction but spilled into the workshops of every artist or skilled craftsman, encompassing every aspect of creative activity.

While Fry enjoyed dressing up as a Renaissance painter with Berenson's authoritative support, he had plenty of other occasions to project into the present the idealized age that George Eliot had evoked in *Romola*. This only goes to show that the actual setting of Florence—with its facades of Santa Croce and Santa Maria del Fiore, Dante's house, and the Palazzo di Parte Guelfa—was most suited to

294

becoming a genuine set through which local citizens could enact events from their glorious past. One significant example is the historical ball organized to celebrate the uncovering of the facade of Santa Maria del Fiore in May 1887. On this occasion, the editor-in-chief of the weekly paper *L'Illustrazione Italiana* informed his readers that the ladies of Florence would be sporting rich and elegant dresses: "The designs by Orcagna, Memmi, and Benozzo Gozzoli from the Spanish Chapel at Santa Maria Novella have been examined, studied, copied, and adapted in the best possible way. Even the frescoes from the cloister of Santa Maria Novella have provided some models; but, most of all, what have been copied are the figures painted on a wedding chest of drawers once belonging to one of the Adimari, and now in the Gallery of the Academy of Fine Arts."[15] Leaving aside the casual attributions made by the journalist, what is most noteworthy here is the fact that this event, in which the city as a whole was involved, had a scenic outcome that is clearly illustrated by the Alinari photographic record. Here we can see armed and robed gentlemen, lords and priors, abbesses and noblewomen: a stream of scarlet robes and skirts with rampant lions and heraldic dragons, and armors and helmets straight off the frescoed walls of churches and palaces, but also based on the endless range of artworks and artifacts that the city museums offered to the curious gaze of international visitors or anyone wishing to translate into his own age the enticing clothing of a period devoted to culture and the imagination. Besides, local exhibitions featured works that met this nostalgic demand for certain images and moods, and which in turn could serve as fascinating prototypes for masquerades and narratives. Examples include the often-copied sculptural group *Lovers' Meeting*, portraying Dianora de' Bardi and Ippolito Buondelmonti, created by Pio Fedi with the aim of harmoniously combining the faithful rendition of period costumes with passionate gestures; Antonio Puccinelli's *Paolo and Francesca*, where a dialogue of love finds resonance in real-life details that seem to have been borrowed from a theater set; and *Simon Memmi Portraying Lady Laura at Petrarch's Behest*, a painting by Pietro Saltini that seems to be set in a room of Palazzo Davanzati chosen for its evocative power—just as in the scene from the film in which Romola is portrayed by Carlo Bucellini, Piero di Cosimo's alter ego.

What best met the expectations of those foreigners in love with the "primitive" eras of the city was the neo-Gothic display at the Bargello, which had been converted into a museum between 1857 and 1860, and which also served as the ultimate source of inspiration for those craftsmen committed to passing down the outstanding Florentine style. The debate surrounding the restoration and transformation of the old Palazzo Pretorio into a museum sprung precisely from the need to assess the most significant and valuable achievements of bygone eras in the light of the present, to "collect those objects that might serve to illustrate the history and customs of the period, and which—to use a modern phrase—exemplify the application of art to the workmanship of those times." The aim was to provide "a not entirely abstract idea of the art, workmanship, and customs of our ancestors, and to study its various

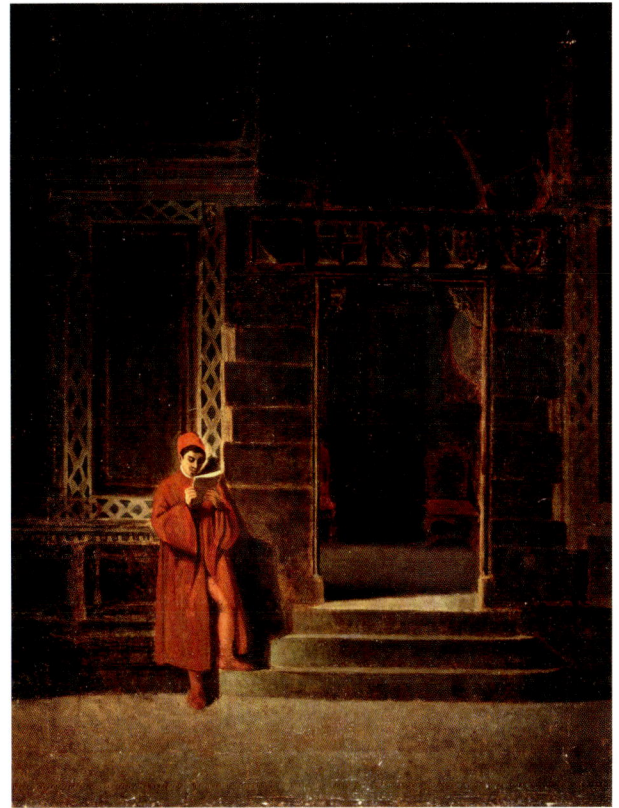

Giuseppe Abbati,
La cappella del Podestà
[The Podestà Chapel],
1861–62
Oil on canvas, 67 x 49 cm
Florence, Gallerie degli
Uffizi, Galleria d'Arte
Moderna, inv. 163

Florentine noblewoman in a dress
reproducing a period costume
worn on the occasion of the
historical ball organized
to celebrate the uncovering
of the facade of Santa Maria
del Fiore in May 1887

Ronald Colman and
Lillian Gish on the
set of *Romola*, 1924

Pio Fedi, *Incontro
tra amanti* [Lovers'
Meeting], 1850
Plaster, height 84 cm
Private collection

Antonio Puccinelli,
Paolo and Francesca, c. 1875
Oil on canvas, 48 x 55 cm
Private collection

stages and the development of that civilization."[16] Upon completion of the project, the Bargello—like many other museums set up in Europe in the wake of the new interest in the applied arts—presented itself as a particularly evocative place, initially launched by the discovery of Dante's portrait in the Chapel of the Maddalena. It then established itself as a perfect example of period restoration, entrusted to artists/restorers the likes of Gaetano Bianchi, who succeeded in transforming the gloomy prison building into a palace capable of evoking Romola's days. Indeed, George Eliot was particularly charmed by the building in question, which she saw when it was still undergoing restoration, catching a glimpse of its wonderful courtyard, with its coats of arms and magnificent stone staircase[17]—the setting of one of the few location shoots of the film.

The setting was an ideal one for revival enthusiasts and for anyone who, like the Macchiaioli, could find in those reconstructed Middle Ages the "spontaneous" matrix of the great Florentine tradition—something to be safeguarded against foreign interferences. The paintings by Odoardo Borrani, Giuseppe Abbati, and Federico Zandomeneghi portray settings in which clear lighting effects offer glimpses of neo-medieval double lancet windows or decorations suited for formal abstraction. These allowed painters to represent everyday life scenes enveloped in the same ambience that in those years marked the recurrent "poetics" of

Ronald Colman and Lillian Gish in a scene from *Romola*, 1924. Visible in the background is a faithful reproduction of the *Procession of the Three Kings*, which Benozzo Gozzoli had frescoed in Palazzo Medici Riccardi
Florence, Museo Salvatore Ferragamo

Pietro Saltini, *Simon Memmi che per incarico del Petrarca ritrae madonna Laura* [Simon Memmi Portraying Lady Laura at Petrarch's Behest], 1863
Oil on canvas, 118 x 142.5 cm
Florence, Gallerie degli Uffizi, Galleria d'Arte Moderna, inv. O.d.A. 1911 no. 784

Giuseppe Abbati, *Armigero in Bargello* [Soldier at the Bargello], second half of the nineteenth century
Oil on canvas, 27 x 47.5 cm
Private collection

masquerades and the pursuit of an integration between antiquity and modernity.[18] The newly restored Palazzo Davanzati instead provided a source of inspiration for the halls of Palazzo de' Bardi that were reconstructed for the film, starting from the luxurious library, which is secretly sold off by the treacherous Tito Melema. In Florence, Palazzo Davanzati was the epicenter of the debate on the renovation of ancient buildings and provided a workshop for eager antiquarians, who casually juxtaposed masterpieces available on the market with skillful imitations, mostly reflecting the same spirit exuded by the many masquerades already described. The "Impannate" Room, in particular, drew the interest of the set designers, with its eclectic furnishing that—in Elia Volpi's intentions—was meant to serve as a prototype for the Florentine Renaissance home. Preserved from the recent demolition work carried out in the city center, it could bring the palace back to life as a charming site of historical memory.[19]

Some film stills show how the study of these rooms made it possible to transfer onto the set the overall ambience and many details of the museum that had been recently inaugurated and authoritatively promoted through an article published in the journal *Les Arts*. This captured the essential significance of the enterprise, at the crossroads between historiographical research and business. It stated: "The tales by the old Italian storytellers, from Boccaccio to Bandello, and the scanty evidence from certain historical documents become integrated, come to life and create a realistic picture filled with movement and life . . . Once again, these small things prove far more informative than many documents laboriously interpreted . . . No doubt, the ancient documents and historians make us acquainted with many details of Florentine life, but when it comes to understanding this whole period of the Italian Renaissance, and truly grasping the soul of its people and of the age, nothing is as evocative as standing in the very setting where such life unfolded."[20] Ultimately, this is the same aim that George Eliot had set herself when visiting Florence and its museums, in search of the most useful library sources to outline the protagonists and events described in her novel. In the end, the writer had fashioned a story centered on Savonarola's city, yet shaped by "mixed human beings,"[21] which is to say characters with complex personalities and modern psychology. This is the case with Romola herself, who

Federico Zandomeneghi,
Palazzo Pretorio, 1865
Oil on canvas, 81 x 64 cm
Venice, Galleria
Internazionale d'Arte
Moderna di Ca' Pesaro,
inv. 1465

does not at all embody the Renaissance woman but reflects instead the thoughts and beliefs of a nineteenth-century puritan: "Romola," Guido Biagi writes in his foreword to the novel, "is English, and she bears a curious resemblance to George Eliot herself, or to what George Eliot's daughter might have been had she had one."[22] What the film mostly emphasizes, with a few variations, are instead those aspects of the novel best suited to providing a visually impressive narrative. It offers a visual transposition of an age that was rediscovered by consistently applying a method of research and imitation that was best cultivated and achieved precisely in Florence at the time of the Kingdom of Italy.

[1] On Florence's myth during the nineteenth century, see L'idea di Firenze. Temi e interpretazioni nell'arte straniera dell'Ottocento, Conference Papers (Florence, 1986), ed. by Maurizio Bossi and Maria Lucia Tonini (Florence: Centro Di, 1989).

[2] Guido Biagi, "Introduction. The making of the romance," in Romola by George Eliot (London: T. Fisher Unwin, 1907), XXX–XXXI.

[3] Kevin W. Sweeney and Elizabeth Winston, "Redirecting Melodrama: Gish, Henry King, and Romola," in Literature/Film Quarterly 23, no. 2 (1995): 137–45.

[4] Biagi, "Introduction" 1907.

[5] Sandra Berresford, "Preraffaellismo ed estetismo a Firenze negli ultimi decenni del XIX secolo," in L'idea di Firenze 1989, 206–08.

[6] Giancarlo Gentilini, "Giovanni Bastianini e i falsi da museo," in Gazzetta Antiquaria 1 (1988): 35-47, 2 (1988): 27–43.

[7] Carlo Sisi, "I macchiaioli e i generi della pittura," in I macchiaioli prima dell'impressionismo, ed. by Fernando Mazzocca and Carlo Sisi (Venice: Marsilio, 2003), 7–9.

[8] Claudio Paolini, "Oggetti come specchio dell'anima: per una rilettura dell'artigianato artistico fiorentino nelle dimore degli anglo-americani," in Gli anglo-americani a Firenze. Idea e costruzione del Rinascimento, Conference Papers (Fiesole, June 19–20, 1997), ed. by Marcello Fantoni (Rome: Bulzoni editore, 2000), 143–63.

[9] William Blundell Spence, The "Lions" of Florence and its Environs, second ed. (Florence: Felix Le Monnier, 1852), 20–21.

[10] Collected Works of Ouida (Hastings: Delphi Classics, 2017), chapter 9.

[11] Carlo Sisi, "Polemiche artistiche intorno alla facciata di Santa Maria del Fiore," in Santa Maria del Fiore. The Cathedral and Its Sculpture, Acts of the International Symposium for the VII Centenary of the Cathedral of Florence (Florence, Villa I Tatti, June 5–6, 1997), ed. by Margaret Haines (Fiesole: Edizioni Cadmo, 2001), 299.

[12] Giancarlo Gentilini, "Arti applicate, tradizione artistica fiorentina e committenti stranieri," in L'idea di Firenze 1989, 161.

[13] Carlo Sisi, "Ore toscane," in Americani a Firenze. Sargent e gli impressionisti del Nuovo Mondo, ed. by Francesca Bardazzi and Carlo Sisi (Venice: Marsilio, 2012), 76.

[14] "Questa fantasia inventata e dipinta da Ruggiero inglese da lui dedicata ai sposi Berenson chi a guisa degli antichi villeggianti della riva mensolana sempre si dilettano cogli amici loro scherzando e favellando delle sciocchezze dell'umano genere." See Luisa Vertova, "Divagazione sul Botticelli (vero e falso)," in Artista, 1989, 98.

[15] Giuliana Chesne Dauphiné Griffo, "Il ballo storico," in La Galleria del Costume. Palazzo Pitti 1 (Florence: Centro Di, 1983), 24–25.

[16] Carlo Sisi, "Scenari del pantheon fiorentino," in Arti fiorentine. La grande storia dell'artigianato, ed. by Maurizio Bossi and Giancarlo Gentilini (Florence: Giunti, 2001), 19–36.

[17] Biagi, "Introduction" 1907, XXI.

[18] Laura Lombardi, "Pittura di storia," in I macchiaioli 2003, 130.

[19] See Roberta Ferrazza, Palazzo Davanzati e le collezioni di Elia Volpi (Florence: Centro Di, 1993).

[20] Ibid., 145–51.

[21] Sweeney and Winston, "Redirecting Melodrama" 1995, 138.

[22] Biagi, "Introduction" 1907, XL.

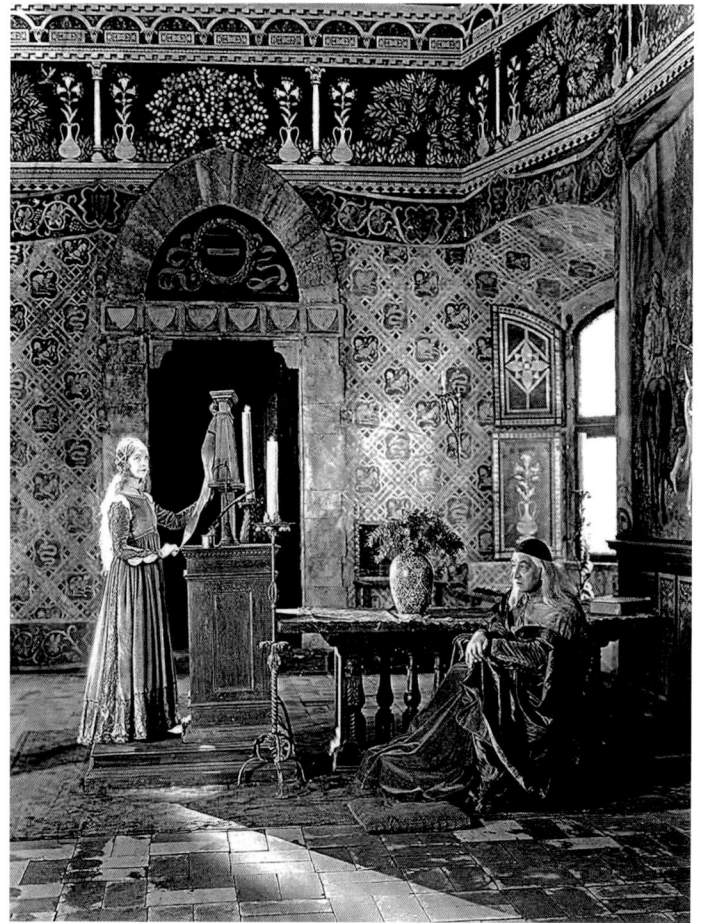

The "Impannate" Room on the third floor of Palazzo Davanzati in Florence, as furnished by Elia Volpi in 1920. The frescoes on the walls were reproduced for Romola

THE AGE OF JAZZ: THE ITALIAN SOUND IN AMERICA AFTER WORLD WAR I

Foreword

The halt in mass immigration during the 1920s allowed the Italian settlements in the United States to become consolidated. The strong Americanization policies implemented in the country after World War I had failed to erase immigrant traditions: on the one hand they continued to follow their "ethnic" professions, while on the other they took advantage of the fertile soil America offered in those years to develop commercial and artistic enterprises rooted in the traditions of their country of origin.

In California, Italian immigrants took part in the formation of the state from the time of the gold rush; such was the case with Domenico Ghirardelli, who was destined to become a chocolate magnate.[1] Like Ghirardelli, Italians entered every sector of an economy that had developed at breakneck speed within a few decades, as novelist Howard Fast has brilliantly narrated in his saga dedicated to Californian immigrants. Fast describes the many occupations Italians and their descendants undertook—from fishing to wine-growing and business to banking—through his main character Dan Lavette, son of a Genoese fisherman, who after the San Francisco earthquake manages to become a successful shipowner.[2] In the history of the young state we come across figures such as Amadeo Peter Giannini, founder of the Bank of Italy, but also of artists like Sabato "Simon" Rodia, who bought land on the outskirts of Los Angeles in 1921 and began to build what would later become the famous Watts Towers.

Nevertheless, in the collective imagination the great Italian immigration to the United States in those years is dominated by the stereotype of poor illiterate farmers who went to America's large industrial cities to work in factories or in the mining centers in the West. At most they figure alongside Chinese workers on the construction sites of the great infrastructural works of the time: railways, roads, bridges, and so forth, forgetting that before its fame for design, the Mediterranean diet, and gangster films, Italy was known as the home of the arts. And Italian immigrants brought this inheritance with them (either as performers or audience members) in order to satisfy the need for recreation and reassurance in the new context: the public was "hungry for entertainment, recognition, a support system and social intercourse, all emotional needs which the theaters and the nightclubs helped to satisfy," wrote Italian-American theater historian Emelise

PINTO
B'KLYN

Eduardo Migliaccio,
alias "Farfariello"
New York, Calandra
American Institute

The soprano Adelina Patti
photographed by Theodore
C. Marceau with her entourage
in Los Angeles in 1910, ready
to leave for her American
tour on her private train

Aleandri.[3] Italian theater arrived
in America at the beginning of the
nineteenth century with Lorenzo Da
Ponte (the first professor of Italian
literature at Columbia College,
Manhattan, in 1825) and was much
appreciated by the immigrant
communities. It soon changed from
amateur to professional status thanks
to such personalities as Eduardo
Migliaccio, whose stage name was
"Farfariello." Migliaccio entertained
Italian-American audiences for years
with a vast repertoire of sketches
taken from the Neapolitan tradition
and adapted to suit the Little Italy
enclave, such as "Lo Sciummecco"
(a pun on "shoemaker").[4] But despite
their great success, the various forms
of regional theater were destined to
remain limited to the ethnic enclave.
Music, on the contrary, spoke a
universal language.[5]

According to musicologist Simona Frasca, the cliché that all
Italians are singers is based on solid foundations, or at least on the
assumption that Neapolitan musicality could be extended to the whole
of Italy: "Recent studies of the activities of the four Neapolitan music
conservatories between the seventeenth and eighteenth centuries,
and in particular the educational practice of the *partimento*, a method
closely related to the concept of improvisation and extremely important
for young composers in Naples, lead us to understand how the mastery of
the medium of musical expression was a matter of skill before it became
a true art form, an expertise acquired through daily practice and passed
on by being continually exercised."[6]

Given Naples' centuries-old musical tradition, Frasca goes on to
explain the city's primacy over other comparative Italian situations:
"The idea of a kind of music with non-local characteristics that contains
the elements of a universal euphony is . . . at least three centuries old,
and in this sense the Neapolitan tradition has certainly stood as an

excellent example at least once in history, thanks to the development of operetta during the eighteenth century, and, to a lesser extent, a second time at the beginning of the twentieth century, when mass emigration established a direct connection between the Neapolitan tradition and the United States, the country that invented and dictated the rules of modern popular music throughout the twentieth century."[7]

Raised in an environment where music beat time to every moment of daily life, immigrants often made it their profession.

The opera

Music in the 1920s represented common ground shared by different ethnic groups, social classes, and musical genres. Opera in particular united Italian immigrants and the world of American WASPs. In fact, it satisfied not only the cultural interests of America, which sought to create a patina of nobility for its financial fortunes (so well illustrated in the novels of Edith Wharton, with her much sought-after European nobles in New York's salons, and the explosion of interest in the Italian Renaissance), but also those of immigrant Italy, which, well aware of the success of Italian composers and masters, considered opera as "its own," despite the fact that the majority of immigrants had a working-class background and limited cultural education.[8] The Italians in San Francisco were famous connoisseurs of opera: "The greatest lyric opera fans are Italian fishermen. They know their music but have no money for a ticket. Whenever we were looking for singers for the choir . . . we used to go down to the port to hire Italian fishermen. You might find them singing *Ernani* or *La Traviata*."[9]

In Italian-American communities, opera was also important in terms of promoting a national identity due to the "American appreciation of Italian composers, singers, and conductors."[10] Ettore Patrizi, the editor of *L'Italia*, the most important Italian newspaper in San Francisco, observed in 1911: "Italian music, like Italian cooking, has helped to facilitate social relations between Americans and Italians . . . San Francisco's Italians . . . love and attend the opera more than any other form of entertainment. Americans too are enthusiastic lovers of our operatic music, but no impresario could fill a season without the patronage of the Italians, who for the most part usually occupy the top gallery, which corresponds to our *loggione*. But from there comes the judgment of artistic success or failure . . . and from there comes the most regular and constant income that guarantees covering expenses, as the impresarios note. Among

The soprano Luisa Tetrazzini singing at Lotta's Fountain in San Francisco, December 24, 1910 Courtesy Museo Italo Americano of San Francisco and Alessandro Baccari

those Italian opera-goers, many are factory workers, greengrocers, and fishmongers, who have to return to their respective market, workplace, or shop in the early hours of the morning . . . a few hours of sleep are enough when one is galvanized by the notes of *Aida*, *Cavalleria*, or *La Bohème*. And with their irrepressible enthusiasm, the Italians drag the Americans along."[11]

Italian opera in America has a long history that can also be traced back to Lorenzo Da Ponte, who played a fundamental role in its diffusion. As early as 1851 in California, the Pellegrini Opera Company Troupe presented Bellini's *Sonnambula*, even though at the time of the gold rush it seemed that Donizetti had conquered audiences with *La figlia del reggimento*.[12] There were numerous successful Italian singers besides the two most famous, Sicilian Luisa Tetrazzini and Roman Adelina Patti. The latter unleashed the *Patti epidemic* in San Francisco: "All of San Francisco went crazy over her; her photos adorned shop windows displaying opera cloaks for the 'Patti season,' and fans painted in *Patti-Style*, as well as handkerchiefs and cases for opera glasses."[13] It was 1884. In 1905, Luisa Tetrazzini also made her debut in San Francisco. Patrizi recounts that five years later, to express her gratitude toward the city that first proclaimed her a diva, Tetrazzini performed outdoors on Christmas Eve "in the city's public streets, at the intersection of Market and Kearny, the two largest, most bustling arteries of San Francisco, in front of about 200,000 people."[14]

The Italians were part of the entire "music chain," starting from the stagehands who set up the shows up to the orchestra directors. Giulio Gatti Casazza, director of the Metropolitan from 1910 to 1935, introduced Arturo Toscanini to this world, where he became a soloist with the Metropolitan Orchestra from 1908 and director of the New York Philharmonic from 1928. In these years in New

The first performance of Giacomo Puccini's *La Fanciulla del West* at the Metropolitan Opera House in New York on December 10, 1910. Left to right, Giulio Gatti Casazza, David Belasco (author of the drama *The Girl of the Golden West* on which the opera was based), Arturo Toscanini, and Giacomo Puccini photographed by Herman Mishkin

A portrait of Enrico Caruso from the 1910s

Enrico Caruso as the Duke of Mantua in *Rigoletto* by Giuseppe Verdi, n.d.

Enrico Caruso as Dick Johnson alias Ramerrez photographed by Herman Mishkin in Puccini's *La Fanciulla del West*, 1910

Enrico Caruso singing opera in the open air, 1918

Album with embroidered
cloth cover that belonged to
Enrico Caruso, containing the
programs and New York press
reviews of the productions
staged at the Metropolitan
Opera House during the
1903–1904 season
35 x 28 cm (closed)
Lastra a Signa (Florence),
Museo Internazionale Enrico
Caruso, inv. 1153

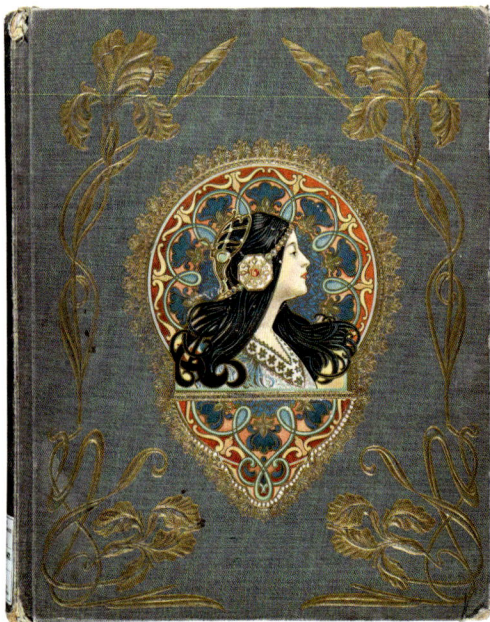

New York Tribune

PAGLIACCI

3 gennaio 1904

...ully. The performance of "Pagliacci" gave Mme. Seygard her first opportunity to appear before a New-York audience as Nedda—an opportunity which she employed successfully, especially in the first act. It was perhaps unfortunate, however, that her efforts were overshadowed by the work of Signor Caruso in the last scene of the first act. He then has the stage to himself, and sang and acted with such dramatic power and vocal finish that he became the hero of the moment. The audience would not be stilled until the scene had been repeated, so little potent are conception of dramatic propriety when brought into conflict with sensuous charm in singing. Signor Scotti repeated his familiar and admirable personation of Tonio. The others in the cast were Messrs. Reiss and Guardabassi, both of whom acquitted themselves well. Signor Vigna conducted both operas with spirit and sympathy.

Non ostante il tempaccio orribile, un gran pubblico accorse alla doppia rappresentazione di *Cavalleria e Pagliacci...* La rappresentazione dei *Pagliacci* dette a Mme Seygard l'opportunità di presentarsi al pubblico di New York nella parte di *Nedda* — una opportunità di cui ella si valse con profitto, specialmente nel primo atto. E fu forse una sfortuna che i suoi sforzi fossero oscurati dal lavoro del signor Caruso nell'ultima scena del primo atto. Qui, egli ha la scena tutta per lui, e cantò ed agì con tale potenza drammatica e con tale squisita arte che divenne l'eroe del momento. Il pubblico non si calmò se non dopo che il monologo fu ripetuto; così poco conta il concetto della convenienza drammatica, quando si trova in conflitto con l'incanto sensuale prodotto da un bel canto.

New York Times

PAGLIACCI

3 gennaio 1904

Mme. Seygard's histrionic talent was well displayed in the tragic scene of the last act, in which she denoted admirably the increasing terror of the faithless wife as she sees the grim purpose of the husband's revenge forcing itself through the mimicry of the little comedy of the strolling players. Mr. Caruso was in superb voice, and never sang with more perfect art and greater opulence and beauty of tone or with more impassioned expression. His 'Canio is one of the parts in which he discloses his best qualities. Mr. Scotti was the Tonio, and, as heretofore, made his impersonation strikingly picturesque.

Mr. Caruso era in superba voce, e non ha mai cantato con arte più perfetta, con più grande opulenza e bellezza di note e con espressione più appassionata. Il suo *Canio* è una delle parti nelle quali egli rivela le sue migliori qualità.

New York Herald

PAGLIACCI

3 gennaio 1904

In "Il Pagliacci" Mr. Caruso, being at his best, was, of course, applauded to the echo and was again compelled to repeat the last scene in the first act entire. Mme. Seygard bettered the impression she made as Nedda a week ago. That her tones were at times thin and somewhat small is due to her recent illness. Mr. Scotti was as artistic as ever in his interpretation of Tonio's disappointed revenge, and Mr. Guardabassi found some increase of impressiveness for his Silvio.

Nei *Pagliacci*, Mr. Caruso, essendo in tutti i suoi mezzi, fu, naturalmente, applaudito fino a farne rintronare la sala, e dové nuovamente ripetere l'intiero monologo.

La Traviata

METROPOLITAN
Opera House

Season
of
Grand
Opera
1903
and
1904

Under
the
Direction
of
Mr.
Heinrich
Conried.

HOERTH

CONRIED METROPOLITAN
OPERA CO.

MICHAEL PRINTING CO.
Publishers, 170 Fulton St. New York.

Orleans, the French Opera House, founded in 1923 by another Italian, Gaetano Merola, became the venue for Italian opera.[15] Arnold "Deacon" Loyacano, a classical musician who soon switched to jazz, reported that the French Opera House was known as the "Italian Conservatory" because all the teachers were Italian.[16] In many U.S. cities "Italians were respected and sought-after musicians, both for the music schools and for the most prestigious orchestras."[17]

According to ethnomusicologists, the key to the success—if not the supremacy—of Italian opera in the United States when compared to French or German opera is substantially ascribable to the particular Italian style of singing: "Italians sang harmony, whereas French usually sang unison. Italians were truly chorists," whereas the French were actors.[18]

Enrico Caruso was the most famous Neapolitan tenor of Italian bel canto; it was the passion and melancholy that were blended in his performances, just as in soul and blues music, that decreed his popularity, which soon led to his appellation as "the first twentieth-century pop star."[19] Caruso made his debut in 1903, playing the Duke of Mantua in *Rigoletto* at the Metropolitan Opera House in New York, where the audience called for an encore of "La donna è mobile."[20] Caruso performed at the Met as many as 706 times. In 1904 he recorded "Vesti la giubba" from Leoncavallo's *Pagliacci*, which in 1907 reached the record of one million copies sold. The opera became highly popular with all his audiences.

Victrola double-sided disc with
the arias "Vesti la giubba" (1907)
and "No, Pagliaccio non son"
(1910) from the opera *Pagliacci*,
both sung by Enrico Caruso
diameter 30 cm
Lastra a Signa (Florence), Museo
Internazionale Enrico Caruso,
inv. 9030

Caruso: *Pagliacci*

Unlike German opera that focused on the text, Caruso emphasized the sung performance, thus overcoming class divisions.[21] He became a social reference model for immigrants and the idol of music lovers of the day. At the Metropolitan Opera House in 1903 he played Radamès in *Aida*; Cavaradossi in *Tosca* (with an encore of "E lucevan le stelle"); Rodolfo in *La Bohème*; Canio in *Pagliacci*; and Alfredo in *La Traviata*. In January 1904 he played Edgardo in *Lucia di Lammermoor* and Nemorino in *L'Elisir d'amore*. In 1909 he recorded a series of twenty-two Neapolitan songs, including "Core 'ngrato," written by Riccardo Cordiferro (born Alessandro Sisca) and Salvatore Cardillo, inspired by Sisca's sentimental adventures. It should be noted that "Core 'ngrato" was composed and recorded in New York and only subsequently brought to Italy.

Caruso knew how to conquer immigrant sympathies, always maintaining a close bond by presenting themes dear to Italian expatriates in his songs, such as the memory of the homeland, or of the mother, or of the beloved left behind in Italy. He demanded exorbitant fees, but would also sing for free to gladden his compatriots. New York's Little Italy was the setting for the 1918 silent film *My Cousin* directed by Edward José, in which he plays a double role, interpreting both himself, a tenor at the Metropolitan, and a poor sculptor, the cousin of the title.[22] The fifty-minute short film contains various Italian-American caricatures: the greengrocer, the restaurateur, and the aspiring singer; and then the banks, and a party in Little Italy.

Caruso's example persuaded many Neapolitan artists to travel to the United States in the years of mass emigration, creating a theatrical and musical network linked to Italy that Frasca has analyzed by exploring the history of Neapolitan music that spread overseas. Music became a significant component of social life in Little Italy and was heard in many recreational venues (such as restaurants, bars, concert halls, and theaters) as well as via the radio, which was a fundamental means for its diffusion. The musical world not only drew on Italian singers, musicians, and conductors but also encompassed Italian teachers, music publishers, and record companies. One of the first music publishing houses was founded by Ludovico Gabici in New Orleans,[23] and in 1914 the Victor catalogue had fifty-six pages listing Italian music, most of

Portable gramophone manufactured by the Victor Talking Machine Co., 1904
Oak case with small plaque reading "Exhibition His Master's Voice" and internal horn; the diaphragm is attached to the end of the metal tone arm
32.5 x 18 x 36.5 cm
Lastra a Signa (Florence), Museo Internazionale Enrico Caruso

it dedicated to opera and operetta, but also including romances and "Neapolitan records."[24]

Victor used different colored labels to distinguish the various musical genres, ranging from "highbrow," that is classical or opera (Red Seal, with higher prices for great names such as Caruso and Patti), to operetta and Vaudeville (blue or purple label), to ethnic discs, sold at less than a dollar (black label).[25] Columbia, the other major record company, identified its ethnic series in green and the letter E, or F for foreign.[26] The market was therefore essentially Italian American, indeed even regional, so much so that the publishers tried to avoid too much sung speech, which would have been incomprehensible to a public that tended to speak only local dialects. Between 1893 and the beginning of World War II, approximately 8,000 matrices of traditional and popular material were registered in the United States exclusively for the Italian immigrant market.[27] However, soon enough, the record companies themselves began promoting the fusion of styles. With the outbreak of World War I, the major record companies were forced to halt imports from Italy and stimulated the spread of instrumental tracks that served the growing popularity of dance music. They reduced the regional recordings in order to address diverse ethnic groups. Leading the way in this sphere was the orchestra called "I Quattro Siciliani": Rosario Catalano, conductor and mandolin, Giuseppe Tarantola, clarinet, Carmelo Ferruggia, guitar, and Girolamo Tumbarello, double bass or bass tuba.[28] Thus the recording industry, and later the radio, made a further contribution to the diffusion of ethnic music.[29]

The New Orleans Rhythm
Kings, photographed
by Duncan Schiedt in
1922: George Brunies
(trombone), Frank
Snyder (drums), Paul
Mares (trumpet), Arnold
Loyacano (bass), Elmer
Schoebel (piano), Jack
Pettis (sax), and Leon
Roppolo (clarinet)

The Original Dixieland
Jazz Band, c. 1920:
Tony Sbarbaro (drums),
Edwin "Daddy" Edwards
(trombone), Dominic
James aka "Nick" La
Rocca (trumpet), Larry
Shields (clarinet), Henry
Ragas (piano)

Cover of the disc *Sensation!*
by the Original Dixieland
Jazz Band, c. 1918
Turin, Centro Altreitalie

Cover of an Eddie Lang vinyl
disc containing eighteen
original recordings, including
seven new tracks, c. 1932
Florence, Museo Salvatore
Ferragamo

Louis Panico (standing with his trumpet) and his swing band, Chicago, c. 1930
Turin, Centro Altreitalie, Italians in Chicago

The Strocchia Band, composed of Italians mainly from the northwest of the country, after a carnival in 1928
Turin, Centro Altreitalie, Italians in Chicago

A still from the movie *King of Jazz* with Paul Whiteman, directed by John Murray Anderson and produced by Universal Studios, 1930

All That (Italian American) Jazz

Some years ago, Lino Patruno wrote: "This music that many people wrongly define as exclusively African American . . . would perhaps be better called Italian American."[30] While the Italian contribution to opera is well established, little is known in Italy about the significant Italian contribution to the birth of jazz, the soundtrack to the Roaring Twenties. Actually, there were dozens of Italian (or of Italian origin) musicians who played in the first bands, adopting English pseudonyms or Americanizing their given names. And it is thanks to an American of Italian origin that we remember the birth of jazz[31]: "We called our music *jazz* after a night in Chicago when someone in the audience kept shouting from the stalls *Jazz it up*, and it really seemed to suit our music. No, I never heard that word in New Orleans. Later I learned that in Chicago it's a swearword. But we've purified it." These are Nick La Rocca's words from an interview with Brian A. L. Rust, published in *Storyville* in 1967 to mark the fiftieth anniversary of the first jazz record.[32]

La Rocca, born in 1889, the son of Sicilian parents who immigrated to New Orleans, is considered a pioneer cornetist of classical jazz. Despite Nick's father's disapproval of his passion for such music, in 1916 the young La Rocca joined Johnny Stein's group, which would later take the name Original Dixieland Jass Band (then the Original Dixieland Jazz Band), and became its leader. The famous band, which included another Italian member, guitarist Michele Ortuso, made the first historic jazz recording in New York, performing "Dixieland Jass One Step" and "Livery Stable Blues," published by RCA Victor. It was 1917.

Original Dixieland Jazz Band

In 1919 the Original Dixieland Jazz Band performed in London as the official orchestra at the Victory Ball, held at the Savoy Hotel to celebrate the signing of the Treaty of Versailles. The band played in front of the royal family, captivating George V. In 1920 they returned to New York, where they continued to enjoy great success until 1922, when they moved to Harlem.

The figure of Nick La Rocca is highly controversial. The orchestra musicians, who liked to call themselves "The Creators of Jazz," were accused of being "the white guys who copied African American music, and called it their own."[33] In the recent reconstruction by musicologist Anna Harwell Celenza, she notes that the coldness with which the orchestra was received derived from the fact that it had questioned the legitimate role of African Americans in the origins of jazz.[34] Later, in the 1930s, La Rocca's arrogant and openly racist behavior made things even worse.[35] Celenza concludes that La Rocca "didn't invent jazz, but he was the first to capitalize on the fact that it was a financially profitable, popular art form that could cross various ethnic and national borders with relative ease. False though it was, La Rocca's claim that he invented jazz played an influential role in Italy's early embrace of the music."[36]

Another notable jazz player who had to deal with the color barrier in those years was Eddie Lang, born Salvatore Massaro, who was considered one of the best rhythm guitar specialists of all time.[37] Under the stage name of Blind Willie Dunn (a baseball player he supported), in 1929 he recorded for the Okeh record company in New York some songs with Lonnie Johnson, an excellent black guitarist. The name "Blind" was often used by black blues players, so Lang adopted it since few African Americans (the main public for blues records, which were known as "race records") would have imagined a white man could play the blues. Eddie Lang initially studied the violin, and by 1918 he was already active as a professional, playing the violin, banjo, and guitar. After working for several orchestras in the northeastern United States, he spent a year in London before settling in New York. In the mid-1920s he was a member of the orchestras of Adrian Rollini, Roger Wolfe Kahn, Jean Goldkette, and Joe Venuti, who was a great friend. With Venuti he recorded "Goin' Places," "The Wild Dog," and "Cheese and Crackers." He performed on the radio and in the burgeoning record industry, recording a great variety of styles and musical genres. In 1929, he and Venuti joined the Paul Whiteman orchestra, with which Lang appeared in the film *King of Jazz* (1930) directed by John Murray Anderson. Lang became an accompanist to Bing Crosby when he left Whiteman, taking part in the 1932 film *The Big Broadcast*.

The connections between classical music and jazz are evident from the biographies of many other musicians. "Bel canto and Italian opera are also to be found in jazz performances by African Americans such as Armstrong, who revisited arias from *Rigoletto*, *Pagliacci* and *Cavalleria Rusticana* in his renditions of the 'New Orleans Stomp,' 'Dinah,' and 'Tiger Rag,'" observed musicologist Joshua Berrett.[38] Italian musicians not only brought the wind instrument tradition from Italian bands to jazz orchestras, paving the way for other Italian Americans destined to become famous (such as Louis Prima, Frank Sinatra, and Dean Martin), but they were also among the first to adopt new technologies, as Caruso did by recording opera arias on disc.

The Società Filarmonica Bella Italia in a 1911 photograph Turin, Centro Altreitalie, Italians in Chicago

The Damante Band of Bridgeport/Chinatown, 1927 Turin, Centro Altreitalie, Italians in Chicago

Italian bands

The boundaries between classical music, bands, and jazz were therefore very tenuous: in the homeland of jazz at the beginning of the twentieth century there were musicians from the conservatories of the large cities of northern Italy and Sicily (in 1910, 90 percent of the Italians in New Orleans came from Sicily). According to Bruce Boyd Raeburn's reconstruction of the birth of jazz, Arnold Loyacano (originally Lojacono), with Jimmy Durante of the New Orleans Jazz Band, resumed his studies of the violin, originally begun at the Milan Conservatory.[39] The horn player George Poletti from Ravenna had Louis Prima among his students. Joseph Fulco performed at the Orpheum Theatre and also specialized as a horn, viola, and violin soloist at the French Opera House. The links between classical music and jazz were such that in 1919 the musical director of the Palace Theatre declared: "jazz and bel canto were juxtaposed to demonstrate their congruity."

Adrian Rollini, born in New York in 1903, had Italian parents. From the age of three and a half he began taking piano lessons. It is reported that "at the age of four, through the mediation of his teacher Madame Negri, he held a fifteen-minute recital at the Waldorf-Astoria Hotel. Among the pieces he performed was Chopin's Minute Waltz."[40] From that moment on he gained a reputation as a child prodigy. To devote oneself to music at that age was not unusual in Italy: between the late nineteenth century and the 1930s a very high percentage of Neapolitan singers had made their debut between seven and ten years of age in the so-called *concertini*: musical interludes comprising guitar, voice, and mandolin during baptisms, name days, and weddings.[41]

By the age of fourteen Adrian Rollini was leading his own group composed of neighborhood boys, in which he played both piano and xylophone. At sixteen he became a member of the popular band The California Ramblers (the orchestra was actually formed in the Midwest in 1920 but chose the name because California evoked more exotic images). Jimmy and Tommy Dorsey were also in the band and recorded many records with Rollini during the 1920s.

The Chicago Heights Concert Band in a 1918 photograph
Turin, Centro Altreitalie, Italians in Chicago

Jimmy Durante in a scene from the
musical comedy *The Phantom President*,
directed by Norman Taurog in 1932

Giuseppe Venuti from Lombardy received a classical training from his grandfather, his first violin teacher. He was six when he joined his family in the United States. Considered one of the most innovative jazz violinists, he played for most of his career with the great guitarist Eddie Lang, his neighbor, school companion, and friend.

Rollini was among the most famous exponents of Dixieland (the particular "white" way of playing the New Orleans style) and played for a long time at the Onyx in New York, a famous club on 52nd Street. He also appeared in the 1930 movie *King of Jazz*; this famous film features the creolization of jazz in the number "Melting Pot," in which American musicians from multiethnic backgrounds play together, introduced by the voice of the presenter who recites: "America is the melting pot of music wherein the melodies of all nations are fused in the one great new rhythm: Jazz!" The piece representing Italy is "Santa Lucia."[42]

Retracing the history of the two most popular musical genres in the first decades of the twentieth century also demonstrates the tenuous boundaries between cultured music and popular music. In an article from 1919 (published in *La Lettura*, newspaper *Corriere della Sera*'s monthly magazine) covering musical innovations from America, the musical hybridization is evident: "Jazz is an orchestra like any other but it has added some 'modern' instruments to the 'ancient' ones, and plays any kind of music. The rhythm is certainly always the same: ragtime or syncopated music, but any aria can be played in that rhythm. In fact, I've often heard jazz bands play 'O sole mio,' Neapolitan songs, and Viennese waltzes."[43]

Relationships between Italian American and African American musicians were complex, ranging from those who rejected jazz to those who tried to appropriate it—as was the case with Nick La Rocca who, together with his pupil Dominick Barocco, who played the banjo in blackface, was accused of wanting to expropriate the genre from African Americans—to figures such as Carlo Curti, the leader of a "typically Mexican" orchestra.[44]

Cover of the disc *Miss Annabelle Lee* by The California Ramblers, 1925–27
Florence, Museo Salvatore Ferragamo

Caricature of the Italian jazz orchestra of the Teatro Pace, New York, published in the monthly magazine *La lettura* of the daily paper *Corriere della Sera*, August 1919
Florence, Biblioteca Nazionale Centrale di Firenze

The Millepiedi were one of the first Italian bands to play New Orleans jazz on the radio. Bobby Matassi (in the center of the photos) continued to play the double bass with the Red Bean Jazzers until the 1990s
Matassi Family Archive

In the New Orleans culture of that period, Sicilians, Jews, Creoles, and Latinos often played with this idea of color. According to Raeburn, the fact that Sicilians were long considered non-exactly-white facilitated the creolization of jazz. Louis Armstrong, himself an admirer of bel canto and the Italian musical tradition, defined jazz as "a rich creolized music tradition."[45] Nevertheless, the jazz-listening public of the day was divided: "Currently, there are two categories of jazz band: those mostly black, who play in the hotels, restaurants, and dance halls of clubs and elegant society, and those, often Italian, who play in cinemas, variety theaters and in countless other theaters where the most genuine theatrical product of North America triumphs: operetta, known as 'musical comedy'."[46]

A field in which Italian musicians were destined to make their mark in the following decades, mainly via cinema, was "crooning," a new familiar singing style that explains the origins of the success of Frank Sinatra, Perry Como, and Dean Martin. Radio was particularly suited to crooners. The advent of the radio and microphones enabled a closer contact with the audience through "a more intimate, seductive sound than had not been possible for opera singers like Caruso. This brought to a new vocal approach, *crooning* as it was called,

in which the microphone served as a kind of electronic ear connected to each and every listener."[47] Thus tenors gave way to baritones, whose lower tone was closer to the sound of the normal voice. One of the first crooners was Rudy Vallée, of Irish Canadian origin, "the vocalist who became famous for the melodious tenor voice which he applied to ballads and jazz pieces." The best known crooner among the Italians was Russ Columbo, born Ruggiero Eugenio di Rodolfo Colombo (1908–1934), a baritone, author, violinist, and actor who began playing the violin as a child and made his debut at thirteen years of age. Bing Crosby was also among the first crooners and sang together with Vallée and Columbo.[48] Columbo, known as "Radio's Valentino,"[49] became the violinist for Pola Negri, the diva of silent movies, who introduced him to the most important film personalities of the time, including Rudolph Valentino, Gloria Swanson, and Joan Crawford. His most famous interpretations were "You Call It Madness (But I Call It Love)" and "Prisoner of Love." He died aged twenty-six as the result of an accidental shooting.

Thanks to the radio, jazz was a huge success from the very start, even in fascist Italy, inasmuch as it was a symbol of energy and modernity. The Futurists had already appreciated its links to African culture and primitivism, and, as Anna Harwell Celenza notes: "When jazz arrived on Italian shores at the conclusion of World War I . . . the Futurists praised its 'virile energy,' Mussolini described it as 'the voice of Italian youth,' and musicians, mesmerized by its 'progressive' sounds, left the conservatories and flocked to dance halls and nightclubs . . . In Italy, the music was embraced early on as a sign of youth and modernization."[50] Here too, radio played an important role, and since the Italian listening public was unable to observe "ethnic and color" differences, "Nick La Rocca (Italian American), Gorni Kramer (Italian), the Trio Lescano (Jewish Dutch) and Louis Armstrong (African American), to name just a few, all found their place in the Italian soundscape."[51]

Conclusion

The journey through the music of the Roaring Twenties has led us to analyze little-known aspects of the dynamics of hybridization that occurred in the artistic sphere of the United States. It has also enabled us to understand in greater depth the WASP society's contradictory assessment of Italy, torn between an appreciation of Italian culture, as demonstrated by the success of composers such as Toscanini and opera, and a negative view of Italian immigrants, criticized for their impulsiveness, violence, passion, and sentimentality. The conjunction of nature and culture coalesced into a harmonious balance in jazz music, and in figures such as Enrico Caruso, who made the most of his natural talents—his voice and body—and refined them through study, technique, and art.

[1] In his early youth, Domenico, the son of Giuseppe Ghirardelli, an exotic food importer, was an apprentice to a local chocolate maker near Genoa. In 1837 he left Italy for South America, opening a chocolate shop in Lima, Peru, where he changed his name to Domingo. Later, on the advice of a friend, he moved to California, initially trying his hand at gold mining, but soon found it more profitable to sell chocolate to the miners, and so opened a general food store in Stockton, followed soon after by another in San Francisco, both of which were later destroyed by fire. Undeterred, in 1852 he opened a prominent specialist chocolate and confectionary store, thus founding the famous Ghirardelli Chocolate Company. Around 1865, a Ghirardelli worker developed a technique for extracting cocoa, which later became the most common method for chocolate production. See http://www.italoamericano.org/story/2014-10-21/Ghirardelli (accessed February 1, 2018).

[2] Howard Fast, *The Immigrants* (Boston, MA: Houghton Mifflin, 1977); *Second Generation* (1978); *The Establishment* (1979); *The Legacy* (1981); *The Immigrant's Daughter* (1985); *An Independent Woman* (1997).

[3] Emelise Aleandri, "Italian-American Theatre," in *Altreitalie* 34 (2004): 131–51: 132; Deanna Paoli Gumina, *The Italians of San Francisco 1850–1930* (New York: CMS, 1978), 58.

[4] Francesco Durante, *La letteratura italoamericana. Storie, autori e opere dal '700 a oggi* (Brescia: La Scuola, 2017), 49; on this vast production, see also Hermann W. Haller, *Tra Napoli e New York. Le macchiette italo-americane di Eduardo Migliaccio* (Rome: Bulzoni, 2006).

[5] The Italian contribution to world music is easily verifiable through the very language of music. "The majority of musical terms are in Italian," http://www.musictheory.org.uk/res-musical-terms/italian-musical-terms.php (accessed December 18, 2017). The site contains as many as 1,139 Italian musical terms used in the universal language of music. For an idea of the wealth of Italian American record production, see Richard Spottswood, *Ethnic Music of Records. A Discography of Ethnic Recordings Produced in the United States, 1893–1942* (Champaign: University of Illinois Press, 1990).

[6] Simona Frasca, "La canzone napoletana negli anni dell'emigrazione di massa," in *Altreitalie* 29 (2004): 34–52: 37–38.

[7] Ibid., 38.

[8] Impoverished Italian nobles appear as characters in numerous novels by Edith Wharton, such as *The Age of Innocence* (1920) and *Twilight Sleep* (1927). On the American passion for the Renaissance, see Roberta Ferrazza, "The Allure of the Florentine Style in the United States," in *1927 The Return to Italy. Salvatore Ferragamo and Twentieth-century Visual Culture,* ed. by Stefania Ricci and Carlo Sisi (Milan: Skira, 2017), 37–53. Anna Maria Martellone, "La 'rappresentazione' dell'identità italoamericana: teatro e feste nelle Little Italy statunitensi," in *La Chioma della Vittoria. Scritti sull'identità degli italiani dall'Unità alla*

Seconda Repubblica, ed. by Sergio Bertelli (Milan: Ponte alle Grazie, 1997), 357–91; "The Formation of an Italian-American Identity through Popular Theatre," in *Multilingual America. Transnationalism, Ethnicity and the Languages of American Literature*, ed. by Werner Sollors (New York: New York University Press, 1998), 240–45.

[9] Paoli Gumina, *The Italians of San Francisco* 1978, 60.

[10] Simone Cinotto, *Una famiglia che mangia insieme. Cibo ed etnicità nella comunità italoamericana di New York 1920–1940* (Turin: Otto, 2001), 386.

[11] Ettore Patrizi, "Gl'Italiani in California. Stati Uniti d'America. Monografia dell'ing. Ettore Patrizi, Direttore del Giornale L'Italia di San Francisco, Cal." (1911), in *Gli italiani in California, L'Italia, San Francisco*, ed. by Augusto Troiani (San Francisco: Stabilimento Tipo-Litografico, 1991), 1–51: 46.

[12] Andrew F. Rolle, *The Immigrant Upraised: Italian Adventurers and Colonists in an Expanding America* (Norman: University of Oklahoma Press, 1968).

[13] Ibid.

[14] Patrizi, "Gl'Italiani in California" 1991, 46.

[15] Bruce Boyd Raeburn, "Italian Americans in New Orleans Jazz: Bel Canto Meets the Funk," in *Italian American Review* 4, no. 2 (Summer 2014): 96.

[16] Ibid.

[17] Cinotto, *Una famiglia* 2001, 386.

[18] Raeburn, "Italian Americans in New Orleans Jazz" 2014, 88.

[19] John Gennari, "A Riff on Italian Americans in Popular Music and Jazz," in *The Routledge History of Italian Americans*, ed. by William J. Connell and Stanislao Pugliese (New York: Routledge, 2017), 415–32: 416.

[20] Ibid., 415.

[21] Ibid., 416.

[22] "Enrico Caruso: The Film *My Cousin* Part 1 of 6, directed by Edward José, written by Margaret Turnbull, with Henry Leone, Carolina White, Joseph Riccardi, A. G. Corbelle, and Bruno Zirato," https://www.youtube.com/watch?v=3_RK87WE9Qo.

[23] Raeburn, "Italian Americans in New Orleans Jazz" 2014, 90.

[24] The other ethnic record publishers were Columbia and Okeh, a manufacturer of low-cost records for the various communities. Giuliana Fugazzotto, "Donne e musica nell'America degli emigrati italiani del primo Novecento," in *Musical Anthropology in Mediterranean Cultures: Interpretation, Performance, Identity*, ed. by Philip V. Bohlman, Marcello Sorce Keller, and Loris Azzaroni (Bologna: Clueb, 2009), 59–70: 62.

[25] Giuliana Fugazzotto, *I quattro siciliani. La straordinaria vicenda di Rosario Catalano e del suo quartetto nell'America degli anni Venti* (Udine: Nota, 2015) 7.

[26] Ibid., 8.

[27] Giuliana Fugazzotto, *Sta terra nun fa pi mia. I dischi a 78 giri e la vita in America degli emigranti italiani nel primo Novecento* (Udine: Nota, 2010), 15.

[28] Fugazzotto, *I quattro siciliani* 2015, 15.

[29] Flaminio Di Biagi, "Scene e suoni della Little Italy," in *Altreitalie* 4 (1990): 77–79.

[30] Lino Patruno was known as "the king of Dixieland and Swing in Italy" due to his long career, which saw him play with the greatest international jazz musicians. Lino Patruno, "Jazz, gli italo-americani nella storia," in *Il Fatto Quotidiano*, January 15, 2015, https://www.ilfattoquotidiano.it/2015/01/15/jazz-gli-italo-americani-storia/1336224/.

[31] In addition to those already mentioned, here are some of the most renowned Italian American jazz musicians of the 1920s: Vincent Barocco, Dominick Barocco, Joseph (Ernie) Cagnolatti, Adrian Rollini, Carlo Curti, Jimmy Durante, Frank Signorelli, Joe Fulco, George Vitale (Jack "Papa" Laine), Giuseppe "Joe" Alessandra, Irene Bordoni, Joseph Benivetto, Santo Pecora, Little Cag, Louis Prima, Arnold Loyacano, Pete Pellegrini, Leon Roppolo, Stephane Grappelli, and Tony Sbarbaro. For more on this subject, see Jonathan Bogart, *100 Great Records of the 1920s* (Spring 2008), www. http://aceterrier.com/?cat=3. In *Other Italian American Jazz Greats of New Orleans*, http://aifed.org/wp-content/uploads/2013/05/5-Other-Italian-American-Jazz-Greats-Of-New-Orleans.pdf (accessed January 8, 2017), sixty Italian jazz musicians are listed for New Orleans alone.

[32] Brian Rust, "Grateful for the Warning," in *Storyville* 9 (February–March 1967). To mark the centenary of the release of the first jazz record in history, on February 26, 1917, many articles were published on the subject, among them the documentaries *E fu subito Jazz* by Renzo Arbore, and Michele Cinque's *Sicily Jass: The World's First Man in Jazz*, https://www.youtube.com/watch?v=8koHwk-Rr7E IT; *Lino Patruno racconta: La storia del Jazz – Nick La Rocca,* https://www.youtube.com/watch?v=Mj44rjLBlOc.

[33] http://www.redhotjazz.com/odjb.html.

[34] Anna Harwell Celenza, *Jazz Italian Style: From its Origins in New Orleans to Fascist Italy and Sinatra* (Cambridge: Cambridge University Press, 2017).

[35] Ibid., 3. A very controversial text due to its chauvinism concerning Italians involved in jazz is the recent book by Bill Dal Cerro and David Anthony Witte, *Bebop, Swing, and Bella Musica: Jazz and the Italian American Experience* (Chicago: Bella Musica Publishing, 2015). The racial question is dealt with in Stefano Zenni, *Che razza di musica: Jazz, blues, soul e le trappole del colore* (Turin: EDT, 2016).

[36] Celenza, *Jazz Italian Style* 2017.

[37] Nick Dellow, *Eddie Lang. The Formative Years, 1902–1925*, http://www.vjm.biz/168-eddie-lang-part-two-web.pdf.

[38] Joshua Berrett is mentioned in Raeburn, "Italian Americans in New Orleans Jazz" 2014, 87–108, 88.

[39] Ibid., 91–106 and *passim*.

[40] Arthur Rollini, *Thirty Years with the Big Bands* (Basingstoke, UK: Palgrave Macmillan, 1987), 4, https://it.wikipedia.org/wiki/Adrian_Rollini.

[41] Frasca, "La canzone napoletana" 2004, 35.

[42] In 2013, the film was selected for conservation in the National Film Registry of the United States Library of Congress.

[43] Bruno Zuculin, "Musiche e danze americane," in *La lettura*, the monthly magazine of *Corriere della Sera* 8 (August 1919): 1–2, 600.

[44] Raeburn, "Italian Americans in New Orleans Jazz" 2014, 95–96.

[45] Ibid., 94, 106.

[46] Zuculin, "Musiche e danze americane" 1919.

[47] Celenza, *Jazz Italian Style* 2017, 421.

[48] On the success of the three crooners in the 1930s, see *Forgotten Crooner: The Extraordinary and Short-Lived Career of Russ Columbo*, https://www.youtube.com/watch?v=ejOs-8X0sTo and https://www.youtube.com/watch?v=Ob-pseT81Eg (accessed January 21, 2018).

[49] "Radio's Valentino," in *Radio Guide* 1, no. 6 (New York, December 5, 1931): 1, 9.

[50] Celenza, *Jazz Italian Style* 2017.

[51] Ibid.

328

JOHN PAUL RUSSO

AMERICAN EYES: ITALY BEFORE AND AFTER WORLD WAR I

The Spanish American philosopher George Santayana left Harvard in 1912 and took up residence in Europe, changing addresses for over a decade. During the Great War he lived in Oxford, moved afterwards to Paris, pondered Avila, where he was born, then Monaco, and Florence, among other places, before settling in the mid-1920s in Rome, where he largely remained until his death in 1952. "It might seem that I turned to Italy and especially to Rome as a last resort, but that was not the case," he wrote. "Italy and Rome were my first choice, my ideal point of vantage in thought, the one anthropological center where nature and art were most beautiful, and mankind least distorted from their complete character."[1] No one had or would say it better. In the humanistic language of the Renaissance—ideal point, center, completeness, nature, beauty, universality—he had summed up the collective experience of travelers to Italy.

In the first decades of the twentieth century, American travelers could scarcely escape seeing Italy along the sightlines of their predecessors, so exceedingly difficult was it to establish a fresh and independent approach to a country that has been described as "the empire of stereotypes."[2] Their predecessors, products of the Grand Tour and the expansion of tourism in the nineteenth century, had created a wealth of writing on Italy in their fiction, history, poetry, and memoirs, but especially in their travel writing. What Augustus Hare protested in 1876, that "there are very few good books of general Italian travel," had been completely reversed.[3] The period from roughly 1880 to 1914 was the golden age of travel writing in the English-language cultural tradition. The train and steamship had opened up the country to writers who penetrated every corner of the peninsula and the islands and depicted all classes of the population. The German cultural historian Rudolf Borchardt placed English and American travel writers in the front ranks of the genre for their robust sense of adventure, their desire to "make use of their own eyes," their empirical detail, and their "nonchalance," by which he did not mean *nil admirari* but something like a lack of fuss. The finer writers did not approach Italy on bended knees, nor lament a lost paradise. Rather, they wrote with "a freshness and realism with which they would speak of Haiti and Uganda."[4] Thanks to their glowing autumnal prose—and mostly minor writers wrote the major books in the genre—one can still "travel" almost anywhere in Italy in these decades, from the major cities to the most remote countryside.

By and large, the travel books of the golden age reflected the level of cultural and historical knowledge of their readers, and could challenge those readers while entertaining them. Edith Wharton paid tribute to Walter Pater, J. Addington Symonds, Vernon Lee, and Paul Bourget for giving her generation "a high but unspecialized standard of culture" in travel writing and art criticism. Unspecialized means non-specialist, for "scientific" specialization increasingly had a claim on the territory of the travel writer. Wharton appreciated the role of the scholar, such as her friend Bernard Berenson, in pruning "sentimental undergrowth." However, travel writing on such a country as Italy was not to be confined to a specialization. "There remains a field of observation wherein the mere lover of beauty can open the eyes and sharpen the hearing of the receptive traveler"; one needed "cultivated sensibilities" to express the "imponderable something" in travel.[5] This would be the accomplishment of her generation on either side of 1900. The American historian William Roscoe Thayer caught the spirit that moved these travel writers to portray "that Enchanted Land, whose beauty is inexhaustible, and whose boundless interests touch, and will always touch, men and women who perceive the deepest concerns of the human soul."[6] Altogether, they brought travel writing to perfection and, in doing

so, demonstrated the extent to which the educational legacy of the humanistic Renaissance survived through the nineteenth century. This was the long historical twilight of a period that Arnold Toynbee would call the "Third Italistic Age" of Western civilization, which was coming to an end in 1914.[7]

If the eighteenth century was the age of the coach, and the nineteenth the age of the train, the twentieth century was the age of the car. While the train had opened up some regions of the country, it had closed off others, as it had done in the American West; there could be just so many rail lines and so many stations, and plenty of space in between. Borchardt put his finger on the problem in 1907: "The Italy of our ancestors has, as we know, since the railroads made it inaccessible, become one of the least known countries of Europe."[8] With the railroad's mechanical power, if never quite its speed, the touring car restored the privatizing virtues of the old horse-drawn carriage. In the first decades of the twentieth century its huge domain included the cities, but where it would eventually reign supreme was in the vast space between them. In 1912 Douglas Sladen dubbed Italy "the motorist's Paradise"—in a book on trains.[9]

To digress, the Italians, just like the Americans, embraced the car immediately. They established an automotive industry in Turin and Bergamo, and set up automobile clubs around the country, which pressured the government for better roads. The Touring Club Italiano (TCI), organized in 1894 for cyclists, soon became a center for automobile news; its guidebooks began appearing in 1900 and scholars would soon praise them for their accuracy and cite them in their references. Between 1901 and 1914 the car went from being the toy of the rich to a bourgeois commodity.

The motor car enabled a generation of new travelers to see far more of Italy than was hitherto easily possible, always excluding those such as Norman Douglas, Edward Hutton, and Ezra Pound, for whom the travel on foot was the gold standard. Before 1900 and the advent of the car, the California cosmopolitan Katharine Putnam Hooker pointed out one of the drawbacks of the train; it was a cramp on freedom. She was "happy in the independence of little open carriages, which can always be found to suit one's desire when the impulse comes to move on." On a train from Ancona across the Marches to Umbria, she felt cheated: "what tantalizing towns did we not see upon the way! [Chiaravalle, Jesi, Castelbellino]. It well nigh tempted us to cast ourselves forth from the [train] car windows in despair at being whirled past them." Hence, early in the new century she adopted the motor car, and tested it out on journey to Apulia, then a rather daring choice, though at least much of Apulia was a plain. The car, and not "automobile-diligences" or small buses, which "move with a rapidity that leaves little opportunity for observation."[10] Chauffeurs, observes Hooker, can be warned to slow down, though they think that they please their patrons by carrying them fast, or at least faster than the buses. (Chauffeurs doubled as mechanics; breakdowns were all too frequent.)

In the Galleria Vittorio Emanuele II in Milan, while buying fruit, Hooker engaged a helpful shop assistant in conversation, and affirmed what many travelers found so appealing in the working and peasant class of Italy, their unselfconscious pleasure in giving pleasure to others: it is the "unembarrassed manner, a self-respect, a cheerful courtesy, and a pleasant sort of confidingness that seldom fail, and it helps to give intercourse with them an ease and charm that renders traveling twice as agreeable." Years before, Stendhal and James Fenimore Cooper had made a similar observations. The Italians of the lower classes were as "distinctly aristocratic as the corresponding orders in certain other nations are vulgar."[11]

Edith Wharton was among the first champions of car travel, and why not when your vehicle was a 1904 Pope-Hartford Touring and the only car on the road? Wharton had lived in Rome and Florence for three years in her childhood and visited the country often thereafter. The so-called "Italian period" extended from 1885 to 1904, during which she made lengthy research trips each year. These resulted in her first novel *The Valley of Decision* (1902), set in late eighteenth-century Italy, and her pioneering work *Italian Villas and Their Gardens* (1904). Her travel book *Italian Backgrounds* (1905) collected essays separately published, now joined into an almost seamless whole. These works had shown that she had, in her own words, "lived in and *with* Italy."[12] She had surpassed William Dean Howells and her own mentor Henry James in her historical understanding and cultural appreciation of Italy.

The car facilitated studies in out-of-the-way villas and gardens; she was tired of either rushing to catch a train or "kicking our heels for hours in some musty railway-station." But it was not just about utilitarian value. "The motor-car has restored the romance of travel," she pronounces, reaching back to her grandparents' generation; "freeing us from the compulsions and contacts of the railway, the bondage to fixed hours and the beaten track, the approach to each town through the area of ugliness and desolation created by the railway itself, it has given us back the wonder, the adventure and the novelty which enlivened the way of our posting grandparents."[13] The idea of "romance" conveys the intimacy and eroticism of the car. The passage expresses an even-handed "tribute to

modernity as well as a commemoration of an older and glorious age of travel," notes Gianfranca Balestra; Wharton's was an "elitist refusal of the limitations of the railway" and "a cry for freedom."[14]

The title *Italian Backgrounds* is not only the key to Wharton's practice of travel writing but to her very understanding of Italy. With regard to the former, it suggests her fondness for the smaller cities and towns, the less visited ones, the unvisited ones, and their uninterrupted spiritual commerce with their deep past. With regard to the latter, however, Wharton extrapolates from the language of the Romantic picturesque: like a landscape painting by Claude Lorrain, Italy is divided into a foreground that is "the property of the guide-book and of its product, the mechanical sight-seer" (Baedeker's starred sites, museums), and a background that belongs to "the dawdler, the dreamer and the serious student of Italy." Knowledge of one enhances an understanding of the other. "The famous paintings and sculptures have become slightly conventionalized by being too long used as the terms in which Italy is defined. They have stiffened into symbols."[15] To bring them to life, one seeks out the "backgrounds," research into the historical and cultural antecedents that entails being a "serious student." At the same time, however, one must indulge "the dawdler, the dreamer," by which she invokes the poetic imagination: "in summer [in Brescia] there is a strong temptation to sit and think of these things [in the gallery] rather than to go and see them." Sometimes the foreground and background rival each other, as in Rome; at other times, they blend imperceptibly into each other, as in Umbria and Tuscany. But, she counsels, in a road metaphor, "there is no short cut to an intimacy with Italy."[16]

In 1903, with her "old friend" the American ambassador George Meyer in the driver's seat, Wharton inspected Villa Caprarola in northern Lazio. It was her first time in a car. "In a thin spring dress, a sailor hat balanced on my chignon, and a two-inch tulle veil over my nose, I climbed proudly to my perch, and off we tore across the Campagna, over humps and bumps, through ditches and across gutters, wind-swept, dust-enveloped." She rode out at noon, inspected the villa, and "tore back" to Rome in time for a dinner party. Although she was laid up for days with acute laryngitis, she swore to purchase a car as soon as she could afford one. She did soon enough, and continued to suffer, "till some benefactor of the race invented the wind-screen and made motoring an unmixed joy."[17]

Her later published report on this excursion in *Italian Backgrounds* illustrates her method of travel writing. As from a prospect, she surveys far and wide. But instead of looking down, she is enabled to look horizontally by the moving car. "The still air had a pearly quality and a mauve haze hung upon the hills": "pearly quality" and "mauve haze hung hills" have inner rhyme, consonance, alliteration, besides a rhythmic energy of motion; "ahead of us the same undulations swept on interminably." Now, lest it intrude upon her vision, her car dematerializes to the sound of its hypnotic "steady rush . . . strangely inspiriting in the call of this fugitive road . . . luring us up slope after slope, and racing ahead of us down the long declivities where the motor panted after it like a pack on the trail." She gathered in the "sun-bathed rugged fields with black cattle grazing in their hollows": "These fortress farms of the Campagna, standing sullen and apart among the pacific ruins of pagan Rome—tombs, aqueducts and villas—give a glimpse of that black age which rose on the wreck of the Imperial civilization. All the violence and savagery of the medieval city, with its great nobles forever in revolt, its popes plotting and trembling within the Lateran walls, or dragging their captive cardinals from point to point as the Emperor or the French King moved his forces—all the mysterious crimes of passion and cupidity, the intrigues, ambushes, massacres with which the pages of the old chronicles reek, seem symbolized in one of those lowering brown piles with its battlemented sky-line, crouched on a knoll of the waste land which its masters helped to devastate."[18]

In a sentence Wharton had set two periods of history in conflict: the Roman Empire at its height, secure and "pacific," and then the following "black age" or dark age with its "sullen" and "crouched" fortresses, the "lowering brown piles" dotting the "waste land" into which the Roman Campagna had fallen.

The idea of speed and escape in the title *A Motor-Flight through France* conveys the exhilaration that Wharton felt on the road. "There is no end to the exploring one can do, in a carriage of which the horses are never tired." "We don't want to give up the trip to go ignominiously by train, missing all the beauties of the road between here [Nice] & Pisa." But she has to admit her letter is dull: "all weather and motor, but really they are my only topics, for one sees no one who is interesting in these places."[19] On morning she set out by car to visit the monastery of La Verna high in the Casentino (4,209 ft.). It was a long day and by 11 p.m. "we were hanging over dizzying precipices . . . unable to turn back and almost unable (but for [her driver] Cook's coolness and skill) to go on. Our luggage was all taken off and hauled behind us on a cart by a wild peasant, others escorted us with big stones to put behind the wheels at the worst ascent." When at length they arrived, they had to wake up the monks for a night's lodging.

"The car had to be *let down by ropes* to a point about 3/4 of a mile below the monastery, Cook steering down the vertical descent, and twenty monks hanging on to a funa [rope] that, thank the Lord, *didn't break*." Inevitably, accidents or near-accidents begin to enter the history of travel. On the main thoroughfare to Milan in foul weather the car ran into a wagon and her maid was thrown out and nearly drowned. With a shattered windshield Wharton rode on holding her umbrella over the occupants, making the Paris train by three minutes.[20]

As with many American travelers, "Wharton's love of Italy did not include a love of Italians,"[21] who figure occasionally in her letters but rarely in her travel writing, and then only incidentally, almost like stage props or figurines. "When I see the stupid Italians I have met here, completely insensitive to their surroundings, & ignorant of the treasures of art and history among which they have grown up, I begin to think it is better to be an American, & bring to it all a mind & eye unblunted by custom."[22] Private letters can be more revealing than published travel books. On the aestheticization of contemporary Italians, Maureen E. Montgomery remarks that Wharton's essential cosmopolitanism "goes a long way toward avoiding the worst elements of a colonialist discourse that seeks to debase the 'other.'" Writers like Howells, Francis Marion Crawford, and Tryphosa Bates-Batcheller also avoided the worst elements, as a few decades later did Hemingway. Nonetheless, whether the Italians are aestheticized or merely ignored by Wharton, "we learn more about [her] than any live person that inhabits her text."[23]

Unlike Wharton who kept her comments on the means of travel to her correspondence, Dan Fellows Platt is a harbinger of those travel writers who make the technique of travel the main theme of their book, edging out knowledge, personal feeling, and local color. For Platt, an American millionaire and art collector, the car was the best way of seeing art and architecture in sites off the beaten track, thus serving the "chief end" of Italian travel. With its extensive itinerary and 200 photographs, *Through Italy with Car and Camera* (1908) does not always achieve its end because Platt's car—a Fiat Brevetti 1905–1906, it would appear from the photograph—vies for attention with the declared goal, and on its account the narrative is interrupted 200 times (as many as there are photographs). Road incidents, gas stations, breakdowns, punctures, and information like the 41.5 km in 44 minutes from Verona to Mantua for a "flying side-trip" are interspersed with sensitive comments on Lotto in Jesi, Gaudenzio Ferrari in Varallo, and Perugino in Fano and Senigallia. Carburetor trouble and pine branches for traction to pull out of a ditch are discussed on the same pages as appears a photograph of the abbey of San Galgano and observations on Lorenzetti's *Madonna and Saints* in Massa Marittima—which tends to equalize their significance. What should one make of his parking his black touring Fiat so that it forms the central point of his photograph of the sixth-century Sant'Apollinare in Classe outside Ravenna? The car seems to be "showing off" to the basilica, as new against old. Platt went where people rarely saw a car, where it scared a child, killed a mule, and went fast enough to rattle a local guide ("it was mean of us"). Though he mocks the tourist who describes Siena as the place where the train backs out of the station, he reports on many towns only for some challenge of vehicular maneuver. "Loitering" Neapolitans "deaf to all sounds of warning" have a nerve to take over *his* road: they "have made of this paradise a hell, in particular a motorist's hell. If Naples be distasteful to the railway tourist, how much more so to the traveller by automobile": the traveler has the upscale car, the tourist rides the train. When an elderly man walked into the mud-guard of his car and had to be taken to a hospital for examination, a judge would not permit Platt to leave Naples. Never one to waste time, Platt asked for an hour to see the ruins at Pozzuoli. Back and forth to Pozzuoli in an hour! The excited judge fetched his nephew and went along for the ride. Though Platt pleaded with his chauffeur, who had a "severe case of speed-mania," to drive slowly, the judge insisted on going faster.[24] The old man was released, the judge lifted his order, and Platt was on his way.

For some reason he could not reach Camerino (2,200 ft.), more likely because of the road, not the car which had already braved the Alps. Instead, he passed through Belforte del Chienti, "never before visited by an automobile," which is a few miles away. "The engine stops. We enter the little church [Sant'Eustachio] and are translated into a peace and quietness produced and dominated by the supreme work of art which faces us. No picture by an early master has so impressed me. Boccatis of Camerino [sic] is the artist who casts his spell upon us. Dignified and spiritual, the archaicness but adds to a charm of whose strength a photograph can convey no idea. May the fame of Boccatis some day become equal to the power of the appeal that he makes to receptive souls!" Time stands still when "the engine stops," and taken by surprise Platt experiences a kind of awe that combines the aesthetic and the mystical. Boccati's polyptych (1468) has over eighty figures, with the Virgin and Child in the center, saints Eustachio and Peter to their right and saints James the Greater and Venanzio to their left. Eustachio, patron saint of hunters, was in the woods and saw Christ on the cross amidst the antlers of a deer, looking almost like an extra set of antlers, an exemplum of divine immanence. Venanzio, a fifteen-year-old boy, refused to abjure his faith before the Roman prefect of Camerinum. He was tortured and dragged by horses across a field but a spring gushed forth, from which the Roman soldiers, in awe of his courage, drank and became converts themselves. Eventually, Venanzio was beheaded. Boccati portrays him as a dashing youth, fastidious in his elegant clothes, restored to himself in paradise; he stands on heavenly grass among flowering poppies, clover, chicory, and dandelion.

In search of "the real Italy, the old Italy" in 1909, Francis Miltoun, another American, said that the automobile could open up the "half-used byways" and help a traveler to know the country "as it was not even possible for his grandfathers to know it." Arezzo, Gubbio, Montepulciano, the Mugello, Ancona, and many "unexploited, little corners" exhibit the "reality of the life of mediaevalism which is difficult to trace" in the major cities. The car should deliver "us into the heart of the life of a country instead of forcing us to travel in a prison van on iron rails." Though he cautions against speeding 60 mph down the Via Emilia, he extols freedom of movement and the new control over time: "That is what the automobile is doing for modern travel—more than the stage or the railway ever did, and more than the aeroplane ever will!" There are drawbacks: expensive gas, few garages, and roads in the plains less good than anywhere in Western Europe except Spain, though for some reason Italian mountain roads are excellent. Criticizing "superficial Italian itineraries," he recommends that a traveler "leave the beaten track at least once"—only once!—and "try to discover something that none of his friends have ever seen." Elsewhere he says that "there is no really unbeaten track any more," lamenting the disappearance of "Romantic, sentimental Italy." Yet there were plenty of unbeaten tracks, many in the major cities, some just a block or two from the major watering holes (and there still are). Miltoun does not lack appreciation—"one never finishes his Italian travels. Once the habit is formed, it becomes a disease"; yet he is always restless and having to move on, and the commentaries are a mere tally. His is the modern hubris: by car we can know more of Italy "in six weeks than could otherwise be acquired in six months."[25] The car that brought him nearer to the genuine experience of Italy in one way distanced him too.

One legendary encounter of an American in Italy happened in late December, 1924 when F. Scott Fitzgerald was visiting Rome. He and his wife Zelda seemed more interested in visiting the set of *Ben-Hur* (1925) and

F. Scott Fitzgerald with his wife
Zelda and their daughter Scottie
during a tour of Italy

meeting fellow celebrities like the American actress Carmel Myers. "Rome," he writes his editor Maxwell Perkins, "does *not* particularly interest me" (December 20, 1924). Late one night, after drinking heavily, "stewed" as he would say, he was returning to his hotel on the Piazza di Spagna and got into a brawl with his taxi-driver (the car again!) over what he considered an exorbitant fare. Soon there were two taxi-drivers to contend with. A bystander attempted to separate the belligerents, but Fitzgerald gave him a punch that landed him on the pavement. The bystander happened to be a plainclothes policeman, for at this time fascist surveillance was on the rise. Fitzgerald ended up at the police station where was given a sound beating and a broken nose and let out the next day. The shock and embarrassment of this episode lingered in his mind for years. The late-night brawl became the sketch "The High Cost of Macaroni," which was the germ of *Tender Is the Night*: it figures prominently in the three separate drafts, finally serving as the climactic episode of Book II, Dick Diver's "catastrophe." But the Fitzgeralds had had enough: "I hate Italy and the Italiens [sic] so violently" (January 23, 1925). "We're moving to Capri. We hate Rome" (February 18, 1925). "Italy depressed us both beyond measure—a dead land where everything that could be done or said was done long ago—for whoever was deceived by the pseudo-activity of Mussolini is deceived by the spasmodic last jerk of a corpse" (April 19, 1925).[26]

In the mid-1930s Anne Bosworth Greene took the wheel with her daughter Babs and left a lengthy account (536 pages) of her travels through northern and central Italy. By now the car had become so familiar as to be infantilized. Her C3 or C4 Citroën is christened the diminutive Nicolette: she "was furious—being scratched over with a beggar's rag"; she was a "great absorber of atmosphere"; she "ambled surprisedly" over the pavements in Pisa; she "ceased trying" to climb on the slopes of Monte Amiata; "liked Umbria" (smoother roads) and "recovered humor"; had a "real burst of enthusiasm"; "had grown feeble again," a "fainting damsel"; at Cesenatico, "left Nicolette cooling her hot nose in the sea breezes." The Greenes race through the towns of southern Tuscany and seem almost proud that they "looked back not even once at medieval Buonconvento," the object of one of Hutton's walking tours. Try as she might, she keeps coming back to the car, which proved a demanding child, so that at one point she says with relief, "we actually began to look about us, instead of concentrating every second on her." It soon breaks down and the cycle is repeated. At bedtime in Orvieto she gives a last look at the Duomo, another at Nicolette. If she had spent less time worrying about her car, she might have seen more of Orvieto and would not have written "everything in it is charming," because Signorelli's *Last Judgment* and *Resurrection of the Dead* are many things, but "charming" is not one of them. Nicolette was in a hurry, "her ears pierced for the road (we hoped)."[27] Nicolette is not in a hurry; Greene has assumed qualities of the machine and projected them onto her car.

"They say that everyone loves Italy once and that it is well to go through it young," wrote Ernest Hemingway.[28] Not yet nineteen, he came of age in Italy on July 8, 1918, when as a Red Cross ambulance driver and canteen supplier he was severely wounded on the Piave front. After a long convalescence in a Milan hospital and a week's visit to Taormina, he returned after eight months to Oak Park (Chicago) where, overly *italianizzato*, he played up his Italian identity and was celebrated as a local war hero.[29] Writing a draft of his last chapter of *Death in the Afternoon* in 1931, he interrupted the narrative to recall his experience: "I loved Northern Italy like a fool, truly, the way I had loved northern Michigan."[30] His memories of the war, the trauma of his near-death experience, the aftermath of falling in love with his nurse, would furnish him the materials for numerous short stories and *A Farewell to Arms*. Hemingway is associated with many locales, Paris, Spain, Cuba, Chicago, Idaho, but as Rena Sanderson writes, "it was in Italy that he became a man, and it was to Italy that he (re)turned for restoration."[31]

In one way Hemingway departed markedly from the general tenor of writing about Italians by Americans at this time, because, Jeffrey A. Schwarz points out, "as an American in Italy, he was submerged within an authentic Italian culture."[32] Whatever prejudice he brought to Italy and Italians (and Italian Americans) from Chicago—and he grew up during the period of massive immigration and local crime—was soon undermined and dispelled. In *A Farewell to Arms* Hemingway's Italians do not belong to the discriminatory American stereotypes of the period but "are portrayed in realistic and individualized ways."[33] Hemingway visited Italy for extended periods in the early and mid-1920s, but ceased after 1927 over his disgust with Mussolini; he did not return for twenty-one years.

When he did return, and saw Venice for the first time, it inspired him to write his second "Italian" novel, *Across the River and into the Trees*. Readers expecting Hemingway to indulge in touristic views were quickly chastened. To be sure, Venetian imagery brings the city to life but it is always in the service of plot and character and the organic work of art as a whole. This much undervalued novel tells the story of the last days in the life of Lieutenant Colonel Richard Cantwell, with a parallel between the prematurely aging colonel (he is fifty-one, the same age as Hemingway at the time) and sinking Venice, the quintessential Romantic city of the beautiful death. Using the free indirect style, Hemingway allows the reader to overhear Cantwell's somber internal monologues as he walks through the city—and Venice is a walker's city. The Grand Canal looks "as grey as though Degas had painted it on one of his greyest days." Nothing seems "dull" along the canals and it "doesn't all have to be palaces and churches." He passes Santa Maria del Giglio on the way to Harry's Bar and compares its "compact," "air-borne" structure to a P47; perhaps the heavy drinking may explain how this heavy baroque church could fly. Cantwell thinks he would enjoy reading up about it; he will never have the chance to learn what Hemingway already knows, that, endowed by the Barbaro, the Venetian military family, Santa Maria del Giglio is one of the few churches in Christendom decorated with carvings of military fortifications on its facade: a soldier's church. Cantwell walks through the "strange, tricky town," it is like "working cross-word puzzles," full of bridges, junctures, crossroads, a symbol for the puzzles of a text. For Venice is "a game you play," fun to be sure, but also an unknown terrain where one gets lost playing "solitaire ambulante" as in the labyrinthine underworld. Taking a gondola across the Grand Canal, he sees the "black-clad people" climbing out of a "black-painted vehicle." Since all gondolas are black, one must assume that this is one of the new motor taxis, a modern intrusion. The power of blackness is doubly unsettling; it would seem that they disembark on the isle of the dead; "nobody would give you a penny for your thoughts." The ancient Roman was to leave a small coin to pay Charon the ferryman—it costs next to nothing.[34]

In 1924, Ezra Pound left Paris and chose to live in Rapallo for the sake of peace and economy. At the time he was at work on that portion of the *Cantos* in which Venice and its history figure prominently. He had first visited Venice, aged twenty-three, in April 1908, and stayed for four months, self-publishing his first book *A lume spento* (1908) there:

And I came here in my young youth
and lay there under the crocodile
By the column, looking East . . .
And at night they sang in the gondolas
And in the barche with lanthorns
(XXVI/121)

First patron saint of Venice, Saint Theodore of Amasea bestrides a crocodile atop one of the two tall columns in Piazza San Marco. He slew the dragon whom Pound interprets as a symbol for usury. Through Pound's eyes, one sees a city transformed into a goddess rising from the water:

Within her cave, Nerea,
she like a great shell curved
In the suavity of the rock
Cliff green-gray in the far
(XVII/76–77)

Down the coast at Ravenna, he celebrates the mosaic tomb of the Empress Galla Placidia (d. 450) next to San Vitale:

Gold fades in the gloom
Under the blue-black roof, Placidia's,
Of the exarchate; and we sit here
By the arena. *Les gradins* . . .
And the palazzo, baseless, hangs there in the dawn
With low mist over the tide-mark.
(21/98)

The golden tesserae fade in color without the light, but return to life by means of the golden light of the imagination:

In the gloom, the gold gathers the light against it.
(XI/51)[35]

This, Pound would aver, is how to "see" Italy.

[1] George Santayana, *Persons and Places: Fragments of Autobiography*, ed. by William G. Holzberger and Herman J. Saatkamp, Jr. (Cambridge: MIT Press, 1986), 529; John McCormick, *George Santayana: A Biography* (New York: Knopf, 1987), 45, 263.

[2] See Andrew M. Canepa, "From Degenerate Scoundrel to Noble Savage: The Italian Stereotype in 18th Century British Travel Literature," in *English Miscellany* 22 (1971): 107–46; Robert Casillo, *The Empire of Stereotypes* (New York: Oxford University Press, 2005).

[3] Augustus Hare, *Cities of Northern and Central Italy* (London: 1876), 1: xxxii.

[4] Rudolf Borchardt, *Città italiane*, trans. M. Marianelli and M. Ingenmey (Milan: Adelphi, 1989), 27–28.

[5] Edith Wharton, *A Backward Glance* (New York: D. Appleton-Century, 1934), 140–41. Edith Wharton proved herself to have both talents, that of the scholar (for her works on Italian decor and Italian gardens) and the cultured amateur; and so too Bernard Berenson wrote exceptional works of travel writing, such as *The Passionate Sightseer* (1960), *Sunset and Twilight. From the Diaries of 1947–1958* (1962).

[6] William Roscoe Thayer, *Italica* (Boston, MA: Houghton Mifflin, 1908), iv.

[7] Arnold Toynbee, *A Study of History* (London: Oxford University Press, 1939–61), 4: 275 and 5: 637–38; see 1: 19, 3: 345–46, 350–63, 375; 12: 522.

[8] Borchardt, *Città italiane* 1989, 23, 25. See also Wolfgang Schivelbusch, *The Railway Journey: The Industrialization of Time and Space in the 19th Century* (Berkeley: University of California Press, 1977).

[9] Douglas Sladen, *How To See Italy by Rail* (London: Kegan, Paul, Trench, Trubner, 1912), xxiv: "it is full of splendid roads, which are kept in excellent order, where they do not compete with railways."

[10] Katharine Putnam Hooker, *Through the Heel of Italy* (1901) (New York: Rae D. Henkle, 1927), ix. Travel writers in these years rarely discussed modes of transportations in their published writings. Compare the majority of Hooker's travels, based on the car, with another travel book on Apulia, *The Land of Manfred, Prince of Tarentum and King of Sicily: Rambles in Remote Parts of Southern Italy* (1889) by Janet Ross, who traveled by train and carriage.

[11] Katharine Putnam Hooker, *Wayfarers in Italy* (New York: Scribner's, 1902), 6, 88, 95; *Byways in Southern Tuscany* (London: T. Fisher Unwin, 1919), viii.

[12] *The Letters of Edith Wharton*, ed. by R. W. B. Lewis and Nancy Lewis (New York: Scribner's, 1988), 76, cited in William L. Vance, "Edith Wharton's Italian Mask: *The Valley of Decision*," in *The Cambridge Companion to Edith Wharton*, ed. by Millicent Bell (Cambridge: Cambridge University Press, 1995), 169.

[13] Edith Wharton, *A Motor-Flight through France* (New York: Scribner's, 1909), 35.

[14] Gianfranca Balestra, "Edith Wharton, Henry James, and 'The Proper Vehicle of Passion'," in "Technology and the American Imagination: An Ongoing Challenge," ed. by Francesca Bisutti De Riz and Rosella Mamoli Zorzi, in *RSA (Rivista di Studi Anglo-Americani)* 8, 10 (1994): 596.

[15] Edith Wharton, *Italian Backgrounds* (New York: Scribner's, 1905), 177–78.

[16] Ibid., 36, 177.

[17] Wharton, *A Backward Glance* 1934, 136–37.

[18] Wharton, *Italian Backgrounds* 1905, 137–39, 142–43.

[19] Eleanor Dwight, *Edith Wharton: An Extraordinary Life* (New York: Abrams, 1994), 120.

[20] R. W. B. Lewis, *Edith Wharton: A Biography* (New York: Harper and Row, 1975), 319.

[21] Robin Peel, "Wharton and Italy," in *Edith Wharton in Context*, ed. by Laura Rattray (Cambridge: Cambridge University Press, 2012), 287.

[22] Cited by Peel, "Wharton and Italy" 2012, 287.

[23] Maureen E. Montgomery, "Possessing Italy: Wharton and American Tourists," in *Edith Wharton and Cosmopolitanism*, ed. by Meredith L. Goldsmith and Emily J. Orlando (Gainesville: University Press of Florida, 2016), 126.

[24] Dan Fellows Platt, *Through Italy with Car and Camera* (New York: G. P. Putnam's, 1908), 8, 11, 74, 210, 268, 276, 316, 453–54.

[25] Francis Miltoun, *Italian Highways and Byways from a Motor Car* (Boston: L. C. Page, 1909), 2, 4, 9, 10, 11, 12, 18.

[26] *Dear Scott/Dear Max: The Fitzgerald-Perkins Correspondence*, ed. by John Kuehl and Jackson R. Bryer (New York: Scribner's, 1971), 88; *F. Scott Fitzgerald: A Life in Letters*, ed. by Matthew Bruccoli (New York: Scribner's, 1994), 94; *The Letters of F. Scott Fitzgerald*, ed. by Andrew Turnbull (New York: Dell, 1965), 177, 479. For an excellent analysis of the episode and its significance to Fitzgerald psychologically and to his later work, see Caterina Ricciardi, "F. Scott Fitzgerald and Rome," *RSA (Rivista di Studi Anglo-Americani)* 10 (1999): 36–43. See also Jeffrey Meyers, *Scott Fitzgerald: A Biography* (New York: Harper Collins, 1994), 119–20, esp. 75.

[27] Anne Bosworth Greene, *Sunshine and Dust: A Journey through Italy and the Alps* (New York: Appleton-Century, 1936), 7, 90, 94, 240–41, 242–45, 261, 262, 324. A similar infantilization of the car is illustrated by Stanley Williams's *Two in a Topolino* (1957), the travelogue of Williams and his wife from Rome to Palermo. Topolino ("Mickey Mouse") was the name of the little Fiat Cinquecento: see *Italian Americana*, 13, 1 (1995): 123–28.

[28] Cited in Donald Junkins, "The Poetry of the Twentieth Chapter of *Death in the Afternoon*: Relationships between the Deleted and Published Halves," in *Hemingway in Italy and Other Essays*, ed. by Robert W. Lewis (New York: Praeger, 1990), 120.

[29] Kim Moreland, "Bringing 'Italianicity' Home: Hemingway Returns to Oak Park," in *Hemingway's Italy: New Perspectives*, ed. by Rena Sanderson (Baton Rouge: Louisiana State University Press, 2006), 51.

[30] Cited in Junkins, "The Poetry of the Twentieth Chapter" 1990, 120.

[31] Rena Sanderson, "Hemingway's Italy: Paradise Lost," in *Hemingway's Italy* 2006: "he loved not only the landscape, but also the foreign culture—the language, food, customs, architecture, paintings, music, and literature" (2).

[32] Jeffrey A. Schwarz, "Who's the Foreigner Now? Rethinking 1920s American Prejudice in *A Farewell to Arms*," in *Hemingway's Italy* 2006, 109; see also Nancy R. Comley, "The Italian Education of Ernest Hemingway," in *Hemingway's Italy* 2006, 41–50.

[33] Schwarz, "Who's the Foreigner Now?" 2006, 110.

[34] Ernest Hemingway, *Across the River and into the Trees* (New York: Scribner's, 1950), 71, 44, 45, 185.

[35] Ezra Pound, *The Cantos* (New York: New Directions, 1993).

338

ELVIRA VALLERI

Only a few words in Italian precede the long audio recording in English where Salvatore Ferragamo tells the story of his life, an account that ends with the publication of *Shoemaker of Dreams*.[1] That recorded material, which for the first time ever is the subject of study and research for this exhibition, contributes to specifying the feelings, emotions, thoughts, but also the most significant parts of Ferragamo's "California Experience" and his relationship with the "Hollywood Story."

The recording[2] has a single narrator, Salvatore Ferragamo; the few, significant words by his wife Wanda interrupt the story to offer some interesting keys to interpretation, which we shall return to later on. It is not an interview, nor is there anything constructed, composed, or solemn about it; it is not a fake portrait offered to the narrator so that he can turn it into a monument to a life of successes. We find ourselves facing a picture of a life and work that cross the entire first half of the twentieth century, between two wars and two worlds: Italy and America.

The "autobiographical pact"[3] that Ferragamo intends to underwrite is aimed at offering an interpretation[4] as to why he chose a trade—he would also refer to it as an art—that in twentieth-century Italy was seen as something of a disgrace.[5]

As he pulls each of the threads of his life and describes them with a firm, deep voice in correct English with no accent, we can hear in the background the sounds of the city in the morning, of life waking up again, alternating with the rhythmical noises of a workshop where we imagine him intent on watching over and checking the work being done by his workers. The sound of a hammer on a small anvil is reminiscent of the tinkling metallic noises of a smithy and accompanies the entire recording.

One of the central knots of this oral source, which is not always diachronic, is the cyclical reflection on the essence of the shoemaker's trade. Ferragamo does not intend to abdicate to artisanal skill and the

THE "AUTOBIOGRAPHICAL PACT" OF SALVATORE FERRAGAMO

pride of knowing how to do something; rather, he wants to foster new knowledge and synergies, which he will express over time thanks to his studies on the anatomy of the foot and the skeletal system, on posture, on the use of leather as well as other uncommon materials, while at the same time seeking the taste and the style that distinguishes the identifying signature of his production.[6]

It is probably around 1957[7] and in that "story about himself," which time has turned into something that is not always easy to listen to and to understand, Ferragamo comments and explains the choice of his intense experience of life and work, before his untimely death in August 1960.

We can hypothesize that the recording was used to draft his autobiography, which saw the collaboration of two English writers, John Desmond Currie and Elisabeth Warner,[8] whom Ferragamo thanks for their help to "prepare the manuscript for publication."[9]

Indeed, *Shoemaker of Dreams* was not just the product of the biunivocal relationship between Ferragamo and the two narrators, but also a tacit agreement that involved many more subjects, in a complex game of reciprocal seduction from which what emerged was the image of a successful man who had pursued a dream and had made it come true. Actually, his voice also expresses the difficulties, the commitment, the absolute devotion: it was a question of "stubbornness," not luck, as Wanda tells us in those few, precious moments in the recording.[10] The passion for work and not simply the dream of its realization.

What you expect from an autobiography in the first place is that the person who writes about him or herself is also the representative of a context, a world, that his or her story is the story of a time and a place. From this point of view Ferragamo's narrative allows us to grasp, in the folds of his personal story, the description of different and interesting realities on both sides of the Atlantic.

In the wake of the strong impulse of study that the autobiographical genre has exerted in the fields of history and sociology, the writings of those who experienced migration can represent an interesting literary chapter; indeed, they can cast light on a real segment of life, not an imaginary one, and in many cases go beyond the individual borders to become exemplary in various directions.

The autobiography, in its form of self-reflection, can in fact signify the restoration of subjective points of view that, subtracted from the sociological generalizations and literary manipulations, become a

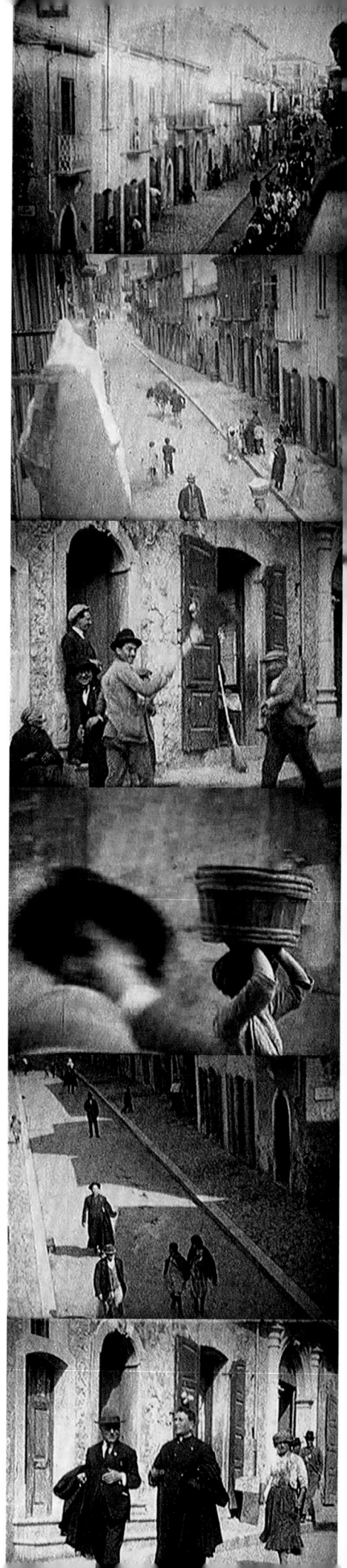

Stills from the movie Salvatore Ferragamo made in Bonito in 1927, upon returning from the United States. The town was not that different from what it had been when he left it in 1915. Clearly visible in the images is his uncle the priest, who gave Salvatore the money he needed to emigrate to the United States

Naples represented in the short silent film made by the Lumière brothers in 1898. The film comprises several scenes shot in Via Marina, Via Toledo, at the port with a view of Vesuvius, and in Borgo Santa Lucia

precious source for the study of collective mentality and psychology.[11]

A precocious apprenticeship

Salvatore Ferragamo was born in 1898 in Bonito, in the Irpinia region. He was the eleventh child in a big family that made many economic sacrifices so that their firstborn son, Agostino, could get a degree at the University of Naples. But Agostino, who was a model student, a "phenomenon" as Salvatore described him, died when he was still very young.[12] Salvatore's other older brothers had no choice but to "try their luck in the United States."[13]

In the early twentieth century, the school in Bonito only went as far as third grade, and at the age of nine Salvatore was too young to leave with his brothers. So his father gave him permission to learn how to be a shoemaker, which, as he tells us in his memoirs, he felt was the "mission" of his life.[14]

In spite of the fact that his mother and father were completely against his choice, which they felt was too distant from the family tradition of working the land,[15] Salvatore began his precocious apprenticeship at the town cobbler's, where shoes were both made and repaired. The workshop-cum-store fulfilled the needs of the customers of modest means who sought an "inexpensive" product.[16] The young boy had no specific schedule or assignments: he began by

EMIGRAZIONE ITALIANA PRIMA E DOPO LA GUERRA

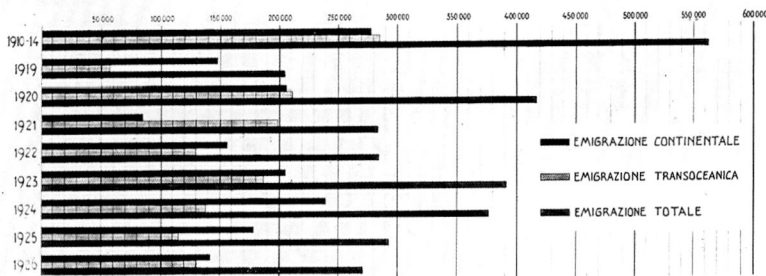

PRIMA DELLA GUERRA
MEDIA 1910 – 14

1920

1924

1922

1926

1919

EMIGRAZIONE CONTINENTALE
EMIGRAZIONE TRANSOCEANICA
EMIGRAZIONE TOTALE

Graphs on Italian emigration
before and after the war toward
continental countries and across
the ocean, exhibited in September
1927 on the occasion of the *Mostra
Geografica dell'Espansione Italiana
all'Estero* held at the Palazzo
della Permanente in Milan

straightening out nails and cleaning the shop and had to be ready to work when other things came up, which even included taking care of his boss's children when necessary. Little by little Maestro Luigi Festa allowed him to learn the basics of the job: for example, to make the twine used to stitch the shoes. "Step by step I learned each part of the art of shoemaking," Salvatore recalled, "not necessarily in the correct order . . . Before the end of the year I had mastered every phase of the craft."[17]

Seven days a week the young son of Mariantonia Ferragamo ("in southern Italy," he annotated in his memoirs, "children are always known as the sons of their mothers"[18]) worked as many as twelve hours a day, at times even more. When his father suddenly passed away, in 1908, the family's situation got worse. Young Salvatore was forced to contribute his modest earnings so that the family could make ends meet, while his brothers and sisters sent their savings over from the United States.[19]

In the early twentieth century, in every Italian village, there were certain figures of reference for the life of a small community. In Bonito these were the teacher and the pharmacist and they encouraged Salvatore, who had shown interest and versatility in the shoemaking trade early on, to go to Naples where he could learn more about it.[20] The young boy was convinced that in the city he would finally learn to measure shoes properly and even produce "new models." He was only eleven and had just a few cents in his pocket when he arrived in the ancient capital city, which since the nineteenth century had represented for the southern populations an attraction in spite of its strong internal contradictions and the signs of an economic expansion that was "limited and disorderly."[21] The 1911 industrial census recorded the presence in the city of a widespread domestic industry network in a variety of sectors, revealing an artisanal rather than industrial structure: shoemakers, manufacturers of wooden buttons, combs, containers, artistic leather and gloves, trunks and pipes.[22]

For a young apprentice who went from one shop to another in the context of such an economic framework, life was quite hard: "sometimes there were whole days when I did not eat . . . In Bonito we had never lived luxuriously, but we had never gone without food. It was in Naples that I first learned what hunger means."[23]

He shared a room with other people who came from his town and were having the same problems.

In the recording he stresses that "I was a young boy and I needed food. And the food was the biggest problem for me. I didn't care where or how I would sleep, or whether I would sleep, but the food was a necessary proposition for me."[24] The annotation is interesting and it helps understand that living conditions got worse when workers and artisans left their country villages to go to the city—a situation that was quite common throughout Europe in the first phase of the Industrial Revolution, which for Italy corresponded to the fifteen years preceding World War I.

Despite the many sacrifices, which we can perceive from Salvatore's recollections, he chose to stay so that he could "learn to take correct measurements the way they did in Naples" and not as "I had learned before."[25] Let's imagine him in Via dei Calzolai, near the San Pietro neighborhood in Patierno. This was an impoverished area, famous for shoemaking since the late nineteenth century with shops that were still run the way they were during the Renaissance. All the same, Ferragamo managed to reach one of the "best shops in the city" where he hoped to finally learn to make well-made shoes: to "make them fit."[26] However, he was not completely satisfied with this method either.

The city that the young Ferragamo discovered, in the early twentieth century, still had the irresistible charm of the ancient capital, which a decade before the Lumière brothers had immortalized in a short documentary. In those images you can grasp a reality that was complex and contradictory, but also unsurpassably and overwhelmingly beautiful; you can also admire scenes from everyday life in the area of Santa Lucia, Via Marina, Via Toledo, and the port. The streets were filled with shops that had wooden windows reminiscent of the style of some of the major European capitals. Looming up in the background was the veritable soul of Naples, Mount Vesuvius, the silent and menacing sovereign who rules over the gulf and whose shape enchants the viewer, much like the siren Parthenope used to do with her amazing voice.

The Neapolitan experience must have deeply affected and fascinated the young Ferragamo, who, having returned to Bonito in 1912 to open up his own business, remembers how he had tried, to no avail, to recreate a store that was similar to the one where he had worked in Naples and that would probably serve as a model for his Hollywood Boot Shop a decade later.

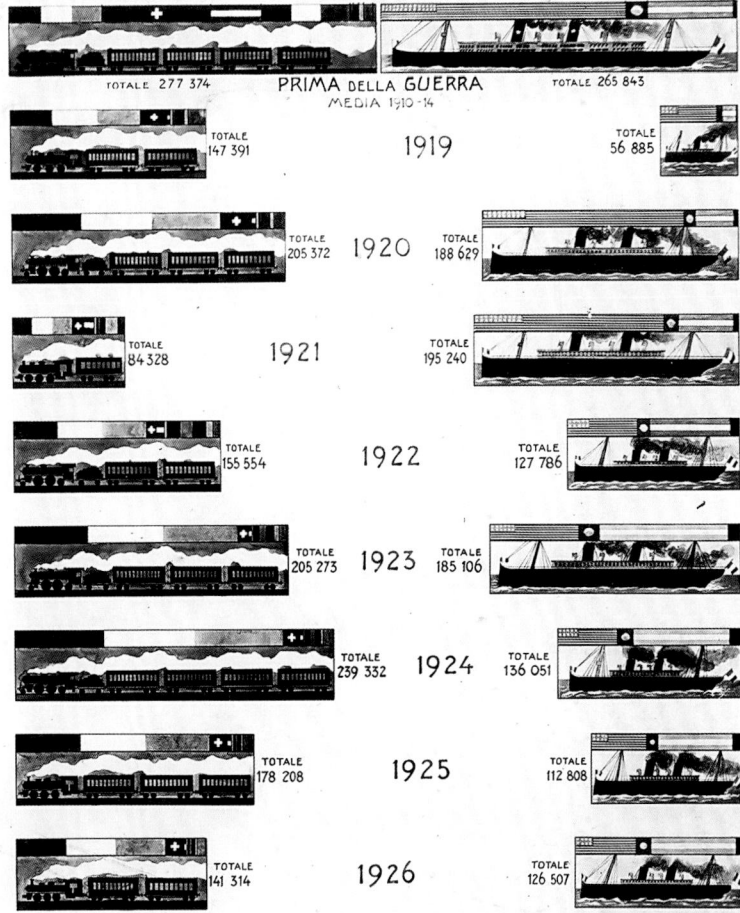

EMIGRAZIONE ITALIANA PER PAESI CONTINENTALI E TRANSOCEANICI

TOTALE 277 374 — PRIMA DELLA GUERRA MEDIA 1910-14 — TOTALE 265 843

1919 — TOTALE 147 391 — TOTALE 56 885

1920 — TOTALE 205 372 — TOTALE 188 629

1921 — TOTALE 84 328 — TOTALE 195 240

1922 — TOTALE 155 554 — TOTALE 127 786

1923 — TOTALE 205 273 — TOTALE 185 106

1924 — TOTALE 239 332 — TOTALE 136 051

1925 — TOTALE 178 208 — TOTALE 112 808

1926 — TOTALE 141 314 — TOTALE 126 507

Historic photo of the building that
hosted Ferragamo's shop in Santa
Barbara, at 1033 State Street
Santa Barbara, Santa Barbara Historical
Society

Side view of the Flying "A"
Studios and the main entrance
on Mission Street in Santa Barbara
Santa Barbara, Santa
Barbara Historical Society

The Italo-American dream

In April 1915, at the age of seventeen, Ferragamo left Bonito and Italy. The American tales his brother Alfonso told convinced him that in that "fabulous country" everything was easier and that machines were of precious help.[27] Once again, the challenge to better understand how to produce shoes that fit, combined with the entreaties of his older brother, convinced Salvatore to leave Bonito in the hopes of returning there one day "rich and famous" and "show all of Italy how shoes are made."[28]

When the young Salvatore landed on Ellis Island he was one of the approximately three and a half million Italians who, from the start of the twentieth century, had arrived in the New World. Very few of them had some form of schooling or their own money, and very few of them were professionals or merchants. Although all the regions of Italy were represented,[29] four-fifths of this significant number of young men came from the south, especially from Campania, Abruzzo, Calabria, Molise, and Sicily. Only a small number of immigrants had been trained to do a specific job and most of the time they were dressmakers, barbers, shoemakers, stonecutters and stonemasons, mosaicists and plasterers, to mention only the most numerous groups.

Based on a study promoted in 1909 by Italy's Ministry of Foreign Affairs, what emerged was a multifarious miscellany of jobs in the United States, and the Italian consulates, in charge of doing the survey, identified at least twenty-three categories of Italian workers: a complex and composite structure that revealed the consistent presence of shoemakers and leather-workers alongside dressmakers, seamstresses, and barbers. An analysis of the historical data has shown how in some cases these trades represented the very elite of the migrant workforce.[30]

Undoubtedly, in this wave of "new immigration"—as it was referred to by the Research Commission of 1911[31]—Italians were the most numerous, followed by large groups of Jews from Eastern Europe, Germans, and the Polish.

For a long time, and perhaps also in today's culture, rural society and migration represented two terms of "an obvious and intimately antithetical pair." The archaic and remote world of southern Italy

countryside was considered the only one capable of generating migration, albeit openly against its traditional stability and demographic immobility. A pair of opposing realities that at a certain point history would bring together almost indissolubly. The truth is that recent research has shown how the social dynamics are much more articulated and complex than this. Having torn away the veil of a simplistic and mannerist representation of rural society, forever interpreted as a closed reality with its slow rhythms of social reproduction and fixed in the immutable residential status of its inhabitants, we can glimpse the surprising variety of work activities that were carried out on a seasonal basis.[32]

The story itself of the Ferragamo family confirms and reflects the tendency for members of the Irpinia society to relocate: men and women accustomed to being uprooted from their towns or villages if this meant earning something, or else aspiring to learn a trade. This was a culture of the journey and of wandering disseminated in the popular world, at least amid its more active and entrepreneurial layers, and indicated a break in the paradigm of a permanent residence. Emigrating, more than an escape from poverty, was in itself a "trade," or the vehicle, the instrument, with which to exercise it.

All these reasons explain, therefore, the desire to migrate for economic reasons in areas, such as southern Italy, that were more conventionally seen as passive containers of the workforce.[33]

A recent analysis of the lists of the Italians who left Naples headed for the United States in the late nineteenth century offers interesting information on the travel companies, the destinations, and the returns, but even more importantly it confirms a presence greater than 60 percent of young Italian males, most of whom from Irpinia, who had been trained to work, especially as dressmakers and shoemakers.[34]

This overall vision provides us with a context for the young Ferragamo when he reached the United States: in the early twentieth century one Italian male immigrant every twenty-five was registered as a shoemaker. Although they had been forced to convert to cobblers, accepting the job of repairing shoes rather than making them, Italian shoemakers had found a way to "monopolize" the market—often beginning from the humble job of shoe-shining—undermining the positions of the Germans.[35] Indeed, the 1922 Santa Barbara Business Directory recorded the widespread presence of "shoemakers" and "shoe repairers," albeit slightly fewer than the previous years.[36]

It may also be of interest to note how on the West Coast, American shoemakers could boast a deep-rooted and widespread presence and a consolidated associative tradition dating back to the seventeenth century. A study of the early twentieth century recorded their presence, described their characteristics, and drew their geographical location.[37]

Salvatore Ferragamo thus learned about a world and a trade that could boast a solid tradition, and it was precisely based on this analysis and his coming to terms with this reality that he developed his brilliant economic plan.

In the new world he searched for stimuli, ideas, and new ways of thinking about an occupation that he felt he was destined to carry out and that engaged him as though it were a mission for his entire life. "I was born to be a shoemaker," he jotted down. "I know it. I have always known it . . . but from whence does my knowledge come . . . *I have remembered*, that is the only way to describe it. I have only to sit down and think, and the answer comes to me out of the memory of the days . . . when I was a shoemaker."[38]

This is not just a marginal thought, nor will it be necessary to evoke the Platonic doctrine of reminiscence. The interpretation that Ferragamo himself provided for his choice to be a shoemaker is undeniably connected to a spiritual dimension, which is not taken for granted, that can perhaps be seen in relation to the spreading of the Theosophical doctrine in American culture at the time.

The idea that underlying all religions there is a unique and universal "divine knowledge" had also been expressed in different ways in Europe; suffice to think of Giuseppe Mazzini who shared the idea of reincarnation, or Giuseppe Garibaldi who, in the mid-nineteenth century, accepted the presidency of an esoteric society in Venice.[39]

Backdrop used for the scenes of movies at the Flying "A" Studios, 1910 Santa Barbara, University of California, UC Santa Barbara Library, Joel Conway/Flying "A" Studios Photograph Collection

On the set of a Western movie produced by the Flying "A" Studios in 1916, published in Robert S. Birchard, *Images of America Silent-Era Filmmaking in Santa Barbara* (Mount Pleasant, SC: Arcadia Publishing, 2007). The actor and director of Italian origin Frank Borzage (center) gets ready to enter the scene while L. Guy Wilky looks into the camera; holding the script to the right is the assistant director Park Frame Courtesy Arcadia Publishing

A scene from *Diamond from the Sky* (1915), a Western series produced by the Flying "A" Studios which is where Ferragamo began collaborating with the cinema. The series was originally supposed to have fifteen episodes, but because it was so successful thirty were eventually produced. William Desmond Taylor directed the first ten, Jacques Jaccard the others

Lillian Gish in *Way Down East*, directed by David W. Griffith in 1920, for which Ferragamo made the shoes

Salvatore Ferragamo behind the wheel of his car, 1920

Jiddu Krishnamurti, who lived in California in the 1920s, was also a member of the International Theosophical Society. We do not know whether and how Salvatore Ferragamo was drawn to these reflections or associations. He undoubtedly breathed that array of religious practices that saw the flourishing in the United States, alongside Catholicism, Protestantism, and Judaism, of different forms of spirituality, identified as one of the origins of the dissemination of the "American model."[40]

The young Italian perceived with great insight and rather quickly some of the features that were typical of the society that had welcomed him and where he was to live for twelve years; a reality where man's ability to self-organize, according to the scholar

Oliver Zunz, was fueled not just by a culture of interpersonal faith but also by a different spiritual model.

Coast to Coast
It has been correctly emphasized how memories above all allow us to penetrate "the mental worlds of immigrants," and how autobiographies in particular provide an "interpretation of a long period" through which the authors seek to gather the story of their life and reorganize their experience of migration around certain themes that they believe to be of fundamental importance.[41] Hence, in the web of memory, silence is perhaps worth more than words.

As concerns the period Salvatore Ferragamo spent in Boston, a guest of his sister Alessandrina and brother-in-law Joseph Covelli, we know very little.[42] The research carried out in the United States for the purposes of this exhibition has confirmed the presence of Salvatore's brothers Alfonso, Girolamo, and Secondino on the other coast, in Santa Barbara, California as early as 1915–16.[43]

Recalling the short period of time he spent in Boston, where he worked at the Queen Quality Shoe Manufacturing Company, one of the most important factories on the East Coast, he describes the sense of loss he experienced before the assembly line: "this was not shoemaking. This was an inferno, a bedlam of rattles and clatters and whizzing

machines and hurrying, scurrying people." A maze of working parts that clashed with the image of work he carried within: "I was a shoemaker, not a finisher or a trimmer or an edger or any other of the piecemeal jobs which went into these mass-produced shoes. There was no craftsmanship here, not an ounce."[44]

Ferragamo was "horrified," not "fascinated" the way his brother Alfonso had hoped, upon seeing this way of working, and became convinced that it was not for him. Those were difficult years for Italians living and working on the East Coast, as proven by the many articles on the subject in the press; but the memoirs remain silent. So after a few months, Salvatore decided to leave Boston and move to Santa Barbara.[45]

From the second half of the nineteenth century, Italian migration to the Golden State had witnessed a considerable rise after gold was discovered there; nonetheless, even after this resource became depleted, many continued to move to the cities, which soon became centers of attraction for the chain migration that called out to other Italians, in particular from the northern regions, based on friendships and kinships.

Ilaria Serra, who comparatively analyzed two major newspapers on the East and West Coast respectively, *The New York Times* and the *San Francisco Chronicle* in the first decade of the twentieth century, emphasized the widespread perception that "many excellent immigrants" had opted for the West Coast. Indeed, there were many Italians who had distinguished themselves for their talent and their abilities and who, thanks to money and power, had become part of the elite in the California cities.[46]

With their skills and with time, as the *Times* emphasized in 1909, the Italians of San Francisco had shown they could contribute to the construction of a greater America.[47] The prestigious newspaper cited the case of Amadeo Peter Giannini who, by studying and working, had succeeded in 1904 in founding a small bank, The Bank of Italy, which now boasted credit all across the United States.[48] Alongside "AP," as he was usually referred to especially by the Italians in America to whom he loaned money with just a "shake of the hand," the article also mentioned Marco Fontana, who established the Del Monte canned fruit company; the intellectual Ettore Patrizi, founder of the newspaper *L'Italia* and of the Italian-Swiss Colony Wine Company; and Andrea Sbarboro, whom also the *San Francisco Chronicle* described in emphatic and enthusiastic tones as the man who had brought the "enchantment of Italy" back to life by building his majestic Pompeiian villa in Asti, California.

S. FERRAGAMO.
TURNBUCKLE.
APPLICATION FILED FEB. 4, 1921.

1,393,614.

Patented Oct. 11, 1921.

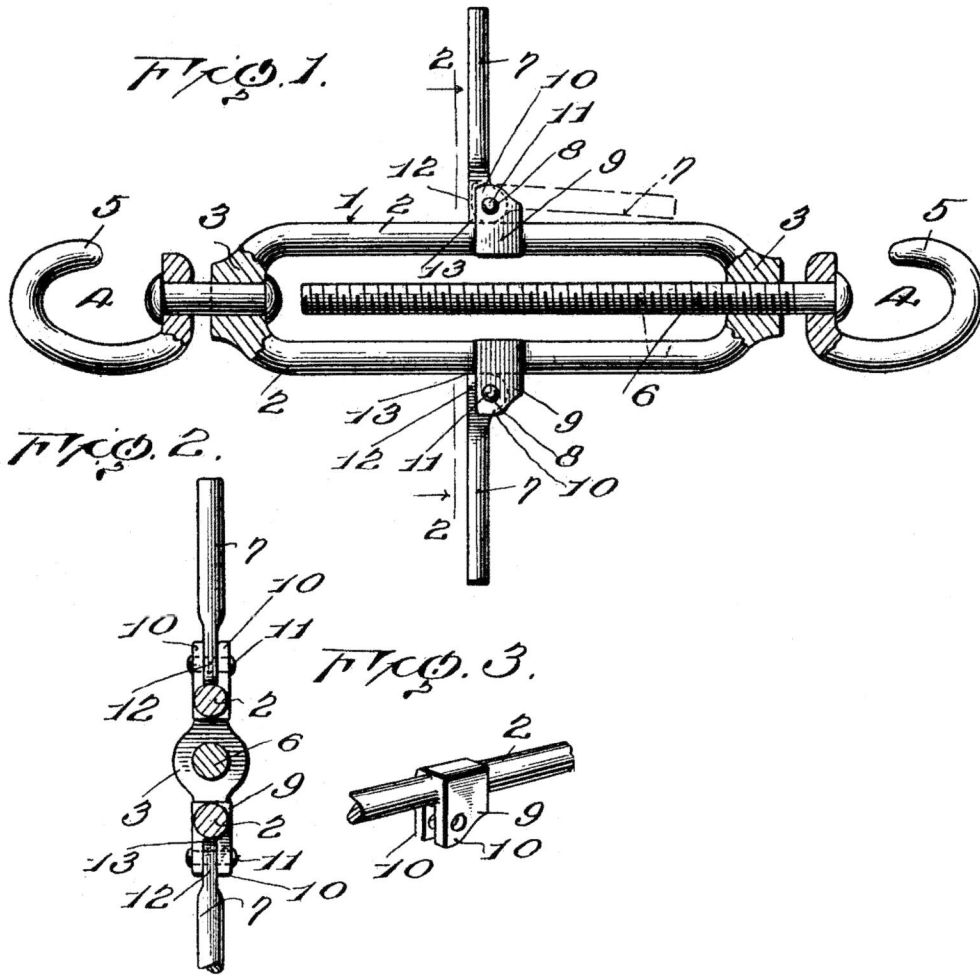

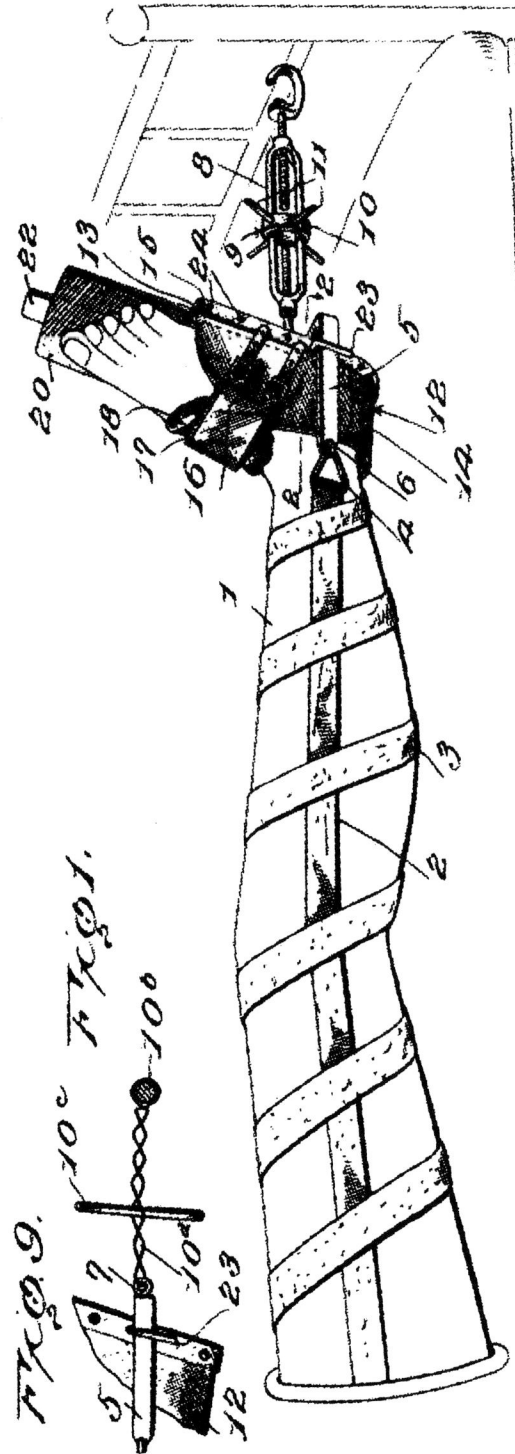

Inventor
Salvatore Ferragamo,
By Wm. E. Dyre,
Attorney

S. FERRAG
SURGICAL APP
APPLICATION FILED

1,399,606.

Patents registered by Salvatore Ferragamo to make a cylinder that would allow for the traction of the limb with a double-screw stretcher and an orthopaedic apparatus:
no. 1,393,614 of October 11, 1921;
no. 1,399,606 of December 6, 1921;
no. 1,479,536 of January 1, 1924

Patented Dec. 6, 1921.

2 SHEETS—SHEET 1.

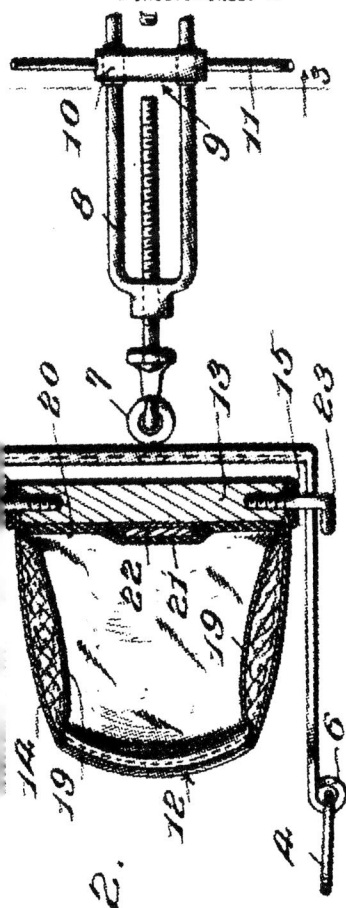

Fig. 2.

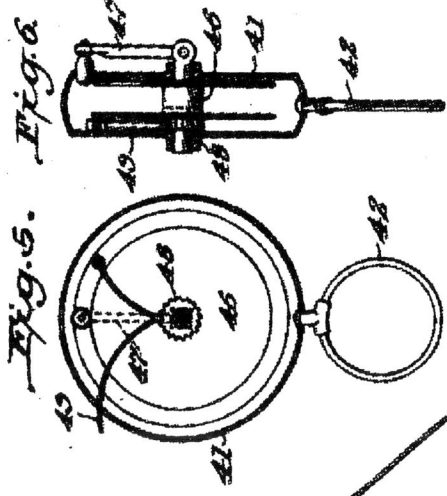

Fig. 6.

Fig. 5.

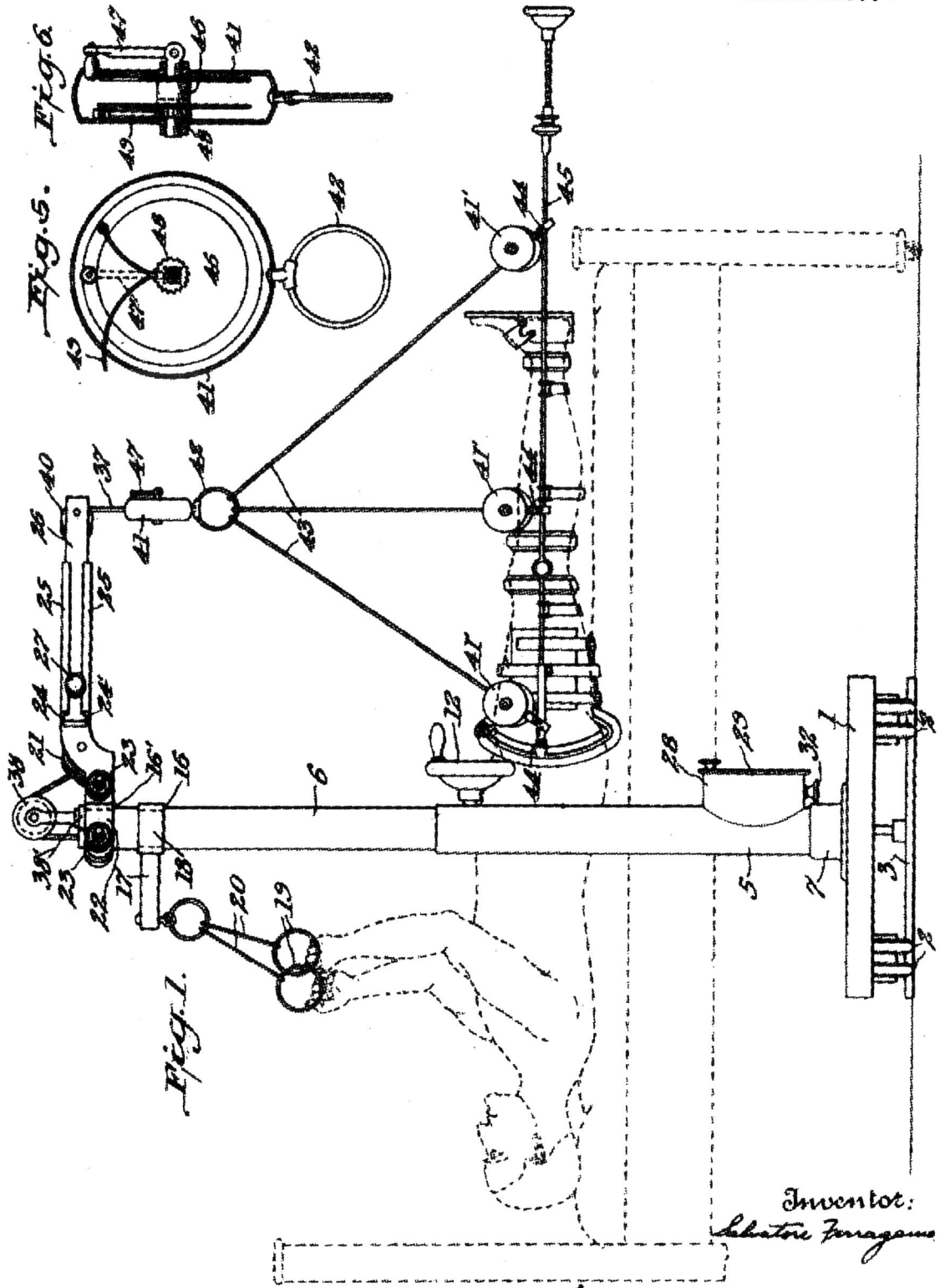

Fig. 1.

Inventor

Salvatore
Ferragamo,

Wm E. Dye, Attorney

Inventor:
Salvatore Ferragamo

by
Byrnes, Townsend & Rubenstein,
Attorneys.

Salvatore Ferragamo's home
at 719 California Street,
Santa Barbara

Generally speaking, the reporters' descriptions seemed to depict a sort of polarity between the Italians on the East and the West Coast. Actually, contributing to shaping this image was a different type of immigration; in particular, the group of prominent Italians in California, enthralled by American success, had been capable of creating the concept of a prosperous colony. And the Italian community today, which is well established in the Golden State, still holds this vision.[49]

Santa Barbara

The journey toward Santa Barbara was filled with surprises and awe for the young Salvatore: the desert of Arizona where the train "ran for hours through cactus and sand," the Rocky Mountains and Mexican workers toiling away on the railway, or some traveler of Italian origin who spoke to him. Once he had arrived in Santa Barbara, he was struck by the beauty of the landscape and felt the desire to tell his mother about it. So he sent her some postcards.[50] Since the late nineteenth century, after Charles Nordhoff's emphatic description,[51] the city had earned the reputation of a "tourist attraction." When Ferragamo arrived, the luxurious Potter Hotel, with its 400 rooms, had already been built and was soon to become the greatest attraction in the area, contributing to create the image of a refined city,

View of State Street, Santa Barbara, c. 1908

The courtyard of the public library in Santa Barbara in a picture from 1919. This is probably where Salvatore Ferragamo conducted his historical research into footwear used in the first costume movies

The square opposite Los Banos del Mar in Santa Barbara, c. 1905. To the left the famous Potter Hotel
Santa Barbara, Santa Barbara Public Library, Edson Smith Photo Collection

The movie studios of Mary
Pickford and Douglas
Fairbanks on Santa Monica
Boulevard, Hollywood, 1922

The movie studios of Mack
Sennett in Edendale, 1921.
Edendale was a town located
close to Hollywood, which
was later named Glendale
or Echo Park

an ideal place in terms of health and well-being. The Southern Pacific Railroad, which had reached the city in 1905, had consolidated its importance. In those years, the railway was seen as a sort of icon of progress and the new times, and was often used as a photographic or advertising set (perhaps even a cinematographic set) to celebrate success and power.[52] Some images of those years preserved at the Santa Barbara Maritime Museum allow us to capture the appeal of this resort with its bathing facilities, swimming pools, hotels, and places where people could meet or simply find comfort, frequented by finance and business tycoons. The years spent by Salvatore Ferragamo in Santa Barbara, where the Flying "A" Studios (American Film Company) had recently moved to, were a very interesting period for both his life and his work—a period that is worth observing carefully because it allows us to grasp how he fostered a new vision of the shoemaker's profession, bestowing it with original ideas and insights that would eventually become some of the fundamental elements for the definition of a new footwear dictionary.

We know that Salvatore's first store was in Mission Canyon, not far from Mission Street where the American Film Company was based; shortly afterwards, the Ferragamo brothers decided to pool their economic resources in a new store at 1033 State Street.[53]

While the United States were preparing to end isolationism to put an end to the German "barbarianism" of the Great War, as President Thomas Woodrow Wilson said, the last Ferragamo brother, Eliodoro, arrived in America to work as a

Entrance to Paramount studios in Hollywood

The Walt Disney studios at 2719 Hyperion Avenue in Los Angeles

Advert appearing in May
1923 in the local newspaper
Holly Leaves, where the
name "S. Ferragamo,
Manager" can be seen on
the left

The Hollywood Boot Shop
sign is clearly visible in the
movie *Show People*, directed
by King Vidor in 1928

New Shipment of
NETTLETON and J. P. SMITH Shoes for Men
and also
K. and L. Shoes for Women
Just Arrived

HOLLYWOOD BOOT SHOP

6687 Hollywood Boulevard

S. Ferragamo, Manager - - Telephone 577-101

The Renaissance-style
interior of Salvatore
Ferragamo's shop, published
in *Boot and Shoe Recorder*,
March 28, 1925

The Hollywood Boot Shop
business card

tailor and Salvatore came into contact with the world of cinema through Alfonso, who, among other things, ironed clothes for the American Film Company. Thanks to the wardrobe manager, Salvatore entered the film studios and was enthralled by what he saw. In his autobiography he tells of having "felt instantly at home among the dresses and cloaks and hats and shoes," and in the audio recording he adds: "my entire life began in this wardrobe," where for the first time ever he saw a pair of cowboy boots[54] for Westerns, a popular genre with the star system back then.[55] He felt he was facing another "challenge"[56] and wondered how he could correct and, if necessary, perfect these shoes. He offered to produce better boots than the ones he had seen, and at the same time he began thinking about staying in America.[57] His became fully aware of the importance of studying and learning English, which would also lead him to become a naturalized citizen. And so English became Salvatore's second language, the language to which he could entrust the story of his life, even thirty years after his definitive return to Italy. It was probably at that time that he began to move about in the world of cinema, where different types of workers, technicians, screenwriters, directors, producers, actors emigrated from Italy and other European countries "took possession of the studios and ended up directing them toward new forms of representation."[58] Celebrating the culture of the countries of origin would not have made any sense; immigrants wanted to be recognized as citizens of the New World, and along this path mastering the language was definitely a decisive step. The trajectory of Ferragamo's entrepreneurial activity was becoming parallel to the fast development of cinema, which has been compared to a sort of "profane pantheon," built up and enhanced by the star system.[59]

Anatomy and glamour

Salvatore Ferragamo soon learned English and felt ready to make the most of the decision that had brought him to America. He chose to study anatomy so that he could fully understand the structure of the foot, on which the health of the entire skeleton depends; he enrolled in the Extension Division (evening classes) of the University of Southern California,[60] and the audio perfectly expresses his great commitment, all the problems encountered, and his constant dedication to the lessons.[61] The teacher was intrigued by the young Italian and his frequent questions, which he answered by suggesting different readings and insights.

Customers relaxing on the sofa of the Hollywood Boot Shop

The actor Charles de Rochefort in the role of Ramesses in the silent film *The Ten Commandments*, directed by Cecil B. DeMille in 1923 and produced by Paramount Pictures. Ferragamo created the shoes for the main characters

Calfskin shoe. Replica of the model created by Salvatore Ferragamo for the movie *The Ten Commandments* Florence, Museo Salvatore Ferragamo

The entrance to Grauman's Egyptian Theatre, opened in October 1922 opposite the Hollywood Boot Shop

The actor H. B. Warner in
a scene from the silent film
The King of Kings, directed
and produced by Cecil B.
DeMille in 1927, for which
Salvatore Ferragamo made
some of the men's sandals

Calfskin sandal.
Reproduction of one
of the models Ferragamo
made for *The King of Kings*
Florence, Museo Salvatore
Ferragamo

Before finishing the academic year, Salvatore remarked, "I had acquired the knowledge of what I wanted to know, and I had a perfect understanding of the relationship between the human body and its feet . . . the plause of my clients grew from month to month . . . Everybody began to feel different in my shoes . . . my new discovery also preserved the line of the shoe . . . By combining the results of anatomic research and the actual experience in the making and the fitting of the shoes, nature fully compensated my efforts."[62]

Salvatore Ferragamo had let himself be guided by his "restlessness" in order to better understand how to create well-made footwear; he had renewed an ancient craft, studying it and analyzing it meticulously, breathing life into it through his constant pursuit of glamour and elegance. He cultivated his reflections on the anatomy and the orthopaedics of the foot and posture and succeeded in bringing footwear to fashion: a complicated, intricate and at times mysterious phenomenon, a place where different attitudes and needs, both individual and collective, all intersect.[63] A kaleidoscopic reality, a true *gnommero* (tangle)—a funny word Inspector Ingravallo coined in Carlo Emilio Gadda's novel *Quer pasticciaccio brutto de via Merulana* to

Rudolph Valentino in a picture taken in 1923 with his beloved dogs. Valentino often visited Salvatore Ferragamo at his home to have a bowl of spaghetti. "He was a beautiful boy, always impeccably debonair," writes Ferragamo in his autobiography. "He liked to dress in the Italian way—put as much as possible on himself—but everything would be tip-top and he was always perfectly groomed"

White nubuck and black calfskin Oxford shoe designed by Salvatore Ferragamo for his friend Rudolph Valentino in 1925
Florence, Museo Salvatore Ferragamo

Rudolph Valentino in the garden of his Hollywood home
Turin, Collection Museo Nazionale del Cinema

John Gilbert in the garden of his home, 1926. Ferragamo would often spend his leisure time relaxing with him, swimming at Lake Arrowhead

describe the sum of the causes that determine a complex and somewhat enigmatic phenomenon.

The study of anatomy helped to draw in his mind a scientific approach to the work of the shoemaker. Salvatore understood that he needed to also gather knowledge about the materials to be used, which is why he enrolled in the chemical engineering correspondence courses of the University of Scranton (Pennsylvania)[64] and maths in Berkeley.[65] Ferragamo himself pointed out that this was an entirely new synergy that no one had tried before.[66]

At the beginning of the twentieth century, Americans had invented new ways of associating business, politics, and science; they had put in place an institutional network of commercial companies, universities and research institutes, government agencies, and private foundations to ensure that producers, intermediaries, and users of knowledge could interact and elaborate together new strategies for acquiring it and growing.[67] In America the reorganization of knowledge, and not simply of economic power, was what generated prosperity at home and expanded the presence of the United States in the world.

Salvatore Ferragamo breathed this atmosphere of trust in the individual skills that made it possible for a young man from Italy without a degree, who had not yet become a U.S. citizen, to attend the university and rethink an ancient trade through a new concept of the product, having as his primary objective the elimination of errors concerning fit and the plantar arch, whose causes he could now understand and for which he could imagine suitable solutions.

The seven years spent in Santa Barbara brought him closer and closer to the studio system and the orders he received for historical and costume films gave him the chance to spend time in the city library so that he could find in the art and history books the style and suggestions he needed for a product that was increasingly in keeping with the requests of the producers and directors.

He realized that films needed "special shoes" for exceptional clients, such as Lottie and Mary Pickford, the Costello sisters, Barbara La Marr, Helen Hayward, Pola Negri, May McAvoy.[68] However, the most important development for his career can be attributed to the orders for shoes he privately received from the actresses themselves: it was the start of a privileged relationship with the "profane pantheon" that Salvatore Ferragamo would cultivate for the rest of his life.

Douglas Fairbanks and John Barrymore in the Warner Brothers studios in 1924. Both of them were friends and clients of Salvatore Ferragamo; Barrymore would often go to the shop on Hollywood Boulevard, not just to buys shoes but also to have a drink, regardless of Prohibitionism

Ferragamo's home at 2222
North Beachwood Drive,
Los Angeles

"The American century"

The years Ferragamo spent in the United States can be considered the beginning of the "American century," as it was famously defined in 1941 by the great journalist and founder of the magazine *Life*, Henry Luce, at least in the perception that U.S. society had of the period following World War I. Within this context, Hollywood's hegemony was considerably strengthened and it conquered the leadership of the world market: the 1920s were characterized by a "dizzying increase in the public, the capital invested, and the number of cinemas."[69] This was a complex "industrial, artistic, rhetorical, linguistic, and narrative universe" that structured itself as "a dynamic, articulated, and multifaceted system"[70] where the plans for production and diffusion of films (the so-called studio system) acquired a special relevance. Ferragamo was able to catch this complexity and probably captured its models and canons, he understood that it was a medium capable of generating a cultural production even beyond the "American Way of Life."

After the American Film Company decided to leave Santa Barbara and move production to Hollywood, Salvatore followed in their steps. Due to fast and intense growth, in those years the studio system was developing a sort of vertical integration structure whereby the production and distribution of the movies were becoming interconnected.[71]

When Ferragamo thought back to that decision, he saw a "parallel between the film industry and my own." He wrote: "Just as the motion picture industry has grown and developed from those fledgling days, so too, I hope, has mine."[72]

But the project seemed to come to a standstill in February 1920, when Salvatore was involved in a serious car accident[73] in which his brother Eliodoro lost his life: "His death was the end of the world for me," he wrote. He himself risked losing a leg from gangrene caused by the splinters from his hip bone sticking into the flesh. A friend, a doctor in Santa Barbara, helped him to convince the surgeons at Bard Memorial Hospital, where he was hospitalized, not to amputate. He was instead submitted to very painful traction treatment of the limb, which was, however, not sufficiently effective. Orthopaedics at the time, in California as well as in Europe, was slowly gaining its independence from general surgery, laying the foundations for the birth of physiotherapy.[74]

Salvatore used his own body to study how to lessen the pain of the traction. By exploiting what he had learned during his course at the University of Southern California, he designed and created a cylinder for

The opening of the Hollywood Boot Shop in February 1925. The many flowers he received attest to the prestige and appreciation that was felt for Salvatore Ferragamo in Hollywood

the traction of the limb, which he would later take out a patent for.[75] His *Apparatus for supporting injured limbs* would later be marketed by a Chicago orthopaedics company.[76]

The Hollywood Boot Shop, "opposite Grauman's theater"

1922 was the last year Salvatore Ferragamo spent in Santa Barbara.[77] By then he had decided to move to Hollywood, where the studios were creating their own organization, the Motion Picture Producers and Distributors of America (MPPDA) directed by the former Postmaster General William Hays, who was busy spreading American culture and products through the movies as well. On more than one occasion, Hays stated that "to every American in the country and to millions of customers in the world cinema brings the vivid and visual perception of products made in United States."[78] And what became classical Hollywood style, ironically, was actually an international style even before the Great War.

From April 1923, circulating in the Hollywood press with more and more insistence was the news that John Bohannon had sold a license for the Hollywood Boot Shop to Salvatore Ferragamo. It was one of the oldest and most elegant businesses in the city, founded ten years earlier by Morgan & Stoll and then purchased by Bohannon.[79] The agreement signed with the Frank Meline real estate company established a ten-year lease for a fee of 57,000 dollars.[80] But it was only in October of that year that the contract was signed and a new company was founded that included Salvatore, Secondino, and Jerome Ferragamo.[81] It is likely that, in the months leading up to the signature, Ferragamo had been the manager of the shop—the announcement published in May 1923 in the local newspaper, whose left side reads "S. Ferragamo, Manager," is proof that this is so.[82] At the very start, the shop proposed one-off sales of shoes "For all the family"; after which, from late May, the Hollywood Boot Shop was described in the frequent advertising as a place that offered its customers elegant products: "We specialize in ladies' fine footwear. The very latest patterns arriving daily."[83]

The place "at the corner of Hollywood and Las Palmas Boulevards," with "two shops and rooms upstairs"[84] enjoyed an enviable location opposite Grauman's Egyptian Theatre, as stated in the advertising that often appeared in the local press.[85] This choice of place was ideal and can be compared to the purchase of Palazzo Spini Feroni in Florence in the 1930s; in both cases Ferragamo showed his unique sensitivity and intuitive skill at

finding the best and most functional locations for the developments he intended to bring about in his economic activity.

Grauman's Egyptian Theatre first opened in October 1922. Sid Grauman had invested in the expansion and wealth of Hollywood, and this, Ferragamo observed, was evident in the magnificent shows held there: "In addition to a major film there was always a floor show in which he would employ as many as a hundred dancers. Each dancer wore identical shoes for each number, but she might be required to change four or five times in each show . . . Thus the demand for my shoes in Hollywood quickly fell into three categories: special shoes for films; shoes to order for individuals; and 'serial line,' stage shows, and individuals, which could be carried in stock sizes and designs in the same way as in a normal retail store. Most of the shoes used by the dancers at Grauman's were carried in stock, in white. In fifteen to twenty minutes we could tint them with spirit dye in the shade required."[86]

Ferragamo's choice of that very place was no accident, not so much because it was one of the main thoroughfares in Hollywood, but above all because the shop was indeed opposite that huge new theater (this was always underscored in the adverts), with over 1,700 seats. Grauman's Egyptian Theatre was inaugurated on October 18, 1922 with Allan Dwan's film *Robin Hood*, featuring Douglas Fairbanks; its numerous repeat screenings continued until April of the following year. The Hollywood daily newspaper (October 13, 1922) stressed the uniqueness of the "photoplay theater" on the West Coast with seats reserved for the two daily shows (matinée and evening performance). Each cinematographic production had its own musical score, which was performed by an orchestra; also of importance, as reported in the Hollywood press, was that a committee of influential people in the city— Salvatore Ferragamo was included in the list—was busy organizing the city orchestra.[87]

On December 4, 1923, the movie *The Ten Commandments* directed by Cecil B. DeMille was screened at the Egyptian Theatre. The shoes for the movie had been commissioned from Ferragamo: the job was a hard one, forcing him to spend long hours in the public library to develop the designs and the

The actress Patsy Ruth Miller in Ferragamo's shop

Salvatore Ferragamo measures the median line of the actress Olive Hasbrouck, 1927

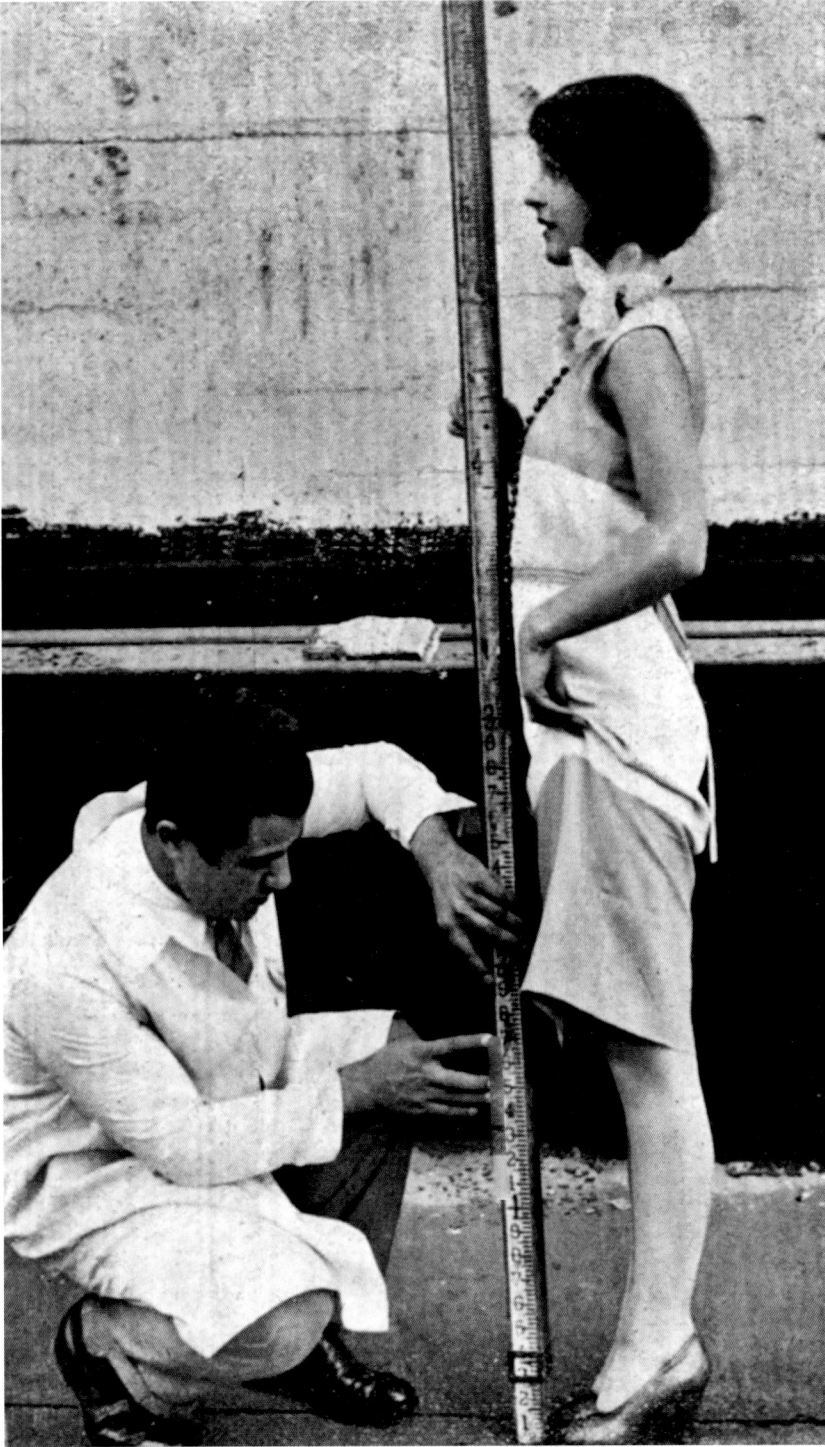

solutions that would go with the costumes designed by Clare West.

While he was busy consolidating his economic position in a part of the city that was becoming increasingly lively and vital both culturally and in terms of the number and variety of businesses, the famous "shoemaker for the cinema" was also trying to become an American citizen, having applied in September 1920. His application was rejected in 1924 but was finally accepted two years later, when he finally received his U.S. passport.[88]

In a long article published on May 4, 1923 the magazine *Holly Leaves* praised the new management of the Hollywood Boot Shop and emphasized how Salvatore Ferragamo, who was a member of the executive board of the Hollywood Retail Merchants' Bureau, established the previous year, could play an important role for the city and its inhabitants. Two years later, the same magazine described him as the man who represented "a new spirit of retailing in the Hollywood community."[89]

It is worthwhile noting how highly the local press spoke of him in those days, describing Salvatore as the shoe designer of the stars, a friend of Rudolph Valentino, John Gilbert, John Barrymore, and Douglas Fairbanks,[90] and a successful "American business man."[91]

"In the 1920s and 30s movies, the close-ups, photography, costumes, make-up, and storyline aimed at celebrating the cult of the stars by identifying a specific style for each of them, a style that would remain the same from one film to another."[92] Ferragamo came into contact with this world, grew familiar and mingled with it; in the 1920s the movie stars were veritable modern myths, embodying the worship of the Graeco-Latin classical world and its complex and contradictory mythology dominated by the image of otherness, as the French philosopher Edgar Morin has suggested. And in designing shoes for the movie stars, as wrote the *Los Angeles Times*, the great "footwear designer" Ferragamo interprets their personality, as well as offering a product of top-notch artisanal quality.[93]

In 1923 Salvatore was living at 2222 North Beachwood Drive, Hollywood,[94] where some of the old buildings from the 1920s still stand (but the one where he lived was rebuilt in the 1960s). On the same street is the house where Marilyn Monroe spent several years, and up on the hill above is the lovely villa owned by Charlie Chaplin. In the background, amidst palms and hibiscus flowers, are the famous letters that spell out Hollywood, at the time Hollywoodland: so close you almost feel like you're on a movie set.

Two countries, two languages

The following years were successful both professionally and economically; the "Hollywood Story" was a hotbed of events in which music, theater, and cinema accompanied the birth and the development of a reality that strongly celebrated the icons of success. One of those icons was Salvatore Ferragamo.

A long and detailed article published in February 1925 lauded the new economic initiative of the talented Italian: Ferragamo's new shop opened, after a thorough renovation, at 6683 Hollywood Boulevard, "one door east of the old [location]."[95] The new shop was described as follows: "The design is of the Italian Renaissance period and furnishings are Venetian, with elegantly upholstered and hand carved chairs and sofas, large mirrors, rich hangings and wrought iron display fixtures and lantern shaped chandeliers"; the light was indirect and the floor, covered with a rug in neutral colors, accentuated the hues of the batiks on the walls, according to the custom of hanging tapestries in Italian Renaissance palaces. A row of columns separated the entrance from the dressing room and gave the place an old-fashioned, solemn sort of air. Ferragamo had wanted to recreate something of a sitting room, continued the journalist: in fact, the shop itself was in a special part of the whole, which the public could not see. The shoemaker's office, where orders were taken, was in the mezzanine.

The opening of the shop speaks volumes about the esteem that the twenty-five-year-old designer of Italian origin, as he was described in the press, enjoyed from the most important members of the city and

The illusionist Maurice Chefalo or Cefalo, a native of Bonito like Salvatore Ferragamo. The two men shared a close friendship for many years

The actress Alice White in 1929

the movie stars; however, most importantly, it tells us about the Renaissance-style taste and atmosphere Ferragamo borrowed from to decorate his new shop.

The snapshot immortalizing that moment shows, in addition to lots of guests, all the flowers that were sent, proof of the popularity and prestige Salvatore enjoyed. At the opening, besides the movie stars Mary Pickford, Gloria Swanson, Pola Negri, Douglas Fairbanks, and Monty Banks, the famous illusionists Magda Palermo and Maurice Chefalo, a native of Bonito, were also present. The Chefalo or Cefalo (both names are found in the press) family had a close friendship with the Ferragamos.[96]

The environment that the shoemaker had tried to recreate alluded to the taste of the American Renaissance praised by the magazines of interior decoration and by the opinion-makers who were experts on fashion.[97] Like other successful artists and artisans in the United States, Ferragamo had brought with him on the journey across the Ocean his creative skills, now geared toward his personal quest for identity and a role.[98] The image of Italy he had left behind gradually faded and took on other meanings, combined with the new representations of the country that American culture was re-elaborating, in which the Italian Renaissance played an all important role.

In the first two decades of the twentieth century, even before becoming an object of study and the topic of university courses and academic research, the multiple expressions of Italian culture—in particular the representations of the arts, the sciences, as well as the luxury and commerce of a city like Florence between the fifteenth and sixteenth centuries—charmed American businessmen and millionaires and would later become the setting of a number of silent movies.[99] Among the main channels for the diffusion of the legend of Florence and the Renaissance were writings and articles that brought these contents into the interior decoration and fashion magazines. The Golden State celebrated the entrepreneurial magnificence of the Florentine merchants of the Renaissance, while houses and public buildings were decorated and furnished in antique style. The major newspaper publisher William Randolph Hearst borrowed from Italian taste and culture to decorate his sumptuous residence in San Simeon in California.

In the early part of 1926, after becoming a U.S. citizen, Ferragamo thought he could connect the successful business he had developed in California with the image of an Italy that he had perhaps begun to know precisely because of his American experience, which allowed him to discover his homeland's diverse identities. While he tried out new forms of advertising and expanded the number of customers for whom he created custom-made shoes to include less famous names like Alice White, who would become Charlie Chaplin's production secretary,[100] the shoemaker of Hollywood developed a whole new company model: it involved seeking the best skilled workers with lower wages to produce

Alice White's white antelope
and blue calfskin *Spectator*
pumps, designed by Salvatore
Ferragamo in 1925–26
Los Angeles, Natural History
Museum

high-quality shoes in Italy and distribute them in the United States and perhaps also in Europe.

This was a bold design, a sort of sui generis and virtuous delocalization for the creation of a quality product on a large scale. The project, both interesting and very ambitious, rose up from the idea of connecting two worlds that seemed to excel for different qualities: the professionalism of the Italian artisans and the wealth and dynamism of the American world.

The idea was clearly explained by the Hollywood newspapers that ran the story: Salvatore Ferragamo was developing a company design that would bring shoes produced in Italy to both Europe and America, opening shops with the brand name Ferra-Gamo. The new five-member corporation included his sister Rosina, along with Girolamo and two outside members, Ethel A. Haun and Jerome J. Mayo.[101]

The Roaring Twenties were years of great economic euphoria for that part of the world, a sort of north star "that determined the directives of the present and dictated the word for the future."[102]

The young designer and creator of the Cecil B. DeMille Studios, as Ferragamo was often referred to in the city's press, was also courted by the radio, where he had a talk show entitled "On Proper Footwear."[103]

Also surprising, in addition to the shoemaker's artistic and creative skills, was the ease with which he related, and not just for commercial reasons, with the East Coast; an article published in June 1928 announced the agreement made between the Brooklyn School of Shoe Design and the Ferra-Gamo Company, "with offices and factories in Hollywood, California and Florence, Italy." The news was interesting also because, in addition to the production of shoes and "hand-painted heels," it referred to clothing accessories and, specifically, to scarves and "hand-knitted shawls" as well.[104]

The years that Salvatore Ferragamo spent in Hollywood also coincided with his approach to the world of music and in particular to melodrama, which was gradually spreading and was greatly appreciated by the Italo-American communities on both the East and the West Coasts.[105] A postcard written in 1924 by Rosina Ferragamo Schiavone to her mother Mariantonia depicted a performance at the Hollywood Bowl and, besides reassuring her

that all was well with the family and work, described the packed musical and opera performances that, it would seem, the Ferragamo siblings attended.[106]

Salvatore definitely bought a grand piano; in publishing the news, the *Los Angeles Times* mentioned how the shoe designer and "world-known fad creator" was another name to add to the list of celebrities and successful businessmen who showed interest in this particular instrument.[107]

In those years, the arias and overtures from Italian operas, besides popular songs, took up about 70 percent of the programs on the American radio stations in Italian. Joseph Tusiani, a native of a small town on the Gargano who had migrated to the United States in the 1940s, a famous poet and translator of Tasso as well as of the poetry of Michelangelo into English, and a prestigious professor at Lehman College in New York, describes in his autobiography how moved he was when, as a young immigrant boy in New York in the 1940s, he listened from a small radio to the aria "Lassù in cielo vicino alla madre/ in eterno per voi pregherò" from *Rigoletto*.[108]

Thanks to the reinterpretation that historical cinema and costumes suggested to him, Salvatore Ferragamo succeeded in grasping the symbolic aspect of the opera, the expression of a national identity and a place for memories of his homeland, and considered it a means to channel the genuine desire to reinforce the connections within the Italo-American community and stimulate Italian culture.

Between two worlds and two languages, music appeared to Ferragamo—a man who had arrived from a small town in Irpinia ten years before with little knowledge of Italy and its cultural tradition—to be a powerfully evocative medium. The melodies were enchanting and engaging and could involve everyone, surpassing any regionalism, in a great sense of Italian belonging marked by feelings and passions that were collectively significant.

Italian musicians, directors, and opera singers performed regularly in a number of American cities: there were the famous names such as Caruso, Toscanini, and the director of the Metropolitan Opera House Gatti Casazza, and less known ones like maestro Pietro Cimini, guest conductor of the Hollywood Bowl and a friend of Salvatore's.[109]

Before returning to Italy, Ferragamo was considered "one of the few shoe experts of the country," the person who had succeeded in delving so deep into his knowledge of orthopaedics[110] that, the newspaper reported, he was often referred to as an authority in "shoe journals" and "the best known progressive businessman of the community."[111]

Hence, not just a successful artisan but an excellent and illuminated entrepreneur who knew how to get his bearings between art and industry, music and cinema, anatomy and glamour. In his day, the press said he was one of those who had helped to give Hollywood an international dimension and thus foster the creation of its image as the "art center of the world."[112]

The Hollywood Bowl, the great theater on the Los Angeles hills, which opened in 1922 and was mainly used for musical and opera performances

1 Salvatore Ferragamo, *Shoemaker of Dreams. The Autobiography of Salvatore Ferragamo* (London: George Harrap & Co. Ltd, 1957). The first edition was in English.

2 The audio recording is preserved in the Archivio Salvatore Ferragamo. The audio files, hereinafter referred to as "Memorie SF," are of different lengths: Memorie SF no. 1: 1 hour, 3 minutes and 10 seconds; Memorie SF no. 2: 1 hour, 5 minutes and 46 seconds; Memorie SF no. 3: 47 minutes and 39 seconds: Memorie SF no. 4: 48 minutes and 57 seconds; Memorie SF no. 5: 31 minutes and 3 seconds.

3 Philippe Lejeune, *Le pacte autobiographique* (Paris: Éditions du Seuil, 1975). Lejeune was the scholar who most contributed to the assessment of this genre of writing. He stressed that the "autobiographical pact" is a statement in which the author makes explicit his intention to tell the story of his own life: a testimony that allows one to enter the "inner garden" of that person. The following Italian contributions are of particular interest: Arnaldo Pizzorusso, *Ai margini dell'Autobiografia* (Bologna: il Mulino, 1986); Andrea Battistini, *Lo specchio di Dedalo. Autobiografia e biografia* (Bologna: il Mulino, 1990).

4 Salvatore Ferragamo explains the reason why he is recording the story of his life as related to the autobiography he is writing, and adds that it is his intention to offer an interpretation that tells us why he chose to renew the image of the professional shoemaker; he calls it a "mission" that he wanted to pursue with passion and great commitment: Memorie SF no. 3, 2:03.

5 Ferragamo, *Shoemaker of Dreams* 1957, 14.

6 The search for American documents, some of which still unpublished, was carried out by Catherine Angela Dewar, who worked as a research assistant in Los Angeles and in Santa Barbara. Heartfelt thanks to Catherine for the care, commitment, and intelligence she has shown. In a previous study on Ferragamo's activity in California, Edward Maeder stressed how this period was not particularly documented, and he hoped that further research on the activity of the great "entrepreneur-artisan" would contribute to clarifying several obscure points: *The Art of the Shoe. 1898–1960*, ed. by Edward Maeder and Stefania Ricci (Milan: Rizzoli International, 1992), 19. The director of the Museo Salvatore Ferragamo, Stefania Ricci, in her "Idee, modelli, invenzioni" (the introduction to the exhibition catalogue *Idee, Modelli, Invenzioni. I brevetti e i marchi d'impresa di Salvatore Ferragamo dal 1929 al 1964*, ed. by Stefania Ricci, Florence: Sillabe, 2004), expressed the hope that more information on the American period would be forthcoming.

7 His wife Wanda, interrupting the recording for a few seconds, speaks of the birth of "five treasures" which she takes good care of so that they will grow up to be physically and morally healthy; this tells us that her youngest son Massimo hadn't been born yet, and that he hadn't turned three when his father died in 1960: Memorie SF no. 4, 40:52.

8 Little is known about John Desmond Currie and Elizabeth Warner; we do know that they went by the pseudonym Douglas Warner and that they wrote together the novel *Death of a Cop* (1964), on which one of the episodes in the series *The Alfred Hitchcock Hour* was based. It is likely they were both close to the world of cinema: the novel *Death of a Snout* inspired the film *Underworld Informers*. The UCLA archive has a list of their novels: *Ghana and the New Africa* (1960); *Death of a Bogey* (1962); *Death on a Warm Wind* (1968).

9 Salvatore Ferragamo, *Shoemaker of Dreams: The Autobiography of Salvatore Ferragamo* (Florence: Giunti Gruppo Editoriale S.p.a., 1985), on the page preceding the Table of Contents.

10 Memorie SF no. 4, 42:42.

11 Sebastiano Martelli, "Letteratura ed emigrazione: congedo provvisorio," in *Il Sogno Italo-Americano. Realtà e immaginario dell'emigrazione negli Stati Uniti*, ed. by S. Martelli (Naples: Cuen, 1998), 431–32.

12 Memorie SF no. 3, 5:42.

13 "One by one," wrote Ferragamo, "my elder brothers and sisters left Italy to try their fortunes in the United States. Secondino went first, when he was twelve years old, and Girolamo went, and Alfonso went after Girolamo, before he was twelve years old. Even my sisters went when they were old enough to. Teodolinda, the eldest daughter, went, and Clotilde, the third daughter; and Alessandrina, the fourth daughter, and Carmela, the fifth daughter . . . By the time I was nine years old. They had all gone except myself and those younger than I: Elio . . . and the sixth and seventh daughters, Giuseppina and Rosina"; Ferragamo, *Shoemaker of Dreams* 1985, 12.

14 Memorie SF no. 3, 2:10.

15 Memorie SF no. 3, 2:22; also in Ferragamo, *Shoemaker of Dreams* 1985, 11.

16 Ferragamo, *Shoemaker of Dreams* 1985, 17.

17 Ibid., 20.

18 Ibid., 20.

19 Ibid., 23.

20 Ibid., 25.

21 The cholera epidemic that struck Naples in 1884 shone a light on the difficult economic and emotional conditions of the people living in the city. This inspired a vast amount of literature, from Pasquale Villari to Jessie White and Mario and Renato Fucini, among others. See the Population Census of 1901 and the Economic Census of 1911. See also Giuseppe Galasso, *Napoli* (Bari: Laterza, 1987) and, by the same author, "Gli studi di storia della famiglia e il Mezzogiorno d'Italia," in *Mélanges de l'école française de Rome* 95–96 (1983): 149–59.

22 Ministero di Agricoltura, Industria e Commercio, Direzione generale della statistica del lavoro, *Censimento degli opifici e delle imprese industriali al 10 giugno 1911* (Rome: Tipografia nazionale G. Bertero, 1913), 5 vols.

[23] Ferragamo, *Shoemaker of Dreams* 1985, 25.

[24] Memorie SF no. 3, 29:20.

[25] Ibid.

[26] Memorie SF no. 3, 31:09.

[27] Before moving to California, Alfonso Ferragamo had also worked in the Boston Queen Quality Shoe Manufacturing Company. In 1912 he returned to Bonito to see the family and insisted that his brother Salvatore go back to America with him, reassuring him as follows: "Look Salvatore, I'll take you, I'll pay your fare and see you get a job the day after you land in America. It won't be hard for you as it was hard for us . . . I had to go through hell. I worked on the railroad as a waterboy and then with a pick and shovel . . . now I make a lot of money. I send money home and still I'm able to put aside something for myself"; Ferragamo, *Shoemaker of Dreams* 1985, 34. These words are important in that they confirm the role and the value of chain migrations in helping relatives and friends make a decision about leaving their country.

[28] In the autobiography, he recalls this moment but without indulging in feelings of nostalgia, which he says he did not experience as he watched his family gather together to see him off: "So I turned and waved to them as they stood in the morning sunshine on the light tan road until they were out of sight . . . Before my boyish mind lay a world of miracles, magic, and adventure, and I was eager to sample it"; Ferragamo, *Shoemaker of Dreams* 1985, 37.

[29] Ercole Sori, *L'emigrazione italiana dall'Unità alla seconda guerra mondiale* (Bologna: il Mulino, 1979), 22.

[30] Robert F. Foerster, *The Italian Emigration of Our Times* (Cambridge, MA: Harvard University Press, 1919). Albeit distant in time, this economic-social analysis is impeccable from several points of view. Rudolph J. Vecoli, "Negli Stati Uniti," in *Storia dell'Emigrazione Italiana, II. Arrivi*, ed. by Piero Bevilacqua, Andreina De Clementi, and Emilio Franzina (Rome: Donzelli, 2002), 59.

[31] The United States Immigration Commission—established in 1907 by Congress and made up of members of the House and the Senate—ended its works in 1911, stressing how immigration from southern and eastern Europe caused a series of problems for American society. The Commission's efforts were used a decade later to justify the *Quota Act* of 1921.

[32] Piero Bevilacqua, "Società rurale e emigrazione," in *Storia dell'Emigrazione Italiana, I. Partenze*, ed. by Piero Bevilacqua, Andreina De Clementi, and Emilio Franzina (Rome: Donzelli, 2001), 95–99.

[33] Ibid., 96–97.

[34] *Tra due mondi. L'avventura americana tra i migranti di fine secolo. Un approccio analitico*, ed. by Riccardo Scartezzini and Roberto Guidi (Milan: Franco Angeli, 1995).

[35] Emilio Franzina, "Emigrazione transoceanica e ricerca storica in Italia. Gli ultimi dieci anni (1978-1988)," in *Altreitalie* 1 (April 1989); Emilio Franzina, *Gli italiani al Nuovo Mondo. L'emigrazione italiana in America, 1492–1942* (Milan: Mondadori, 1995). See also Patrizia Audenino, "Mestieri e professioni degli emigrati," in *Storia dell'Emigrazione Italiana, II. Arrivi* 2002, 335–350.

[36] Santa Barbara Business Directory 1922.

[37] John R. Commons, "American Shoemakers 1648–1895: A Sketch of Industrial Evolution," in *The Quarterly Journal of Economics* 24, no. 1 (November 1909): 39–84.

[38] Ferragamo, *Shoemaker of Dreams* 1985, 59.

[39] Lucetta Scaraffia and Anna Maria Isastia, *Donne ottimiste. Femminismo e associazioni borghesi nell'Otto e Novecento* (Bologna: il Mulino, 2002), 46–47.

[40] Olivier Zunz, *Perché il secolo americano?* (Bologna: il Mulino, 2002).

[41] Emilio Franzina, "Le traversate e il sogno," in *Il Sogno Italo-Americano* 1998, 27.

[42] Also living in Alessandrina and Joseph Covelli's home was his sister Clotilde. As we mentioned before, Salvatore Ferragamo arrived in the United States after the departure of his elder brothers and sisters. Chain migrations—such as in this case—involved whole families.

[43] Santa Barbara City Directory 1915–1916. The Santa Barbara City Directory from 1916–1917 to 1922 reveals some interesting data: when Salvatore arrived in Santa Barbara he worked with Secondino and Alfonso at Ferragamo Bros. in Mission Canyon, while Girolamo was registered as a tailor. From 1917 to 1918 Ferragamo Bros. included Girolamo, Secondino, and Salvatore and was recorded as being at 1033 State Street; however, Salvatore lived with Girolamo and Eliodoro (tailor). From 1918 to 1922 Salvatore shared a house with Secondino and his wife Jennie.

[44] Ferragamo, *Shoemaker of Dreams* 1985, 42.

[45] In 1916-1917 the name Salvatore Ferragamo is listed in the Santa Barbara City Directory.

[46] Ilaria Serra, "L'immagine dell'immigrante italiano," in *Il Sogno Italo-Americano* 1998, 247–78. See also Sebastian Fichera, *Italy on the Pacific. San Francisco's Italian Americans* (New York: Palgrave Macmillan, 2011).

[47] Ibid., 254.

[48] Guido Crapanzano, *Amadeo Peter Giannini. Il banchiere che investiva nel futuro* (Rome: Graphofeel, 2017). In twenty years' time the Bank of Italy became one of the most important financial institutes in the world.

[49] *Struggle and Success. An Anthology of the Italian American Experience in California*, ed. by Paola Sensi Isolani and Phyllis C. Martinelli (New York: Center for Migrations Studies, 1993), 4.

[50] Ferragamo, *Shoemaker of Dreams* 1985, 44–46.

[51] Charles Nordhoff, *California, a Book for Travelers and Settlers*, 1872.

[52] There is a very interesting picture of Salvatore Ferragamo helping the actress Kathleen Key, who is posing on the railing of a train, put on a pair of shoes. Clearly visible at the center is the logo of the Southern Pacific and the train in question is the *Argonaut*, which connected Los Angeles to New Orleans. The photograph was probably used to advertise the train, at the time second only to the luxurious

Sunset Limited. It is interesting as it proves the importance that was attributed to the work of Ferragamo in Los Angeles. One of the most famous images of Amadeo Peter Giannini is that of him with his wife, in 1922, on the Southern Pacific *Larck*, an overnight train featuring high comfort. The name was chosen because the lark announces the arrival of the day, not without a literary reference to Chaucer or Shakespeare.

53 Santa Barbara City Directory 1916-1917.

54 Memorie SF no. 4, 9:50.

55 Peter Decherney, *Hollywood* (Bologna: il Mulino, 2016), 39. The author advocates the close link between the star system and the different genres of movies. The initial success of Western films in the first decade of the twentieth century was another one of the factors responsible for moving film production from New York to Fort Lee, New Jersey, and finally to Los Angeles, in search of rugged land and sunlight.

56 Ferragamo, *Shoemaker of Dreams* 1985, 47–48.

57 Memorie SF no. 4, 9:59. Ferragamo remembers this moment, stressing how he decided to stay in California.

58 Cristina Jandelli, *Breve storia del divismo cinematografico* (Venice: Marsilio, 2007), 58.

59 Edgar Morin, *Les stars* (Paris: Éditions du Seuil, 1957). At the end of the 1950s—the height of splendor for international stardom—the French philosopher argues that movie stars embodied modern myths—a sort of revisitation of Greek and Latin mythology.

60 The USC Medical School, founded in 1885, offered evening classes between 1917 and 1922. However, the research conducted in the institute's archives did not produce any results. The university replied that those who enrolled in evening classes were not registered; however, the USC Alumni Magazine (2010) did publish a photo of Salvatore Ferragamo with this caption: "Faced with the challenge of creating shoes that were as comfortable as they were beautiful, Ferragamo turned to USC, where he studied human anatomy." I wish to thank Claude Zachary, USC Libraries Special Collection, for this information. Virginia Ferragamo Schilling, Secondino's daughter, gave an interview in June 1991 (as reported in Edward Maeder's essay "The California Experience," in *The Art of the Shoe* 1992, 15), where she recalled that Uncle Salvatore frequently made tiny sketches of his shoes in the margins of the pages he read for his Human Anatomy course. The City Directories of Santa Barbara confirmed that Salvatore and Secondino Ferragamo lived in the same house.

61 Memorie SF no. 4, 19:54.

62 Memorie SF no. 4, 26:32.

63 Maria Giuseppina Muzzarelli, *Breve storia della moda in Italia* (Bologna: il Mulino, 2011), 17.

64 Student records for International Correspondence Schools at the University of Scranton are no longer available.

65 Berkeley no longer has any records for its correspondence courses.

66 Memorie SF no. 4, 32:48. "I saw that my clients could no longer put their old shoes without suffering and told me that my principles worked . . . and so I made my fortune . . . my new discovery kept the shoes line. I combined the anatomical research and the experience of fitting, nature compensated my efforts and the mystery was revealed when I applied my discoveries . . . the weight of the body falls vertically on the arch of the foot . . . the body weight is supported by the plantar arch of the shoe."

67 Zunz, *Perché il secolo americano?* 2002, 22.

68 Memorie SF no. 4, 38:14.

69 Giulia Carluccio and Matteo Pollone, "Il cinema classico hollywoodiano," in Giulia Carluccio, Luca Malavasi, and Federica Villa, *Il Cinema. Percorsi storici e questioni teoriche* (Rome: Carocci, 2015), 67.

70 Ibid., 70

71 Decherney, *Hollywood* 2016, 25–26.

72 Ferragamo, *Shoemaker of Dreams* 1985, 84.

73 "Auto Races Train: Accident Results: One Dead and Three Injured," in *Los Angeles Times*, February 5, 1920. The article by the local reporter described what had occurred near Ventura on February 4, 1920.

74 M. A. J. Schoenefeld, "Orthopedic Surgery in the United States Army: An Historical Review," in *Military Medicine* 176 (2011).

75 The patent was registered on November 3, 1921 and it was the first of a very long and varied series of patents and inventions; see *Idee, Modelli, Invenzioni* 2004.

76 Ferragamo, *Shoemaker of Dreams* 1985, 79.

77 Santa Barbara City Directory and Santa Barbara Business Directory 1922.

78 Quoted by Mary Anne Doanne, "The Economy of Desire: The Commodity Form in/of the Cinema," in *Movies and Mass Culture*, ed. by John Belton (New Brunswick, NJ: Rutgers University Press, 1996), 121.

79 "Announcing that Salvatore Ferragamo has bought The Hollywood Shop from J. M. Bohannon and will run it under the same high class management which proved so successful in his Santa Barbara shop for the last seven years," in *Holly Leaves*, April 6, 1923. On April 15 of the same year, in the article "Shoe Store in Hollywood Is in New Hands," which appeared in the *Los Angeles Times*, this change of hands was emphasized.

80 Quoted in Maeder, *The California Experience* 1992, 16.

81 The deed written up by the State Notary George D. Copeland was signed on October 20 and ratified on October 23, 1923; Catalog# GC-1145-1-282-29232 1923 Incorporation Record Hollywood Boot Shop, Seaver Center for Western History Research, Natural History Museum of LA County.

82 *Holly Leaves*, May 4, 1923; see also the calling card in the Archivio Salvatore Ferragamo.

[83] See Tommy Dangcil, *Hollywood 1900–1950 in Vintage Postcards* (Charleston, SC: Arcadia Publishing, 2002).

[84] Ferragamo, *Shoemaker of Dreams* 1985, 80.

[85] *Holly Leaves*, May 4, 1923.

[86] Ferragamo, *Shoemaker of Dreams* 1985, 86.

[87] "Bias Musical Tea," in *The Pacific Coast Musician*, May 29, 1925. The article refers to a "musical tea" in the home of the singer Rober Bias, listed among the promoters of a committee to support the realization of the Opera Company in Hollywood. Salvatore Ferragamo and maestro Pietro Cimini were among the participants.

[88] Salvatore Ferragamo, *Document Petitions*, http//:ancestry.com (accessed August 28, 2017). The naturalization did not arrive until February 19, 1926. This first and only denial of U.S. citizenship probably had to do with the accident that had occurred in Ventura in February 1920, which had led to the investigation of Eliodoro Ferragamo's death.

[89] "A Passion for Shoes," in *Holly Leaves*, February 20, 1925.

[90] Ferragamo, *Shoemaker of Dreams* 1985, 89.

[91] *Holly Leaves*, April 6, 1923.

[92] Jandelli, *Breve storia del divismo* 2007, 60. According to Dario Tomasi, the previous performances of the stars created a sort of "horizon of expectation" with which the movies that came later had to come to terms. Dario Tomasi, *Cinema e racconto. Il personaggio* (Turin: Loescher, 1988), 116.

[93] "Hollywood boot shop a place of rare beauty," in *Holly Leaves*, February 25, 1925.

[94] Los Angeles City Directory 1929. See also Maeder, *The California Experience* 1992, 19.

[95] *Holly Leaves*, February 20, 1925.

[96] I wish to thank Valerio Massimo Miletti for the information.

[97] Elisa Camporeale, "Visioni americane d'interni del Rinascimento italiano: dalla Gilded Age agli anni Venti," in *Archivio Storico Italiano* III (2015): 514.

[98] Regina Soria, *Fratelli lontani. Il contributo degli artisti italiani all'identità degli Stati Uniti (1776-1945)* (Naples: Liguori, 1997).

[99] Camporeale, *Visioni americane* 2015, 484.

[100] Chaplin himself encouraged Alice to act. She debuted in 1927 in Francis Dillon's *The Sea Tiger*, but she was not particularly appreciated by the critics, who often compared her to Clara Bow only because of her aesthetic qualities.

[101] The signature, before the State Notary, for the founding of the new Ferra-Gamo Inc. is dated April 29, 1926; the contract was registered on May 4, 1926. Catalogue # GC 1145.1-23-35995 1926 Incorporation Record for shoe manufacturers Ferra-Gamo, Inc., Seaver Center for Western History Research, Natural History Museum of LA County.

[102] These were the words of Riccardo Gualino, an industrialist active in international markets and a major art collector, in a story with a highly evocative title, "Uragani," which he published in 1933, while he was in forced confinement on the island of Lipari.

[103] *Los Angeles Times*, August 11, 1926: "A lecture on Proper Footwear was given yesterday over KHJ by Salvatore Ferragamo, who designs shoes and boots for most of the motion picture and stage stars." The same radio show hosted Arthur Goodstein, a "night blues singer."

[104] News appearing in *Shoe Retailer*, June 23, 1928.

[105] Anna Maria Martellone, "Little Italy e Opera," in *Il Sogno Italo-Americano* 1998, 177.

[106] The postcard belongs to the President of Salvatore Ferragamo S.p.a., Ferruccio Ferragamo. In a June 1926 article, Cedric E. Hart reported a meeting to establish an "executive committee" made up of various personalities in the world of music, including maestro Pietro Cimini, composer and librettist Leon Ardin, the English dancer Maud Allan, a contradictory and interesting figure at the time, together with Salvatore Ferragamo, whose "sound advice and cooperation" is acknowledged ("Hollywood Musical Topics," in *Hollywood Magazine*, May 25, 1926).

[107] *Los Angeles Times*, October 22, 1926.

[108] Joseph Tusiani, *La parola difficile. Autobiografia di un italoamericano* (Fasano: Schema editore, 1988), 72–74.

[109] Pietro Cimini, *Ten Commandments for Correct Voice Production* (Los Angeles: Freeman-Matthews Music Co., 1936). Autograph copy kept at the International Museum and Library of Music in Bologna. Maestro Pietro Cimini had been the director of the Imperial Theater in Warsaw, of the Chicago Opera, and of the Los Angeles and San Francisco Opera, and guest conductor at the Hollywood Bowl for eight years. In 1926 he directed the film *La Bohème*, which was to be brought to Bologna, Italy, by Salvatore Ferragamo upon his return home. On June 4, 1926 an article was published in the Sunday edition of *El Heraldo México* entitled "Vibraciones de Hollywood," describing the atmosphere in Hollywood and recalling, among the most representative figures, those of Salvatore Ferragamo and maestro Cimini. A note sent by Pietro Cimini to Remington, a typewriter manufacturing company, is preserved in the Archivio Salvatore Ferragamo. In it he says he is very happy with his purchase, suggested to him by his friend Salvatore Ferragamo.

[110] It appears that the Hollywood Boot Shop had a space in the local newspapers called the "Hollywood Boot Shop Section," where it was stated that the shop could also boast of an "Orthopaedic Expert."

[111] "Corner of Boot Shop," in *Holly Daily Citizen*, March 26, 1925.

[112] C. D. Heart, "Business Aspect of Art Center," in *Southern California Transmitter*, July 1926. See the adverts published in the *Hollywood Daily City* from May 31 to December 2, 1926.

380

SALVATORE FERRAGAMO

DAYS
IN HOLLYWOOD

The Hollywood to which I came in the spring of 1923 was still more than a village in the sun. The studios were few and, compared with their future, modest in size and budgets. There was a scattering of palatial homes—Harold Lloyd's, Mary Pickford's, Barbara La Marr's, Pola Negri's, Rudolph Valentino's, Charlie Chaplin's—in which magnificent parties could be thrown; the majority of the remainder had neither the size nor the facilities for the large-scale entertainments soon to become so familiar. On the surface of the Hollywood of 1923 there was a good deal of substance in my brothers' contention that there was an insufficient population to support our repair shop and little hope for my future in hand-made shoes, particularly considering the limitations of my output.

When I left Hollywood in 1927—never to return, as it happened, except as a visitor—all was changed. The studios were larger, more magnificent, wealthier. Some of the concentration of capital had already taken place—for instance, the American Film Company had disappeared into Fox Films, and Metro Goldwyn Mayer had been born. The million-dollar spectacle which in 1923 was a dream occasionally reaching realization in 1927 was a commonplace. The number of stars, extras, bit players, and technicians had multiplied and, in the main, had thrived on the growing, apparently endless, prosperity of this giant industry. The exotic villas of the wealthy were creeping inexorably up the surrounding hillsides as each new star strove to make good the claim that he or she was "tops in Hollywood." More significant still, the silent film was on the edge of death, with all the upheavals which that occurrence meant to stars and studios.

For the Hollywood Boot Shop on the corner of Las Palmas and Hollywood Boulevards—it is still there, though the name and the owner are not the same—those years were glittering and glorious and yet, in a curious sense, unsatisfying. My shoes sold in ever-increasing numbers. The comfort of my new creations reached into every corner of the United States. I captured virtually the entire theatrical trade, and my shoes were on the feet of the most fabulous movie stars in the world, on the feet of dancers, showgirls, bit-players, directors, and producers. I was, by my own standards if not the standards of Hollywood, an immensely wealthy man, richer than I had ever dreamed I could be in the days in Bonito. I had many friends. Yet I had to throw it all away, as I had thrown away my shop in Bonito and my shop in Santa Barbara.

As I look back now I seem to see a parallel between the film industry and my own. The era has vanished for the movies, and my part in it, too, has gone these many years. Yet, just as the motion picture industry has grown and developed from those fledgling days, so too, I hope, has mine.

My life in Hollywood during these years fell into three sections: my hand-made shoes, my flirtation with machine-made shoes, and my experiences with the people for whom I worked. From the beginning my working problem was plain: how to make enough shoes to supply the demand. In Santa Barbara my output of hand-made shoes had never been large; except in the really busy weeks it was scarcely greater than the quantity I had managed to produce years before in Bonito. Therefore I knew before even I opened the Hollywood Boot Shop that I could not cope with the requirements of possibly half a dozen studios instead of one and hundreds of customers instead of scores. As it turned out, Hollywood's growth outstripped even my optimistic assessment of its future development and intensified my problem. To begin with, I took up my connexion with the American Film Company and all my old friends from Santa Barbara, but within a few weeks my customers had grown steadily. In those days the rival studios co-operated closely enough to hire shoes (and costumes and other props) among each other, with the result that other studios were brought into contact with my shoes without my having to go canvassing for the business. The immediate effect was an influx of orders to make shoes for entire pictures.

As in Santa Barbara, they sent me the scripts and I was required to design and make the entire wardrobe of shoes in the styles of the period required. The difference now was that, instead of the films being shorts or serials or modest first features only a few reels long, the industry was tackling the enormous spectacle picture which employed hundreds and even thousands of extras in addition to the stars and bit players.

The first of these films with which I was concerned was Cecil B. DeMille's *The Ten Commandments*—almost the first of that great director's many great pictures. In addition to *The Ten Commandments*, I also worked on *The King of Kings*, DeMille's story of Christ. Our friendship, cemented in those early days, still endures, and to-day I make his shoes still, and those of his daughter and of his nieces Agnes and Margaret.

The Ten Commandments presented me with a problem similar to the one I had solved in Santa Barbara when I was first asked to provide shoes for a costume film. It was my first commission for a shoe wardrobe of a spectacle film of such immensity, and it staggered me. I had never designed shoes for the Babylonian-Egyptian-Hebraic period, and my knowledge of the times was nil. On an inspiration I sat down and designed a high-fronted shoe with a mask reaching half-way up the shinbone, and on the masks I placed the heads of beasts—lions and leopards and strange mythical creatures. For the Egyptian I designed an open half-shoe with sandal effect. When the girl I now employed to turn my rough pencil sketches into detailed instructions had completed her work I took the results to DeMille. I knew him already as a man with an immense capacity for detail. He is the most cultured director in Hollywood. I do not think there has been a man to compare with him and I doubt if there will be another for many years. When he is working on a film he carries the whole scope and detail of it in his mind. He organizes everything, from the shoes to the sun. A fly cannot go by without DeMille knowing it. Therefore I wondered how my inspiration would look in the eyes of his mastery of period.

He was delighted and enthusiastic. He had no corrections to make, but I had—or thought I had. To satisfy my curiosity I went to the local library and scanned every book I could find which might give me a clue to the closeness of my imagined ideas to the actual footwear of the real Mosaic period. I found virtually nothing. It

Mary Pickford in the 1920s.
"Mary Pickford's feet,"
writes Ferragamo in his
autobiography, "were the most
graceful, the most shapely, and
the smallest of all the stars
I had the opportunity to make
shoes for"

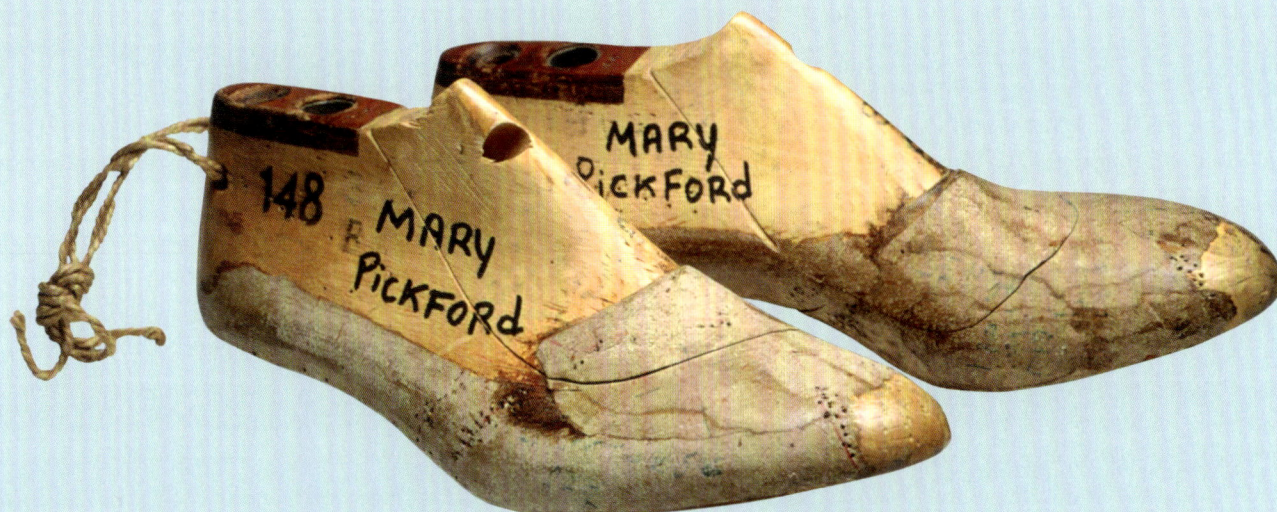

remains a fact—still true to-day—that the footwear of the ancients has never been adequately described or catalogued. Dresses, yes; head-dresses, yes in plenty; but shoes, no. I found here and there a hint of sandals—plain, one-strap sandals with a flat heel—and here and there the evidence of no shoes at all. Otherwise there was nothing. (Incidentally, it is not only the ancients who have been neglected by those who record fashions. If you cast your mind over the portraits you have seen painted by the great masters how many can you recall which show the shoes?)

I was thus unable to confirm my inspiration from the records, yet my designs harmonized perfectly with the costumes of the Mosaic period—because, I believe, I had remembered them.

After DeMille—and also concurrently with him—came D. W. Griffith and James Cruze. Griffith's masterpieces, *The Birth of a Nation* and *Intolerance*, were already behind him, but there were many more films to come, including *Way Down East* and *The White Rose*. Cruze's most famous picture, on which I worked, was *The Covered Wagon*. Then the great studios followed, one by one: Fox Films, Universal, Warner Brothers, Metro Goldwyn Mayer. I made shoes for the films of Clara Bow, Rudolph Valentino, Lillian Gish, the Costello sisters, John Barrymore, John Gilbert, Theda Bara, and, of course, my stars of the Santa Barbara days, Mary Pickford, Douglas Fairbanks senior, and Pola Negri. Soon individ-

The wooden forms for Mary Pickford's feet, which Ferragamo used to make shoes for the actress Florence, Museo Salvatore Ferragamo

Black satin pump with white rhinestone buckle ornament, 1927–30. The model was designed by Salvatore Ferragamo for Mary Pickford Florence, Museo Salvatore Ferragamo

ual actors, both known and unknown, who had worn my shoes in films, came to me with personal orders, and later on, as visitors to Hollywood took my shoes farther afield, people came to me from all over the States. Within months of my arrival in Hollywood came the event which marked the city's victory as the film centre of the United States, and eventually of the world: the establishment of Grauman's Egyptian and Chinese Theatres. Grauman's confidence in Hollywood's wealth, growth, and future was shown by his fabulous shows. In addition to a major film there was always a floor show in which he would employ as many as a hundred dancers. Each dancer wore identical shoes for each number, but she might be required to change four or five times in each show. I was specializing in dancers' shoes, and so the orders came to me. I kept the ballerina shoe, so fashionable to-day, always in good stock, alongside dancers' shoes with a soft toe, one strap, and a completely flat heel; those with a box toe; those with a heavy, hard toe; and those with a medium soft toe on a perfectly plain shoe which pulled on and tied at the instep.

Thus the demand for my shoes in Hollywood quickly fell into three categories: special shoes for films; shoes to order for individuals; and "serial line," stage shows, and individuals, which could be carried in stock sizes and designs in the same way as in a normal retail store. Most of the shoes used by the dancers at Grauman's were carried in stock, in white. In fifteen to twenty minutes we could tint them with spirit dye to the shade required.

I organized as many shoemakers as I could on the serial lines, and Taylor, Dietrich, and I, together with as many other men as I could find, concentrated on custom-made shoes to individual order. Many of my work-people at this time were Italians and Mexicans who were capable—especially the Italians—of making the whole shoe by hand at home. I could not use them for serial lines because no two pairs of shoes thus made would be alike, but they were competent enough on single pairs. Yet even with this assistance I could not always meet demand and there were many occasions when I knocked from door to door in Hollywood in search of anyone who could help me to make a pair of shoes. Some of my difficulties were my own fault, because I changed my styles so quickly. Of every ten shoes made for me by my workers, six would be satisfactory and the remainder would have to be discarded, largely because as soon as they had learned to make one line perfectly I switched them to another, newer model.

The period, indeed, is studded with styles and designs. At the beginning I modified my "French" toe, making it a trifle sharper, and called it the "Stage" toe. At the end of the period, in answer to the pleadings of short girls who wanted to look taller, I created the platform sole. I continued to make my "Roman" sandals in many styles, and my "First" model stayed in vogue almost to the 1930s. I remember some of the more exotic individual orders: the corkscrew heels, studded with imitation pearls, for Gloria Swanson; the multicoloured satin slippers for Lillian Gish; the rainbow-coloured evening shoes with ankle straps and tall gold heels for Dolores del Río; and the "Serpent" shoes for Esther Ralston. These were a pair of black and gold slippers with a spike hel. To the vamp of each shoe I glued the head of a snake and their sleek, flexible bodies, with golden scales painted as life-like as I could make them, writhed half-way up her beautiful legs. They cost 150 dollars and were designed for a jungle film. Esther was supposed to wear them as a totem to scare away wild animals. Instead she wore them one night to the Cocoanut Grove and scared the life out of the *habitues*.

Best of all I remember the Indian princess who had made my sandals popular, and for whom I made perhaps the most exquisite and certainly the most rare pair of shoes of my career.

After buying my sandals in Santa Barbara the princess returned to India. Years later she came back to Santa Barbara and, finding me gone, she sought me out in Hollywood. Her request now was for a pair of shoes that would be "completely different"—shoes no one had ever seen before. They must not be made

Salvatore Ferragamo with the actress Kathleen Key on Southern Pacific's *Argonaut*, the train connecting Los Angeles to New Orleans, often the ideal set for many of Hollywood's promotional pictures. The new railway line was inaugurated in 1926 (the year when this picture was taken), as proven by the many articles that published it, preserved in the Archivio Salvatore Ferragamo in Florence

Southern Pacific
ARGONAUT

Chateau Art
Studios
LH
#4

Marion Davies, a customer of Salvatore Ferragamo, in 1928

Two-piece shoe by Salvatore Ferragamo in dyed calfskin, with strap fastened by a lock, 1929
Florence, Museo Salvatore Ferragamo

Black satin pump with rhinestone dust appliqué. The shoe is a faithful reproduction of the model created by Ferragamo in 1927 and published in the California press
Florence, Museo Salvatore Ferragamo

Freulich

of leather or any material commonly in use; they must be "entirely different." She was so insistent on this word "different" that it occurred to me that it might be possible to make shoes of bird's feathers. Excited, I began to experiment. I tried the feathers of many birds, but when it came to sticking them on the shoes they proved too clumsy or too big. Finally, almost in despair at many failures, I asked a Mexican boy who worked for me to bring me the smallest bird's feathers he could buy. He returned with duck's feathers, which were uglier still. The following Sunday, the problem still unsolved, I went to stay for the week-end on my brother-in-law's ranch at Mission Canyon. There I looked and looked, examining every flying thing. I could see nothing suitable; none of the birds had feathers luminous enough or small enough for my purpose. I had almost decided to give up the idea of feathered shoes and seek another solution when I saw a humming-bird. It was so small and its tiny feathers were set so closely on its body that it seemed the answer to my prayers. I asked my brother-in-law if there were many of these birds about, and he told me: "Here, one or two. They are mostly called honey-suckers, because that's what they do: they suck the honey from the flowers. But they are more common in Southern California, down towards the Mexican border. You might get some feathers there."

The following day I approached my Mexican boy again. He looked puzzled at first and then, as my explanation broke through the language barrier, he nodded and said, in Spanish: "Oh! The bird with the long invisible bill." He added that he thought he might be able to get some of the feathers from relatives living in Southern California. At last they arrived—a small bunch for which I paid ten dollars. I set to work, and when the princess saw the result she was almost lyrical with excitement and joy. She at once decided that she must have humming-bird feathers on this model and that model and the other model.

I said: "Your Highness, these are just about the only humming-bird feathers that can be obtained in the United States. There were not really enough for even one pair of shoes." I pointed out to her the spots where, in order to be sure of covering the whole shoe, I had been none too generous with the feathers. She insisted, however, that she would like one more pair, on a model with a more sandalized effect. I searched and searched, but I could not find any more humming-bird feathers before the princess was due to leave America for India, and I was forced to decorate her sandals with birds and other effects.

There are two other points about this story. When the princess asked me the price of the feathered shoes I did not know what to charge. The order was so unusual that my normal standards of payment did not apply. As I was making up my mind what to ask I told her of my difficulty in obtaining the feathers, of my many experiments, of the high price I had paid for the small bunch. I added: "I hardly know how to fix a price. If you paid me five hundred dollars it would hardly cover all the time and trouble and expense I have been put to." Before I could say anything else she said: "That's all right." And she handed me five hundred dollars. It is the highest price I have ever received for a single pair of shoes.

In the years to come I made many pairs of shoes for the princess. She returned again and again to Hollywood and when I established my salon in Florence she visited me several times. I lost touch with her only at the outbreak of the Second World War. I heard from her family that she had remarried, and I imagine that she had changed her religion and now belonged to a sect which prevented her from moving in the world of fashion.

My relationship with the stars was now on a completely different basis to my relationship with those who had known me in Santa Barbara. In Santa Barbara I was a youth, something of a curiosity to be making shoes so young and, as I have hinted, was occa-

The actress Lola Todd wearing
a total leopard look designed by
Salvatore Ferragamo in 1925

Model of sandal featuring thin black kidskin straps designed by Salvatore Ferragamo in 1930. Whether the sandal was made for a Hollywood star is unknown, but certainly it was influenced by the shoes that he made for the silver screen in the 1920s
Florence, Museo Salvatore Ferragamo

Model of a kidskin and golden velvet sandal designed by Salvatore Ferragamo in 1930
Florence, Museo Salvatore Ferragamo

Two-piece shoe in black suede and
silver kidskin designed by Salvatore
Ferragamo in 1925–27
Salem (MA), James Raye Collection

sionally the target of good-natured fun. In Hollywood I was a man in my twenties; still young, of course, but many of the stars in the film city were no older and some were younger. I immediately began to mix with them in my private life as well as in business—men and women like Valentino, John Barrymore, John Gilbert, DeMille, D. W. Griffith, Joan Crawford, Clara Bow, and Corinne Griffith.

Valentino and I, of course, were two good Italians together. He would drop into my house on Beechwood Drive to eat a bowl of spaghetti cooked as he had liked it in Italy. He was a beautiful boy, always impeccably debonair. He liked to dress in the Italian way—put as much as possible on himself—but everything would be tip-top and he was always perfectly groomed. He would never tolerate hair like mine, which crinkles and tends to get out of hand. Every hair had to sleeked down, and every movement of his body, every gesture, was thoughtfully measured.

John Gilbert, tall and thin, Valentino, Douglas Fairbanks, and another Italian actor named Lucio Flamma—he might have stepped into Valentino's shoes after Rudolph's death if he had allowed himself to act more and pose less—and I went swimming one day at Arrowhead Lake. We organized a series of swimming races, but the water was so bitterly cold that only two of us completed the course: myself and John Gilbert. John Barrymore, that perfect actor, used to drop into my shop for a drink as well as to buy shoes. His feet were beautifully shaped, but bad shoes as a boy had made him a trifle flat-footed. I always tried to keep a bottle of something tucked away in the back of the salon; it was the only welcome gift you could make to the stars. They had all the money and all the possessions they needed, but, it being the time of Prohibition, drink was difficult to obtain, and anyone who was lucky enough to come across a spare bottle promptly drank it. D. W. Griffith was fond of pretty feet, and pretty legs and ankles as well. Early in my career in Hollywood he suggested that I run a

beauty competition for the best feet, ankles, and legs in the city. He would offer the first prize—a six months' film contract—and I could give second and third prizes of shoes. It might be a good stunt, he thought. So did I.

The event was organized, and the winner, according to the panel of judges, was a girl named Marjorie Howard. My own choice was a girl with beautiful legs who was trying hard to break into films. Her name was Joan Crawford. I forget whether she won second or third prize; but I know that those were the first shoes of mine she ever wore, and she is my customer still.

I also knew Clara Bow long before she was the famous "It" girl—and at a weight, I may say, of 150 pounds. She was a plummy lass who wore the highest heels I have ever made—they were four inches high, and I swear I defied the law of gravity with them. She had enormously strong, high-arched dancers' feet, and when she was in my shoes she walked on tip-toe. Needless to say, ten blocks along Hollywood Boulevard was about the limit of her walking in those shoes.

It was while I was driving with Clara Bow that I gave up smoking. We were crossing Death Valley, California, when I ran out of cigarettes. I was in torment. At every place—there are not many—where a human being could be found, no matter what sort of human being, I endeavoured to beg a smoke. I failed. It was not until the end of the journey that I was able to buy a package and slake my craving. As I drew the smoke into my lungs I suddenly realized that I was only a miserable slave to a habit. I promptly threw the cigarette away and I have never smoked since.

Maria Palermo and Maurice Chefalo were two of the greatest illusionists who have ever lived. Maurice could give the illusion the auditorium was filling with water, while Maria could make you disappear from a room without your knowing it. One day, in my house, she did the trick with myself and my three brothers. We four

Gloria Swanson photographed by Edward Steichen for *Vanity Fair* in 1928. The actress was one of Ferragamo's first customers and was famous for her extravagant requests

Pump in brushed calfskin
with a white bow in soft
leather designed by Salvatore
Ferragamo in 1928 for
Gloria Swanson
Florence, Museo Salvatore
Ferragamo

Gloria Swanson during the
filming of *Sadie Thompson*,
directed by Raoul Walsh
in 1928

David W. Griffith in 1915. Ferragamo made many shoes for his films. Griffith was also a frequent customer of the Hollywood Boot Shop together with his wife Linda Arvidson

Cecil B. DeMille in 1928. Ferragamo's collaboration and friendship with the famous director lasted throughout the years he stayed in the United States

were all in the room and we could talk to each other—yet as long as the illusion lasted we could not count more than three of ourselves.

Then, too, I went to parties—occasions which I at once enjoyed and detested. I liked the company and the fun, and it was good for business, too. The people who wore my shoes would praise and show my creations. The people who could not show my shoes tucked their feet under the table in embarrassment and came into the salon next day to be fitted. But I hated the drinking and the late hours. I always had work to do the next morning.

I learned my lesson at my first party. It was thrown by Barbara La Marr one Saturday night a few months after I had gone to Hollywood and, as far as my hazy recollection goes, was attended by virtually every star in Hollywood—those who could tolerate one another—from Mary Pickford and Douglas Fairbanks downward. It was tremendously exciting. Every one was pleasant and charming and kept thrusting drinks at me. It seemed ungracious not to accept, so, although I have never been more than a light wine drinker, I swigged away with the best. After the fourth drink—I think it was, though I wasn't keeping an accurate score—I passed out.

I woke up at ten o'clock the next morning, still in the house. Hurriedly I rose, taking my hangover with me, and picked my way among the others lying on chairs and floor; some still sleeping the sleep of just-kept-sober; others, as I had been, unconscious. I went home, had a bath—and felt so sleepy I simply had to go to bed again. The next thing I knew it was Monday morning.

After that I accepted party invitations warily until Monty Banks accidentally showed me the way to combine pleasure and sobriety. We were discussing Italian drinks at a party one night when he mentioned *grappa*. As I had left Italy as a boy I knew the liquor only by name and had no idea what it was made of, but Monty said: "Can you mix one?" "Yes, of course," I said, trying to give myself airs. "It's so simple." "Then go ahead," he said.

I went behind the improvised bar and juggled with a few bottles. Monty tasted the result and thought it good. He yelled to others to come and taste, and when it was all gone I had to make some more. Unfortunately I had forgotten the proportions, but I put a bold face on it and tried again. Nobody worried about the difference in taste, if there was any difference. That little incident gave me the clue to my future rôle at parties: I would act as a bar-tender. From that date onward I became know as a mixer of splendid drinks, and eventually I was asked to parties more as a barman than as a guest. It suited me, and I did what I could with the limited ingredients. Drink was difficult to get, expensive when you could get it, and usually dreadful. I was forced to improvise, and I remember that I invented two drinks, "Roscata" and a green concoction, which became popular. "Roscata" was an awful mixture: gin—they called it gin though it was practically pure alcohol—angostura bitters, a dash of brandy, and lots of ice. The "Green" was simply mint and rum. "Roscata" was liked because if left a pleasant aroma in the mouth, and the "Green" because it was cool. While the guests were drinking my concoctions I stood nonchalantly behind the bar with a glass of ginger ale, chosen because it looked like whisky. Once, I remember, Barbara La Marr came up in a great hurry for a drink and, not waiting while I mixed it, took a mouthful of my ginger ale. The unfamiliar taste so startled her that she sprayed it back, demanding to know why I was drinking such horrible stuff at a party. The habits of film stars are apparently a source of inexhaustible fascination for most people, and I have been asked a thousand times how I managed to get on with them, the implication being that they are all temperamental, difficult, and often unbearable. I have not found them so, except when there was an excellent excuse: an excuse which would have been good enough to bring an explosion from the least temperamental person. I have been appalled and horrified at the treatment some stars have received from the people who minister to them. I have heard stars insulted by their dressmakers and hair-dressers when the stars have wanted one thing and the dress-maker or hairdresser has wanted them to have another—usually for their business reason: to show off a new hair style or reveal a new creation. Stars who were foolish or insufficiently fashion-conscious and allowed themselves to be talked into what they did not want might even find themselves humiliated on the set when the director, looking at the unsuitable "creation," stormed: "Where did you get that dress? What the hell have you done to your hair? Get out of here! Get off the set!" It has always seemed wrong to me for those whose job it is to serve people to impress their new ideas upon their customers solely from a desire to establish their own reputation. The world's stars do not come to my salon to buy my reputation; they come to buy shoes that fit and flatter them. I have always tried to give them what they wanted and, on the occasions when I knew that what they wanted was wrong, have used every wile to persuade them out of it.

If film stars are more liable to "fly off the handle" than other mortals the answer surely lies in the conditions under which they work—and especially the conditions under which they worked during the era of the silent films. To-day film-acting is much easier because the players have the power of speech. In the 1920s they could express themselves only by mime, and so they had to be good. Every actress and actor I ever met in those days who ranked as a star had first-class qualifications for the part, which is more than can be said for some of the actresses who parade before the cameras these days. Indeed, it seems to me that the films today have ceased to concentrate on the actors and are more concerned with the background. It was not so in the silent days.

Portrait of the silent movie
actress Lolita Lee with
a dedication to Salvatore
Ferragamo, "creator
of exquisite footwear"
Florence, Museo Salvatore
Ferragamo

To
Salvador Ferragamo
creator of exquisite footwear
Lalita Lee

Dolores Del Río
in 1926

The great actors and actresses, whether on stage or screen, always give of themselves, drawing upon their exceptional depths of emotion and sensation to convey those emotions and sensations to their audiences. In the 1920s the great actresses prepared themselves for days and sometimes weeks beforehand. They would retire from public life, seeing only those people absolutely essential for the necessities of living, relaxing as best as they could. One would drink, another would chain-smoke, yet another would play endless games of solitaire, a fourth would prefer cards with a load of idle chatter. But all were strung up to what I sometimes thought was an inhuman pitch of concentration: Gloria Swanson, a marvellous actress, a born actress with an art entirely her own; Dolores del Río; Lillian and Dorothy Gish; Marlene Dietrich; Greta Garbo, the greatest actress of them all; Paulette Goddard, the incorruptible; Pola Negri, in her own way. I have seen Pola Negri acting before the cameras with such intensity that I feared she would not live through the performance.

Then, too, unlike the stage actress, the film star must sit afterwards and watch herself. It must be agony to the conscientious artist to see her "rushes" and to pick out her errors: the gesture, the step, the emotion which did not quite register. Then to go to the première, with rivals and critics ready to tear your reputation to shreds. In these conditions explosions are not surprising; it is only surprising that they do not occur more often.

I was the centre of storms from time to time, of course, but it was always my own fault. I remember Paulette Goddard kicking off my shoes with two swift movements so that they flew from her feet like bullets from a gun—because I had been less careful than I should and the shoes had pinched her a trifle. Miss Goddard has a mind of her own. In those days she was much sought after. Every director chased her with contracts. She would break one contract, pay the damages, and some one else would take over. She was the one star who did that over and over again—she started films for DeMille which she never finished. She has a beautiful body and legs—even to-day she has the legs of a girl of eighteen—and she loves beautiful shoes. She will never wear anything that might spoil her lovely feet.

Then there was the night when Jean Harlow threw my shoes out of the window. Luckily, the window was open. But that was my fault, too. It was the evening of the world première of the film which made her a star: *Hell's Angels*. She and I were good friends—she was beautiful and charming—and she adored my shoes. For this event, the most important in her life, she had ordered a pair of pale lavender evening slippers with a rhinestone heel. I had taken a great deal of trouble over them, and it was only an hour or two before the première was due to start that I managed to finish them. Then, as the boy was packing them, he spilled a bottle of stain. They were ruined. Desperately I hunted through my stock and found a pair I knew would fit. I hastily dyed them the correct shade and, as they did not possess rhinestone heels, I painted the heels with glue and stuck on diamond dust. Then, armed with both pairs of shoes, I went in person to her apartment. There I made the grave error of showing her the ruined shoes first. I wanted her to know the trouble I had gone to.

"I'm afraid there's been a mistake," I began. Miss Harlow looked at the shoes and then at me and said: "There's been a mistake, has there? Well, here's another!"

Portrait of the actress
Clara Bow, 1929. She
"had enormously strong,
high-arched dancers' feet,"
wrote Ferragamo

Brown lizardskin
and beige and brown
kidskin pump with a
woven mat motif
designed by Salvatore
Ferragamo in 1923–24
Florence, Museo Salvatore
Ferragamo

Portrait of the American actress and screenwriter Anita Loos taken by Edward Steichen in 1920. Anita Loos was famous for her 1925 book *Gentlemen Prefer Blondes* and was a lifetime customer of Salvatore Ferragamo. In 1954 she accompanied Audrey Hepburn to Florence to order shoes from the famous Italian creator

Laced shoe in suede and calfskin with alternating bands designed by Salvatore Ferragamo in 1928
Florence, Museo Salvatore Ferragamo

Laced shoe in brown lizardskin designed by Salvatore Ferragamo in 1929
Florence, Museo Salvatore Ferragamo

Charlie Chaplin and Pola
Negri after announcing their
engagement, February 2, 1923.
They were both customers
of Ferragamo

Greta Garbo in Los Angeles
in 1928. "Greta Garbo,"
wrote Ferragamo, "arrived in
Hollywood just before I returned
to Florence, and that is where
I made her first pair of shoes,
in the mecca of cinema. She
continued to buy my shoes at the
Hollywood Boot Shop for as long
as I was the owner"

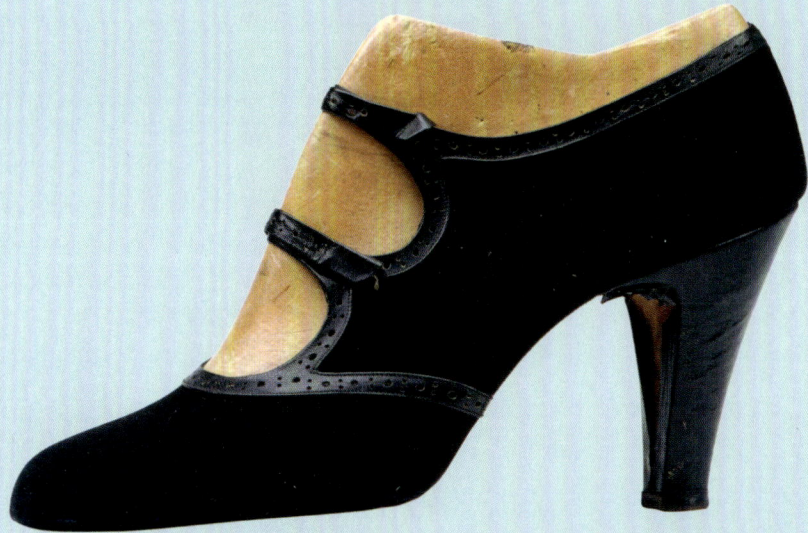

She snatched the stained shoes from my hand and out of the window they went. She stormed round the room, with me close behind trying to explain that I had solved the problem. She did not listen, she would not listen. Jars from her dressing-table smashed on the floor, bottles of scent followed the shoes through the window, while she raged: "You know the première is in an hour! The dress is ready, everything is ready—and you make a mistake in the shoes!" At last I managed to calm her down and showed her the substitutes. It took more persuasion to get them on her feet, and when I had finally succeeded she discovered that they fitted perfectly and matched her dress. She was happy again, but she looked at me witheringly and said: "Why the hell didn't you show me these shoes first and tell me about the accident afterwards?"

It was a lesson in psychology I have never forgotten.

Excerpted from Salvatore Ferragamo, *Shoemaker of Dreams: The Autobiography of Salvatore Ferragamo* (Florence: Giunti Gruppo Editoriale S.p.a., 1985), Chapter 10, 83–94.

Model of a black suede and calfskin shoe designed by Salvatore Ferragamo in 1927–30 for Pola Negri Florence, Museo Salvatore Ferragamo

Model of a black calfskin shoe designed by Salvatore Ferragamo in 1927–30 for Pola Negri Florence, Museo Salvatore Ferragamo

DEBORAH NADOOLMAN LANDIS

HOLLY-WOOD BEGINS 1908-1929: CLOTHES, COSTUME & COUTURE

Long before motion pictures were invented, audiences went to the theater for entertainment to see their favorite actors and to see what they were wearing. The romance, the glamour, celebrity, and costume were irresistible to audiences. When an actress captured the public's imagination, they ran to their dressmaker to copy what she wore on stage. Stage costume helped set the fashion. In a 1908 *Chicago Daily Tribune* article titled "Most New Styles First Seen on the Stage" the journalist wrote, "The department stores of Chicago and New York rely for their latest modish designs in gowns upon the real creators, the people of the stage." *Moving Picture World*, one of the earliest and most influential cinema trade papers, agreed: "It is an undoubted fact that innumerable women go to the theater in London or Paris to study the latest modes and styles."[1] The theater was an influencer for those audiences who could afford the tickets to attend. Yet, there were some obstacles for the fashion forward theater enthusiast: dress details and embroidery were impossible to see from a distance, which was compounded by bright stage lighting. Stage actresses played parts from teenage ingénue to elderly widow, another setback for the costume conscious matron in search of sartorial inspiration. Soon, cinema audiences would be able to scrutinize their favorite fashions up close and in sumptuous detail shimmering on the silver screen.

The arrival of motion pictures democratized audiences. This working-class entertainment with its lack of dialogue and rough and tumble fast-paced stories (Westerns were a favorite) suggested vaudeville skits rather than the traditional theater. In the earliest days, films were also screened as part of vaudeville shows.[2] As a testimony to its immediate popularity, nickelodeons (showing short films for the price of a nickel) sprang up in urban areas across the United States; there were often multiple theaters on one block alone. With their short running time and new titles released daily, nickelodeons were serving 200,000 customers a day. But their mass-market popularity did not please everyone. In a 1907 article in *The Billboard* magazine industry leaders voiced their concern that nickelodeons encouraged a "hoodlum element." They argued that these theaters deterred classier and wealthier patrons. "It is coming to be recognized as a principle that no theater can be a success unless it caters to the patronage of women and children."[3] The new strategy devised by these exhibitors included refining the titles, the substance, and the look of their productions and upgrading the overall quality of their releases and their theaters. A decade later, exhibitors would open fabulous movie palaces with reserved seating for a premium movie going experience. In 1912, French stage icon Sarah Bernhardt starred in the forty-four minute (four reel) *Queen Elizabeth*, forever securing the legitimacy of the motion picture. Her costume designer was the famed French couturier, Paul Poiret. With the import of this film from France, Adolf Zukor, founding mogul of the Famous Players Film Company (later Paramount Pictures), established the prestige of the long-form "feature" film.

In her book *When the Movies Were Young*, Linda Arvidson, the wife of David W. Griffith, recalls a time when she went shopping for a costume for a young Mary Pickford for the 1909 film *The Lonely Villa*.[4] With tight budgets, this special purchase was a rare occasion for an actress. Prior to the formation of stock companies, clothes for period films were hired from theatrical providers, while actors provided their own clothes for modern films. A player's personal wardrobe was so essential to their casting that Arvidson, when discussing three prospective actors for one role, remembered, "Though they all owned well-tailored dress suits, Frank Powell's was featured most often."[5] Powell got the job. Men owned, borrowed, and rented their modern suits, tuxedos and wardrobe, a common practice that lasted in Hollywood until the end of the studio era in the 1950s.

In the earliest days of Hollywood, when films were informally produced and before the establishment of the studio system, the director communicated the costuming requirements directly with casting. Consideration would be given by the casting department to the script, characters, and story arc, within the stylistic perimeters of each genre. Then, casting announced the clothes that were needed for the dramatic scene, whether it be for workers on a factory floor or guests attending a wedding. Each actor arrived with a variety of ensembles, which the director would approve. Personal advertisements in early trade journals promoted actresses' luxurious wardrobes—an asset to be marketed. One from 1915 declares, "April 17 brings Kitty Gordon and her famous wardrobe and her illustrious personality, back in her second World Film production, *Her Maternal Right*."[6] If an actress became a featured player, her bigger paycheck was often used for the purchase of new gowns to enhance her chances for employment. Leading actresses in Hollywood traveled regularly to New York to shop at the most expensive and exclusive couturiers of the time such as Lucile Ltd., Henri Bendel, Hickson, and Madame Frances.

Wherever the fashion originated, it was agreed that the style needed to perfectly fit the character. It was understood that performance and costume were one and indivisible. Silent film super star Mary Pickford was a devoted client of Lucile (Lady Duff Gordon), the premiere American designer. During the period between 1910 and 1922 Lucile dominated ladies' high fashion, designed for the stage and screen, ran a thriving couture business in New York and wrote fashion columns for a few different publications. Pickford was

Left to right: the American actress Alden Gay with Marion Morehouse and Miss Collier in a photograph by Edward Steichen published in *Vogue* in 1927. Gay, famous for her refined elegance, wears a chiffon dress designed by Madame Frances

a perfectionist and cared deeply that her cinema clothes supported her dramatic roles. She noted, "Many of my gowns come to me from London and Paris, but if they do not suit me I have them made over."[7] Early screen star Florence Lawrence summed up the eternal purpose of costume design in an early interview: "I do not wish to dress so that people can label my clothes with the designer's name whenever I appear. I want them to see me, not my gown. Each gown must fit the situation so well that it supplements instead of detracting from the effect. My audience must feel that I look the character I am playing in every detail. That is why I must make a thorough study of my role before I dress it. I could not get the gowns beforehand."[8]

Actresses also sewed their own clothes in a time when home sewing was commonplace. Silent film star Alma Taylor said, "It often means a great deal to know that the gown one is wearing is expressive of the mood one has to express and that one's own fingers can, with a little training and experience, carry out such a design more easily than trying to impress someone else with the effect that the gown should convey."[9] In those early years, before fan magazine audience members found outlets to discuss their favorite styles on screen in the modestly produced two-reelers, fashion commentary of actresses' ensembles were already being reported daily in newspapers and followed with fervor by fans.

By 1915, the Los Angeles-based studio chiefs agreed that employing a full time in-house costume designer made the most sense financially. Keeping the entire film production on a studio campus made for less wasted time. The actress could stay close for fittings and alterations. This addition of a costume designer on the studio lot was less common on the East Coast due to the proximity and competition of the New York fashion business. After years of

Lillian Gish in *The Birth of a Nation*, directed by David W. Griffith in 1915. The costumes were designed by Robert Goldstein and Clare West

production, the Hollywood film companies began to accumulate costume in bulk. They recycled their costumes and built substantial storage space for police and military uniforms and character clothes.

In Hollywood, clothes could be altered and created by professionals in the wardrobe department on the studio lot next to filming. Designers were encouraged to invent new styles and to create theatrical looks for each dramatic scene. The seismic shift from outsourcing fashion to anchoring the entire costume design process to the studio lot allowed actresses to spend more time in front of the camera. A time and money saving studio strategy. Keeping everyone together also helped with last minute script and casting changes. Costume designer Mrs. Frank Farrington described this moment: "A young woman rushes in to the department with a rush call for a dress that will fit a vampire part that has suddenly been written into the picture."[10] Costume design in the studio system became streamlined and standardized before 1920 as film production was becoming formalized in the lead up to the Golden Age of Hollywood.

These new costume professionals shared a variety of titles: costume designer, wardrobe mistress, and costume director. Whatever the title, they were de facto costume designers; creating a dress, choosing items from

Mary Pickford in a dress designed by Lucile for the film *Stella Maris*, directed by Marshall Neilan in 1918

stock, and shopping for readymade clothes. In 1914, when interviewed about her research, Mrs. Madden, the "wardrobe woman" from New York City's Reliance Studio, was very clear about her role as a cinema storyteller. She said of her process, "I never have any pattern, not even theatrical plates to go by. I just work from a description of my idea of the character. I use my own imagination and judgment."[11] Early designers came from the worlds of fashion design, dressmaking, and theatrical costume design. The absence of screen credits during this period makes it challenging for historians to chart the careers of the first costume designers. Some of the most notable pioneering Hollywood designers include Clare West (Famous Players-Lasky), Jane Lewis (Vitagraph), Melville Ellis (Ince), Peggy Hamilton (Triangle), Ethel Chaffin and Alpharetta Hoffman (Lasky), Harry Collins (Universal Film Manufacturing Company), Virginia Norden (Ince), Mrs. Frank Farrington (Thanhauser), and Sophie Wachner (Goldwyn Studios). As the directors of costume, these designers were responsible for all the contemporary and character clothes for the female stars and supporting cast. With the aid of specialist tailors and seamstresses and a robust costume workroom, many of these designers traveled for inspiration and fabric in New York and in Europe.

Film companies exploited their stars and their celebrity encouraged attendance and ticket sales. This included promoting and differentiating their films with the "latest fashions" that would draw more women to the pictures. Publicity departments churned screen style and make-up "tips" and star gossip for newspapers' lady's pages. Interviews with actresses and costume designers became common. Fan magazines, collaborating closely with the Hollywood studios, allowed readers to follow their favorite stars' glamorous on and off screen clothes and romances, although these accounts were often written by studio press agents. Costume budgets were grossly inflated to conjure must-see excitement. Newsreels and "Fashion Films," often with a slim storyline, showed the latest collections in theaters from Paris designers like Worth, Lanvin, and Paquin—a prequel to the catwalk show. Prior to World War I, Paris dictated fashion. However, after the war started and couture houses closed in 1914, Paris styles became less accessible to women worldwide.

After 1917 and America's entry into the war, President Wilson encouraged women to be thrifty, to practice conservation and frugality. But the war benefited Hollywood film studios, who did not miss Paris's domination of fashion and who were very happy to fill American style pages promoting their contract players in their gorgeous studio-created gowns. Duplication of a Paris couture dress, that is another actress in a different film wearing the identical French dress, had always caused some anxiety. Ethel Chaffin worried, "What disillusionment, for instance, if Claire Windsor and Gloria Swanson were each to show on the screen the same brocaded satin gown!"[12] Costume designer Peggy Hamilton heralded Hollywood as fashion forward as editor of the rotogravure fashion page at *The Los Angeles Times*, while boosting studio designers by setting up fashion shows of Hollywood costumes. After the war, publicity departments proclaimed that America was now the hub of international fashion. American movies, not Paris, were setting the style and fueling the imagination of the female audience.

Hollywood ignited fashion trends because the gowns created for the movies were seen to the utmost advantage; the romantic story, the setting, the make-up, hair, lighting: all conspired to elicit emotion. Designer Clare West explained, "This costume is worn under circumstances as nearly perfect as can be and it is shown throughout the country. Women who never saw New York or Paris styles are now thoroughly familiar with the latest fashions as presented in the motion pictures and have come to regard the clothes worn in the pictures as authoritative from a fashion point of view."[13] Actress Corinne Griffith agreed that cinema style had become a dynamic portal for current fashion

Theda Bara wearing a dress by the costume designer George Hopkins in the film *Cleopatra*, directed by J. Gordon Edwards in 1917

The Cast of "Monsieur Beaucaire" In the Costumes Barbier Designed For Them

The Designer's Dreams Come True

Two articles from an unknown publication celebrate the costumes designed by George Barbier for the film *Monsieur Beaucaire*, directed by Sidney Olcott in 1924, with Rudolph Valentino in the lead role

Rudolph Valentino in his dressing-room during the shooting of *Monsieur Beaucaire*; in the background is his wardrobe
Turin, Collection Museo Nazionale del Cinema

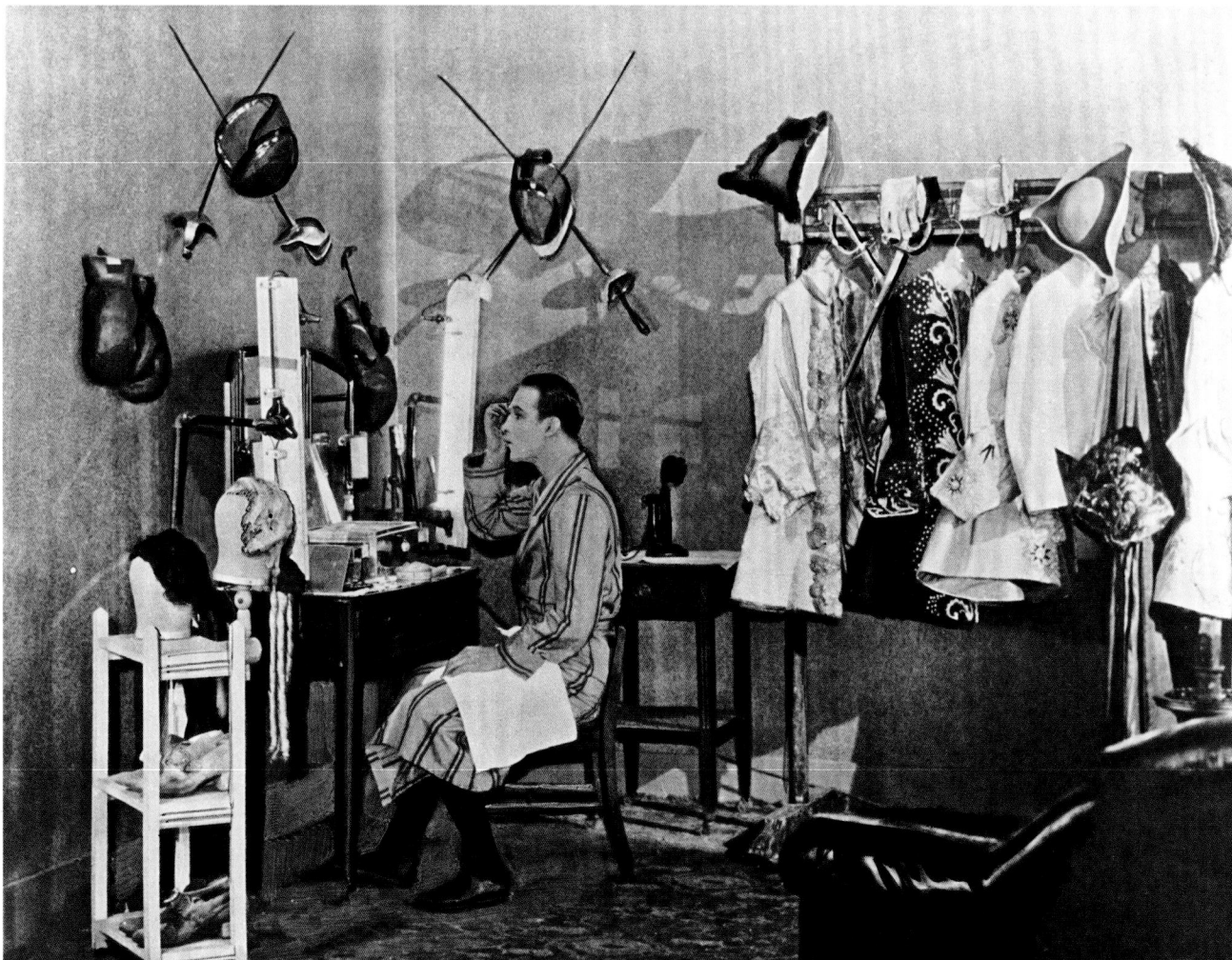

news and trends. Griffith reflected, "The movie fashions are a godsend to the small-town girl. They keep her alive as to what is going on. Time was when the local dressmaker took in a fashion magazine and a few paper patterns and did her best. Now there is plenty of opportunity to study the designs on the screen and see exactly what they are and how they should be worn."[14] If studio publicity departments worked hard to tout their stars and their costumes, they did not necessarily expect their designs to start a trend amongst their audience. Clare West understood that the theatrical exaggeration of cinema costuming would serve as an inspiration and not as something to copy: "Of course, while the dressmaker who wants new ideas or the little girl in the small town who is planning her trousseau probably would not want an evening gown such as I design for Bebe Daniels, she can get an idea for a new draping of her skirt or an unusual way of cutting the neckline from it."[15]

Outrageous silhouette, sweeping trains and low décolletage were

Eighteenth-century style costume in peach velvet with lace soutache at the neck and on the cuffs, probably one of those worn by Rudolph Valentino in *Monsieur Beaucaire*. The label "R. Valentino EO-3" is sewn onto the lining
Pasadena, Bryan Johns Collection

Silk caftan created for Rudolph
Valentino by the costume
designer Adrian, under
the supervision of Natacha
Rambova, for the unfinished
film *The Hooded Falcon*,
directed by Joseph Henabery
in 1924
Pasadena, Bryan Johns
Collection

Federico Beltrán Masses, *Portrait of Rudolph Valentino*, 1925
Oil on canvas, 250 x 156.2 cm
Pasadena, Bryan Johns Collection

Inside the home of Rudolph Valentino, with the portrait of the actor painted by the Cuban-born Spanish artist Federico Beltrán Masses. Valentino is portrayed in the guise of El Cid, whose story is told in *The Hooded Falcon*

not the only elements that were inappropriate for street wear. Film costumes were designed to be photographed and seen in two dimensions projected on a big screen. The silhouette of the gown with exposure of powdered neck, arms, and backs was a crucial tool for the Hollywood designer working on black-and-white movies. These gowns featured long extended or extra wide or puffed sleeves, festooned with high collars, lavish furs, feathered turbans, ropes of pearls and monumental tassels hanging from the waist. Motion picture costume designers understood that their role as interpreters of the screenplay was different than that of a fashion designer. Costumes were obliged to fit within the dramatic narrative, suit the character and (if possible) flatter the performer. Costume designer Ethel Chaffin noted that fashions designed for retail sale were not always cinematic: "A dress that a woman could wear in the street would look badly in a picture. Some of the straight-line dresses just look slab-sided before the camera. The greater number of our women are small, and we must select the styles that are suited to small women and that do not make them look large."[16] Actress Marguerite Courtot agreed that her job was complex, "My clothes are not simply so many lovely gowns. When I select them for plays I have to study their capabilities to cooperate with

Outfit in cream-colored wool
composed of a Norfolk jacket
and knickerbockers, designed by
J. Dege & Sons Ltd. and Everitt
& Macklin in the early 1920s
and belonging to the personal
wardrobe of Rudolph Valentino.
The actor is seen wearing the
outfit in several photos taken
during a visit to the family villa
of his wife Natacha Rambova,
Château Juan-le-Pins in Antibes
Pasadena, Bryan Johns
Collection

me. Some clothes act, others never could."[17]

The black-and-white on-screen image could be frustrating for the fashion forward audience seeking the guidance. Most cinematographers, complaining of the glare from their very hot lights, prohibited the use of white on the set or on the clothes. Screen testing fabrics after much trial and error, costume designers replaced white with a light pink fabric, which still "read" as white in a black-and-white film. Red photographed as black. Following the lead of early cinematographers, costume designers were in possession of a blue viewing glass to determine how fabrics would look on black-and-white film. Designers were obliged to rely upon startling contrast in pattern and accessories, plaids and stripes, details such as lace and embroidery, texture like big feathers and fluffy furs, and shiny fabrics like silk charmeuse, duchesse satin, and an abundance of crystals and sequins that reflected light. By necessity, sometimes clothes were created in colors that had no bearing to what they looked like on screen, a fact that was unsettling to sensitive actors. Sophie Wachner countered, "I find that a woman's mood will unconsciously change to fit the style of the garment in which I dress her. I try to make everything exactly as it would be if it were to be worn in real life instead of reel life."[18]

By the early 1920s, the Hollywood studios were established as film factories with a veritable production line. The structure of the wardrobe department was formalized, with chief designers who designed for the lead actresses and oversaw all other production. The fully staffed costume workrooms clothed the dozens of films studios were producing each year. Back in 1915 the wardrobe at Lasky Studio consisted of "two racks of clothing for which a kind-hearted junk man might have offered $200," but just four years later it had grown into a costume department that "has its own two-story building, employs fifty people, and has a costume stock valued at $200,000."[19] The design and manufacturing of costumes became streamlined as the number of films being produced by Hollywood grew exponentially. A few of the major film companies, including Vitagraph, began to create costumes for their extras (atmosphere) for period and for modern pictures. Previously, background players were well-dressed wealthy elites with deep closets, but they could not be counted on to show up for film production with regularity. This shift in costume production allowed a professional class of film performer, the "extra," to thrive.

Hats, which were constantly worn by all men, were made by the specialty millinery haberdashery in the studio. And while period shoes were sometimes outsourced, studios would later employ a cobbler and specialist shoemaker to create them. Finding the right shoes for modern films was the responsibility of each actress. Shoes were always considered part of the costume and an essential accessory. They had to do more than to simply match the costume, they were acknowledged early as a key to character. Sophie Wachner noted, "Even shoes and stockings need thought. The players must furnish these themselves."[20] Costume director of the Paramount Studios in New York H. M. K. Smith weighed in, "Regarding accessories, such as bags, hats, gloves, shoes and fans, the actress usually can exercise her personal preference so long as the articles chosen do not conflict with the ensemble."[21]

Actresses were scrutinized for imperfection and their ensembles were required to be pitch perfect for the dramatic moment. This maniacal attention to detail became the signature of a Hollywood film; glossy, sophisticated, and refined. No distracting dress or accessory would be allowed to sabotage the story and the scene. There were also those professionals who did not want their costumes to overwhelm their performance; as Lillian Gish reminisced, "We hoped we were making timeless films, and we would always try to dress our heroines in a classical way. I was conscious of style, as most young women are, but I knew that if my costumes

The actress Anna Q. Nilson in a photo from 1926 showing her receiving beauty treatment from the make-up artist Percy Westmore. Make-up was no less important than clothing, especially in the context of silent film

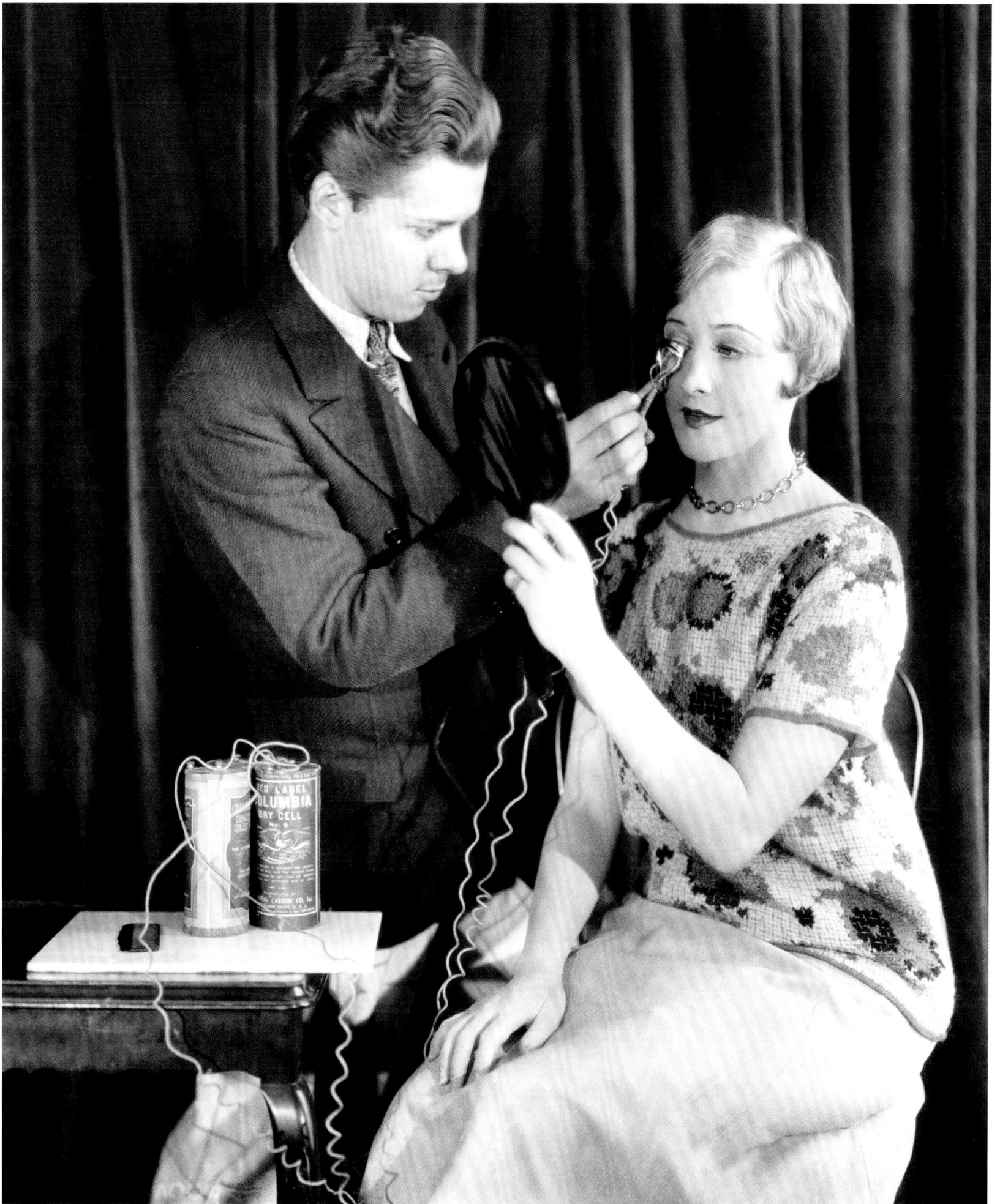

were in style one year they would look out of style five or ten years later."[22] The final costuming decision was made by the directors; and with their approval, the camera could roll and the scene could begin.

At the dawn of the 1920s the motion picture business was booming and costume design was being recognized by plentiful coverage in the film, fashion, and general press. As producers aggressively promoted costume design as a lure for movie attendances, they sought bigger international design talent for their stars. As part of studio public relations and marketing strategy, Hollywood began importing Parisian (and Paris-trained) fashion designers. These imports had mixed and sometimes disappointing results. In 1920, Famous Players-Lasky announced the hiring of Paul Iribe. He was a multi-talented artist known for his Art Deco fashion illustrations and spoke movingly about the impact of cinema: "Impressions received through the eye are many times more vivid than those received from cold print and a gown actually seen creates greater interest than one described. I believe that the screen is the logical messenger of art and beauty."[23] He found some success working as a costume designer, art director, production designer, and even co-directed. But he returned to Paris after his Hollywood career ended abruptly after a catastrophic budget battle[24] with director Cecil B. DeMille during the filming of the epic *The King of Kings* (1927).

The Parisian Russian costume and fashion designer Erté was already famous for his fabulous Art Deco illustrations and outrageous costumes for the Folies Bergère. Although he had designed the Egyptian costumes for the exotic "Ball of the Gods" scene in Paramount's *The Restless Sex* (1920), he did not "officially" arrive in Hollywood until 1925. He had been invited by Louis B. Mayer with great fanfare to MGM Studios. Like Iribe, Erté was convinced of Hollywood's impact on fashion and culture: "I came to this country because I realize that films may do more toward establishing fashions than any other influence in the world. It is because they speak the international language of the eye and they reach the masses."[25] MGM had hoped to keep him permanently, but according to veteran costume director Ethel Chaffin, Erté failed to understand the multifaceted role of the costume designer for motion pictures. He worked only seven months before breaking his contract due to his frustration over the constant rewriting of the script that he had been hired to design. Erté disliked actresses, who had their own opinions and their complaints of his designs. He bemoaned the short pre-production schedule. It was not long before Erté left MGM and returned to Paris.

Already an international superstar, Coco Chanel arrived in Hollywood at the invitation of mogul Samuel Goldwyn. Chanel's aspirations were high: "I am not going to convert any of Mr. Goldwyn's players to my clothes or to my style. With a method and a technique that are entirely new to me, I am going to try to create in their clothes the same excitement, the same allure, the same interest that they and their designers have always attempted. As a work, designing for cinema stars is a great unfathomed field. It fascinates me. I am proud to have a part in it. I feel that the movies are having a tremendous influence on costume and dress. That is why I am intrigued with designing clothes for the screen."[26]

Surprisingly, although Chanel had signed a contract with Goldwyn to design three films, she never finished the third production. Her clothes for *The Greeks Had a Word for Them* (1932) left the producers and actresses unimpressed. Chanel's gowns were remade for the studio by costume designer Milo Anderson, who would later recall, "Goldwyn had imported Chanel from Paris to design some pictures, but it just didn't work out. Once she caused a long delay in production while she waited for a certain kind of pin to arrive from Paris."[27] To everyone's surprise, this fashion & film marriage was a mismatch of culture and failed spectacularly. Movies had established a mode of production with their own rules regarding the cohesive design of

A scene from *The King of Kings*, directed by Cecil B. DeMille in 1927, which saw the collaboration of the French costume designer Paul Iribe. Salvatore Ferragamo made the shoes for the main characters

the character within the story and the body in the frame. Chanel had revolutionized fashion for the modern woman but she did not understand that costume design for cinema had become a professionalized and sovereign endeavor.

The most successful and enduring transition from fashion design to film could be credited to actress Gloria Swanson, who brought Swiss designer René Hubert from Paris to the United States in 1924. Hubert designed Swanson's film costumes and personal wardrobe, commonplace at the time. A major silent film star, Swanson understood the power of costume stating, "I claim no credit for acting. Clothes make me act. I never rehearse in street clothes—it is for me a waste of time because I feel no sympathy with the part unless I am dressed for the part. I do not mean that I must be 'dressed up' to feel the urge. But if I am to do a gypsy I must wear gypsy rags. Clothes are everything." Hubert had designed for the theater in France and had also assisted the great couturier

Jean Patou. Thanks to this bifurcated background, he enjoyed an extremely long and successful career in Hollywood: he designed many modern and period films and received two Academy Award nominations.[28]

The American designers who honed their skills in the silent film era made their mark in Hollywood for decades to come. These "greats" designed the stars and the icons of the Golden Age and the Hollywood classics that we revere as pillars of American and international popular culture. Gilbert Adrian started designing costumes at MGM in the mid-1920s. As director of wardrobe at MGM, he closely collaborated with Greta Garbo, Joan Crawford, Katharine Hepburn, Jean Harlow, and others throughout their careers. They were all wearing Adrian, who helped them create their individual screen personalities. At Paramount, Travis Banton, who had honed his talent while designing at Lucile, Ltd. in New York, created Marlene Dietrich's signature style, luminous designs for Carole Lombard, Mae West's silhouette, and Claudette Colbert would not do a film without him.

Golden Age costume designers actually created what the world thinks of today as a Hollywood movie. From their Los Angeles offices, they designed hundreds of productions and their expertise was unparalleled by any measure. Every studio wardrobe department employed generations of talented craftspeople; many of them were new immigrants. These tailors, cutters, embroiderers, beaders, milliners, and cobblers brought their skills and virtuosity to each costume, which graced every single frame of film. Hollywood films and their stars were created and supported by this superbly organized framework of artists. That was genius of the Hollywood system. In 1928, at the close of the silent era, attendance at movie theaters had reached sixty-five million people per week. Hollywood's influence on fashion and popular culture continues today and its pioneering artisans have inspired generations of American and international designers.

Gloria Swanson in a dress created by the Swiss costume designer René Hubert for the film *The Love of Sunya*, directed by Albert Parker in 1927

Bolero designed by Natacha
Rambova and worn by
Rudolph Valentino in *Blood
and Sand*, directed by Fred
Niblo in 1922
Silk, metal thread, silver
sequins, glass beads
and rhinestones
Courtesy of The Colletion
of Motion Picture Costume
Design: Larry McQueen,
Los Angeles

Rudolph Valentino in *Blood
and Sand*, directed by Fred
Niblo in 1922
Turin, Collection Museo
Nazionale del Cinema

Louise Brooks in *The Canary Murder Case*, directed by Malcolm St. Clair and Frank Tuttle in 1929. She is wearing an outfit created by the costume designer Travis Banton

Claudette Colbert photographed in 1929 by Nickolas Muray for *Vogue*. She is wearing a long black dress designed for her by Travis Banton

1 "Dress and the Picture," in *Moving Picture World*, July 9, 1910: 73.

2 For one vaudeville act, two of the performers, Albert Edward Smith and James Stuart Blackton, went on to form the Vitagraph Company in 1897. See Anthony Slide, *The New Historical Dictionary of the American Film Industry* (New York: Routledge, 2013), 222–23.

3 Oliver M. Gale "The Chicago Film Business," in *The Billboard (Archive: 1894–1960)*, vol. 19, no. 49, December 7, 1907, 74–75.

4 Linda Arvidson, *When the Movies were Young* (New York: Dover Publications, 1925), 110.

5 Ibid., 112.

6 "Around the 'World'," in *Motograph* XV, no. 16 (April 15, 1916): 876.

7 Grace Kingsley, "Clothes," in *Photoplay*, May 1915: 100.

8 Gladys Jones, "A Breakfast Chat with Florence Lawrence," in *Feature Movie Magazine*, March 1916: 15.

9 Alma Taylor, "Cinema Talk," in *Cinema Chat: Number 1*, May 26, 1919: 6.

10 Mrs. Frank Farrington, "In the Costume Room," in *Moving Picture World,* July 21, 1917: 389–90.

11 "Making Wardrobe for the Movies," in *Reel Life*, March 28, 1914: supplement, iii.

12 Jack Jungmeyer, "Costuming Gives Films Personality," in *The Independent* (evening edition), St. Petersburg, FL, January 12, 1924: 6.

13 "Motion Pictures to Create New Fashion Center," in *Women's Wear*, November 8, 1919: 1.

14 Campbell MacCulloch, "Beating the Fashion Clock," in *Liberty*, February 25, 1928: 57–60.

15 Louise Williams, "A Painter in Fabrics," in *Picture-Play Magazine*, February 1920: 41–43.

16 "Paris Commercialized, Says Ethel Chaffin: Famous Players Designer Comments on Necessity of Individual Styles for Films," in *Women's Wear*, November 27, 1920: 2.

17 Lillian Howard, "How I Teach My Gowns to Act," in *Photoplay*, February 1916: 89–93.

18 "Los Angeles District: 'Movie' Studio Has Its Costume Department: Miss Wachner Supervises Wardrobe and Makes Fashion Rules for Goldwyn," *Women's Wear*, December 27, 1920: 30.

19 Adela Rogers St. Johns, "From the Skin Out," in *Photoplay*, 15, 6 (May 1919): 32–35, 97–101.

20 "Film Fashion Features," in *The New York Times,* December 2, 1923: 1.

21 "Costume Director Tells of Clothing Characters," in *The New York Times*, January 10, 1926: X5.

22 Lillian Gish with Ann Pinchot, *Lillian Gish, The Movies, Mr. Griffith and Me* (Englewood Cliffs, NJ: Prentice Hall, 1969), 230–31.

23 "Dresses," in *Women's Wear*, February 5, 1921: 15.

24 Presley DeMille, Cecilia and Mark A. Vieira, *Cecil B. DeMille: The Art of the Hollywood Epic* (Philadelphia, PA: Running Press, 2014), 132–34.

25 "Paris Style King In Film Debut," in *Los Angeles Times*, March 18, 1925: 1.

26 Marcella Burke, "Fashion Mandates from a Famous French Expert," in *Hollywood* 20, no. 8 (September 1931).

27 David Chierichetti, "Milo Anderson: Quiet Man with Resounding Talent for Costumes," in *Los Angeles Times*, August 19, 1983: G1.

28 Hubert received Academy Award nominations for Best Costume Design, Black-and-White, for *The Visit* (1964) and Best Costume Design, Color, for *Désirée* (shared with Charles LeMaire).

Greta Garbo and costume designer Adrian on the set of *The Single Standard*, directed by John S. Robertson in 1929

SILVIA LUCCHESI

TWO YOUNG ITALIANS IN HOLLYWOOD

For *Italy in Hollywood*, filmmaker Yuri Ancarani and photographer Manfredi Gioacchini, two young Italian artists working in Los Angeles, have expressly created a video-installation and a series of fifteen photographic portraits respectively, ideally exploring the exhibition subject. What is it about this legendary city of cinema that captures Italian artists once they arrive there? And who are the Italians working in Hollywood today?

West of Malibu is Zuma Beach, a stunning naturally scenographic environment surrounded by high rocks that every evening turn ochre and red in the sunset. Thanks to its beauty, Zuma Beach has been a location for cult films such as Franklin J. Schaffner's *The Planet of the Apes* and the Coen brothers' *Barton Fink*; during the 1990s, at the height of the TV production season, the famous *Baywatch* series was also shot here.

Today's art film crisis, with distribution becoming increasingly hard and cinemas closing down due to the spread of new technologies, has led Yuri Ancarani to explore the theme of Hollywood by observing Zuma Beach as a symbol of change. An award-winning artist whose production spans from contemporary art to cinema, Ancarani reflected on how this famous beach today has become a spontaneous set for common people. Every day at sunset you can see four of five sets with aspiring young actresses, actors, and models taking selfies or posing before the camera, all sharing the same goal: create their personal show they will then share on the social networks.

The very presence of those youths is the sign of a cultural shift, one affecting cinema too. No longer spectators, these people are able to capture the attention and take control by irrupting into the two-dimensional image and by affirming themselves as the lead characters of their self-produced web content. This social-anthropological shift from user to protagonist, a shift that characterizes the world of social network, where anyone can become filmmaker, actor, actress, or model can be witnessed on Zuma Beach, a fabulous cinema and TV location whose audio-visual fruition has today radically changed.

This short circuit could not escape the attention of Ancarani, who created his *Zuma Beach* looped video installation on the very observation of this phenomenon. Taken at sunset over a period of two weeks, each film still composing the work portrays one of these spontaneous sets against the majestic natural setting kissed by red sunset light. The video creates a highly pictorial ensemble, a sort of landscape gallery where movement appears to be minimal due to the distance from which the subjects were filmed.

Interestingly, for this project about the Hollywood of today and the lost tradition of great cinema, Ancarani did not use state-of-the-art cameras but chose a common iPhone, an anonymous easy tool that enabled him to capture the scenes as they were happening, the iPhone being an audio-visual recording device that anyone can use to photograph, shoot, or "capture," as in this case, the legendary atmosphere of the cinema productions of the past. But at the hands of Ancarani, the everyday ritual is transformed into a narrative of great visual and seductive power. His seemingly amateur shoots form a spectacular narration of small stories containing a surprising *coup de théâtre*, a reference to Schaffner's famous film, which combines the level of reality with that of artifice. Ancarani himself appears in one of the scenes with his friend Manfredi Gioacchini taking a photo of him while he is in turn shooting the "selfie-takers." This creates an intersection of glances with the viewer that is typical of cinema and that makes the interconnections and the different readings of the work explicit.

Manfredi Gioacchini's project leads us into the life of Hollywood through the portraits of Italian professionals working there today. We have seen their names in the credits of the most highly successful films of the last thirty years; some of them were nominated and even awarded an Oscar. Gioacchini photographs them in their homes, which often are also their workplaces, in Santa Monica, Venice, Pacific Palisades, West Hollywood, and Los Angeles. In Los Angeles, where he moved to from Rome in 2013, thirty-year-old photographer Gioacchini published his *Portraits of Artists* (2016), a photo book with portraits of artists living in California—a series that was also displayed at the Los Angeles County Museum of Art: an experience that led him to this exhibition at the Museo Salvatore Ferragamo.

Gioacchini presents a visually consistent all black-and-white gallery with indoor and outdoor shots, all in a vertical format inviting the viewer to concentrate on the character's humanity and personality, be it a close up or a full figure picture: a gallery of producers, cinematographers, screenwriters, film editors, actors, special effects specialists, men and women, young and old, whose skills and competence contribute, just as their predecessors did one century ago, to the world's leading cinema industry. We see famous professionals such as Milena Canonero, nine times Academy Awards nominee and four times winner for best costumes with *Barry Lyndon*, *Chariots of Fire*, *Marie Antoinette*, and *The Grand Budapest Hotel*, or Giorgio Moroder, Oscar winner for the soundtracks of *Midnight Express*, *Flash Dance*, and *Top Gun*, or film editor Pietro Scalia who won an Oscar for Oliver Stone's *JFK* and another for Ridley Scott's *Black Hawk Down*. And also less known personalities, but each with their outstanding story. Pasquale Fabrizio, former hockey player and then advertising sales agent who became the shoemaker of the stars following the footsteps of his uncle who had a shoe repair shop in Beverly Hills. Along his thirty-year Hollywood career he made shoes for Uma Thurman in *Kill Bill*, for Will Smith in *Mohamed Ali*, and for Christina Aguilera in *Burlesque*. Gioacchini captures this master craftsman holding his tools while standing at his workbench. The producer Silvia Bizio, who has been living in Hollywood for over twenty years, working as the correspondent from Los Angeles for the newspaper *la Repubblica* and the magazine *L'Espresso*, is portrayed nonchalantly in the garden of her home. And then Carlo Siliotto, composer of over seventy film scores who traveled for years across Kazakhstan to capture the sound of the drums, one of which he lovingly hugs in the photo. Young costume designer Christian Cordella (*Spider-Man: Homecoming* and *Guardians of the Galaxy 2*, among others) poses before the iconic *Psycho* house, unaltered since 1960 and today a Universal Studios tourist attraction. In the full figure portrait of producer Gisella Marengo, the luxuriant green palm landscape is reflected in the large windows of her dimly lit home.

Gioacchini prefers to photograph his subjects during their first meeting, before any sort of familiarity may develop. He needs to keep an emotional distance in order to create that moment of fleeting empathy that guides him in the making of the photo. This particular approach explains certain details that seem out of place, some imperfections that are actually expressions of his personal style. Gioacchini calls them his "flawed photos" because, although being posed portraits, each of them includes deliberate but yet unpredictable imperfections, as if they were really candid photos, or reportage shots where the photographer must capture that exact moment before it is gone. In the portrait of Pietro Scalia, his right arm is left out of the frame and his glasses and mobile phone casually left on the garden table, while his face is lit by a beautiful open smile.

YURI ANCARANI

Zuma Beach, 2018
video stills

His work has been featured in numerous national and international exhibitions and museums, among which Art Basel Unlimited, the Venice Biennale, the Centre Pompidou in Paris, the Fondazione Sandretto Re Rebaudengo in Turin, the Hammer Museum in Los Angeles, the MAXXI Museo Nazionale delle Arti del XXI secolo in Rome and the Kunsthalle Basel, as well as in a number of national and international festivals.

ZUMA BEACH

A VIDEO BY YURI ANCARANI

UN PROGETTO RATE CON
LA BIENNALE DELL'ARTE FILM FESTIVAL
MUSEO SALVATORE FERRAGAMO

MANFREDI GIOACCHINI

**Portraits from
Hollywood**

After studying at Central Saint Martins–UAL–University of Arts London and the Istituto Europeo di Design in Milan, in 2006–08 he has been an assistant to Mario Testino in London and in 2012–13 to Daniele & Iango in New York. He won Les plus grand concours Photo du Monde 2012 and was a finalist at the Prix d'Or de la Photographie in Paris in 2011. In 2016 he published the book *Portraits of Artists* (UTG LLC, New York), in which he assembled a number of portraits of artists living and working in California. His photographs are included in the collections of LACMA in Los Angeles and the Centre Pompidou in Paris. His work has been published in major international magazines.

Christian Cordella
Costume designer

Carlo Siliotto
Composer

Daniele Auber
Designer

Emanuela Postacchini
Actress

Ivan Olita
Director

Gisella Marengo
Producer

Giorgio Moroder
Composer and record
executive

Pasquale Fabrizio
Shoemaker

Silvia Bizio
Film producer

Stefania Cella
Set designer

Yuri Ancarani
Video artist

Alessandro Jacomini
Cinematographer

Pietro Scalia
Film editor

Milena Canonero
Costume designer

EXHIBITION CHECKLIST

ROOM 1

ITALIAN EMIGRATION TO CALIFORNIA

_ARTWORKS

Raffaello Gambogi
Emigranti [Emigrants], 1894
Oil on canvas, 146 x 196 cm
Livorno, Museo Civico Giovanni
Fattori, inv. 1109

_VIDEOS

Emigration, 2018
Video by Daniele Tommaso, 9:34
Sources: *Nuovomondo* by
Emanuele Crialese (2006); *Good
Morning Babilonia* by Paolo and
Vittorio Taviani (1987); *L'emigrante*
by Febo Mari (1915)
Turin, Collection Museo Nazionale
del Cinema

Italians in California, 2018
Edited by Fabio Iaquone and Luca
Attilii, 8:00
Sources: Amadeo Peter Giannini,
founder of the Bank of Italy, later
the Bank of America, in his office,
1923; Facade of the Bank of Italy,
San Francisco; Italian miners at
Angels Camp, California, 1910; The
Costantini Store in Los Angeles;
The restaurant and grocery store
Little Joe's on North Broadway, Los
Angeles; Di Carlo bakery bread
cart, Los Angeles; The railroad at
the Italian Vineyard Company;
The Italian Workers Club in Los
Angeles, 1920s; Members of
the Garibaldina Society with
their families in Griffith Park, Los
Angeles, 1920s; Italian fishermen
at San Pedro, Los Angeles,
Italian American Museum of Los
Angeles; Model of the Jacuzzi
J-7 monoplane, Courtesy Museo
Italo Americano of San Francisco;

Italian street sweepers in San
Francisco, c. 1915; The cart that
distributed the Italian newspaper
L'Italia, 1910, Courtesy Museo
Italo Americano of San Francisco
and Paola Sensi Isolani; The
soprano Luisa Tetrazzini singing at
Lotta's Fountain in San Francisco,
December 24, 1910, Courtesy
Museo Italo Americano of San
Francisco and Alessandro Baccari;
Female Italian workers canning
fruit at the California Fruit Canners
Association, San José (CA), History
San José Research Library and
Archives; The Società Filarmonica
Bella Italia in a photo from 1911,
Turin, Centro Altreitalie, Italians in
Chicago

ITALY AT THE PANAMA-PACIFIC INTERNATIONAL EXPOSITION IN SAN FRANCISCO, 1915

_ARTWORKS

Eugenio Pellini
L'idolo [The Idol], [1906]
Bronze, 74 x 73 x 66 cm
Bologna, Fondazione Lercaro

Plinio Nomellini
Baci di sole [Kisses of the Sun],
[1908]
Oil on canvas, 93 x 119 cm
Novara, Galleria d'Arte Moderna
Paolo e Adele Giannoni

Amleto Cataldi
La spiga [Wheat], [1909]
Bronze, 52 x 19 x 15 cm
Rome, Galleria d'Arte Moderna
di Roma Capitale, inv. AM247

Giuseppe Graziosi
Susanna, 1910
Bronze, 46 x 42 x 30 cm
Piacenza, Galleria d'Arte Moderna
Ricci Oddi, inv. 264

Luigi Russolo
Case e fanali [Houses and
Lights], 1911
Oil on canvas, 40 x 70 cm
Bologna, Fondazione Massimo
e Sonia Cirulli

Giacomo Balla
*Disgregazione X velocità
Penetrazioni dinamiche
d'automobile* [Disintegration X
speed, Dynamic penetrations
of an automobile], 1913
Tempera, watercolor, and Indian
ink on paper, 67.7 x 95.7 cm
Bologna, Fondazione Massimo
e Sonia Cirulli

Ettore Tito
La perla [The Pearl], 1914
Oil on canvas, 88.5 x 66 cm
Private collection

_BOOKS

Arduino Colasanti and Ettore
Ferrari, *International Panama-
Pacific Exhibition San Francisco
California 1915. Italian Fine Art
Section* (Rome: Stabilimento di arti
grafiche E. Calzone, 1915)
Florence, Museo Salvatore
Ferragamo, inv. BIBL. 0000943

*Della Cittadella Italiana alla
Esposizione di San Francisco*, ed.
by the Royal Italian Commission
for the San Francisco International
Exposition (Rome: Stabilimento
Tipografico "Aternum" di Enrico
Sabucchi, 1915)
Florence, Museo Salvatore
Ferragamo, inv. BIBL. 0000861

_PHOTOGRAPHS

Gabriel Moulin
*Gallery 141 with the works by
the Futurists displayed at the
Panama Pacific International
Exposition of 1915*
San Francisco, San Francisco
History Center, Public Library

_VIDEOS

The Italian Citadel at the Panama-Pacific International Exposition in San Francisco, 1915, 2018
Synchronized video installation, 7:40
Concept: Fabio Iaquone, Luca Attilii, and Stefania Ricci; art direction and execution by Iaquone e Attilii Studio, Rome, multimedia service AVUELLE s.r.l.

Italian Architectural Influences in California, 2018
Edited by Fabio Iaquone and Luca Attilii, 3:00
Sources: Studies by Bernard Maybeck for the Bank of Santa Barbara, the Packard Dealership in Oakland, and the pool of the Women's Gym at the University of California in Berkeley, Berkeley, University of California, Environmental Design Archives, Bernard Maybeck Collection, Earle C. Anthony Packard Dealership 1927–1931; The inner courtyard of the building housing the chapel and music room of the Occidental College Campus in Los Angeles; The west facade of the Bertha Harton Orr Hall, 1925, Los Angeles, Occidental College Library; The gardens of the Gurdon Wattles residence, 1917, Sacramento, California State Library; The actor Harold Lloyd's Tuscan-style villa with cypress-lined driveway (called "Greenacres") at Beverly Hills, late 1920s; The exterior and vestibule of one of the guest houses (called "B") of William Hearst's residence at San Simeon; View of Gordon Blanding's residence on Belvedere Island, San Francisco Bay, San Luis Obispo (CA), California Polytechnic State University, Julia Morgan Papers and Julia Morgan–Sara Holmes Boutelle Collection; Pola Negri in the garden of her Hollywood home, 1927

THE INFLUENCE OF ITALIAN CINEMA IN CALIFORNIA

Hebrew pectoral, 1916
From a costume for the film *Intolerance* (1916), directed by David W. Griffith
Gilded bronze set with glass gems
Courtesy of The Collection of Motion Picture Costume Design: Larry McQueen, Los Angeles

Salvatore Ferragamo
Shoe, 1923 (1985)
Bronze calfskin upper with incised fish-scale motif and brown calfskin lining. Oriental-style curled toe. Oval ornament in burnished brass at the ankle. Leather sole, 27 x 2 cm. Replica of the sandal created by Salvatore Ferragamo in Hollywood in 1923 for *The Ten Commandments*, directed by Cecil B. DeMille
Florence, Museo Salvatore Ferragamo, inv. SC0010503

_VIDEO

Three Epics Compared, 2018
Video by Daniele Tommaso, 5:39
Sources: *Cabiria* (1914), directed by Giovanni Pastrone, Turin, Collection Museo Nazionale del Cinema; *Intolerance* (1916), directed by David W. Griffith; *The Ten Commandments* (1923), directed by Cecil B. DeMille

ROOM 2

CABIRIA

_ARTWORKS

Leopoldo Metlicovitz
Maciste, [1914]
Lithographic poster for *Cabiria* (1914), directed by Giovanni Pastrone and produced by Itala Film, 207 x 144.5 cm
Turin, Collection Museo Nazionale del Cinema, inv. P30034

Leopoldo Metlicovitz
Fiamme [Flames], [1914]
Lithographic poster for *Cabiria* (1914), directed by Giovanni Pastrone and produced by Itala Film, 206 x 145 cm
Turin, Collection Museo Nazionale del Cinema, inv. P30008

Cecchetto
L'appuntamento [The appointment], 1932
Lithographic poster for the French sound version of *Cabiria* (1932), 157.5 x 118 cm
Turin, Collection Museo Nazionale del Cinema, inv. P01327

_PHOTOGRAPHS

Series of 12 stills on hand-colored slides. The slides were displayed inside the movie theaters and were also used in 1931 to launch the sound version of *Cabiria*. The shots are the ones taken for the original version of 1914
Turin, Collection Museo Nazionale del Cinema

_CLOTHING

Costume for Fulvio Axilla, 1914
Metal breastplate with studs and shoulder pieces. The helmet indicated the soldier's rank
Turin, Roberto Devalle Collection

Costume for centurion, 1914
Metal helmet and breastplate with studs and shoulder pieces
Turin, Roberto Devalle Collection

Costume for Hannibal, 1914
Moleskin cuirass with studs. The fur has been added, in keeping with the images of the scene in which Hannibal crosses the Alps to descend into Italy
Turin, Roberto Devalle Collection

Costume for Massinissa, 1914
Leather cuirass with decorated metal scales. Helmet with decoration and black pigtail reminiscent of a horse's mane. The cloak has been remade
Turin, Roberto Devalle Collection

Roman Standards, 1914
Gilded metal. Recto: S.P.Q.R. Verso: Flower Sun with fasces below; hand making Roman salute above the head of an illustrious man; head of an illustrious man with wreath
Turin, Roberto Devalle Collection

ROOM 3

ENRICO CARUSO, LINA CAVALIERI, TINA MODOTTI, RUDOLPH VALENTINO: ITALIAN ICONS IN HOLLYWOOD BETWEEN NATURE AND ART

ENRICO CARUSO

_ARTWORKS

Hugo Ballin
Portrait of Enrico Caruso, 1906
Oil on canvas, 96.5 x 71.8 cm (106.7 x 81.9 cm including frame)
New York, The Metropolitan Opera

Enrico Caruso
Self-portrait as the Duke of Mantua in Rigoletto *by G. Verdi*, Hamburg, 1906
Pencil on paper, 21 x 13 cm (35 x 29 cm including frame)
Lastra a Signa (Florence), Museo Internazionale Enrico Caruso, inv. 1450

Enrico Caruso
Self-caricature with humorous caption in Neapolitan, New York, 1909
Pencil on paper, 40 x 53 cm
Caruso depicts himself while smoking a pipe featuring the face of the baritone Eduardo Missiano. The caption reads: "Statte sore Missiá/ I me t'aggia sfeziá/ Tu te crire' e pazziá/ I à pipp' aggiá fumã/ Enrico Caruso/ NY 1909" (Don't worry, Missiano/ I've got to have some fun with you/ You think you're the joker/ But I'm the pipe smoker/ Enrico Caruso/ NY 1909)
Lastra a Signa (Florence), Museo Internazionale Enrico Caruso, inv. 1776

Enrico Caruso
Self-portrait as Alfredo in La Traviata *by G. Verdi*, Hamburg, 1912
Pencil on paper, 21.5 x 14.5 cm (35.2 x 282 cm including frame)
Lastra a Signa (Florence), Museo Internazionale Enrico Caruso, inv. 1448

Paolo Troubetzkoy
Enrico Caruso performing in La Fanciulla del West, 1912
Bronze, 55 x 32 x 37 cm
Lastra a Signa (Florence), Museo Internazionale Enrico Caruso, inv. 8074

_OBJECTS

Waldorf Luggage touring trunk, early twentieth century
This traveling trunk with two compartments, in galvanized iron and wood, and lined with fabric, belonged to Enrico Caruso who used it on his American tours
102 x 56 x 56 cm
Lastra a Signa (Florence), Museo Internazionale Enrico Caruso, inv. 2052

Album with embroidered cloth cover that belonged to Enrico Caruso, containing the programs and New York press reviews of the productions staged at the Metropolitan Opera House during the 1903–1904 season
35 x 28 cm
Lastra a Signa (Florence), Museo Internazionale Enrico Caruso, inv. 1153

Portable gramophone manufactured by the Victor Talking Machine Co., 1904
Oak case with small plaque reading "Exhibition His Master's Voice" and internal horn; the diaphragm is attached to the end of the metal tone arm
32.5 x 18 x 36.5 cm
Lastra a Signa (Florence), Museo Internazionale Enrico Caruso

Victrola double-sided disc with the arias "Vesti la giubba" (1907) and "No, Pagliaccio non son" (1910) from the opera P*agliacci*, both sung by Enrico Caruso
diameter 30 cm
Lastra a Signa (Florence), Museo Internazionale Enrico Caruso, inv. 9030

_CLOTHING

The costume Enrico Caruso wore as Canio in the opera *Pagliacci* by Ruggero Leoncavallo, early twentieth century
Jacket and pants in sandy yellow woolen cloth with pom-pom buttons in beige wool on brown felt. Measurements: shoulders 46 cm, circumference of jacket 114 cm, length of jacket in front 85 cm, length of jacket at the back 88 cm, waist 98 cm, length of pants 106 cm. Pierrot hat in felt in the same color with brown woolen pom-poms, diameter 27.5 cm
Lastra a Signa (Florence), Museo Internazionale Enrico Caruso, inv. 7904

Enrico Caruso's costume as Osaka in the opera *Iris* by Pietro Mascagni, Metropolitan Opera House, New York, 1907
Costume composed of two cloths with a central opening and slit at the side. The entire surface of the garment is decorated with a motif of trees in bloom and butterflies, hand-worked in polychrome embroidery in satin stitch executed with silk thread, metal thread, and applications with small round mirrors edged with gilded metal. Measurements: shoulders 80 cm, chest 168 cm, total length 150 cm
Lastra a Signa (Florence), Museo Internazionale Enrico Caruso, inv. 2070

_PHOTOGRAPHS

Portrait of Enrico Caruso, n.d.

Enrico Caruso as the Duke of Mantua in *Rigoletto* by Giuseppe Verdi, n.d.

Enrico Caruso in London, n.d.

A portrait of Enrico Caruso from the 1910s

Herman Mishkin
Enrico Caruso as Dick Johnson alias Ramerrez in Puccini's La Fanciulla del West, 1910

Enrico Caruso in a 1910 photo

Enrico Caruso in a 1912 photo of with autograph dedication: "Saluti/ da Salso[maggiore] Enrico Caruso/ 1912" [Greetings from Salsomaggiore Enrico Caruso 1912]. The image is part of an album acquired in 1973 from Giuseppe Carfagna in Rome
Naples, Biblioteca Lucchesi Palli, section of the Biblioteca Nazionale di Napoli, inv. 1414821

Enrico Caruso seated at the piano in his New York apartment, c. 1915

Portrait of Enrico Caruso, c. 1915. The photo was taken for Bain News Service, New York

Enrico Caruso singing opera in the open air, 1918

Herman Mishkin
Enrico Caruso, 1918
Taken on the set of the film *My Cousin*, the photo shows Caruso as the tenor Cesare Caroli singing in *Pagliacci* by Leoncavallo, one of his most famous interpretations
New York, The Metropolitan Opera

Enrico Caruso in Sorrento, c. 1920

_VIDEO

My Cousin (1918), directed by Edward José
Gemona, La Cineteca del Friuli

LINA CAVALIERI

_ARTWORKS

Vittorio Corcos
Portrait of Lina Cavalieri, c. 1903
Oil on canvas, 265 x 178 cm
Private collection

Cesare Tallone
Portrait of Lina Cavalieri, c. 1905
Oil on canvas, 96 x 70 cm
(109.5 x 84 cm including frame)
Milan, Archivio Galleria Campari

Piero Fornasetti
Theme and Variations
Lithograph and serigraph on
porcelain, diameter 26 cm
36 variations on Lina Cavalieri's
face from 1952 to the 1970s (009,
016, 017, 043, 047, 056, 082, 098,
105, 107, 138, 140, 145, 148, 152, 166,
168, 171, 174, 176, 181, 189, 190, 193,
199, 202, 219, 220, 250, 260, 268,
276, 281, 282, 285, 302); 4 variations
from the 2000s (363, 365, 369, 373)
Milan, Archivio Fornasetti

_CLOTHING

Italian manufacture, *Evening
gown. Attributed to Lina Cavalieri*,
c. early 1906
Lace and black velvet ribbon on
pink ivory satin base decorated
with sequins and black glass
beads, length 185 cm
Rome, Sorelle Gazzoni,
Fondazione Tirelli Trappetti

_PHOTOGRAPHS

Lina Cavalieri photographed for a
postcard, late nineteenth century
Florence, Archivi Alinari, Fondo
Mary Evans

Portrait of Lina Cavalieri in
a Reutlinger postcard, late
nineteenth century

Portrait of Lina Cavalieri in a
Reutlinger postcard, 1890

Portrait of Lina Cavalieri in a
Reutlinger postcard, 1890

Portrait of Lina Cavalieri, c. 1890

Francesco Paolo Michetti
*Portrait of Lina Cavalieri wearing
a voluminous hat*, 1909 (series of
three photographs)
Florence, Archivi Alinari, Archivio
Michetti

Lina Cavalieri in the title role of
the courtesan in Jules Massenet's
lyric comedy *Thaïs*, published in
The Bystander, July 13, 1910

Lina Cavalieri in the garden of her
summer residence in Waterford,
Connecticut, 1910

Herman Mishkin
Lina Cavalieri, New York, 1916
Taken in the period of her debut
in silent film with *La rosa di
granata* (*The Rose of Granada*,
1916), directed by Emilio Ghione

_VIDEO

Sposa nella morte! (*The Shadow
of Her Past*, 1915), directed by
Emilio Ghione
Bologna, Cineteca di Bologna

TINA MODOTTI

_PHOTOGRAPHS

Tina Modotti in San Francisco, 1915

Tina Modotti in San Francisco,
1920

Portrait of Tina Modotti at the
time when she performed in *The
Tiger's Coat* (1920), directed by
Roy Clements
Florence, Archivi Alinari/Roger
Viollet

Tina Modotti in a scene from
The Tiger's Coat (1920), directed
by Roy Clements

Tina Modotti in Hollywood,
1920–21
Pordenone, Cinemazero, Archivio
Fotografico Zeroimage

Tina Modotti in Hollywood,
1920–21
Pordenone, Cinemazero, Archivio
Fotografico Zeroimage

Johan Hagemayer
Tina, San Francisco, 1921
(series of three photographs)

M. Geely
Tina Modotti, Los Angeles, 1921

Edward Weston
Tina, California, 1921

Edward Weston
The White Iris, Los Angeles, 1921

Edward Weston
Tina, Tacubaya, 1923

Edward Weston
Tina, 1924

Edward Weston
Tina on the Azotea, Mexico, 1924
(pair of photos)

Edward Weston
Tina, Mexico, 1924

Edward Weston
Tina Acting, Mexico, 1925
(series of five photographs)

Edward Weston
Tina, 1925

Tina Modotti
The Hands of Assunta Modotti,
California, 1926
Pordenone, Cinemazero, Archivio
Fotografico Zeroimage

Tina Modotti
Hands Washing Laundry,
Mexico, 1927
Pordenone, Cinemazero,
Archivio Fotografico Zeroimage

Tina Modotti
Hands on Shovel, Mexico, 1927
Pordenone, Cinemazero,
Archivio Fotografico Zeroimage

Tina Modotti
Hands of the Puppeteer,
Mexico, 1929
Pordenone, Cinemazero,
Archivio Fotografico Zeroimage

_VIDEO

The Tiger's Coat (1920), directed
by Roy Clements
Gemona, La Cineteca del Friuli

RUDOLPH VALENTINO

_ARTWORKS

French poster for the film
A Sainted Devil (1924), directed
by Joseph Henabery
Lithographic print, 162.3 x 122.6 cm
Turin, Collection Museo Nazionale
del Cinema, inv. P30034

Federico Beltrán Masses
Portrait of Rudolph Valentino, 1925
Oil on canvas, 250 x 156.2 cm
Pasadena, Bryan Johns Collection

Poster for the film *The Eagle* (1925),
directed by Clarence Brown
Offset print, 140 x 100 cm
Turin, Collection Museo Nazionale
del Cinema, inv. P00980

French poster for the movie
The Son of the Sheik (1926),
directed by George Fitzmaurice
Lithographic print, 160 x 120 cm
Turin, Collection Museo Nazionale
del Cinema, inv. P01475-001

_CLOTHING

Natacha Rambova
Bolero
Worn by Rudolph Valentino in *Blood and Sand* (1922), directed by Fred Niblo. In dark red silk, the bolero is richly decorated with French wire in silver and gold metal thread, silver sequins, white glass beads, and blue rhinestones. On the lining is printed in black ink "Paramount Wardrobe" and handwritten in black "Rudolph Valentino"
Courtesy of The Collection of Motion Picture Costume Design: Larry McQueen, Los Angeles

Eighteenth-century style costume in peach velvet with lace soutache at the neck and on the cuffs, probably one of those worn by Rudolph Valentino in *Monsieur Beaucaire* (1924), directed by Sideny Olcott. The label "R. Valentino EO-3" is sewn onto the lining
Pasadena, Bryan Johns Collection

Adrian and Natacha Rambova
Silk caftan
The caftan was designed for Rudolph Valentino for the unfinished film *The Hooded Falcon* (1924), directed by Joseph Henabery
Pasadena, Bryan Johns Collection

J. Dege & Sons Ltd. and Everitt & Macklin
Suit, early 1920s
Part of Rudolph Valentino's personal wardrobe, the cream-colored wool suit is composed of a Norfolk jacket with four pockets and knickerbocker pants
Pasadena, Bryan Johns Collection

_PHOTOGRAPHS

Rudolph Valentino kissing his wife Natacha Rambova, 1920s
Turin, Collection Museo Nazionale del Cinema

Rudolph Valentino and spaghetti in a photo from the 1920s

Half-length portrait of Rudolph Valentino in profile, 1920s

Rudolph Valentino in the garden of his Hollywood home, 1920s
Turin, Collection Museo Nazionale del Cinema

Rudolph Valentino as an Indian warrior, 1921

Rudolph Valentino as an Indian chief, 1921

Helen MacGregor
Rudolph Valentino as Vaslav Nijinsky in a faun costume, 1921

Rudolph Valentino on the set of the film *The Conquering Power* (1921), based on the novel *Eugénie Grandet* by Honoré de Balzac and directed by Rex Ingram

Rudolph Valentino and Alice Terry photographed for the advertising of His Master's Voice gramophone, 1921

Rudolph Valentino and Beatrice Dominguez in *The Four Horsemen of the Apocalypse* (1921), directed by Rex Ingram
Turin, Collection Museo Nazionale del Cinema

Rudolph Valentino reading a fan letter, New York, 1922

Rudolph Valentino and Natacha Rambova in their house at Whitley Heights, Los Angeles, 1922

Rudolph Valentino relaxing in his Los Angeles home, 1922

Rudolph Valentino training with weights in Palisades Park, Santa Monica, 1922
Turin, Collection Museo Nazionale del Cinema

Rudolph Valentino training with weights in Palisades Park, Santa Monica, 1922

Rudolph Valentino, 1922
(pair of photographs)

Rudolph Valentino and his wife Natacha Rambova, 1922

Rudolph Valentino in a publicity shot for *The Young Rajah* (1922), based on a novel by John Ames Mitchell and play by Alethea Luce, and directed by Phil Rosen

Rudolph Valentino in a publicity shot for *The Young Rajah* (1922), based on a novel by John Ames Mitchell and play by Alethea Luce, and directed by Phil Rosen

Rudolph Valentino wearing a fencer outfit outside his home in Los Angeles, 1922

Henry Waxman
Rudolph Valentino
The photo was taken on the set of the film *Beyond the Rocks* (1922), adapted from the novel by Elinor Glyn and directed by Sam Wood

Henry Waxman
Rudolph Valentino and Gloria Swanson
The photo was taken on the set of *Beyond the Rocks* (1922), adapted from the novel by Elinor Glyn and directed by Sam Wood

Rudolph Valentino with his beloved dogs in a 1923 photo

Rudolph Valentino on the set of the film *Moran of the Lady Letty* (1923), directed by George Melford

Rudolph Valentino, 1924

Rudolph Valentino as Monsieur Beaucaire in the eponymous film (1924), adapted from the novel by Booth Tarkington and directed by Sidney Olcott

Rudolph Valentino and Nita Naldi in a 1924 publicity shot for the film *A Sainted Devil*, directed by Joseph Henabery

Rudolph Valentino, 1925

One of the last official portraits of Rudolph Valentino, 1926

_VIDEO

Rudolph Valentino in Movies, 2018
Video by Daniele Tommaso, 3:03
Sources: *The Four Horsemen of the Apocalypse* (1921), directed by Rex Ingram; *Blood and Sand* (1922), directed by Fred Niblo; *Camille* (1921), directed by Ray C. Smallwood; *Beyond the Rocks* (1922), directed by Sam Wood; *Conquering Power* (1921), directed by Rex Ingram; *The Eagle* (1925), directed by Clarence Brown; *Monsieur Beaucaire* (1924), directed by Sidney Olcott; *The Young Rajah* (1922), directed by Phil Rosen; *Cobra* (1925), directed by Joseph Henabery; *The Sheik* (1921), directed by George Melford; *The Son of the Sheik* (1926)*, directed by George Fitzmaurice

ROOM 4

ITALIANS IN HOLLYWOOD

_PHOTOGRAPHS

Mario Nunes Vais
Portrait of the actress Mimì Aguglia in costume, c. 1910

Luciano Albertini in the title role of *Sansone contro i filistei* (1918), directed by Domenico Gaido
Bologna, Cineteca di Bologna

Albert Roccardi in a scene from the film *The Virtuous Model* (1919), directed by Albert Capellani

Monty Banks (Mario Bianchi) in a photo from the 1920s

Lido Manetti in the 1920s
Florence, Museo Salvatore Ferragamo

The director Robert Vignola in the 1920s

Miriam Battista and Frank Borzage on the set of *Humoresque*, 1920

Frank Puglia in *Orphans of the Storm* (1921), directed by David W. Griffith

Bull Montana (Luigi Montagna) in 1922

Portrait of the director Frank Borzage, 1923

Director Frank Capra with Clark Gable and Claudette Colbert on the set of *It Happened One Night* (1923)

Mario Carillo (Mario Caracciolo) in a scene from the film *The Only Thing* (1925), directed by Jack Conway

Cinematographer Tony Gaudio with the director Fred Niblo on the set of *The Temptress* (1926)

Tullio Carminati in the movie *Honeymoon Hate* (1927), directed by Luther Reed

The director Gregory La Cava with Bebe Daniels during the shooting of *Feel My Pulse* (1927, released in 1928)

The actor Alberto Rabagliati, winner of the competition organized by Fox in a 1928 photograph

Sol Polito and Bette Davies together on the set in a rare photograph from 1942

_VIDEO

Video by Daniele Tommaso, 2018
Sources: *Street Angel* (1928), directed by Frank Borzage, starring Henry Armetta and Guido Trento; *The Street of Forgotten Men* (1925) by Herbert Brenon, starring Agostino Borgato; *The Eagle* (1925), directed by Clarence Brown, starring Albert Conti; *La Bohème* (1926), directed by King Vidor, starring Gino Corrado; *Merry-Go-Round* (1923), directed by Erich von Stroheim, starring Cesare Gravina; *Poor Little Peppina* (1916), directed by Sidney Olcott, starring Antonio Maiori; *Forbidden Paradise* (1924), directed by Ernst Lubitsch, starring Fred Malatesta; *Broadway* (1929), directed by Paul Fejos, starring Paul Porcasi

TWO YOUNG ITALIANS IN HOLLYWOOD

Manfredi Gioacchini
Yuri Ancarani, video artist, 2018
Black-and-white photograph, 37 x 47 cm
Florence, Museo Salvatore Ferragamo

Manfredi Gioacchini
Daniel Auber, designer, 2018
Black-and-white photograph, 37 x 47 cm
Florence, Museo Salvatore Ferragamo

Manfredi Gioacchini
Silvia Bizio, film producer, 2018
Black-and-white photograph, 37 x 47 cm
Florence, Museo Salvatore Ferragamo

Manfredi Gioacchini
Milena Canonero, costume designer, 2018
Black-and-white photograph, 37 x 47 cm
Florence, Museo Salvatore Ferragamo

Manfredi Gioacchini
Stefania Cella, set designer, 2018
Black-and-white photograph, 37 x 47 cm
Florence, Museo Salvatore Ferragamo

Manfredi Gioacchini
Christian Cordella, costume designer, 2018
Black-and-white photograph, 37 x 47 cm
Florence, Museo Salvatore Ferragamo

Manfredi Gioacchini
Pasquale Fabrizio, shoemaker, 2018
Black-and-white photograph, 37 x 47 cm
Florence, Museo Salvatore Ferragamo

Manfredi Gioacchini
Alessandro Jacomini, cinematographer, 2018
Black-and-white photograph, 37 x 47 cm
Florence, Museo Salvatore Ferragamo

Manfredi Gioacchini
Gisella Marengo, film producer, 2018
Black-and-white photograph, 37 x 47 cm
Florence, Museo Salvatore Ferragamo

Manfredi Gioacchini
Giorgio Moroder, composer and record executive, 2018
Black-and-white photograph, 37 x 47 cm
Florence, Museo Salvatore Ferragamo

Manfredi Gioacchini
Ivan Olita, director, 2018
Black-and-white photograph, 37 x 47 cm
Florence, Museo Salvatore Ferragamo

Manfredi Gioacchini
Emanuela Postacchini, actress, 2018
Black-and-white photograph, 37 x 47 cm
Florence, Museo Salvatore Ferragamo

Manfredi Gioacchini
Pietro Scalia, film editor, 2018
Black-and-white photograph, 37 x 47 cm
Florence, Museo Salvatore Ferragamo

Manfredi Gioacchini
Carlo Siliotto, composer, 2018
Black-and-white photograph, 37 x 47 cm

Manfredi Gioacchini
Dante Spinotti, cinematographer, 2018
Black-and-white photograph, 37 x 47 cm
Florence, Museo Salvatore Ferragamo

CORRIDOR AND ROOM 5

AMERICAN PRODUCTIONS SET IN ITALY AND THE INFLUENCE OF ITALIAN ART ON HOLLYWOOD CINEMA

BEN-HUR

_OBJECTS

Laurel wreath, 1925
Gilded metal trimmed with
gold lamé ribbon
Worn by Ramón Novarro
as Judah in *Ben-Hur* (1925),
directed by Fred Niblo
diameter 30.5 cm
Courtesy of The Collection of
Motion Picture Costume Design:
Larry McQueen, Los Angeles

_PHOTOGRAPH

Fred Niblo studying the battle
scene for *Ben-Hur* (1925)
Courtesy Kevin Brownlow
Collection, UK

_VIDEO

Ben-Hur (1925), directed by Fred
Niblo, video by Daniele Tommaso,
3:04

_ARTWORKS

Pio Fedi
Incontro tra amanti
[Lovers' Meeting], 1850
Plaster, height 84 cm
Private collection

Stefano Ussi
Il supplizio di Savonarola [The
Execution of Savonarola], c. 1850
Oil on glass, 30 x 43.5 cm
Florence, Gallerie degli Uffizi,
Galleria d'Arte Moderna, inv. 66

Giovanni Bastianini
Bust of Piccarda Donati, c. 1855
Patinated plaster,
53.5 x 45 x 28 cm
Florence, Gallerie degli Uffizi,
Galleria d'Arte Moderna, inv. 722

Vincenzo Cabianca
Novellieri toscani del XIV secolo
[Tuscan Storytellers of the
Fourteenth Century], 1860
Oil on canvas,78 x 99 cm
Florence, Gallerie degli Uffizi,
Galleria d'Arte Moderna, inv. 300

Giuseppe Abbati
La cappella del Podestà [Chapel
of the Podestà], 1861–62
Oil on canvas, 67 x 49 cm
Florence, Gallerie degli Uffizi,
Galleria d'Arte Moderna, inv. 163

Pietro Saltini
*Simon Memmi che per incarico del
Petrarca ritrae madonna Laura*
[Simon Memmi Portraying Lady
Laura at Petrarch's Behest], 1863
Oil on canvas, 118 x 142.5 cm
Florence, Gallerie degli Uffizi,
Galleria d'Arte Moderna, inv. O.d.A.
1911 n. 784

Federico Zandomeneghi
Palazzo Pretorio, 1865
Oil on canvas, 81 x 64 cm (106 x 88
x 7.5 cm including frame)
Venice, Galleria Internazionale
d'Arte Moderna di Ca' Pesaro,
inv. 1465

Antonio Puccinelli
Paolo and Francesca, c. 1875
Olio on canvas, 48 x 55 cm
Private collection

Giuseppe Abbati
Armigero in Bargello [Soldier at
the Bargello], second half of the
nineteenth century
Oil on canvas, 27 x 47.5 cm
(42.5 x 63 cm including frame)
Private collection

Anonymous
*Madonna of the Magnificat
by Sandro Botticelli*, first–third
decade of the twentieth century
Oil on canvas, diameter 109 cm
(149 cm including frame)
Private collection, Heirs Bianca
Capoquadri Tommasi

_BOOKS

Guido Biagi, *The Private Life of the
Renaissance Florentines* (Florence:
R. Bemporad and Son Publishers,
1896)
Florence, Biblioteca Nazionale
Centrale di Firenze, inv. 20520.5

Guido Biagi, *Men and Manners of
Old Florence* (London and Leipzig:
T. Fisher, 1909)
Florence, Biblioteca Nazionale
Centrale di Firenze, inv. MAGL.
53.3.333

_PHOTOGRAPHS

Ronald Colman, the director Henry
King, Dorothy Gish, and Lillian Gish
relaxing during the shooting of
Romola, 1924

Ronald Colman and Lillian Gish
in a scene from *Romola*, 1924
Florence, Museo Salvatore
Ferragamo

Photograph taken on the set
of *Romola* featuring the scene
of Girolamo Savonarola's
execution, 1924
Gemona, La Cineteca del Friuli

Lillian Gish on the set of
Romola, 1924
Courtesy Kevin Brownlow
Collection, UK

Lillian Gish on the set
of *Romola*, 1924.
Florence, Museo Salvatore
Ferragamo

Ronald Colman and Lillian Gish on
the set of *Romola*, 1924

The "Impannate Room" on the
third floor of Palazzo Davanzati in
Florence, as furnished by Elia Volpi
in 1920. The frescoes on the walls
were reproduced for *Romola*
Florence, Archivi Alinari

_VIDEO

Romola (1924), directed by Henry
King, video by Daniele Tommaso,
2:11

ROOM 6

**ITALIAN SOUND IN AMERICA
AFTER WORLD WAR I**

Immersive and site-specific video
installation
Concept: Fabio Iaquone, Luca
Attilii, and Stefania Ricci; art
direction and execution by
Iaquone e Attilii Studio, Rome;
multimedia service AVUELLE s.r.l.

ROOM 7

ZUMA BEACH

Video installation by Yuri Ancarani
Concept, art direction and
execution by Yuri Ancarani, Milan;
multimedia service AVUELLE s.r.l.
In collaboration with
Lo Schermo dell'Arte Film Festival
Museo Salvatore Ferragamo
Florence, Museo Salvatore
Ferragamo

ROOM 8
HOLLYWOOD BOOT SHOP

_ARTWORKS

Paolo Troubetzkoy
Mary Pickford, 1919–1920
Plaster, 45 x 35 x 26 cm
Verbania, Museo del Paesaggio,
inv. T 307

Arturo Martini
Portrait of Lillian Gish, 1929
Terracotta, 39 x 31 x 23 cm
Venice, Galleria Internazionale
d'Arte Moderna di Ca' Pesaro,
inv. 2173

_FOOTWEAR

Salvatore Ferragamo
Riding boot, 1921 (2018)
Dark brown calfskin, with
removable thong around the
ankle and underneath the sole,
secured by a butterfly buckle,
30.5 x 3 cm, shaft 43 cm.
Facsimile of a model created
for Rudolph Valentino
Florence, Museo Salvatore
Ferragamo, inv. SC0014507

Salvatore Ferragamo
Pump, 1923–24
Toe and heel in brown lizard. The
rest of the upper, open on either
side of the toe, is composed of
closely interwoven strips of beige
and brown kid. The slightly flared
wooden heel and the insole are
covered in beige kid. Leather sole,
23.5 x 7.5 cm
Florence, Museo Salvatore
Ferragamo, inv. SC0001205

Salvatore Ferragamo
Prototype for sandal, 1924
Gold kid and red suede upper,
23 x 7 cm
Florence, Museo Salvatore
Ferragamo, inv. SC0000580

Salvatore Ferragamo
Prototype for sandal, 1924
Black satin and gold kid upper,
20 x 7 cm
Florence, Museo Salvatore
Ferragamo, inv. SC0000736

Salvatore Ferragamo
Prototype for sandal, 1924
Gold and silver kid upper with
black satin strip, 24 x 7 cm.
The model was expressly designed
for Mary Pickford
Florence, Museo Salvatore
Ferragamo, inv. SC0000767

Salvatore Ferragamo
Oxford, 1925
Calfskin and nubuck upper in
black and magnolia colors with
decorative perforation along the
edges, 30 x 30,5 cm. The model
was expressly designed
for Rudolph Valentino
Florence, Museo Salvatore
Ferragamo, inv. SC0014508

Salvatore Ferragamo
Lottie closed shoe, 1925
Black suede with fan motif around
the ankle and heel, wavy stripe
decoration in various shades of
beige suede on the upper,
20 x 10 cm. The shoe is a
reproduction of a historic model
designed by Salvatore Ferragamo,
known of thanks to a photograph
taken at the Hollywood Boot
Shop, preserved in the Archivio
Salvatore Ferragamo
Florence, Museo Salvatore
Ferragamo, inv. SC0014332

Salvatore Ferragamo
Spectator pump, 1925–26
White antelope and blue
calfskin. The model was expressly
designed for the actress Alice
White
Los Angeles, Natural History
Museum

Salvatore Ferragamo
Two-piece shoe, 1925–27
Black velvet and silver kid,
24 x 8 cm
Jimmy Raye Collection

Salvatore Ferragamo
Prototype for sandal, 1925–30
Gold kid upper, 20.5 x 7 cm
Florence, Museo Salvatore
Ferragamo, inv. SC0001131

Salvatore Ferragamo
Prototype for sandal, 1926–28
Canvas upper embroidered with
a red roses motif on an ecru
Gobelin-pattern background,
trimming and heel in gold kid,
21 x 7 cm
Florence, Museo Salvatore
Ferragamo, inv. SC0000737

Salvatore Ferragamo
Oxford, 1926
Calfskin and nubuck upper in
cognac and mud colors with
matching decorative stitching
along the edges, 30 x 4 cm.
The model was expressly
designed for Rudolph
Valentino
Florence, Museo Salvatore
Ferragamo, inv. SC0014509

Salvatore Ferragamo
Autumn closed shoe, 1926
Model with upper close to the
collar of the foot in hand-painted
linen with a plant motif in shades
of light green, 20 x 10 cm. The
shoe is a reproduction of a historic
model designed by Salvatore
Ferragamo, known of thanks to
two articles published in two
American newspapers in August
and October 1926, preserved in
the Archivio Salvatore Ferragamo
Florence, Museo Salvatore
Ferragamo, inv. SC0014333

Salvatore Ferragamo
The Star two-piece shoe, 1926
Black suede model with strap and
rhinestone glitter star-motif,
20 x 10 cm. The shoe is a
reproduction of a historic model
designed by Salvatore Ferragamo,
known of thanks to two articles
published in two American
newspapers in August and
October 1926 and a photograph
taken at the Hollywood Boot
Shop, preserved in the Archivio
Salvatore Ferragamo
Florence, Museo Salvatore
Ferragamo, inv. SC0014334

Salvatore Ferragamo
Fortuna pump, 1927
Black satin upper with a
rhinestone glitter decoration
featuring an arrow through a
circle, 22 x 7 cm. The shoe is a
reproduction of a historic model
designed by Salvatore Ferragamo,
known of thanks to a photograph
accompanying an article
published in California on June 26,
1927
Florence, Museo Salvatore
Ferragamo, inv. SC0014335

Salvatore Ferragamo
Mule, 1927
Crocheted multicolored raffia
upper, gilded brass circular
heel, 21.5 x 4 cm. The model was
expressly designed for Joan
Crawford
Florence, Museo Salvatore
Ferragamo, inv. SC0000268

Salvatore Ferragamo
Sandal, 1927
Black velvet and grosgrain and
gold kid, 23 x 8.5 cm
Florence, Museo Salvatore
Ferragamo, inv. SC0011584

Salvatore Ferragamo
Prototype for sandal, 1927
Gold kid upper, 21 x 8 cm
Florence, Museo Salvatore
Ferragamo, inv. SC0000788

Salvatore Ferragamo
Prototype for sandal, 1927
Gold kid and black satin,
20.5 x 7 cm
Florence, Museo Salvatore
Ferragamo, inv. SC0000890

Salvatore Ferragamo
Prototype for sandal, 1927
Black velvet and grosgrain and
gold kid, 21 x 8 cm
Florence, Museo Salvatore
Ferragamo, inv. SC0003108

Salvatore Ferragamo
Prototype for laced shoe, 1927
Calfskin and suede upper in two
shades of brown, 20 x 7 cm.
The model was expressly designed
for Gloria Swanson
Florence, Museo Salvatore
Ferragamo, inv. SC0010352

Salvatore Ferragamo
Charles IX shoe, 1927–30
Brown lizard upper, 22 x 6 cm
Florence, Museo Salvatore
Ferragamo, inv. SC0001687

Salvatore Ferragamo
Vetia pump, 1927–30
Brown suede and crocodile,
22 x 8.5 cm
Florence, Museo Salvatore
Ferragamo, inv. SC0000221

Salvatore Ferragamo
Pump, 1927–30
Black satin upper with white
rhinestone buckle decoration,
21 x 8.5 cm. The model was
expressly designed for Mary
Pickford and was also purchased
in Florence by Countess
Alessandra della Gherardesca
Spalletti
Florence, Museo Salvatore
Ferragamo, inv. SC0000753

Salvatore Ferragamo
Sandal, 1927–30
Bright blue suede and silver kid
upper, 20.5 x 8 cm
Florence, Museo Salvatore
Ferragamo, inv. SC0000210

Salvatore Ferragamo
Closed shoe, 1927–30
Brown suede and calfskin upper,
22.5 x 8.5 cm. The model was
expressly designed for Pola Negri
Florence, Museo Salvatore
Ferragamo, inv. SC0000203

Salvatore Ferragamo
Prototype for sandal, 1927–30
Aquamarine sequins and silver kid
upper, 21 x 7,5 cm
Florence, Museo Salvatore
Ferragamo, inv. SC0000735

Salvatore Ferragamo
Prototype for closed shoe,
1927–30
Black calfskin upper, 21 x 8 cm.
The model was expressly designed
for Pola Negri
Florence, Museo Salvatore
Ferragamo, inv. SC0000891

Salvatore Ferragamo
Prototype for closed shoe,
1927–30
Black suede and calfskin upper,
20 x 8 cm. The model was
expressly designed for Pola Negri
Florence, Museo Salvatore
Ferragamo, inv. SC0010313

Salvatore Ferragamo
Pump, 1928
Brushed calfskin with ankle
strap in the same material
and color, decorated with an
asymmetric bow in magnolia
napa, 19.5 x 10 cm. The model
was expressly designed for
Gloria Swanson
Florence, Museo Salvatore
Ferragamo, inv. SC0014505

Salvatore Ferragamo
Laced shoe, 1928–30
Brown suede and calfskin,
21.5 x 10 cm
Florence, Museo Salvatore
Ferragamo, inv. SC00000004

Salvatore Ferragamo
Two-piece shoe, 1928–30
Black satin upper embroidered
with a polychrome floral motif,
23 x 8 cm
Florence, Museo Salvatore
Ferragamo, inv. SC0011450

Salvatore Ferragamo
Laced shoe, 1928–30
Brown suede and beige kangaroo
upper, 22 x 8 cm
Florence, Museo Salvatore
Ferragamo, inv. SC0000707

Salvatore Ferragamo
Prototype for sandal, 1928–30
Red Tavarnelle lace and gold kid
upper, 21 x 7 cm
Florence, Museo Salvatore
Ferragamo, inv. SC0000603

Salvatore Ferragamo
Prototype for mule, 1928–30
Black satin embroidered with a
floral motif in multicolored satin
thread, 21 x 7 cm
Florence, Museo Salvatore
Ferragamo, inv. SC0000789

Salvatore Ferragamo
Prototype for mule, 1928–30
Blue velvet embroidered with
multicolored threads, 21 x 7.5 cm
Florence, Museo Salvatore
Ferragamo, inv. SC0000915

Salvatore Ferragamo
Prototype for sandal, 1928–32
Black grosgrain upper, 22.5 x 7 cm
Florence, Museo Salvatore
Ferragamo, inv. SC0010299

Salvatore Ferragamo
Prototype for two-piece shoe,
1928–32
Printed silk crepe and black satin
upper, 22.5 x 7.5 cm
Florence, Museo Salvatore
Ferragamo, inv. SC0010315

Salvatore Ferragamo
Laced shoe, 1929
Black lizard upper, 22.5 x 8 cm
Florence, Museo Salvatore
Ferragamo, inv. SC0000222

Salvatore Ferragamo
Sandal, patent no. 6938
dated November 27, 1929
(withapplication no. 307
dated July 2, 1929)
Suede upper in shades of beige
and brown, 21 x 8 cm
Florence, Museo Salvatore
Ferragamo, inv. SC0002971

Salvatore Ferragamo
Strap shoe, patent no. 6959
dated November 27, 1929
(withapplication no. 330
dated July 4, 1929)
Beige suede upper with suede
decorations in the same shades,
21.5 x 8 cm
Florence, Museo Salvatore
Ferragamo, inv. SC0002973

Salvatore Ferragamo
Pump, patent no. 6960
dated November 27, 1929
(with application no. 333
dated July 4, 1929)
Black suede upper with half-moon
suede decorations in shades of
beige, 21 x 8 cm
Florence, Museo Salvatore
Ferragamo, inv. SC0002972

Salvatore Ferragamo
Closed shoe, 1929
Magnolia suede with black kid toe
and double lace around the ankle,
21.5 x 8.5 cm. The model was
expressly designed for
Mary Pickford
Florence, Museo Salvatore
Ferragamo, inv. SC0014504

Salvatore Ferragamo
Pump, patent no. 7028 dated
March 8, 1930 (with application
no. 376 dated July 4, 1929)
Beige grosgrain upper
embroidered with a beige
soutache spriral motif, 21 x 8.5 cm
Florence, Museo Salvatore
Ferragamo, inv. SC0014352

Salvatore Ferragamo
Prototype for pump, 1929
Black-painted calfskin covered
in mesh made from silk thread
mechanical chain dégradé
stitching in shades of red,
21.5 x 7 cm
Florence, Museo Salvatore
Ferragamo, inv. SC0000772

Salvatore Ferragamo
Prototype for pump, 1929
Dark gray calfskin covered in mesh
made from silk thread mechanical
chain stitching of the same color,
20.5 x 7 cm
Florence, Museo Salvatore
Ferragamo, inv. SC0005587

Salvatore Ferragamo
Strap shoe, patent no. 7173 dated
July 25, 1930 (with application
no. 472 dated October 29, 1929)
Pearl gray lizard and black-
painted kid upper, 22 x 10 cm
Florence, Museo Salvatore
Ferragamo, inv. SC0014168

Salvatore Ferragamo
Two-piece shoe, patent
no. 7024 dated March 8, 1930
(with application no. 328
dated July 4, 1929)
Painted calfskin upper with
strap and burnished metal lock,
22 x 7.5 cm
Florence, Museo Salvatore
Ferragamo, inv. SC0014336

Salvatore Ferragamo
Two-piece shoe, 1930
Embroidered black satin upper,
Tavarnelle lace and silver kid,
24 x 8 cm
Florence, Museo Salvatore
Ferragamo, inv. SC0000028

Salvatore Ferragamo
Sandal, 1930
Black satin upper, square heel
covered in silver metal lamina,
21 x 7.5 cm
Florence, Museo Salvatore
Ferragamo, inv. SC0011718

Salvatore Ferragamo
Pump, 1930
Upper in brown calfskin,
suede and crocodile sewn in a
patchwork pattern, 21.5 x 8 cm
Florence, Museo Salvatore
Ferragamo, inv. SC0000014

Salvatore Ferragamo
Two-piece shoe, 1930
Black satin and silver kid upper,
20.5 x 7 cm
Florence, Museo Salvatore
Ferragamo, inv. SC0000208

Salvatore Ferragamo
Two-piece shoe, 1930
Black canvas and silver kid upper,
22.5 x 8 cm
Florence, Museo Salvatore
Ferragamo, inv. SC0000209

Salvatore Ferragamo
Sandal, 1930
Black and multicolored grosgrain
upper and gold kid, 22 x 8 cm
Florence, Museo Salvatore
Ferragamo, inv. SC0000020

Salvatore Ferragamo
Prototype for sandal, 1930
Gold kid upper and pyramid-
shaped brass heel, 23 x 6 cm
Florence, Museo Salvatore
Ferragamo, inv. SC0000018

Salvatore Ferragamo
Prototype for sandal, 1930
Black kid strips and high heel
covered in kid, 20.5 x 7 cm
Florence, Museo Salvatore
Ferragamo, inv. SC0000019

Salvatore Ferragamo
Prototype for sandal, 1930
Gold kid and velvet upper,
21.5 x 7 cm
Florence, Museo Salvatore
Ferragamo, inv. SC0000025

Salvatore Ferragamo
Prototype for sandal, 1930
Gold upper decorated with black-
painted circular bubbles edged
with red silk thread chain stitching,
20 x 7.5 cm
Florence, Museo Salvatore
Ferragamo, inv. SC0000697

Salvatore Ferragamo
Prototype for laced shoe, 1930–32
Black calfskin and suede,
23 x 7.5 cm
Florence, Museo Salvatore
Ferragamo, inv. SC0003110

Salvatore Ferragamo
Two-piece shoe, 1930–35
Brown suede upper, 23 x 7.5 cm
Florence, Museo Salvatore
Ferragamo, inv. SC0000024

Salvatore Ferragamo
Cenerentola, 1930–35
Black Tavarnelle lace sandal
embroidered with a floral motif in
multicolored silk thread, 22 x 9 cm
Florence, Museo Salvatore
Ferragamo, inv. SC0000027

Salvatore Ferragamo
Pump, 1930–35
Burgundy suede and calfskin
upper, 21 x 8.5 cm
Florence, Museo Salvatore
Ferragamo, inv. SC0000214

Salvatore Ferragamo
Prototype for laced shoe, 1930–35
Black suede and calfskin upper,
22.5 x 7.5 cm
Florence, Museo Salvatore
Ferragamo, inv. SC0003099

Salvatore Ferragamo
Prototype for laced shoe, 1930–35
Brown suede upper, 22 x 7.5 cm
Florence, Museo Salvatore
Ferragamo, inv. SC0010253

Salvatore Ferragamo
T-strap shoe, 1932
Snakeskin upper with strips and
heel trimmed with magnolia kid,
21.5 x 7.5 cm. The model was
expressly designed for Joan
Crawford
Florence, Museo Salvatore
Ferragamo, inv. SC0014506

Salvatore Ferragamo
Equilibrium two-piece shoe,
early 1930s
Crocheted upper, designed by
Ferragamo's Creations in 2014 on
the occasion of the *Equilibrium*
exhibition, based on a photograph
preserved in the Archivio Salvatore
Ferragamo, 19 x 10 cm
Florence, Museo Salvatore
Ferragamo, inv. SC0009908

_VIDEO

Hollywood Boot Shop, 2018
Immersive site-specific video
installation, 10:00
Concept: Fabio Iaquone, Luca
Attilii, and Stefania Ricci; art
direction and execution by
Iaquone e Attilii Studio, Roma;
multimedia service AVUELLE s.r.l.
Sources: Actress Bertha Bell
photographed by Albert Walter
Witzel, with dedication to
Salvatore Ferragamo, 1920s,
Florence, Museo Salvatore
Ferragamo; Portrait of actress
Clara Bow, Florence, Museo
Salvatore Ferragamo; Portrait
of actress Clara Bow, Florence,
Museo Salvatore Ferragamo;
Portrait of actress Clara Bow,
1929, Florence, Museo Salvatore
Ferragamo; Portrait of actress
Joan Crawford with a lamé
headdress, 1928, Florence,
Archivi Alinari; Joan Crawford
with Salvatore Ferragamo in the
Hollywood Boot Shop, 1920s,
Florence, Museo Salvatore
Ferragamo; Joan Crawford in
Salvatore Ferragamo's shop,
Florence, Museo Salvatore
Ferragamo; Portrait of Marion
Davies, 1928, Florence, Museo
Salvatore Ferragamo; Portrait
of Marion Davies, 1930; Dolores
Del Río, 1926; Portraits of
actress Dolores del Río, 1920s

(three photographs), Florence,
Museo Salvatore Ferragamo;
Actress Edna Mae Cooper
photographed by Melbourne
Spurr, with dedication to Salvatore
Ferragamo, 1920s, Florence, Museo
Salvatore Ferragamo; Actress
Esther Ralston photographed by
Henry Waxman, with dedication
to Salvatore Ferragamo, 1920s,
Florence, Museo Salvatore
Ferragamo; Gloria Swanson
photographed by Edward
Steichen, published in *Vanity
Fair*, 1928, Florence, Museo
Salvatore Ferragamo; Portrait of
Gloria Swanson in front of a NBC
microphone, 1925, Florence, Museo
Salvatore Ferragamo; Portrait
of Gloria Swanson, Florence,
Museo Salvatore Ferragamo;
Gloria Swanson, 1920; Portrait
of Gloria Swanson, Florence,
Museo Salvatore Ferragamo;
Gloria Swanson during the
shooting of *Sadie Thompson*
(1928), directed by Raoul Walsh;
Greta Garbo photographed by
Clarence Sinclair Bull on the set
of *Inspiration* (1930), directed
by Clarence Brown, Florence,
Museo Salvatore Ferragamo;
Greta Garbo photographed by
Frank Grimes on the set of *Anna
Karenina* (1927), directed by John
Gilbert, Florence, Museo Salvatore
Ferragamo; Greta Garbo with
costume designer Adrian on the
set of *The Single Standard* (1929),
directed by John S. Robertson,
Florence, Museo Salvatore
Ferragamo; Salvatore Ferragamo
with actress Olive Hasbrouck,
1927, Florence, Museo Salvatore
Ferragamo; Salvatore Ferragamo
with actress Kathleen Key in the
Southern Pacific *Argonaut* train,
1926, Florence, Museo Salvatore
Ferragamo; Actress Lolita
Lee photographed by Bruno,
with dedication to Salvatore

Ferragamo, 1920s, Florence, Museo
Salvatore Ferragamo; Actress
Anita Loos photographed by
Edward Steichen, 1920; Pola Negri
as a flapper icon, 1950s, Florence,
Museo Salvatore Ferragamo; A
Ross Verlag postcard portraying
Pola Negri, 1920s, Florence,
Museo Salvatore Ferragamo; Pola
Negri in profile, 1920s, Florence,
Museo Salvatore Ferragamo;
Pola Negri photographed by G.
Vettori, 1920s, Florence, Museo
Salvatore Ferragamo; A Ross
Verlag postcard portraying
Pola Negri in Santa Monica, c.
1928, Florence, Museo Salvatore
Ferragamo; Actress Mary Pickford,
1920s, Florence, Museo Salvatore
Ferragamo; Actress Lola Todd
wearing a total leopard look
designed by Salvatore Ferragamo,
1925, Florence, Museo Salvatore
Ferragamo; Actress Alice White,
1929; Some clients in Salvatore
Ferragamo's shop in Hollywood,
1926 (two photographs), Florence,
Museo Salvatore Ferragamo; John
Barrymore and Douglas Fairbanks
in the Warner Brothers' studios,
1924; Charlie Chaplin and Pola
Negri, February 2, 1923; Portrait
of director Cecil B. DeMille, 1914;
John Gilbert photographed in the
garden of his home, 1926; Portrait
of David W. Griffith, 1915; Rudolph
Valentino photographed by Henry
Waxman on the set of *Beyond
the Rocks* (1922), directed by Sam
Wood; Rudolph Valentino in his
dressing-room during shooting
of *Monsieur Beaucaire* (1924),
directed by Sidney Olcott, Turin,
Collection Museo Nazionale del
Cinema

PHOTO CREDITS

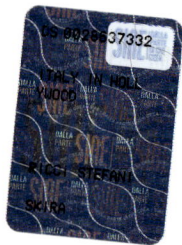